Australia in World Affairs 2016–2020

A Return to Great-Power Rivalry

Between 2016 and 2020 Australia's foreign and security policies were significantly affected by profound changes in geopolitics and geoeconomics, particularly as great-power competition re-emerged between the United States and China. *Australia in World Affairs 2016–2020: A Return to Great-Power Rivalry* examines Australia's engagement on the international stage in light of these events.

The 13th volume in the *Australia in World Affairs* series, this text builds on the history of Australia's foreign policy covered in other volumes to identify patterns of continuity and change. It catalogues the key developments in this period of world history from an Australian perspective. Organised thematically, chapters cover Australia's foreign policy response to climate change, Australia's strengthened ties to the Indo-Pacific region, and its security interests in South-East Asia. Australia's increasing security dependence on the United States in an age of great-power rivalry is evident throughout.

Written by a team of highly respected Australian experts, *Australia in World Affairs 2016–2020* offers clear coverage of Australia's contribution to world affairs in this five-year period and will appeal to specialists, researchers and students alike.

The **Australian Institute of International Affairs** was established in 1933 as an independent non-political body to promote interest in and understanding of international affairs.

Baogang He is Alfred Deakin Professor, Chair in International Relations, School of Humanities and Social Sciences, Faculty of Arts and Education, Deakin University, and a Fellow of the Academy of Social Sciences in Australia.

David Hundt is an associate professor of International Relations in the School of Humanities and Social Sciences, Deakin University.

Danielle Chubb is an associate professor of International Relations in the School of Humanities and Social Sciences, Deakin University.

Titles in the *Australia in World Affairs* series

Australia in World Affairs 1950–1955

Australia in World Affairs 1956–1960

Australia in World Affairs 1961–1965

Australia in World Affairs 1966–1970

Australia in World Affairs 1971–1975

Australia in World Affairs 1976–1980: Independence and Alliance

Australia in World Affairs 1981–1990: Diplomacy in the Marketplace

Australia in World Affairs 1991–1995: Seeking Asian Engagement

Australia in World Affairs 1996–2000: The National Interest in a Global Era

Australia in World Affairs 2001–2005: Trading on Alliance Security

Australia in World Affairs 2006–2010: Middle Power Dreaming

Australia in World Affairs 2011–2015: Navigating the New International Disorder

Australia in World Affairs 2016–2020: A Return to Great-Power Rivalry

Cambridge University Press acknowledges the Australian Aboriginal and Torres Strait Islander peoples of this nation. We acknowledge the traditional custodians of the lands on which our company is located and where we conduct our business. We pay our respects to ancestors and Elders, past and present. Cambridge University Press is committed to honouring Australian Aboriginal and Torres Strait Islander peoples' unique cultural and spiritual relationships to the land, waters and seas and their rich contribution to society.

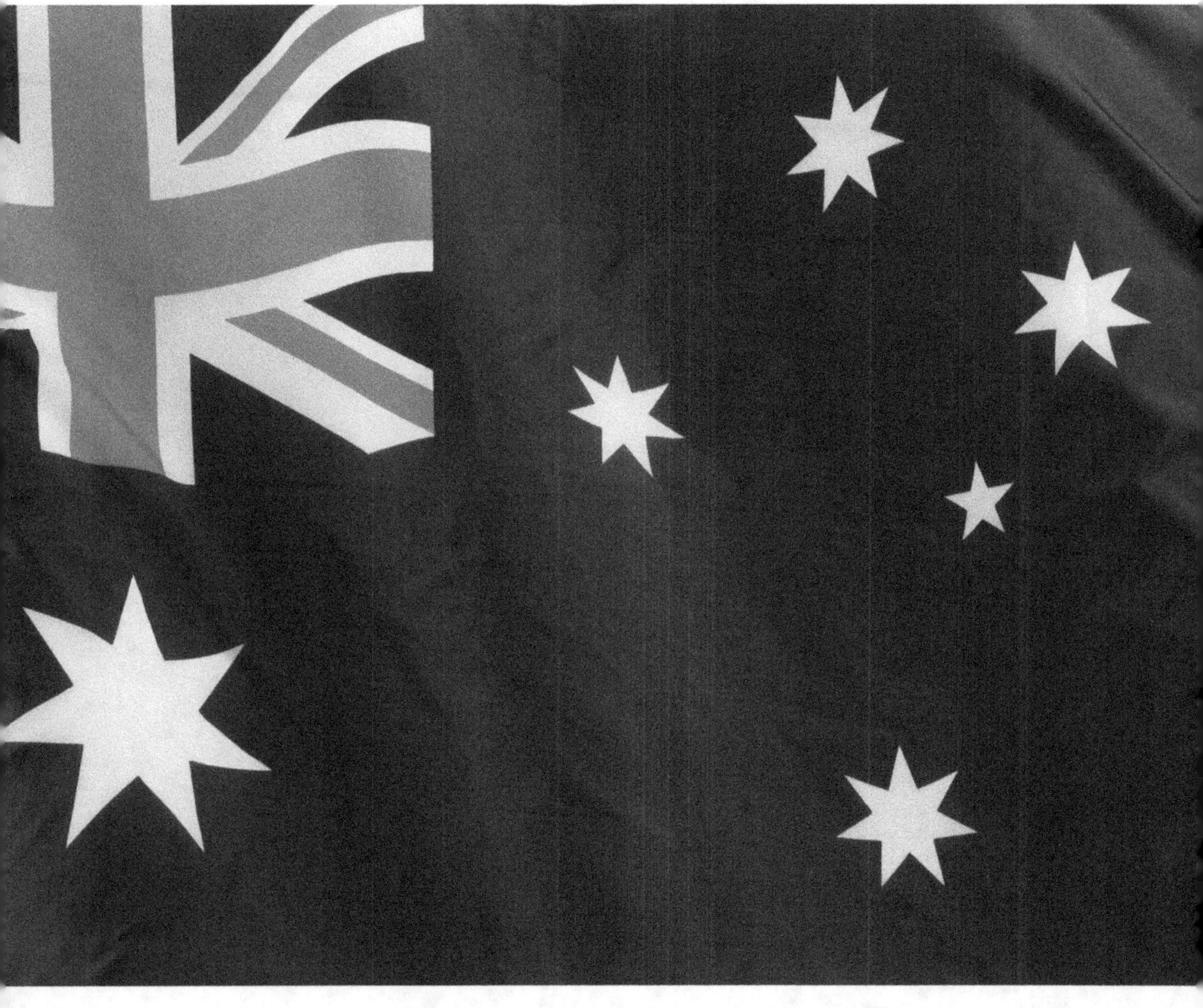

Australia in World Affairs 2016–2020

A Return to Great-Power Rivalry

EDITED BY BAOGANG HE, DAVID HUNDT AND
DANIELLE CHUBB

CAMBRIDGE UNIVERSITY PRESS

Shaftesbury Road, Cambridge CB2 8EA, United Kingdom

One Liberty Plaza, 20th Floor, New York, NY 10006, USA

477 Williamstown Road, Port Melbourne, VIC 3207, Australia

314–321, 3rd Floor, Plot 3, Splendor Forum, Jasola District Centre, New Delhi – 110025, India

103 Penang Road, #05–06/07, Visioncrest Commercial, Singapore 238467

Cambridge University Press is part of Cambridge University Press & Assessment, a department of the University of Cambridge.

We share the University's mission to contribute to society through the pursuit of education, learning and research at the highest international levels of excellence.

www.cambridge.org
Information on this title: www.cambridge.org/9781009479196

© Australian Institute of International Affairs 2024

This publication is copyright. Subject to statutory exception and to the provisions of relevant collective licensing agreements, no reproduction of any part may take place without the written permission of Cambridge University Press & Assessment.

First published 2024

Cover designed by Sardine Design
Typeset by Straive

A catalogue record for this publication is available from the British Library

A catalogue record for this book is available from the National Library of Australia

ISBN 978-1-009-47919-6 Paperback

Reproduction and communication for educational purposes
The Australian *Copyright Act 1968* (the Act) allows a maximum of one chapter or 10% of the pages of this work, whichever is the greater, to be reproduced and/or communicated by any educational institution for its educational purposes provided that the educational institution (or the body that administers it) has given a remuneration notice to Copyright Agency Limited (CAL) under the Act.

For details of the CAL licence for educational institutions contact:

Copyright Agency Limited
Level 12, 66 Goulburn Street
Sydney NSW 2000
Telephone: (02) 9394 7600
Facsimile: (02) 9394 7601
E-mail: memberservices@copyright.com.au

Reproduction and communication for other purposes
Except as permitted under the Act (for example a fair dealing for the purposes of study, research, criticism or review) no part of this publication may be reproduced, stored in a retrieval system, communicated or transmitted in any form or by any means without prior written permission. All inquiries should be made to the publisher at the address above.

Cambridge University Press & Assessment has no responsibility for the persistence or accuracy of URLs for external or third-party internet websites referred to in this publication and does not guarantee that any content on such websites is, or will remain, accurate or appropriate.

Please be aware that this publication may contain several variations of Aboriginal and Torres Strait Islander terms and spellings; no disrespect is intended. Please note that the terms 'Indigenous Australians', 'Aboriginal and Torres Strait Islander peoples' and 'First Nations peoples' may be used interchangeably in this publication.

Contents

List of tables and figures	page vii
Preface	ix
About the AIIA	xi
Contributors	xii
Abbreviations	xvi

1   **Australian responses to great-power rivalry**   1
     Baogang He, David Hundt and Danielle Chubb

PART I   THE DOMESTIC POLITICS OF AUSTRALIAN FOREIGN POLICY   15

2   **The foreign policy process: adjusting to a new era**   17
     Nick Bisley

3   **Australian public opinion on world affairs: China, the United States and climate change**   31
     Danielle Chubb and Ian McAllister

4   **Values, gender and foreign policy**   47
     Jacqui True and Tamara Ernst

5   **Countering foreign interference: domestic laws and international repercussions**   61
     Melissa Conley Tyler and Julian Dusting

6   **Asian Australians, foreign policy and identity in Australia**   76
     Juliet Pietsch

PART II   GLOBAL ISSUES   89

7   **Australian perspectives on the 'rules-based order'**   91
     Huiyun Feng and Kai He

8   **International security challenges**   105
     Sarah Percy and Rebecca Strating

9   **A perfect storm? Climate change and Australian foreign policy**   119
     Matt McDonald

10   **Health security and Australian foreign policy**   131
     Sara E. Davies

PART III   REGIONAL ISSUES   145

11   **Reimagining Australia's regional security for the Indo-Pacific century**   147
     Thomas Wilkins

12   **Australia's security interests in South-East Asia and the Pacific**   161
     Joanne Wallis and Huong Le Thu

13 Australia's engagement with ASEAN: Singapore as a conduit   174
    See Seng Tan
14 Australian foreign economic policy and the Belt and Road controversy   188
    Baogang He, Geoffrey Stokes and David Hundt

Index   204

List of tables and figures

Tables

3.1	Views of China and other countries, 2019–20	page 36
3.2	China as economic partner or security threat, 2015–20	39
3.3	Climate change and party support, 2020	42
3.4	Social background and attitudes towards the United States, China and global warming, 2020	43
6.1	Perceptions of foreign policy threats by birthplace, 2019	82
6.2	Attitudes towards Australia's alliance with the United States by birthplace, 2019	83
6.3	Attitudes towards free trade by birthplace, 2019	84

Figures

3.1	Trust in the United States to act responsibly, 2006–20	33
3.2	Support for the US alliance, 1993–2020	35
3.3	China as a threat, 1967–2020	37
3.4	Levels of Chinese investment in Australia, 2009–19	38
3.5	Public opinion towards climate change and global warming, 2006–20	41

Preface

This volume builds on a venerable tradition, the *Australia in World Affairs* (AiWA) series, which the Australian Institute for International Affairs has sponsored since 1955. In keeping with that tradition, the book's primary goal is to provide a definitive account of Australia's engagement in world affairs during the five years from 2016 to 2020. It does so by cataloguing and analysing the key developments in this momentous period in world history, which began with the Brexit vote in the United Kingdom, Australia's deepening of its ties to the Indo-Pacific region through the Trans-Pacific Partnership, and the election of Donald Trump in the United States, and which ended with the outbreak of the COVID-19 pandemic, Australia's embroilment in a trade war with China, and Trump's replacement as US president by Joe Biden.

The chapters in this volume speak primarily to the past five years while simultaneously drawing on past volumes to identify patterns of continuity and change. When taken in their entirety, one clear theme stands out: Australia's increasing security dependence on the United States in an age of great-power rivalry. This volume dissects Australian responses to and perspectives on these events and others in the five years under review, focusing on Canberra's response to the continuing rise of China. It analyses the domestic politics of foreign policy-making in Australia and the factors that influence it before proceeding to analyse Australian engagement into various subfields, such as security, economy and politics, at the global and regional (Asia/Indo-Pacific) levels.

It was always going to be a challenge to do justice to all these events and processes in sufficient breadth and depth, so one of our tasks as editors was to decide which topics would and would not be covered. We had intended to include stand-alone chapters on such topics as Australia's involvement in debates about human rights, its engagement with the United Nations more broadly, and the politics of international and regional trade agreements, but it was not possible to include such chapters, in part due to the very real constraints that the COVID-19 pandemic placed on the ability of some would-be contributors to complete their work. While some absences can therefore be explained by forces beyond our control, others were due to decisions by the editors. Readers of previous volumes of *Australia in World Affairs* will, for instance, notice that there are no chapters devoted to specific bilateral relationships, such as with the United States and China. In keeping with our commitment to a thematic structure, we have ensured that all these important topics are covered to some degree in the 13 chapters that follow.

The editors are grateful to the School of Humanities and Social Sciences at Deakin University for its support for our work on this project. We also wish to thank the Australian Institute for International Affairs for its support for the production of the volume. We owe special thanks to Tom Barber for providing literature reviews and summaries of previous volumes for each chapter. The editors are grateful to the three anonymous peer reviewers, each of whom provided tremendously valuable feedback on an earlier version of the manuscript. Finally, we are immensely grateful to all the contributors for producing such fine work under extremely trying conditions during

2020 and 2021. Despite the many and varied challenges of the COVID-19 era, especially, delaying the publication for two to three years, we believe this volume is something that will be valuable to all students of Australia's engagement with the world.

David Hundt

Danielle Chubb

Baogang He

Deakin University, Melbourne, 2024

About the AIIA

The Australian Institute of International Affairs (AIIA) is an independent, non-profit organisation promoting interest in and understanding of international affairs in Australia. It provides a forum for discussion and debate but does not develop or promote its own institutional views. Each year, the AIIA stages more than 200 public and specialist lectures, seminars and other events around Australia. It also sponsors leading research and publications, including the *Australian Journal of International Affairs* and the blog *Australian Outlook*. Established in New South Wales in 1924, and in Victoria in 1925 as branches of London's Royal Institute of International Affairs (Chatham House), the AIIA is the only nationwide organisation of its kind in Australia and has been recognised as one of the leading think tanks in South-East Asia. It is financed by members' contributions, a small government subvention and tax-deductible donations from individuals and businesses. For further information, contact (02) 6282 2133 or visit.internationalaffairs.org.au.

Contributors

Nick Bisley is dean of the School of Humanities and Social Sciences and professor of International Relations at La Trobe University. Nick is a Fellow of the Australian Institute of International Affairs, President of the Australasian Council of Deans of Arts, Social Sciences and Humanities, a member of the advisory board of China Matters and a member of the Council for Security and Cooperation in the Asia Pacific. Between 2013 and 2018 he served as editor-in-chief of the *Australian Journal of International Affairs*. Nick is the author or editor of many works on international relations, including *The Belt and Road Initiative and the Future of Regional Order in the Indo-Pacific* (with Matthew Sussex and Michael Clarke; Lexington Books, 2020;), *Issues in 21st Century World Politics*, 3rd edition (Palgrave, 2017) and *Great Powers in the Changing International Order* (Lynne Rienner, 2012).

Danielle Chubb is an associate professor of International Relations in the School of Humanities and Social Sciences at Deakin University. She is a co-author of *Australian Public Opinion, Defence and Foreign Policy: Attitudes and Trends Since 1945* (Palgrave, 2021), the author of *Contentious Activism and Inter-Korean relations* (Columbia University Press, 2014), and a co-editor of *North Korean Human Rights: Activists and Networks* (Cambridge University Press, 2018).

Melissa Conley Tyler FAIIA is an honorary fellow in the Asia Institute at the University of Melbourne. She is Executive Director of the Asia-Pacific Development, Diplomacy and Defence Dialogue (AP4D), a new platform for collaboration between Australia's development, diplomacy and defence communities. Melissa served as national executive director of the Australian Institute of International Affairs for 13 years. She was recognised as a Fellow of the AIIA in 2019 for her service to Australia's international relations.

Sara E. Davies is professor of International Relations at Griffith University and Deputy Director (Indo-Pacific Research) at ARC Centre for the Elimination of Violence Against Women (CEVAW). Her research focuses on global health diplomacy and the Women, Peace and Security agenda. She has a forthcoming book, *Hidden Wars: Gendered Political Violence in Asia* (with Jacqui True, 2024), is co-editor of *The Oxford Handbook on Women, Peace and Security* (with Jacqui True; 2019) and is author of *Containing Contagion: The Politics of Disease Surveillance in Southeast Asia* (2019); and *Disease Diplomacy* (with Adam Kamradt-Scott and Simon Rushton; 2015).

Julian Dusting is a PhD student at Monash University.

Tamara Ernest has completed a Bachelor of Laws (Honours) and Bachelor of Arts (International Relations) at Monash University. Her research interests include the Women, Peace and Security agenda, women's leadership and feminist methodologies in international relations and law. Tamara works as a lawyer in an international commercial law firm.

Huiyun Feng is professor of international relations at Griffith University. Her recent publications include a co-authored book, *Contesting Revisionism: China, the United States, and the Transformation of International Order* (Oxford University Press, 2021), and a co-edited volume, *China's Challenges and International Order Transition: Beyond Thucydides's Trap* (University of Michigan Press, 2020).

Baogang He is Alfred Deakin Professor, Chair in International Relations, School of Humanities and Social Sciences, Faculty of Arts and Education, Deakin University, and a Fellow of the Academy of Social Sciences in Australia. Since graduating with a PhD in Political Science from the Australian National University in 1994, Professor He has become widely known for his work in Chinese politics, in particular the deliberative politics in China as well as in Asian politics covering regionalism, international relations, federalism and multiculturalism in Asia.

Kai He is a professor of international relations at Griffith University. His latest book is *Contesting Revisionism: The United States, China, and Transformation of International Order* (co-authored with Steve Chan, Huiyun Feng and Weixing Hu; Oxford University Press, 2021).

David Hundt is an associate professor of international relations in the School of Humanities and Social Sciences, Deakin University. His research interests include the politics, foreign policy and political economy of Asia and the Pacific, with a particular emphasis on Australia and South Korea. In 2022 he co-edited *China and Human Rights in North Korea: Debating a 'Developmental Approach' in Northeast Asia* (Routledge), along with Baogang He and Chengxin Pan.

Ian McAllister is Distinguished Professor of Political Science at the Australian National University. His most recent book is *An Advanced Introduction to Elections and Voting* (Elgar, 2022). He has been director of the Australian Election Study since 1987, and is a Fellow of the Academy of Social Sciences in Australia and a corresponding Fellow of the Royal Society of Edinburgh.

Matt McDonald is professor of international relations in the School of Political Science and International Studies, University of Queensland. His research is in the area of critical theoretical approaches to security, the relationship between environmental change and security, and Australian foreign and security policy. He has published widely on these themes in a range of journals, and is the author of *Security, the Environment and Emancipation* (Routledge, 2012), co-author (with Anthony Burke and Katrina Lee-Koo) of *Ethics and Global Security* (Routledge, 2014) and author of *Ecological Security* (Cambridge University Press, 2021).

Sarah Percy is associate professor of International Relations in the School of Politics and International Studies at the University of Queensland. Her research focuses on unconventional combatants and security challenges, and the relationship between international law and international relations.

Juliet Pietsch is head of the School of Government and International Relations at Griffith University and a professor of Public Policy and Comparative Politics whose specialist interests include immigration, race and ethnic politics in Australia and the Asia-Pacific region. Her recent work includes a manuscript with Cambridge University Press entitled 'Lost Opportunities: Temporary Migrants across the Asia Pacific'. She is working on a large international interdisciplinary project on population movements across Asia and the Pacific Islands with a focus on migration estimation in instances where data are inadequate or missing.

Geoffrey Stokes was emeritus professor in the Graduate School of Business and Law, RMIT University. He was the author, co-author or editor of 11 books on topics ranging from Australian politics and democratic theory to the philosophy of Karl Popper. Stokes was a senior editor of the *Australian Journal of Political Science* and the *Australian Journal of Politics and History*. From 1990 to 1991, he was senior adviser to the Minister for Trade and Overseas Development. He died in November 2023.

Rebecca Strating is director of La Trobe Asia and professor of Politics and International Relations in the School of Humanities and Social Sciences at La Trobe University. She researches maritime disputes in Asia and Australian foreign and defence policy.

See Seng Tan is president and CEO of International Students Inc., a faith-based non-profit organisation in the United States, and concurrently research adviser at S. Rajaratnam School of International Studies and senior associate at the Centre for Liberal Arts and Social Sciences, both at Nanyang Technological University in Singapore. His latest books include *Awaiting the Impossible: A Dialogue with Derrida, Deconstruction, and the Endless Wait for Messiah* (2022), *The European Union's Security Relations with Asian Partners* (2021) and *The Responsibility to Provide in Southeast Asia* (2019).

Huong Le Thu is the Chair of the Australia–Vietnam Policy Institute Board and is an Expert Associate at the National Security College of the Australian National University. Her recent publications include: 'How to survive great power competition: Southeast Asia's precarious balancing act' and 'Hanoi's American hedge: Why a new US partnership is unlikely to change Vietnam's multialignment strategy' in *Foreign Affairs*. At the time of writing, she was a senior fellow at the Australian Strategic Policy Institute.

Jacqui True FASSA, FAIA is professor of International Relations, director of the ARC Centre of Excellence for the Elimination of Violence against Women and a Global Fellow at the Peace Research Institute, Oslo. Her recent books include *Hidden Wars: Gendered Violence in Asia's Civil Conflicts* and *The Oxford Handbook on Women, Peace and Security* co-edited with Sara E. Davies.

Joanne Wallis is professor of international security in the Department of Politics and International Relations at the University of Adelaide. She is the author or editor of 10 books, including *Constitution Making during State Building* (Cambridge University Press, 2014), *Pacific Power? Australia's Strategy in the Pacific Islands* (Melbourne University Publishing, 2017) and *Girt by Sea: Re-imagining Australia's Security* (La Trobe University Press, 2024; with Rebecca Strating). Joanne is the chief investigator of an Australian Research Council Discovery project analysing the Australia–New Zealand alliance, of a Defence Strategic Policy Grant project analysing statecraft in the Pacific Islands, and of the Regional Perspectives Project in collaboration with the Defence Science and Technology Group and partners in Solomon Islands and Vanuatu. Between 2023 and 2028 she is the editor of the *Australian Journal of International Affairs*.

Thomas Wilkins is an associate professor in international security at the University of Sydney. He is also a (non-resident) senior fellow at the Australian Strategic Policy Institute

(ASPI), Pacific Forum and Japan Institute for International Affairs (JIIA) think tanks. He specialises in Indo–Pacific security affairs, Australian and Japanese foreign policy, and the bilateral Strategic Partnership. His latest monograph is *Security in Asia Pacific: The Dynamics of Alignment* (Lynne Rienner Press, 2019).

Abbreviations

ADF	Australian Defence Force
AES	Australian Election Study
AI	artificial intelligence
AIFFP	Australian Infrastructure Financing Facility for the Pacific
AIIB	Asian Infrastructure Investment Bank
ANZUS	Australia, New Zealand and United States
APc	Asia-Pacific community
APEC	Asia-Pacific Economic Cooperation
APS	Australian Public Service
APSC	Australian Public Service Commission
ARF	ASEAN Regional Forum
ASEAN	Association of South-East Asian Nations
ASIO	Australian Security Intelligence Organisation
ASPI	Australian Strategic Policy Institute
BRI	Belt and Road Initiative
ChAFTA	China-Australia Free Trade Agreement
COAG	Council of Australian Governments
CoP	Conference of the Parties
CPC	Communist Party of China
CPTPP	Comprehensive and Progressive Agreement for Trans-Pacific Partnership
CSP	Comprehensive Strategic Partnership
DFAT	Department of Foreign Affairs and Trade
DSUFSP	Defence Strategic Update and Force Structure Plan
DWP	Defence White Paper
EIDs	emerging infectious diseases
FITS	*Foreign Influence Transparency Scheme Act 2018* (Cth)
FOIP	Free and Open Indo-Pacific
FONOPs	Freedom of Navigation Operations
FPDA	Five Power Defence Arrangements
FPWP	Foreign Policy White Paper
GDP	Gross Domestic Product
GFC	Global Financial Crisis
ICBM	Inter-Continental Ballistic Missiles
IMF	International Monetary Fund
IONS	Indian Ocean Naval Symposium
IORA	Indian Ocean Regional Association
MOU	memorandum of understanding
NAP	national action plan
NATO	North Atlantic Treaty Organization
NEG	National Energy Guarantee

NGO	non-government organisation
NSC	National Security Committee of Cabinet
PCA	Permanent Court of Arbitration
PCR	polymerase chain reaction
PIF	Pacific Islands Forum
PMO	Prime Minister's Office
PPE	personal protective equipment
PRC	People's Republic of China
'Quad, the'	Quadrilateral Dialogue/Quadrilateral Security Initiative
RCEP	Regional Comprehensive Economic Partnership
SAFTA	Singapore-Australia Free Trade Agreement
SARS	Severe Acute Respiratory Syndrome
SCO	Shanghai Cooperation Organisation
TPP	Trans-Pacific Partnership
UN	United Nations
UNCLOS	United Nations Convention on the Law of the Sea
UNDP	United Nations Development Program
UNFCCC	United Nations Framework Convention on Climate Change
UNSCR	United Nations Security Council Resolution
USSC	University of Sydney United States Studies Centre
WHA	World Health Assembly
WHO	World Health Organization
WIL	Women in Leadership
WPS	Women, Peace and Security
WTO	World Trade Organization

Australian responses to great-power rivalry

Baogang He, David Hundt and Danielle Chubb

The first two decades of the 21st century witnessed profound changes in geopolitics and geoeconomics. Between 2016 and 2020, the erstwhile steady trend away from US unipolarity and towards a more truly multipolar international system accelerated, with significant implications for Australian foreign and security policy. As Hugh White (2017) argued in an influential *Quarterly Essay*, the unipolar moment of American primacy appeared to be over. Related to this development was the return of great-power rivalry to the centre stage of international relations (Wright, 2018). Toh Han Shih (2017: 255) described this as a new form of imperial contestation, in which both Washington and Beijing possessed and displayed certain attributes of empire. This shift presaged a new era in international relations, but whether this 21st-century version of strategic competition would constitute a 'new Cold War' (albeit a 'warm' one) was unclear when this volume was being completed in early 2022. Likewise, whether it would precipitate a power transition in favour of China remained to be seen. Irrespective of the terms used to describe this dynamic superpower struggle and its outcome, however, the world witnessed the intensification of this strategic competition from 2016 to 2020. This competition appeared likely to persist well into the new century (Wolf, 2019).

The main goal of this chapter is to describe the re-emergence of great-power competition between the United States and China, discuss how it reshaped the external environment and strategic space for Australia's foreign policy, and examine how Canberra responded to it. The chapter provides a detailed examination of the concept of great-power rivalry, a theme that is evident throughout the book. There is therefore some degree of overlap between this introduction and the chapters that follow, and between individual chapters, which focus on specific aspects of Australia's engagement in international affairs.

The remainder of this chapter proceeds as follows. The first section, 'Great-power competition', describes the emergence of great-power competition between the United States and China in several key realms of international affairs in the period under review, in particular the high-tech field. The second section, 'Great-power rivalry and Australian foreign policy', discusses how the Sino-American rivalry shaped Australia's foreign policy, while the third section, 'Australia's responses', surveys the variety of Australian responses to it. The chapter summarises the main trends and key characteristics of Australian foreign policy from 2016 to 2020, before concluding in the fourth section, 'Prospects', by considering the prospects for the decade ahead.

GREAT-POWER COMPETITION

A key accelerant of US–China competition from 2016 to 2020 was leadership and in particular China's attempts to consolidate its growing regional and global influence. After taking power in 2012, Xi Jinping launched the Belt and Road Initiative (BRI) in 2013, initiated the Asian Infrastructure Investment Bank (AIIB) in 2014, and sped up reclamation and island-building in the South China Sea in 2015 and 2016. Xi further consolidated his position through purges (often ostensibly on the grounds of fighting corruption) and a constitutional amendment in March 2018 that abolished term limits. Flowing from these changes was a more aggressive foreign policy that aimed at reclaiming a central place for Beijing on the world stage. There was also a strong economic dimension to this expansion of national power: China enhanced its reach in global production and supply chains (French, 2014), launched initiatives like the 'Made in China 2025' program, and replicated Japan's economic expansion policy in the 1980s and 1990s through foreign acquisitions of land and ports and the building of regional institutions (Chen & Shepherd, 2017; He, 2020).

The US view of China had begun to shift before 2016, with consensus on the engagement approach to China waning. As 2016 opened, the United States continued to call on China to halt dredging in the South China Sea, particularly its reclamation and island-building activities on Subi Reef in the Northern Spratlys (Gaouette, 2016). The election of Donald Trump to the presidency heralded a shift in Washington's China policy, which became characterised by strategic competition and confrontation. In 2017, the Trump administration's National Security Strategy labelled China a revisionist challenger to US power, influence and interests. It also asserted that the BRI was aimed at drawing Latin America into Beijing's orbit and locking African countries into 'debt-traps'. Trump affirmed US adherence to the One China policy (Chen & Lee, 2017) and hosted Xi at Mar-a-Lago to discuss trade and the North Korea nuclear issue (Phillips, 2017).

In March 2018, the Trump administration initiated a trade war with China and imposed sweeping tariffs on Chinese imports, which prompted retaliation from Beijing (Paletta, 2018). As relations deteriorated, Vice President Mike Pence affirmed in a speech to the Hudson Institute – described by some commentators as the 'biggest shift in US–China relations since Henry Kissinger's 1971 visit to Beijing' (Mead, 2018) – that the United States would prioritise competition over cooperation in its relations (Pence, 2018). In late 2018, and at Washington's request, Canadian authorities arrested Huawei's chief financial officer, Meng Wanzhou, at Vancouver airport. One year later, Trump signed a bill in support of Hong Kong pro-democracy protestors even as the United States sought a deal with China to end the trade stand-off (Williams & Mitchell, 2019). The two sides signed 'phase 1' of a trade deal in January 2020, but the deal's potential was undermined by the economic devastation brought on by the COVID-19 pandemic soon after the signing and the war of words that the United States and China engaged in over the origins of the virus and who bore responsibility (Brown, 2021).

Strategic competition between the United States and China was evident in terms of both hard and soft power, through the continued modernisation of military equipment and increases in expenditure and in the growing competition over each country's respective development model and approaches to human rights (see He, Hundt & Pan, 2022), respectively.

The two sides sparred over the function and purpose of regional multilateral organisations, with each seeking to consolidate their positions and pursue their interests via organisational means, such as the Shanghai Cooperation Organisation (SCO) and the Quadrilateral Dialogue ('the Quad'). China's regionalism increasingly became a new instrument for weakening and undermining the US-led alliance system (He, 2020). In 2017 China expanded the SCO to include India and Pakistan, turning it into a kind of Indo-Central Asia organisation to prevent the Washington-led Quad from being institutionalised (He, 2018a; 2020). It also developed and deepened Association of Southeast Asian Nations (ASEAN) plus 1 (China) with the aim of developing a new Code of Conduct regarding the South China Sea in 2019–20 (He, 2018b).

Economic aspects of great-power rivalry

Competition expanded in the economic realm too, largely at Beijing's instigation. China, for instance, formed a 'Yuan zone' to erode the dominance of the US dollar, created the AIIB and related projects, and sought to establish regional production and supply chains focused on its own industrial zones. The construction of maritime networks and infrastructure to support China's regional production networks, most notably through the BRI, was also part of a broader competition with the United States over regional infrastructure investment mechanisms. As Baogang He, Geoffrey Stokes and David Hundt illustrate in Chapter 14, the BRI was a source of great consternation for Australian foreign policy-makers.

Technology became a new site for strategic competition, particularly with respect to cutting-edge developments, as exemplified by the events surrounding Huawei. The Chinese firm, and its role in building 5G networks, almost became shorthand for Sino-American technological competition. Sectors such as semiconductors and artificial intelligence (AI), in addition to 5G, witnessed intensifying competition between Beijing and Washington. Control over critical raw materials like rare earths and supply chains was a key driver in the economic decoupling between the two economies. The United States tried to reduce its and its allies' reliance on Chinese technology (Kahata, 2020), while China looked to develop its own domestic semiconductor industry to reduce its reliance on US semiconductor manufacturing (You, 2021).

Global economic institutions were not spared from the influence of great-power competition. The US Ambassador to the WTO, Dennis Shea, for instance, took issue with China's 'market access barriers, forced technology transfers; intellectual property theft, discriminatory use of technical standards; massive government subsidies, a highly restrictive foreign investment regime'. Shea's Chinese counterpart, Ambassador Zhang Xiangchen, blamed what he called 'an unprecedented crisis of the multilateral trading system' on the United States, which he accused of 'blocking the normal proceedings and forcing a WTO body out of operation [which] is definitely not our way of doing things'.

China criticised the Trump administration's tariffs on steel and aluminium imports but dismissed concerns that Chinese state-owned enterprises were not market entities. From Australia's perspective, the situation was deeply unsatisfactory: a country whose foreign policy has long been premised on engagement with the 'rules-based international order' faced a situation whereby the world's two most powerful economies were wilfully violating those very rules.

GREAT-POWER RIVALRY AND AUSTRALIAN FOREIGN POLICY

The evolving competition between the United States and China reshaped Australia's external environment, with implications for its foreign policy in the five years under review. Washington, as Australia's closest ally, and Beijing, its biggest trading partner, both sought to pressure Canberra and influence its decisions. In 2020, for instance, China engaged in economic coercion in an unsuccessful effort to pressure Australia to break with the United States on various policies. The United States, meanwhile, leveraged diplomatic pressure to have Canberra adopt positions favourable to the US on issues such as Huawei and the BRI. As detailed by Sarah Percy and Rebecca Strating (Chapter 8), Australia faced difficulties in balancing its American-related security interests against its Chinese-related economic interests due to the close interrelationship of the security and economic realms, and the usurpation of geopolitics by geoeconomics. As Huiyun Feng and Kai He argue (Chapter 7), Australia sided with the United States.

Reducing the autonomy and breadth of Australian foreign policy options

Australia is generally portrayed as the archetypal middle power: neither influential enough to warrant great-power status nor so inconsequential as to be considered a minor player (Cooper, Higgott & Nossal, 1993; Beeson, 2011). This middle-power status has at times significantly shaped Australia's self-identity. The 2006–10 volume of *Australia in World Affairs*, for instance, was subtitled 'Middle Power Dreaming'. During the period examined in that volume, the Rudd government advocated middle-power diplomacy to establish an 'Asia–Pacific community' that would constrain the power of China *and* the United States, with the goal of reducing and managing conflict during a time of great-power transition. In the early 2000s, middle powers grew in importance and gained currency as Beijing and Washington competed to win them over. This afforded Canberra the strategic space in which to explore – often creatively – the possibility of innovative policies and practices.

Regional dynamics shifted significantly, however, and as US–China relations deteriorated between 2016 and 2020, Australia's scope for such policy experimentation was diminished. In particular, the assessment of the Trump administration – and indeed the US establishment more broadly – that the previous policy of engagement with China had largely failed and had in fact strengthened a powerful rival meant that Australia had to tread more carefully in its pursuit of its own policy lest it upset Washington.

Aligning more closely with Washington raised questions about the independence of Australia's foreign policy. Canberra had previously compartmentalised decisions on security and economic matters to a certain degree (see He, Stokes & Hundt, Chapter 14), but Nick Bisley (Chapter 2) argues that this was untenable in the new international strategic milieu. Australia's international economic policies towards China were unavoidably subjected to security scrutiny and, to an extent, subordinate to the security interests of Washington due to its rivalry with China. This further reduced Canberra's strategic autonomy.

Australia had previously developed a wide variety of policy instruments to manage its alliance with the United States and simultaneously deal with the rise of China (see for example Bell, 1988). As Sarah Percy and Rebecca Strating argue (Chapter 8), navigating the 'high politics' of superpower rivalry is a longstanding feature of Australian foreign policy. Responses by Australia have been described, *inter alia*, as accommodation (Manicom & O'Neil, 2010), buck-passing (Schweller, 1999: 16–17), hedging (Medeiros, 2005), avoidance (Goh, 2008), socialising (Ba, 2006), integration (Blair, Hills & Jannuzi, 2007), containment (Rachman, 1996), 'constrainment' (Shambaugh, 1996), norm preservation (Strating, 2020) and soft balancing (McDougall, 2012). By 2020, however, accommodation appeared to be impossible due to China's more hard-line approach and economic coercion. Buck-passing had become much more difficult given Washington's calls on its allies for greater contributions and Australia's desire to demonstrate that it was a good ally and to consolidate the US presence in Asia. Hedging and soft balancing likewise seemed no longer to be viable. In place of alternatives, the dominant framework appeared to be confrontation. Thomas Wilkins (Chapter 11) explores how this was played out in Australia's commitment to the US Indo-Pacific Strategy. Further evidence could be found in Australia's decisions to modernise its military and capability enhancement plans (such as the acquisition of long-range strike capability) as well as bellicose comments by senior ministers and bureaucrats (Daly, 2021).

Australia's uneasy position amid great-power rivalry

Australia was not alone in seeing the emergence of great-power rivalry as contrary to its interests. Initially at least, international public opinion turned against the United States and in favour of China, largely because of Trump's disregard for the concerns of even close US allies. When Gallup asked respondents in Asia, Africa and Europe which of the two great powers provided better international leadership, narrow majorities in all three regions nominated China in 2018. When asked the same question a year later, a small shift was evident: the United States had edged in front of China (Reinhart & Ritter, 2019: 3). In 2020, this trend continued. Pew Research reported that negative views of the great powers had 'soared in many countries' and were 'at or near historic highs', but international public opinion was significantly more positive about the United States than China (Silver, Devlin & Huang, 2020).

Amid this 'reversion to the mean', Australia's position is worthy of analysis. In the 2020 Pew survey, favourable views of the United States among respondents in most European countries were only marginally ahead of those of China. By contrast, two North-East Asian allies, South Korea and Japan, were by far and away the most favourable in their views of American leadership as opposed to the Chinese variant. Australian assessments were somewhere in between these two poles: most Australians were positively disposed towards the United States but still offered it less than a ringing endorsement (Silver, Devlin & Huang, 2020).

This somewhat jaundiced view of the United States coexisted with a serious and sudden decline in Australian public opinion about China. As Danielle Chubb and Ian

McAllister discuss (Chapter 3), the US alliance and China, alongside climate change, were the three main foreign policy issues that concerned Australians during the period under review. As recently as 2018, Australians had viewed China about as favourably as they did South Korea, Indonesia and the European Union. By 2020 (and into 2021), Australian favourability of China was at a similar level to that of Iran and North Korea (Kassam, 2021). Despite this decline in sentiment, there remained a strong sense in public opinion and among policy-makers that Australia had no real choice but to continue to engage China. Former Department of Foreign Affairs and Trade (DFAT) Secretary Peter Varghese (2020), for instance, argued that Australia – unlike the United States – needed to adopt a hybrid approach of 'engage and constrain' due to a function of its geographic and power realities.

AUSTRALIA'S RESPONSES

Australia, like other countries in the Indo-Pacific region, faced the growing challenge of China's coercive statecraft between 2016 and 2020. Australia was particularly vulnerable to China's economic statecraft, as exemplified by the sanctions placed on a range of Australian goods in 2020 (see Chapter 14). Australia made various responses to these changes.

At the domestic level, power was returned to the Prime Minister's Office. The line between foreign affairs on the one hand, and domestic economic matters and political and cultural life on the other, is increasingly blurred in contemporary politics. On issues of foreign affairs, Australian prime ministers must coordinate with a variety of departments. Kevin Rudd, for instance, accelerated the practice through the formation of a mini-Cabinet involving the Treasurer, Finance Minister and Deputy Prime Minister (Taylor, 2009), and the centralisation of political appointments (Carr & Roberts, 2010: 241–3). Thereafter Julia Gillard 'restored a highly disciplined foreign policy decision-making process', and the period from 2011 to 2015 saw a reassertion of DFAT's role in the foreign policy process (Wesley, 2016: 243).

This trend of centralisation was not reversed between 2016 and 2020, but it did reach something of an equilibrium. Australian foreign policy leadership was relatively more stable after the Coalition won government in 2013, which saw Julie Bishop attain and hold the position of Foreign Minister until 2018. While Bishop was not known for grand foreign policy visions, her term was nonetheless characterised, in the words of Rory Medcalf (2018), by 'the unglamorous work of ... actually building capability'. Thus, under Bishop, DFAT at least partially reasserted its authority over foreign policy.

The Morrison government largely continued the trend of centralisation. A key criticism was a lack of transparency in decision-making, which some characterised as arrogance. For instance, the National Cabinet was formed during the emergency conditions of the COVID-19 pandemic but was extended indefinitely as a de facto replacement for the Council of Australian Governments (Tulich, Reilly & Murray, 2020). Coordination was vital during the pandemic, but the prolongation of the National Cabinet continued the trend towards the centralisation of power in Australian politics.

Not only was power being centralised but also this was occurring within a federal system of government. Beijing was aware of the weaknesses inherent in federalism and sought to exploit them to create inconsistencies or the appearance of national division.

A notable example was China's success in getting the state government of Victoria to sign a BRI memorandum of understanding. This stoked tension between the Australian Government in Canberra and the state of Victoria, given that their positions were inconsistent. It also highlighted the difficulty in distinguishing between economic and security policy: Canberra argued that the BRI was a foreign policy matter and therefore the prerogative of the national government, whereas Victoria claimed that it had signed the memorandum to address state-level economic issues. As Melissa Conley Tyler and Julian Dusting argue (Chapter 5), the Australian parliament in 2020 passed legislation allowing it to terminate any agreements made by state governments – and public institutions such as universities – that it deemed were not in the national interest.

Speaking out on (and to) China

Another response from Australia was to voice security concerns openly in its relationship with China and to criticise China's heavy-handed style of tough Hong Kong policy and its human rights violations. Other interests, including those of trade and such sectors as higher education, were overlooked as a more hard-line approach came to dominate policy. The merging of geopolitics and geoeconomics benefited from the inclusion of security issues in foreign policy-making, but the securitisation of Australian foreign policy went well beyond what could reasonably be expected under the circumstances. A prime example of such overreach was Treasurer Josh Frydenberg's proposal that the 'Five Eyes', an intelligence-sharing arrangement between Australia, the United States, the United Kingdom, Canada and New Zealand, be used to develop a post-COVID-19 economic recovery plan (McKinley, 2020).

Canberra's vocal criticism of China's human rights record was not entirely new, but it attracted renewed attention. Speaking at the Institute for International Strategic Studies in Singapore in March 2017, Foreign Minister Bishop strongly defended democracy and democratic values. Along with liberal economics, Bishop claimed, democracy underpinned the stability and prosperity of the Indo-Pacific region via the establishment and maintenance of the 'rules-based order'. She implied that democracy was a normative prerequisite for China, should it wish to become a regional leader in Asia (Bishop, 2017).

Prime Minister Malcolm Turnbull's Shangri-La Speech, delivered in Singapore four months after Bishop's, warned of the 'gathering clouds of uncertainty and instability' that might threaten the rules-based order in the region and result in the emergence of a Chinese 'Monroe Doctrine' (Turnbull, 2017). Like Bishop, Turnbull referred to democracy, along with freedom and the rule of law, as the values from which US leadership derived its 'greatest potency' (Turnball, 2017). This was both a call to the United States to maintain its leadership of the liberal order in Asia and a reiteration of Bishop's argument that democracy was a prerequisite for China's regional leadership ambitions.

In addition to these unilateral statements, Canberra worked with like-minded countries to criticise China's human rights. In 2016, for example, Australia signed a joint statement that 'highlight[ed] China's ongoing problematic human rights record' along with 11 other countries in the United Nations Human Rights Council. In 2017, Australia signed a joint letter with 10 other countries, sent to the Chinese Minister of Public Security, Guo Shengkun, that expressed concern over 'credible claims of torture' inflicted on rights activists and lawyers. In 2019, Canberra again signed a letter, together with 21 other countries, to the chairperson of the Human Rights Council, claiming that China's actions in Xinjiang were 'inconsistent with its national laws and international obligations' (Laurenceson, 2019). Marise Payne, who replaced Bishop as Foreign Minister in late 2018, said that China needed to be held to account for its human rights abuses, particularly in Xinjiang: 'Speaking our minds does not constitute interfering in another country ... We will not surprise any country by advocating consistently for human rights. It will remain part of our conversations, including with China, as our relationship with our Comprehensive Strategic Partner continues to evolve. We will remain constructive and respectful.' (Doherty, 2019)

Another issue that attracted attention from Australia was the 2019 pro-democracy protests in Hong Kong. Initially, Australia expressed hope that the situation would be resolved in a way that 'upholds the rights and freedoms enshrined in Hong Kong's Basic Law under the "one country, two systems" framework' (Minister for Foreign Affairs, 2019). In April 2020, Australia criticised the arrests of 'high-profile pro-democracy figures' in Hong Kong: 'The advantages protected under the "One Country, Two Systems" framework include open and accountable law enforcement which meets society's expectations and the professional and unbiased application of justice. Both are vital to restore confidence and stability in Hong Kong, never more so than now.' (Minister for Foreign Affairs, 2020)

There was also a domestic component to Australia's newly assertive stance on China. In response to Beijing's foreign penetration of Australian institutions and undue influence over some of its politicians, in 2018 and 2020 parliament passed three pieces of legislation relating to 'foreign influence' (see Chapter 5). In this way, Australia used legal countermeasures to defend its democracy and freedom. At the same time, Asian Australians, and in particular those of Chinese descent, played little role in determining the government's confrontational policy towards China, which ran contrary to the interests of this segment of the population (He, 2018c). Juliet Pietsch (Chapter 6) argues that Chinese Australians favoured good relations between the two countries and consistently rejected the confrontational policy, as their perception of China's threat was lower than that of their non-Asian counterparts.

Articulating values in foreign policy

As these references to human rights indicate, Australia became more explicit in articulating values in its foreign policy. Indeed Benjamin Reilly (2020) claims that values 'assumed a central place in [the] foreign policy rhetoric'. This coincided with a greater willingness by China to champion its own governance model, and the values associated with it, internationally. Reilly (2020) charts the evolution of Australia's diplomatic language and identifies the adoption of the phrase 'rules-based order' as heralding the beginning of the shift towards a more values-laden foreign policy rhetoric. He claims that the term 'values' became more prominent in Defence and Foreign Policy White Papers and that the term was used to highlight, usually but not always implicitly, Australia's commitment to defend the status quo international order against the contrasting values of authoritarian governments like China's. 'Like-minded' is another term that was increasingly used to suggest a coalition of countries that share and are committed to certain shared values. This reflected, as Stephen Kuper suggests (2019), a branching of US–China competition into the values domain.

In keeping with the emergence of values in foreign policy, the promotion of gender equality in international politics became a key part of Australia's soft power strategy. Jacqui True and Tamara Ernest (Chapter 4) illustrate how the promise of promoting a gender-equality agenda helped Australia to secure a non-permanent seat on the UN Security Council (2013–14) and UN Human Rights Council membership (2018–20). Gender equality was relevant to great-power politics in at least two ways. First, it helped Australia to strengthen the US-led alliance, as both Washington and Canberra were committed to this core value and its practice. Second, it was an effective way for Australia to build its soft power to compete with Chinese influence in the Pacific islands (see Chapter 12). Australia's aid program featured women's empowerment and leadership, unlike China's, which mainly focused on infrastructure, raw materials and mining interests.

Turnbull, as noted above, was a strong advocate for the 'rules-based international order'. The 2016 Defence and 2017 Foreign Policy White Papers reflected his approach. In the former, the 'concept was explicitly integrated in defining [Australia's] "strategic defence interests" and "strategic defence objectives"' while the latter explicitly focused on the defence of the 'rules-based order' (Medcalf, in Scott, Nyst & Roggeveen, 2020). References to the rules-based order reached all-time highs in 2017 and 2018, with the phrase being used 169 and 174 times respectively in national security and foreign policy speeches by senior ministers. By way of comparison, the next most frequent use of the term was in 2011, when the Gillard government made 46 such references (Scott, Nyst & Roggeveen, 2020).

There was a subtle change under Morrison, with the focus shifting somewhat pragmatically from advocating and defending the rules-based order towards a focus on power and deterrence in the 2020 Defence Strategic Update. This is perhaps not surprising, given Australia's deteriorating strategic environment (Scott, Nyst & Roggeveen, 2020). Nevertheless, there was continuity in the deliberate characterisation of the international order as 'rules-based' rather than 'liberal'. The liberal elements were not disavowed and were mentioned in key speeches, but giving more focus to 'the rules' seemed to be a way for Morrison to make non-democratic states in the Indo-Pacific more receptive to cooperating with Australia in defence of the status quo (Bisley & Schreer, 2018).

Adoption of the Indo-Pacific strategy and revival of the Quad

Australia developed and adopted several initiatives as part of its implementation of an Indo-Pacific strategy. Perhaps the most visible of these was the strengthening and institutionalisation of the Quadrilateral Security Dialogue. This informal grouping of Australia, Japan, India and the United States was established in the mid-2000s ostensibly to discuss regional security issues, but it appeared to many to be aimed at competing with and even containing China. The Quad went into hiatus after 2008, when Australia withdrew over concerns it was upsetting China, but the increasingly revisionist behaviour of Beijing 'galvanized motivations in each Quad nation to further integrate', with the narrative of a free and open regional Indo-Pacific order serving as 'the foundation for bilateral, trilateral, and eventually quadrilateral action to realize that vision' (Buchan & Rimland, 2020).

In November 2017, following the official adoption of the term 'Free and Open Indo-Pacific' by its members, the newly revived Quad officially met in Manila. Further meetings were held in Singapore (June and November 2018) and Bangkok (May 2019). In September 2019, foreign ministers met for the first time under the official auspices of the Quad in New York. In March 2020, the first 'Quad plus' meeting was held to discuss COVID-19 and involved New Zealand, South Korea and Vietnam. While this momentum did not equate to the formation of a formal alliance, particularly given India's tradition of non-alignment, it represented 'an incremental deepening of Quadrilateral relations, with escalation remaining flexible and responsive to Chinese action, and building the capability to act jointly should the need arise' (Lee, 2020).

In addition to the high-level summitry, the Indo-Pacific strategy was evident in Australian foreign policy towards two vital subregions: the Pacific and South-East Asia. In the Pacific, Australia made a long-overdue response to China's developmental sub-regionalism. In 2006 the PRC had established the China–Pacific Island Countries Economic Development and Cooperation Leaders Forum, and in 2019 an Action Plan was agreed to by key players in the region. Australia saw China as an outsider in the South Pacific, but China's endorsement and enlargement of the concept of the Indo-Pacific enabled it to re-present itself as a Pacific country and a critical actor in the region. This is a theme that Joanne Wallis and Huong Le Thu address (Chapter 12). In response to what it perceived as Chinese attempts to dilute Australian influence, they argue, Canberra implemented a Pacific 'Step-up' in conjunction with its adoption of the FOIP language and its Quad commitments. There was overlap between these initiatives, including some involving all four Quad members (Pankaj, 2021).

Canberra also significantly increased its diplomatic presence and funding for development in the Pacific from 2017, while during the coronavirus pandemic Australia pledged additional funding to distribute vaccines in the region (Zhou & Walsh, 2020). Sara Davies (Chapter 10) examines how Australia has sought to engage in health diplomacy in the region. Taken together, these various efforts amounted to an attempt to rebuild Australia's influence in the Pacific, alongside other elements of power enhancement such as the Quad and military modernisation.

A criticism of the Step Up was that it would divert funding away from South-East Asia (Wyeth, 2020), a region with a far greater population and of more geopolitical incompetence to the regional order than the Pacific (Lemahieu, 2020). Perhaps acknowledging this seeming gap in its Indo-Pacific policies, in late 2020 Canberra unveiled a raft of initiatives targeted at South-East Asia. These included pledges to fund and donate vaccines to the region, both through the COVAX Advance Market Commitment and unilaterally, and more than half a billion dollars worth 'of economic, development and security measures to support the region's recovery from COVID-19'. It also included a A$1.5 billion loan to Indonesia and A$104 million to address the region's emerging security needs (Maude, 2020).

Canberra also secured support for an annual bilateral summit with ASEAN, putting it on the same level as the United States, China, Japan and India (Maude, 2020). This reflects a long-running but only modestly successful campaign by Australia to exert influence in South-East Asia, often through key partners such as Singapore, as See Seng Tan notes (Chapter 13). Similarly, Australia was a party to the Regional Comprehensive Economic Partnership, a multilateral trade deal conceived of by ASEAN members in the 2010s, completed in late 2020 and becoming effective on 1 January 2022. Taken together, these developments showed Australia's intent to substantiate its Indo-Pacific strategy.

PROSPECTS

From 2016 to 2020, Australia increased its security dependence on the United States in an age of great-power rivalry. The United States continued its relative decline, as was evident in the Trump administration's self-defeating behaviour in sustaining global leadership and its active abdication of such a role, but Australia maintained and even strengthened its relationship with Washington. However, this came at the price of increased uncertainty and vulnerability. As it hewed closely to the United States, Australia became increasingly isolated when dealing with other countries on issues like climate change (see Chapter 9).

China demonstrated an increasing willingness to challenge the US-led 'rules-based order' and sought to revise it and promote its own hybrid version of order. China's BRI covered the vital regions of Asia, Europe, the South Pacific, Latin America, and Africa, and thus represented Beijing's first step on a new Sinocentric order-building project. Such a continental system, if realised, would challenge the rules-based order associated with, if no longer led by, the United States.

Looking ahead, great-power competition between the United States and China seems set to dominate international relations for the foreseeable future. Cooperation between the great powers is a functional necessity, but confrontation and even armed conflict cannot be confidently ruled out. History is replete with examples of conflicts that stem from miscalculation and bad luck. Given the lack of hegemonic predictability, it would be prudent for Australia to learn how to 'Live with Leviathans' in the third decade of the 21st century.

References

Ba, A.D. (2006) Who's socializing whom? Complex engagement in Sino-ASEAN relations. *Pacific Review* 19(2): 157–79

Beeson, M. (2011) Can Australia save the world? The limits and possibilities of middle power diplomacy. *Australian Journal of International Affairs* 65(5): 563–77

Bell, C. (1988) *Dependent Ally: A Study in Australian Foreign Policy*. Melbourne: Oxford University Press

Bishop, J. (2017) Change and uncertainty in the Indo-Pacific: Strategic challenges and opportunities. 28th IISS Fullerton Lecture, Singapore, 13 March. https://foreignminister.gov.au/speeches/Pages/2017/jb_sp_170313a.aspx

Bisley, N. & Schreer, B. (2018) Will Australia defend the 'rules-based order' in Asia? Australian Strategic Policy Institute, 18 April. https://www.aspistrategist.org.au/will-australia-defend-rules-based-order-asia

Blair, D.C., Hills, C.A. & Jannuzi, F.S. (2007) *US–China Relations: An Affirmative Agenda, a Responsible Course: Report of an Independent Task Force*. New York: Council on Foreign Relations

Brown, C. (2021) Anatomy of a flop: Why Trump's US–China phase one trade deal fell short. Peterson Institute for International Economics, 8 February. https://www.piie.com/blogs/trade-and-investment-policy-watch/anatomy-flop-why-trumps-us-china-phase-one-trade-deal-fell

Buchan, P.G. & Rimland, B. (2020) Defining the Diamond: The Past, Present and Future of the Quadrilateral Security Dialogue. Center for Strategic and International Studies, 16 March. https://www.csis.org/analysis/defining-diamond-past-present-and-future-quadrilateral-security-dialogue

Carr, A. & Roberts, C. (2010) Foreign policy. In C. Aulich & M. Evans (eds), *The Rudd Government: Australian Commonwealth Administration 2007–2010*, pp. 241–57. Canberra: ANU Press

Chen, T.-P. & Lee, C.E. (2017) Donald Trump commits to 'One China' Policy in Call with Xi Jinpin. *Wall Street Journal*, 20 February. https://www.wsj.com/articles/donald-trump-affirms-commitment-to-one-china-policy-in-call-with-xi-jinping-1486699771

Chen, Y. & Shepherd, C. (2017) E-sports to chocolates: Chinese cities rush into risky specialization. *Reuters*, 8 December. https://www.reuters.com/article/us-china-economy-rejuvenation-insight/e-sports-to-chocolates-chinese-cities-rush-into-risky-specialization-idUSKBN1E2020

Cooper, A.F., Higgott, R.A. & Nossal, K.R. (1993) *Relocating Middle Powers: Australia and Canada in a Changing World Order*. Vancouver: University of British Columbia Press

Daly, P. (2021) Dutton and Pezzullo talk up the beating drums of war – but it is not them who will have to fight. *Guardian*, 29 April. https://www.theguardian.com/commentisfree/2021/apr/29/dutton-and-pezzullo-talk-up-the-beating-drums-of-war-but-it-is-not-them-who-will-have-to-fight

Doherty, B. (2019) Marise Payne says China must be held to account for human rights abuses. *Guardian*, 30 October. https://www.theguardian.com/australia-news/2019/oct/30/marise-payne-says-china-must-be-held-to-account-for-human-rights-abuses

French, H.H. (2014) *China's Second Continent: How a Million Migrants are Building a New Empire in Africa*. New York: Alfred A. Knopf

Gaouette, N. (2016) Obama calls for halt to new construction, militarization in Asian waters. *CNN Politics*, 16 February. https://edition.cnn.com/2016/02/16/politics/obama-halt-militarization-south-china-sea/index.html

Goh, E. (2008) Great powers and hierarchical order in Southeast Asia: Analyzing regional security strategies. *International Security* 32(3): 113–57

He, B. (2018a) Chinese expanded perceptions of the region and its changing attitudes toward the Indo-Pacific: A hybrid vision of the institutionalization of the Indo-Pacific. *East Asia: An International Quarterly* 35(4): 117–32

——(2018b) Security regionalism: A new form of strategic competition or cooperation between the United States and China in the South China Sea? In H. Feng and K. He (eds), *US–China Competition and the South China Sea Disputes*, pp. 151–69. London: Routledge

——(2018c) Diversity leadership multiculturalism: The challenge of the securitization of Chinese migrants in Australia. *International Social Science Journal* 68(227–228): 119–31

——(2020) Regionalism as an instrument for global power contestation: The case of China. *Asian Studies Review* 44(1): 79–96

He, B., Hundt, D. & Pan, C. (eds) (2022) *China and Human Rights in North Korea: Debating a 'Developmental Approach' in Northeast Asia*. Singapore: Routledge

Kahata, A. (2020) Managing US–China Technology Competition and Decoupling. Center for Strategic and International Studies, 24 November. https://www.csis.org/blogs/technology-policy-blog/managing-us-china-technology-competition-and-decoupling

Kassam, N. (2021) *2021 Lowy Institute Poll: Understanding Australian Attitudes to the World*. Sydney: Lowy Institute for International Policy. https://poll.lowyinstitute.org/files/lowyinsitutepoll-2021.pdf

Kuper, S. (2019) Balancing values, Australia's China relations and its position in the region. *Defence Connect*, 15 October. https://www.defenceconnect.com.au/key-enablers/4953-balancing-values-australia-s-china-relations-and-the-position-in-the-region

Laurenceson, J. (2019) The efficacy of being very vocal: Australia and human rights in China. *Australian Outlook*, 24 July. http://www.internationalaffairs.org.au/australianoutlook/the-efficacy-of-being-very-vocal-australia-and-human-rights-in-china

Lee, L. (2020) Assessing the quad: Prospects and limitations of quadrilateral cooperation for advancing Australia's interests. Lowy Institute, 19 May. https://www.lowyinstitute.org/publications/assessing-quad-prospects-and-limitations-quadrilateral-cooperation-advancing-australia

Lemahieu, H. (2020) The case for Australia to step up in South-East Asia. *Australian Financial Review*, 23 October. https://www.afr.com/policy/foreign-affairs/the-case-for-australia-to-step-up-in-south-east-asia-20201021-p56743

Manicom, J. & O'Neil, A. (2010) Accommodation, realignment or business as usual? Australia's response to a rising China. *Pacific Review* 23(1): 23–44

Maude, R. (2020) Australia gets more diplomatic firepower in Southeast Asia. Asia Society Australia, 16 November. https://asiasociety.org/australia/australia-gets-more-diplomatic-firepower-south-east-asia

McDougall, D. (2012) Responses to 'Rising China' in the East Asian Region: Soft balancing with accommodation. *Journal of Contemporary China* 21(73): 1–17

McKinley, M. (2020) Accelerating securitisation and militarisation in Australian politics: Symptoms of democracy in decline. *Pearls and Irritations*, 18 June. https://johnmenadue.com/michael-mckinley-accelerating-securitisation-and-militarisation-in-australian-politics-symptoms-of-democracy-in-decline/

Mead, W.R. (2018) Mike Pence announces Cold War II. *Wall Street Journal*, 8 October. https://www.wsj.com/articles/mike-pence-announces-cold-war-ii-1539039480

Medcalf, R. (2018) Julie Bishop's authentic Australian foreign policy must continue. *Australian Financial Review*, 2 September. https://www.afr.com/opinion/julie-bishops-authentically-australian-foreign-policy-must-continue-20180902-h14ttx

Medeiros, E.S. (2005) Strategic hedging and the future of Asia–Pacific stability. *Washington Quarterly* 29(1): 145–67

Minister for Foreign Affairs (2019) Statement on protests in Hong Kong. Media release, 12 June. https://www.foreignminister.gov.au/minister/marise-payne/media-release/statement-protests-hong-kong

———(2020) Statement on arrests of pro-democracy figures in Hong Kong. Media release, 19 April. https://www.foreignminister.gov.au/minister/marise-payne/media-release/statement-arrests-pro-democracy-figures-hong-kong

Paletta, D. (2018) Trade war escalates as China says it will impose tariffs on 128 US exports, including pork and fruit. *Washington Post*, 2 April. https://www.washingtonpost.com/news/business/wp/2018/04/01/trade-war-escalates-as-china-vows-to-impose-tariffs-on-128-u-s-exports-including-pork-and-fruit/

Pankaj, E. (2021) Australia's Pacific step-up and the Quad. *Interpreter*, Lowy Institute, 19 January. https://www.lowyinstitute.org/the-interpreter/australia-s-pacific-step-and-quad

Pence, M. (2018) *Vice President Mike Pence's Remarks on the Administration's Policy towards China*. Hudson Institute, 4 October. https://www.hudson.org/events/1610-vice-president-mike-pence-s-remarks-on-the-administration-s-policy-towards-china102018

Phillips, T. (2017) Chinese president Xi Jinping arrives for first meeting with Donald Trump. *Guardian*, 7 April. https://www.theguardian.com/us-news/2017/apr/06/trump-china-meeting-xi-jinping-mar-a-lago

Rachman, G. (1996) Containing China. *Washington Quarterly* 19(1): 129–39

Reilly, B. (2020) Why is 'values' the new buzzword in Australian foreign policy? (Hint: it has something to do with China). *Conversation*, 5 August. https://theconversation.com/why-is-values-the-new-buzzword-in-australian-foreign-policy-hint-it-has-something-to-do-with-china-143839

Reinhart, R.J. & Ritter, Z. (2019) China's leadership gains global admirers. *Gallup*, 4 March. https://news.gallup.com/poll/247196/china-leadership-gains-global-admirers.aspx

Schweller, R.L. (1999) Managing the rise of great powers: History and theory. In A.I. Johnston & R.S. Ross (eds), *Engaging China: The Management of an Emerging Power*, pp. 1–33. New York: Routledge

Scott, B., Nyst, M. & Roggeveen, S. (2020) Australia's Security and the Rules-based Order: Tracking a Decade of Policy Evolution. Lowy Institute. https://interactives.lowyinstitute.org/features/rules-based-order

Shambaugh, D. (1996) Containment or engagement of China? Calculating Beijing's response. *International Security* 21(2): 180–209

Silver, L., Devlin, K. & Huang, C. (2020) Negative views of both US and China abound across advanced economies amid COVID-19. Washington: Pew Research Center, 6 October. https://www.pewresearch.org/fact-tank/2020/10/06/negative-views-of-both-us-and-china-amid-COVID-19/

Strating, R. (2020) Norm contestation, statecraft and the South China Sea: Defending maritime order. *Pacific Review*. https://doi.org/10.1080/09512748.2020.1804990

Taylor, L. (2009) Coalition sure of one thing: It's Rudd's fault. *Australian*, 22 August. http://www.theaustralian.com.au/news/opinion/coalition-sure-of-one-thing-its-rudds-fault/story-e6frg6zo-1225765002457

Toh, H.S. (2017) *Is China an Empire?* Singapore: World Scientific

Tulich, T., Reilly, B. & Murray, S. (2020) *The National Cabinet: Presidentialised Politics, Power-sharing and a Deficit in Transparency*. Australian Public Law, 23 October. https://auspublaw.org/2020/10/The-National-Cabinet-Presidentialised-Politics-Power-Sharing-And-A-Deficit-In-Transparency/

Turnbull, M. (2017) Keynote address at the 16th IISS Asia Security Summit, Shangri-La Dialogue, 3 June. https://www.malcolmturnbull.com.au/media/keynote-address-at-the-16th-iiss-asia-security-summit-shangri-la-dialogue

Varghese, P. (2020) What should Australia do to manage risk in its relationship with the PRC? *China Matters*, 26 June. https://johnmenadue.com/what-should-australia-do-to-manage-risk-in-its-relationship-with-the-prc-china-matters-26-6-20/

Wesley, M. (2016) The foreign policy process. In M. Beeson & S. Hameiri (eds), *Navigating the New International Disorder: Australia in World Affairs, 2011–2015*, pp. 242–53. Melbourne: Oxford University Press

White, H. (2017) Without America: Australia in the new Asia. *Quarterly Essay* 68: 1–81

Williams, A. & Mitchell, T. (2019) Donald Trump signs Hong Kong pro-democracy bills. *Financial Times*, 28 November. https://www.ft.com/content/7a7ae10c-1170-11ea-a7e6-62bf4f9e548a

Wolf, M. (2019) The looming 100-year US–China conflict. *Financial Review*, 5 June. https://www.ft.com/content/52b71928-85fd-11e9-a028-86cea8523dc2

Wright, T. (2018) The return to great-power rivalry was inevitable. *Atlantic*, 12 September. https://www.theatlantic.com/international/archive/2018/09/liberal-international-order-free-world-trump-authoritarianism/569881/

Wyeth, G. (2020) Australia's Southeast Asian step down. *Diplomat*, 17 March. https://thediplomat.com/2020/03/australias-southeast-asian-step-down/

You, H. (2021) Semiconductors and the US–China innovation race geopolitics of the supply chain and the central role of Taiwan. *Foreign Policy*, 16 February. https://foreignpolicy.com/2021/02/16/semiconductors-us-china-taiwan-technology-innovation-competition/

Zhou, C. & Walsh, M. (2020) Australia pledged to 'step up' in the Pacific amid growing Chinese influence, but are we on track? *ABC News*, 18 January. https://www.abc.net.au/news/2020-01-18/australia-pacific-step-up-in-review/11863150

Part I

The domestic politics of Australian foreign policy

The foreign policy process

Adjusting to a new era

Nick Bisley

This chapter is concerned with how the Australian foreign policy process developed during a period in which great-power politics returned to the centre stage of world politics and how it interacted with and was shaped by these transformations. In particular, this chapter examines the foreign policy process through the lens of three main developments: the significant change in Australia's approach to the People's Republic of China, the dominance of security in Australian foreign policy, and the wholesale and enthusiastic adoption of the Indo-Pacific strategic construct. Rather than adopting a conventional 'institution-by-institution' approach for the analysis of these developments, the chapter instead focuses on the shifting relationship between the institutions that shape Australian foreign policy and the ideas and individuals involved in that process. These three features of the policy process are worthy of close analysis in their own right, so the chapter examines each in turn. The conclusion reflects on what these developments tell us about the foreign policy process and in particular the role played by key institutions, individuals and actors, such as think tanks, parliament and the media, during this period.

To begin, it is important to explain how I am using the notion of the foreign policy process. Despite its everyday usage, foreign policy is a surprisingly slippery concept (Hill, 2015). Some argue that it refers to the actions of a state in dealings with other states. While intuitive, this definition has problems; states deal with many other kinds of actors beyond their borders than just states. Equally, foreign policy entails a complex and difficult-to-corral process unfolding over time. This chapter focuses on foreign policy understood as the process through which states navigate and manage their interactions with international actors.

This involves two key components. The first is the understanding of it as inherently dynamic, a set of interactions that develop over time in which ideas, individuals and institutions interact and compete to influence outcomes. The second relates to the actors, and here the understanding is that the participants in the process are not only states and their component parts but also organisations, interest groups and others with a capacity to shape outcomes at the international level, such as firms, the media and non-government organisations (NGOs). This process-focused understanding of foreign policy is needed as even in a country of Australia's size the range of individuals and institutions that shape the ideas that eventually become policy decisions, and that are then implemented in uneven and imperfect ways, is significant. The perspective of this chapter is one that looks at foreign policy as the product of the interaction of processes with key structures that evolve over time.

It follows that to make sense of a country's foreign policy over a particular period one needs not just to consider the most obvious questions relating to decision-making in a narrow mechanistic sense (who is the foreign minister? What is her relationship with the prime minister?) but also to examine the institutional forms that shape the process and how they have changed over time. Above all, one should focus on the ideas and concepts that are jostling for influence. Analysts should try to work out how and why certain ideas prevail over others. What shaped the competition, how did it play out and what proved decisive in the outcome? It is for this reason that this chapter is organised not through an examination of each bureaucratic actor but through key thematic developments that occurred in the functional and conceptual domains of Australian foreign policy between 2016 and 2020.

CHANGING CHINA POLICY

Australia's relations with China have for some time been the most challenging and complex aspect of Australian foreign policy (Thayer, 2011). Since 2007 it has been Australia's largest two-way trading partner, in 2009 it became the country's largest export market, and the share of trade that it accounts for has risen virtually every year thereafter. It has also become an increasing source of inbound investment; it is by some margin Asia's most important resident power. But as China's wealth has grown, the Sino-American relationship has become increasingly competitive. By the end of 2020, it had become clear that each country saw the other as a significant threat to its regional and global interests. How does one manage a relationship with one's most important trading partner when it has moved to being in outright geopolitical competition with your pre-eminent security partner? During the period examined in this book, the Australian Government reached a different answer to this question from what had previously prevailed.

Once the nature of China's economic revitalisation became clear to Australian leaders in the late 1990s, Australia's approach to the PRC became one of active engagement managed through a compartmentalisation process in which the commercial aspects of the relationship were foregrounded and the more challenging aspects to do with democracy, human rights and security were walled off (Bisley, 2018). Publicly, politicians declared that Australia 'did not have to choose' between Beijing and Washington, and privately they hoped that this was true. Occasionally, problems would emerge, such as when Kevin Rudd's government issued a Defence White Paper in 2009, which mentioned, in relatively muted terms, that China's rise may be destabilising to the region's strategic balance, but on the whole governments of both hues felt that things could be managed, at least in the short term. Australia could benefit from the rapid economic development of the world's most populous country while retaining a close security relationship with Washington.

This changed decisively during the period under review. When Malcolm Turnbull became prime minister following an internal party vote in 2015, many assumed that, much as when Rudd was elected in 2007, he would have a positive influence on ties with China (Murray, 2015). Turnbull's pro-business instincts and pragmatic politics would, it appeared, lead him to follow the same path as his predecessors; active engagement with China would continue with a strong focus on shared economic interests while the difficult political and security questions would be kept off the agenda. Yet under his leadership Australia decisively shifted its posture towards the PRC. This began with a series of set-piece speeches in 2017 in which China was explicitly portrayed as a source of regional instability, a rule breaker and a country meddling in the affairs of others. The speeches, first by Foreign Minister Bishop at the Fullerton Forum in Singapore in February (Bishop, 2017), followed by Turnbull at the Shangri-La Dialogue in June (Turnbull, 2017), and rounded off by Defence Minister Marise Payne at the Seoul Security Dialogue (Payne, 2017), represented a coordinated effort to signal a new attitude in Canberra. From the almost inflammatory – Bishop essentially said that the PRC could not be a legitimate power without democratisation – to the subtly cutting – Turnbull's use of a traditional Chinese saying to portray the country as a bully – the message was clear and consistent: Australia was no longer going to leave its concerns about controversial matters unaddressed or quietly discussed behind closed doors.

In 2018 the rhetorical hard line was matched with two further developments which indicated that in some domains Australia was prepared to match its deeds with its words. In June of that year Australia passed legislation intended to prevent foreign interference in the domestic political process (Australian Government, 2018). The wide-ranging legislation sought to curtail foreign efforts to interfere in domestic politics and to make visible foreign lobbying of politicians and public affairs. It included industrial espionage as a widening of existing counter-espionage laws. While the government was at pains to say it was not all about China, given the level of reporting about Chinese interference, including an unusually visible role played by intelligence agencies, it was plainly prompted by concerns about the People's Republic.

In July 2018 the government also banned PRC firms Huawei and ZTE from playing any role in the introduction of Australia's 5G telecommunications network (BBC, 2018). The government's reasoning was simple: while the firms were market leaders, their links to the Party-state posed an unacceptable risk to Australia's critical infrastructure. The government was open about the decision and its concerns, which were centred on the opaque ownership structure and underlying problems of trust that this created. Contrary to much speculation – and overt efforts by Beijing to spin the narrative – the decision was an Australian one and not influenced by the United States or other intelligence partners (Cave, 2019). This followed the 2016 decision to block Chinese firms from acquiring part of Ausgrid, an energy firm responsible for much of Sydney's power distribution and supply. Australia's concerns about Chinese firms were unmistakable and very much in the public eye.

In August 2018 Turnbull attempted to soften the public rhetoric at a speech at the University of New South Wales (Turnbull, 2018), but he was removed from office by his Liberal Party colleagues the next day and replaced by Scott Morrison. While the Morrison government sought to distance itself from some of Turnbull's policies, it did not alter what became the new Canberra consensus on China. In April 2020, when the scale of the COVID-19 pandemic was not fully understood, Foreign Minister Marise Payne called for an independent investigation into the origins of the virus, insisting that the World Health Organisation should not run it (Worthington, 2020). This was done alone and without building a broader diplomatic coalition.

Between 2016 and 2020 Australia moved from a policy of active engagement to being one of China's most vocal critics. Beijing responded with a slow but steady escalation of punitive measures. These began with the PRC increasingly distancing itself from Australia, refusing access to officials in Beijing and preventing regular meetings, leading some scholars to describe Australia as being in a diplomatic 'deep freeze' (Strating & Leibold, 2018). It then further signalled dissatisfaction through some trade disruption – most visibly holding up imports of Australian wine due to purported concerns about labelling (*Sydney Morning Herald*, 2018) – and issuing warnings about the risks of studying in Australia via embassy websites (Knauss, 2017). Notwithstanding these efforts, the trade relationship did not suffer in any tangible way and exports to China continued to grow, as did the number of students from the PRC studying in Australia. This may have led to a false sense of security, leading Canberra to conclude that it could talk tough to Beijing and not pay a price. Following the push for the investigation into COVID-19's origins in 2020, Australia saw some exports hit with a range of non-tariff barriers. By the end of 2020, the PRC had imposed restrictions on Australian beef, barley, wine and seafood (Wilson & King, 2020). It also sent very clear signals about tourism and education, although travel restrictions related to COVID-19 muted the full impact in these sectors.

What was the reason for what some have described as Australia's 'reality check' (Medcalf, 2018) on China? And what does this tell us about Australia's foreign policy process? The first reason for Australia's new approach to the PRC relates to China's behaviour and the second to domestic politics. On the former, PRC behaviour in the region, particularly in relation to the South China Sea and its dispute with Japan, showed that the optimism that lay behind the compartmentalisation approach of the past was misplaced. Security matters of that magnitude and risk could no longer be walled off from other aspects of the relationship. Equally, China's authoritarian turn further hardened views in Canberra. The approach of the past was not naïve – few policy-makers or political leaders had believed that the PRC was likely to liberalise in any meaningful sense – but the authoritarian face that the Party presented to the world since Xi Jinping's ascension was a key reason for Australia's changed approach to Beijing.

On the domestic front, a principal driver was the increasing concern among key figures in the Prime Minister's Office (PMO) and security branches of government that China was using the openness of a liberal society to try to influence Australian policy. More broadly, in the past Australian elites had believed that China's interests, particularly in ensuring a stable region and rapid economic growth, would corral PRC foreign policy and keep dangerous tendencies in check. During this period, that belief changed. Together, these factors led to a decisive shift in Canberra's attitude towards Beijing.

It is also worth reflecting on the extent to which China policy reflects the centralising tendencies of the policy process. The shift in China policy can, for instance, be contrasted with Australia's approach to participation in the Asian Infrastructure Investment Bank (AIIB). Under Prime Minister Abbott the government was divided on whether to join Beijing's infrastructure initiative. The Cabinet was split largely along functional lines: those from areas with an interest in economic matters, such as Trade Minister Andrew Robb and Treasurer Scott Morrison, advocated for Australia to join, while those with a more national security brief argued against it (Garnaut & Wen, 2015). In that case, the Prime Minister's Office was not in command of the policy approach and was itself divided, given that Abbott had hawkish instincts towards the PRC but equally saw the benefits of economic engagement. Australia decided to join. This was not due to the victory of one side over the other, however, but because so many other US allies and democracies joined, prompted by the British decision to join, which made critics' arguments unsustainable (Harris-Rimmer, 2015).

In contrast, the move to harden Australia's stance on the PRC illustrated the unity of the government, with the initiative coming from the PMO and being unaffected by the transition from Turnbull to Morrison. Cabinet was clearly in line and, unlike the AIIB case, those with economic portfolios also agreed with the decision even in the face of quite visible criticism in public forums (e.g. Raby, 2018) and concern in the private sector about the risks of this type of approach towards Beijing. As foreign policy matters rarely require legislation, major issues tend not to be exposed to the complexity of parliament and the need to navigate a divided Senate. But in this case, it did in the form of the foreign interference legislation introduced in 2018. Here again the PMO effectively coordinated the various elements of government and managed to secure the support of the opposition ALP, even though Labor had begun to position itself ahead of the 2019 election as having a different approach to Asia (Wong, 2018). Although the prompt for the legislation was the PRC, framing it as a general national security matter gave the ALP relatively limited room for legislative manoeuvre.

Changing such a major part of Australia's foreign policy – its relations with its most important trade partner and the region's most significant resident power – was not just a function of a hawkish turn in the PM's office but also resulted from a clear alignment of attitudes in all the key bureaucratic institutions. During this period the Department of Foreign Affairs and Trade (DFAT) was headed firstly by Peter Varghese, who had taken an unusually public profile as department head, articulating a sceptical tone about the geopolitical consequences of China's rise. He was succeeded by Frances Adamson, who had previously been Australia's ambassador to the PRC as well as its representative in Taiwan and then Turnbull's senior foreign policy adviser. The interests of those atop the government institutions promoting diplomacy and trade were closely aligned with the PMO's strategic outlook.

During this period the government also established the Department of Home Affairs to integrate policy components that had, over time, come to be seen as linked and requiring coordination, most obviously those related to immigration, border security, and domestic intelligence and security. The head of Home Affairs, Mike Pezzulo, as well as the head of the Australian Security Intelligence Organisation (ASIO), Duncan Lewis, played unusually prominent public roles in arguing for a harder line on China as well as key behind-the-scenes parts (Shields, 2018; Pezzullo, 2019).

The coordination and alignment of the various arms of government to advance a risky approach to the PRC was supported by the views of key departmental secretaries. Since its establishment in 1996, the National Security Committee of Cabinet (NSC) has played an increasing role in Australian foreign policy, reflecting the growing role of security matters. If the question of how to handle China is in essence an effort to balance economic and security concerns, by 2017 security was beginning to outweigh the economic. This brought the NSC much more clearly into operation, which provided a clear structure through which command, coordination and implementation could be centrally managed. Finally, the norm of bipartisanship on foreign and security policy worked to reinforce this process. As Andrew Carr has shown, the logic that underpins the tendency towards bipartisanship is questionable (Carr, 2017), and in this case it stifled debate about the pros and cons of the government's decision to change its approach to the country's biggest customer.

Foreign policy has long ceased to be the exclusive domain of DFAT and Defence: the globalised nature of Australia's economy and society has meant that virtually all branches of the federal government undertake some interactions with foreign counterparts. But in the period under review a forgotten element of the Australian system (or at least one forgotten by international relations scholars) illustrated that not all aspects of foreign policy are at the beck and call of the prime minister. Federalism became part of the foreign policy debate due to the Victorian government's completion in May 2018 of a memorandum of understanding with the PRC in relation to the Belt and Road Initiative (BRI) (see Chapter 14).

In response to this development, as well as broader concerns that universities and other institutions had become too close to Beijing, the Australian Government passed legislation that gave the Foreign Minister the power to invalidate any agreement with foreign governments or their affiliates (such as universities) that would 'adversely affect' or be 'inconsistent with Australia's foreign policy' (Australian Government, 2020). Notwithstanding the negative consequences of this heavy-handed approach (see Chapter 5), Victoria's action and the Australian Government's response illustrated both the complex nature of foreign policy in a federation whose economy is highly globalised and the striking influence of China's rise on the foreign policy process.

SECURITY DOMINANCE

Central to the changes in China policy was the way security came to overshadow the economic, cultural and social dimensions of relations between the PRC and Australia. This was a second major trend in the Australian foreign policy process during the period under review: its increasing dominance by security concerns.

In his authoritative study of Australian foreign policy, Allan Gyngell described the ten years between 1998 and 2008 as the 'national security decade', during which security came to dominate the policy mind, institutional structures and the resourcing of foreign policy (Gyngell, 2017). Yet security has continued to be the dominant concept in Australian foreign policy. Indeed, during the period under review security matters played almost a defining role in the policy process.

By security matters I mean policy questions that focus on what are perceived to be acute threats to the state and society. Traditionally these were the military threats that states pose to one another, but in recent years the concept has broadened. The COVID-19 pandemic illustrated all too painfully how damaging infectious diseases can be to society's well-being. Observing that the existential nature of questions of security means a suspension of the normal political and financial rules of the game, scholars from the Copenhagen school show that an issue can receive disproportionate resources and influence by linking itself to security, a process they call *securitisation* (Buzan, Waever & de Wilde,

1998). In describing the foreign policy process as being dominated by security matters, I am referring to two discrete but related elements. First, there was an empirical dimension in which financially, institutionally and in policy activity security matters dominated the agenda. Second, in conceptual terms, security almost entirely consumed the way the government thought about advancing its international interests.

Perhaps the most visible example of the dominance of security was in its allocation of scarce resources. In 2016, the Turnbull government released a Defence White Paper – the third in seven years – which laid out an ambitious expenditure program. The biggest expansion in Australia's defence capabilities outside wartime (Department of Defence, 2016) included the acquisition of a fleet of 72 F35 fighter jets and 12 new long-range submarines to replace the ageing Collins class. Annual defence expenditure was set to increase for many years, and by 2020–21 it amounted to more than A$42 billion, around 2 per cent of GDP. In 2020 the government published a Strategic Update, effectively a new Defence White Paper, which presented a much more pessimistic account of the likely strategic future and confirmed another decade of increases in defence spending. By 2030 it was projected that Australia would spend A$73.7 billion on defence (Department of Defence, 2020). Defence has long commanded a much greater share of foreign policy resources due primarily to the expensive nature of warfighting. Australia's defence policy has long been predicated on having equipment superior to any in the region, and its personnel are expensive.

At the same time as Defence and the intelligence agencies were gearing up for a significant expansion, other facets of the foreign policy machinery were suffering significant budgetary constraints. Foreign Minister Bishop secured some additional funding for DFAT early in her term, but between 2016 and 2020 funding for the non-security dimensions of Australian foreign policy was significantly decreased. Diplomatic capacity had been a target for cost-cutting for some years, but it came under renewed pressure between 2017 and 2020. In 2019 the budget for DFAT was at a low ebb of 1.3 per cent of the federal budget, and in 2020 communications within the department signalled the possibility of further job cuts and no end to financial constraint (Galloway, 2020a). The reduction in the DFAT budget included not just the diplomatic components of statecraft but also aid. As a result, Australia significantly scaled back the share of GDP allocated to aid (Development Policy Centre, 2020), narrowed its geographic scope, and increasingly saw aid in instrumental terms tied to a security logic.

Over the five years covered by this volume, reductions in expenditure in non-security-related domains of foreign policy were significant, but investment in those areas had been declining for some time. According to some analysts, 2020 would mark nearly two decades of disinvestment. As far back as 2010, alarm bells were ringing about the declining standing of Australian diplomacy because of continual cuts (Shearer & Oliver, 2010), and when that is put in the context of record expansion in defence expenditure, matters of security were coming to dominate the operation of Australia's international policy machinery. The emergence of defence diplomacy is illustrative of this trend. Efforts to build trust and improve communication between militaries have a long history in Asia and beyond (Kerr & Taylor, 2013). But defence diplomacy has moved beyond the narrow confines of officer exchanges, defence college partnerships and people-to-people links, and has expanded to be seen as an important tool for strategic influence (Taylor et al., 2014). As Carr and Baldino have shown, the potential for defence diplomacy at the higher level of foreign policy strategy is limited (Carr & Baldino, 2016). In effect, Australia is using well-resourced defence and security agencies to do work that diplomats have historically done because the latter are insufficiently resourced. There is a role for military engagement in the broader diplomatic endeavour and defence ministerial speeches have an important role to play in policy signalling. However, there is a growing tendency to use military and defence officials because there simply is not sufficient diplomatic capacity.

Security concerns suffuse many of the key foreign policy initiatives developed in the five years under consideration. The 'Pacific Step-up' (see Chapter 12), as the Morrison government has styled the reinvigoration of Australian engagement with the Pacific, was prompted by fears about Chinese strategic influence in the region and the security implications for Canberra. A central problem with the policy is that its prime motivation was obscured by a message of common interests and goodwill. The ability of the policy to make good on its ambitions was hamstrung by the fact that Australia was not being transparent about its underlying motives. The long-term criticism that Australia was not genuinely interested in the well-being and interests of the South Pacific nations remained valid even in the face of public declarations to the contrary (Smith, 2020).

The Quadrilateral Security Initiative ('the Quad'), a collaborative security program among the United States, Japan, India and Australia, was revived after its abandonment in 2007 (Bisley, 2022). It moved from being a gathering of mid-level officials to an annual ministerial meeting and, with Australia's 2020 invitation to participate in the Malabar military exercise program with the United States, Japan and India, it began to go beyond policy-signalling and information-sharing to the realm of military exercise. The Japan–Australia Security relationship, which had been strengthened and broadened since the 2007 Joint Declaration on Security Cooperation, was further reinforced with a space cooperation agreement signed in 2020 (Galloway, 2020c) as well as considerable cooperation occurring in minilateral contexts like the Trilateral Security Dialogue. Security matters were not just snaring significant financial resources; they were also central to the government's more dynamic policy initiatives.

The most immediate reason why security assumed this dominant role was the growing salience of these issues in the international system. Given the return of geopolitics and the growing role of great-power rivalry, it was not surprising that security assumed the position that it did. The principal fault line in this new global competition was in Australia's own region. The old cliché of the tyranny of distance was replaced by a kind of existential anxiety of proximity. Much of the reporting of China seeking bases in the South Pacific lacked credible sourcing, but the implications of such an eventuality for Australian defence and security planning would have been significant even if security was not such a big part of the foreign policy process. By their existential nature, security matters can appear more compelling to policy-makers and politicians than more other, less urgent policy domains.

A second reason for the salience of security relates to the increasingly difficult task of distinguishing between security and non-security matters. Today who and what poses a threat of sufficient magnitude to warrant what follows when the security label is affixed to it is much less clear cut. This is most evident in high technology and the near impossibility of distinguishing between legitimate business operations and matters of strategic and security risk. The reason Australia opted to ban Huawei from participating in the 5G network was because policy-makers could not generate sufficient trust in the company and its equipment. Not all countries reached the same conclusion: the United Kingdom was faced with essentially the same information as Australia but allowed Huawei to take part in its 5G program. But for Australia and other countries, the dilemma posed by Huawei was illustrative of the much more complex and challenging security environment. The inability not just to disentangle the questions of ownership and motivations of Chinese firms but also to draw clear lines between economic matters and political and security concerns prompted Australian decision-makers to take a conservative approach to the matter. Where there were doubts, the security risks trumped economic considerations. In such a context, foreign policy struggled to maintain its balance of the past.

The trend in the period under review was the dominance of security over the other domains in Australian foreign policy. The establishment of the Department of Home Affairs in 2017 illustrated this trend. The creation of a large institution bringing together immigration, law enforcement and the security and intelligence services reflected not just bureaucratic empire-building or institutional efficiencies but also a securitised view of the policy domain.

THE INDO-PACIFIC CONSTRUCT

Until the middle of the 2010s, Australia described the region of which it was a part as the 'Asia Pacific'. At this point the 'Indo-Pacific' began to be advocated as a 'new mental map' by think-tankers and analysts in Australia (Medcalf, 2012) and beyond (Scott, 2014). It appeared in Australian official documents and speeches, and slowly gained greater prominence. It was first used in the *Australia in the Asian Century White Paper* (2012) produced by the Gillard government. Appearing as a brief discussion of a possible 'trans-regional' concept (PMC, 2012), it was flagged in the 2013 Defence White Paper as part of Australia's strategic outlook as an 'emerging strategic arc' (Department of Defence, 2013).

During the period this volume examines, the Indo-Pacific replaced the Asia Pacific as the term that Australia used to describe its region. In 2016 the Coalition government launched its ambitious Defence White Paper, which marked the arrival of the Indo-Pacific as the new master concept of Australian strategic geography. Indeed, not only was the Indo-Pacific the core geographic zone for Australian defence planning but also the stability of this new mega-region became one of Australia's three core interests (Department of Defence, 2016: 68). The 2017 Foreign Policy White Paper followed the precedent set by its Defence twin, cementing the idea of an integrated strategic system of the western Pacific and the Indian Ocean Region as the principal theatre of operations for Australian foreign policy (DFAT, 2017). While the Coalition retained government for the duration of this period, it is notable that the embrace of the Indo-Pacific idea was thoroughly bipartisan, being supported by Stephen Smith, David Johnston and Julie Bishop. By 2020, anyone who had the temerity to use such quaint notions as Asia or the Asia Pacific as Australia's region was regarded with the casual amusement of someone hearing their grandparents describe the radio as the wireless or movies as the talkies.

One of the most notable ways in which this occurred was in the organisational structure of DFAT. In the past the main organisational divisions had been geographic with some issue and policy entities also receiving distinct instantiation. In 2016 there were five main pillars of the department, two of which were focused on geographic regions. One covered the Americas, Europe, the Pacific, Africa and the Middle East, and South and West Asia, as well as policy planning and protocol. The other included North Asia, South-East Asia continental and South-East Asia maritime affairs, as well as international security, counter-proliferation and consular affairs. A further group was devoted to development and aid following the merger with AusAID; one was focused on trade policy; and the fifth focused on administrative services such as the legal office, passports and information technology (DFAT, 2016).

By 2020, the department's organisational structure was quite different. There were now six key groups: (1) Global Cooperation, Development and Partnerships, (2) Trade Investment and Business Engagement, (3) Indo-Pacific, (4) International Security, Humanitarian and Consular Group, (5) Office of the Pacific and (6) Service Delivery Group. The geographic zones of interest were scattered. The Indo-Pacific group included South-East Asia, North-East Asia, the United States and Indo-Pacific strategy, and South and West Asia, but not the Pacific, oddly enough. Europe and Latin America were found in the Trade group, Africa and the Middle East were buried in the International Security Group, while the half of the Indo-Pacific not in that group had an organisationally significant stand-alone grouping. The point here is not that things should always remain as they were and that ministries of foreign affairs, particularly when struggling with funding challenges, must be creative. But giving the Indo-Pacific such an all-encompassing organisational embodiment raised several issues, particularly relating to the reality of the Indo-Pacific as a substantive region and the consequences of adopting the label in the department's organisational life, particularly given its normative baggage.

One of the most peculiar facets of the Indo-Pacific, beyond the speed with which it was embraced, was the lack of fit between the term and the security and trade structures of the region. There was no meaningful Indo-Pacific strategic system. There were clear points of connectivity between the markets and polities of East Asia and the Indian Ocean region, but the core security complexes of North-East Asia and South-East Asia, which centre on the strategic rivalries and frictions of strong states, were fundamentally different from and largely unconnected from the security complexes of the Indian Ocean region. Equally, trade and investment patterns were not Indo-Pacific beyond the transit of cargo moving energy, commodities and finished goods into and out of factory Asia. Given that at the time of writing the structure of DFAT remained new and its implications in terms of function unclear, it was puzzling that the institutional entities tasked with managing Australian foreign policy in most corners of the globe were organised according to claims about strategic and economic linkages that did not yet exist.

The Indo-Pacific emerged relatively swiftly and came to have both a rhetorical as well as a substantive influence on the foreign policy process. Yet the gap between what it purported to describe and the region as it was remained significant. Moreover, the Indo-Pacific concept was likely to reinforce the trends driving the dominance of security matters in Australian foreign policy.

CONCLUSION

One of the most striking aspects of the issues discussed in this chapter is how they reveal the growing influence of think tanks in the policy process. Australia does not have a strong tradition of think tanks more broadly, and in the foreign policy field they have only really emerged as players in the 21st century. But organisations that develop and advocate for novel approaches to international policy issues, whether about trade or strategy, have become active, visible and quite influential in the policy process. The idea of the Indo-Pacific has been actively promoted by analysts at the Lowy Institute for International Policy since at least 2012, while more recently the National Security College of ANU has become a platform to articulate and develop the strategic construct. The University of Sydney's United States Studies Centre's (USSC) foreign and defence policy program has also been an effective player in reinforcing the construct and developing policy initiatives to reinforce the idea's centrality to Australian foreign policy. Since 2014 the Perth US–Asia Centre, a sibling of the USSC, has reinforced these efforts and particularly buttressed the instinctive appeal of the Indo-Pacific construct for Western Australian elites.

Think tanks have also been prominent in pushing for and defending the shift in policy towards the PRC. The Defence Department–supported Australian Strategic Policy Institute was by some margin the most prominent critic of the PRC and an advocate for a shift in Australia's approach. This entailed both frequent media commentary from CEO Peter Jennings and former senior Defence official Michael Shoebridge directly on these questions. But during this time ASPI also produced significant research shining a light on China's behaviour, particularly in Xinjiang. The groundbreaking project 'Uyghurs for Sale' illustrated the approach (Xu et al., 2020). The team used open-source material to ascertain that significant numbers of Uyghurs were being used effectively as slave labour in a range of sectors across China. While important as a piece of research and as a human rights issue, it nevertheless had a clear influence on the policy process in that it reinforced the negative aspects of China's behaviour and made political opposition to Canberra's new approach difficult to sustain. To be clear, think tanks do not determine policy, but they are an influential new non-government voice that can navigate and influence the policy process. They have played a key role in the five years under review in this volume.

If think-tank influence was a new component in the process, the strong guiding hand of the Prime Minister's Office between 2016 and 2020 was not. In each of the issues discussed in this chapter, the PMO was crucial: it was the key determinant of policy change, it ensured a unity of position across portfolios in Cabinet, and it coordinated and managed the many branches of government that develop and implement foreign policy. That trade matters were not at loggerheads with strategic decisions in relation to the PRC most obviously illustrated this. Although not a new development, it was notable that even as foreign policy concerns became more widely embedded in government departments, reflecting the globalised nature of Australian society and economy, ensuring unity of policy and managing disparate interest groups was more challenging than in previous eras. The government also passed several pieces of legislation related directly to foreign policy matters, bringing the legislative branch into play in ways that were not particularly common. Here again the PMO navigated a divided Senate shrewdly and saw off potential challenges to its approach to the PRC that the representative aspects of government might have brought to bear.

What do these issues tell us about Australia's key foreign policy institutions? The department most closely associated with foreign policy, DFAT, remained in a subordinate position. It lacked the resources and capacity to influence strategic decision-making and continued to play the part of a key implementor of foreign policy rather than a determinant of its course and operation. This in part reflected the dominance of security matters: diplomacy, trade and aid were at a disadvantage at a time when security and geopolitics had come to dominate. But it was telling that it was not as effective as it could be in linking the core elements of its operations to broader strategic ambitions. This speaks both to the constrained capacity of the department and the broader approach that dominated the period under review, during which policy was not viewed holistically: for example, defence and development might have worked together to drive strategy, but one element was seen as more appropriate to managing the challenging context. The development of a new ministry, Home Affairs, also reinforced this by making the competition for influence that bit more challenging and by embodying a highly securitised conception of Australia's strategic milieu. And, of course, Defence had become the most important institutional player in Australian foreign policy, understood not just in the narrow sense that its scale and resources gave it an outsized role but also in how defence matters were understood to be at the heart of Australia's foreign policy challenges.

As Australia entered another national security decade, the foreign policy process was unbalanced. The central idea of Australia's place in the world lacked grounding in strategic reality, security concerns had a disproportionate influence in the realm of ideas and the call on resources, and Australia had a dysfunctional political relationship with the region's most important resident power and its most important export customer. This reflected a particular constellation of individuals, institutions and ideas that formed between 2016 and 2020. If this approach remained in place, the policy process would not be well placed to navigate the coming years in which a greater level of flexibility would be required and a broader sense of Australia's interests and the policy mechanisms to advance those interests would be necessary to chart Australia's path most effectively.

References

Australian Government (2018) *National Security Legislation Amendment (Espionage and Foreign Interference) Act 2018*. https://www.legislation.gov.au/Details/C2018A00067

——(2020) Australia's Foreign Relations (State and Territory Arrangements) Bill 2020. https://www.legislation.gov.au/Details/C2020B00125

BBC (2018) Huawei and ZTE handed 5G network ban in Australia. *BBC News*, 23 August. https://www.bbc.com/news/technology-45281495

Bishop, J. (2017) Change and uncertainty in the Indo-Pacific: Strategic challenges and opportunities. 28th IISS Fullerton Lecture, Singapore, 13 March. http://foreignminister.gov.au/speeches/Pages/2017/jb_sp_170313a.aspx

Bisley, N. (2018) Australia's engagement with China: From fear to greed and back again. *International Journal* 73(3): 379–98

——(2022) Contested Asia and the return of the Quadrilateral Security Initiative. *Melbourne Asia Review*, Edition 9, 18 March. https://melbourneasiareview.edu.au/contested-asia-and-the-return-of-the-quadrilateral-security-initiative/

Buzan, B., Waever, O. & de Wilde, J. (1998) *Security: A New Framework for Analysis*. Boulder: Lynne Rienner

Carr, A. (2017) Is bipartisanship on national security beneficial? Australia's politics of defence and security. *Australian Journal of Politics and History* 63(2): 254–69

Carr, A. & Baldino, D. (2016) Defence diplomacy and the Australian defence force: Smokescreen or strategy? *Australian Journal of International Affairs* 70(2): 139–58

Cave, D. (2019) Huawei's 'trust deficit' kept it out of Australia's 5G network. *Global Asia* 14(3): 18–22. https://www.globalasia.org/v14no3/cover/huaweis-trust-deficit-kept-it-out-of-australias-5g-network_danielle-cave

Department of Defence (DOD) (2013) *2013 Defence White Paper*. Canberra: Department of Defence. https://www.defence.gov.au/about/strategic-planning/defence-white-paper

——(2016) *2016 Defence White Paper*. Canberra: Department of Defence. https://www.defence.gov.au/about/strategic-planning/defence-white-paper

——(2020) *2020 Defence Strategic Update*. Canberra: Department of Defence. 1 July. https://www.defence.gov.au/about/strategic-planning/2020-defence-strategic-update

Department of Foreign Affairs and Trade (DFAT) (2016) *Annual Report 2015–16*. Canberra: DFAT. https://www.dfat.gov.au/about-us/publications/corporate/annual-reports/Pages/department-of-foreign-affairs-and-trade-annual-report-2015-2016.aspx/annual-report-2015-2016/home/section-1/departmental-overview/index.html#figure-1-modal

——(2017) *2017 Foreign Policy White Paper*. Canberra: DFAT. https://www.dfat.gov.au/sites/default/files/2017-foreign-policy-white-paper.pdf

Department of the Prime Minister and Cabinet (2012) *Australia in the Asian Century White Paper*. Canberra: Department of the Prime Minister and Cabinet. https://www.murdoch.edu.au/ALTC-Fellowship/_document/Resources/australia-in-the-asian-century-white-paper.pdf

Development Policy Centre (2020) *Australian Aid Tracker*. http://devpolicy.org/aidtracker/trends/

Galloway, A. (2020a) Department of Foreign Affairs and Trade to slash dozens of jobs. *Sydney Morning Herald*, 15 July. https://www.smh.com.au/politics/federal/department-of-foreign-affairs-and-trade-to-slash-dozens-of-jobs-20200715-p55c8a.html

——(2020b) 'Flagrantly reckless': Victoria signed China infrastructure deal without consulting DFAT. *Age*, 26 May. https://www.theage.com.au/politics/federal/flagrantly-reckless-victoria-signed-china-infrastructure-deal-without-consulting-dfat-20200526-p54wfn.html

——(2020c) Australia and Japan to sign space deal, discuss deeper security ties. *Sydney Morning Herald*, 8 July. https://www.smh.com.au/politics/federal/australia-and-japan-to-sign-space-deal-discuss-deeper-security-ties-20200708-p55a92.html

Garnaut, J. & Wen, P. (2015) Cabinet split over 'Asian bank' after UK's shock support. *Sydney Morning Herald*, 13 March. https://www.smh.com.au/politics/federal/cabinet-split-over-asian-bank-after-uks-shock-support-20150313-143jya.html

Gyngell, A. (2017) *Fear of Abandonment: Australia in the World Since 1942*. Melbourne: La Trobe University Press

Harris-Rimmer, S. (2015) Why Australia took so long to join the AIIB. *Interpreter*, Lowy Institute, 30 March. https://www.lowyinstitute.org/the-interpreter/why-australia-took-so-long-join-aiib

Hill, C. (2015) *Foreign Policy in the Twenty-first Century*, 2nd edn. London: Red Globe Press

Kerr, P. & Taylor, B. (2013) Track-two diplomacy in East Asia. In P. Kerr & G. Wiseman (eds), *Diplomacy in a Globalizing World: Theories and Practices*, pp. 226–43. New York: Oxford University Press

Knauss, C. (2017) 'Chinese government warns students in Australia are at risk of attack', *Guardian*, 22 December. https://www.theguardian.com/australia-news/2017/dec/22/chinese-government-warns-students-in-australia-are-at-risk-of-attack

Medcalf, R. (2012) Pivoting the Map: Australia's Indo-Pacific System. *Centre of Gravity Series*, paper no. 1. Canberra: Australian National University, Strategic and Defence Studies Centre. http://sdsc.bellschool.anu.edu.au/sites/default/files/publications/attachments/2020-10/cog_1_2018_softproof_v4.pdf

——(2018) Australia and China: Understanding the reality check. *Australian Journal of International Affairs* 73(2): 109–18

Murray, L. (2015) Malcolm Turnbull's China connections change outlook for relationship. *Australian Financial Review*, 15 September. https://www.afr.com/politics/malcolm-turnbulls-china-connections-change-outlook-for-bilateral-relationship-20150915-gjmrg3

Payne, M. (2017) Sixth Seoul Defence Dialogue keynote. Seoul, 11 September. https://www.minister.defence.gov.au/minister/marise-payne/speeches/sixth-seoul-defence-dialogue-keynote

Pezzullo, M. (2019) Seven gathering storms: National security in the 2020s. Address to Australian Strategic Policy Institute, Canberra, 13 March. https://www.homeaffairs.gov.au/news-media/speeches/2019/13-march-australian-strategic-policy-institute

Raby, G. (2018) China relations can only be unfrozen with Julie Bishop's sacking. *Australian Financial Review*, 14 May. https://www.afr.com/opinion/china-relations-can-only-be-unfrozen-with-julie-bishops-sacking-20180514-h100w9

Scott, D. (2012) India and the allure of the 'Indo-Pacific'. *International Studies* 49(3–4): 165–88

Shearer, A. & Oliver, A. (2010) Diplomacy in ruins. *Australian*, 26 March. https://www.theaustralian.com.au/news/inquirer/diplomacy-in-ruins/news-story/351bb78d756035d01d1a850a97e69ac8?sv=2e5ea4bbc1b44cfba5185d198679938e

Shields, B. (2018) ASIO chief Duncan Lewis sounds fresh alarm over foreign interference threat. *Sydney Morning Herald*, 24 May. https://www.smh.com.au/politics/federal/asio-chief-duncan-lewis-sounds-fresh-alarm-over-foreign-interference-threat-20180524-p4zhdk.html

Smith, L. (2020) Despite its Pacific 'step-up', Australia is still not listening to the region, new research shows. *Conversation*, 11 February. https://theconversation.com/despite-its-pacific-step-up-australia-is-still-not-listening-to-the-region-new-research-shows-130539.

Strating, B. & Leibold, J. (2018) Coping with the Beijing freezer. *Strategist*, Australian Strategic Policy Institute, 28 June. https://www.aspistrategist.org.au/coping-with-the-beijing-freezer/

Sydney Morning Herald (2018) Australian wine shipments held up at Chinese ports amid political tensions: Report. *Sydney Morning Herald*, 15 June. https://www.smh.com.au/business/the-economy/australian-wine-shipments-held-up-at-chinese-ports-amid-political-tensions-report-20180615-p4zloj.html

Taylor, B., Blaxland, J., White, H., Bisley, N., Leahy, P. & Tan, S.S. (2014) Defence diplomacy: Is the game worth the candle? *Centre of Gravity Series*, paper no. 17. Canberra: Strategic and Defence Studies Centre, Australian National University. http://sdsc.bellschool.anu.edu.au/sites/default/files/publications/attachments/2016-03/cog_17_web.pdf

Thayer, C. (2011) China's rise and the passing of US primacy: Australia debates its future. *Asia Policy* 12(1): 20–6

Turnbull, M. (2017) Keynote address at the 16th IISS Asia Security Summit, Shangri-La Dialogue. 3 June. https://www.malcolmturnbull.com.au/media/keynote-address-at-the-16th-iiss-asia-security-summit-shangri-la-dialogue

——(2018) Speech at the University of New South Wales. Sydney, 7 August. https://www.malcolmturnbull.com.au/media/speech-at-the-university-of-new-south-wales-sydney-7-august-2018

Wilson, J. & King, G. (2020) *Political Risks for Australia–China Agriculture Trade.* Indo-Pacific Anaysis Briefs 2020, No. 11. Perth: Perth USAsia Centre. https://perthusasia.edu.au/getattachment/60ff3fef-f357-441e-9f77-8e85536b13d5/PU-176-V11-AU-CH-Agri-WEB.pdf.aspx?lang=en-AU

Worthington, B. (2020) Marise Payne calls for global inquiry into China's handling of the coronavirus outbreak. *ABC News*, 19 April. https://www.abc.net.au/news/2020-04-19/payne-calls-for-inquiry-china-handling-of-coronavirus-COVID-19/12162968

Wong, P. (2018) Peace and prosperity in a time of disruption. Speech to Lee Kuan Yew School of Public Policy, National University of Singapore, 24 January. https://www.pennywong.com.au/media-hub/speeches/peace-and-prosperity-in-a-time-of-disruption-lee-kuan-yew-school-of-public-policy-singapore-24-01-2018/

Xu, V.X., Cave, D., Leibold, J., Munro, K. & Ruser, N. (2020) *Uyghurs for Sale: 'Re-education', Forced Labour and Surveillance Beyond Xinjiang,* Policy Brief, Report No. 26. Canberra: International Cyber Policy Centre, Australian Strategic Policy Institute. https://www.aspi.org.au/report/uyghurs-sale

Australian public opinion on world affairs

China, the United States and climate change

Danielle Chubb and Ian McAllister

Between 2016 and 2020, Australian public debate over foreign affairs and security issues was dominated by the question of how Australia should manage three pressing international issues: relations with China, the US alliance, and the threat of climate change. These conversations took place against the backdrop of increased rivalry between China and the United States in Australia's region, the importance of which was not lost on the general public. In this chapter we examine public opinion around these three issues using the insights available from the polling data.

The role of public opinion in foreign affairs has been the subject of considerable debate in international relations. Foreign policy realists have traditionally viewed public opinion as capricious and unpredictable. In this view, what the public thinks about foreign affairs is at best a distraction and at worst an impediment to effective policy-making. In contrast, liberals have emphasised the importance of accountability and democracy in helping to create a fairer and more peaceful world. From this perspective, public opinion has a central role to play. For example, the idea that public opinion can place limits on the narrow pursuit of national interests is embedded within liberal institutionalist strands of thought (see Chubb & McAllister, 2021a, Chapter 1, for more on these debates). This latter view is the dominant one within Australian thinking about foreign affairs and defence.

The impetus towards analysing the role of public opinion on foreign affairs in Australia is relatively recent. In the immediate post-war years there was a bipartisan elite consensus on most foreign policy issues. This consensus was challenged during the late 1960s with the debate about Australia's role in the Vietnam War, and public opinion played a key role in Labor's decision to withdraw from the war in 1972. A second factor has been the rapidly changing sociocultural composition of the population, with new social groups displaying very different perspectives on foreign affairs compared to the native-born population. Finally, opinion surveys have become more frequent, more technically sophisticated and able to tap into an ever-widening range of opinions.

In their introduction to the 2011–15 volume of *Australia in World Affairs*, Beeson and Hamieri (2016: 2) remarked on what they saw as a concerning disconnect in Australian political debate: public discourse had taken on an increasingly populist tone around foreign policy issues, but there was relatively little public scrutiny of these issues. This is usually attributed to the high level of bipartisanship over important issues on foreign and defence policy, with little significant difference evident between the approaches of the major parties (Carr, 2017). This broadly bipartisan approach within the policy elite continued during the period 2016–20: the policy platforms of the major parties remained largely intact and in harmony, with few, if any differences. This bipartisanship was mirrored within the mass public but, as we indicate below, within certain clearly defined boundaries.

Despite the continued adherence of the foreign policy elites to bipartisanship, there was increasing public debate around some of the most significant changes taking place in the Asia/Indo-Pacific region – and within Australia itself. The relatively calm tone witnessed in parliamentary debate stood in stark contrast to the heightened divisiveness around such issues as Chinese influence in Australia. These divisions were evident also in public opinion polling, as Australians' views of China changed significantly. This in turn led many to believe that Chinese interference represented an ongoing threat to democratic values and procedures.

Previous volumes of *Australia in World Affairs* have not included standalone chapters on public opinion (the exception being Goot's (2007) contribution to the 2001–05 volume), but this topic is possible and timely for the current volume. Not only has public debate around foreign policy gained increased prominence but also high-quality data is available for analysis.

In this chapter, we examine public opinion around the three issues on which the biggest shifts were evident. The first section, 'Trust in the United States', deals with trust in the United States and focuses particularly on long-term trends in public opinion. The second section, 'Public concerns about China', examines the public's view that China represented a security threat, while the third section, 'Climate change', evaluates the extent to which the public saw climate change as important. In the fourth section, 'The role of social background', we examine how far these three areas of concern were shaped by individuals' social background. Finally, the conclusion discusses the role of public opinion in shaping policy on these three areas of concern.

TRUST IN THE UNITED STATES

The US presidential election of 2016 was more significant for the Australian public than any in the past few decades. While presidential elections had never before produced a sizeable shift in Australian public opinion, it was widely understood that a Trump foreign policy doctrine would deliver a meaningful departure from post-war US leadership. Evident in public discourse was what one analyst has called a 'new sense of nervousness about the alliance' (Zala, 2017: 613), which spoke to questions of alliance durability as well as broader questions about how the foreign policy establishment should respond to Trump's anti-globalist rhetoric. One commentator wondered whether, should an inept handling of Australia's volatile region lead to economic ruin or a call to engage in military action unpopular among the public, this would have significant downstream consequences for an alliance that had hitherto been extraordinarily durable (Bowen, 2017).

These fears were amplified early in the Trump presidency by reports of a hostile telephone exchange between Trump and Prime Minister Malcolm Turnbull over an agreement made with the Obama administration to accept refugees from Australian detention centres in Nauru and Papua New Guinea (Miller & Rucker, 2017). The call attracted widespread national and international attention, given the bluntness of Trump's comments. While Australian officials sought to reassure the public that all was well in relations with the United States, some commentators revived a debate that had been simmering in the background for many years about the durability and desirability of the alliance. In a speech to the National Press Club, Rory Medcalf (2017), head of the National Security College at the Australian National University, summarised the concerns raised by foreign policy elites including Hugh White, Allen Gyngell, Paul Dibb and Paul Keating. This airing of the most critical views of the strong bipartisan commitment to the US alliance was made possible in an environment in which the public was becoming more open to considering the alliance's shortcomings.

Despite efforts by the government to reject any such concerns, the public was aware of the risk that Trump's apparent disdain for the usual patterns of US alliance behaviour might translate into an unwillingness to continue to play a stabilising role in the region. Since 2006 the Lowy surveys have asked a question concerning trust in the United States to act responsibly in the world. As Figure 3.1 shows, trust was high during the Obama presidency, peaking in 2011 when four in 10 of the respondents said that they had a 'great deal' of trust in the United States. When the question was asked again in 2017, one year after Trump's inauguration, that proportion had halved, to 20 per cent. From 2018 onwards, a plurality of the survey respondents said that they had little or no trust in the United States. This is a significant shift in public opinion over a relatively short period.

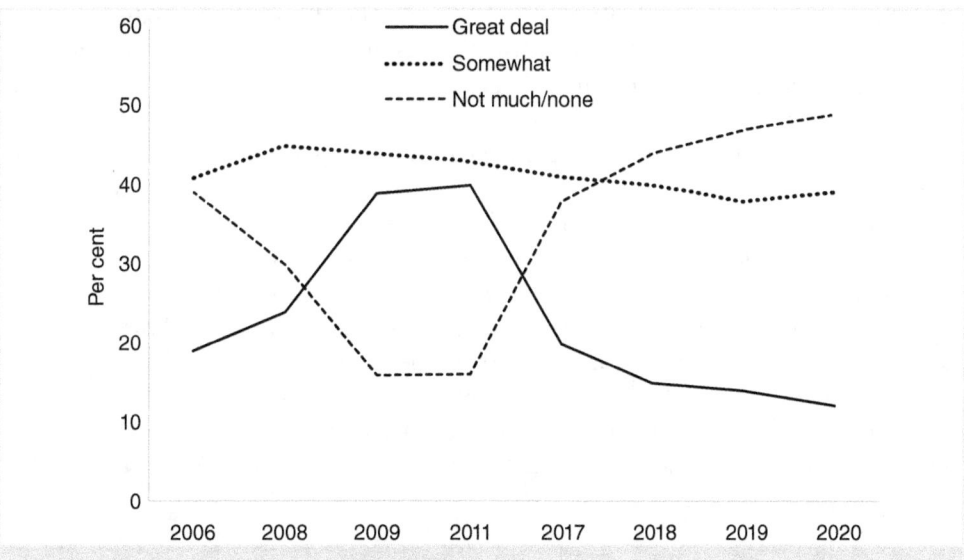

Figure 3.1 Trust in the United States to act responsibly, 2006–20

Note: 'How much do you trust the following countries to act responsibly in the world? ... the United States'
Source: based on data from Lowy Institute Polls (2006–20).

Trump attracted a considerable negative reaction from the Australian public, but other presidents have also been unpopular at certain points in time. For example, the 2007 and 2017 Lowy surveys asked the respondents if the US president caused them to have an unfavourable opinion of the United States. In 2007, 69 per cent said that George W. Bush caused them to have an unfavourable opinion; the figure for Trump in 2017 was less, at 60 per cent. Nevertheless, Trump remained one of the most unpopular world leaders in the Lowy surveys, with a ranking similar to China's Xi Jinping and Indonesia's Joko Widodo. For the leader of Australia's closest ally, this was a cause of significant concern.

The decline in trust in the United States under the Trump presidency did not, however, appear to reflect a dramatic decline in public support for the ANZUS alliance. Since 1993 the Australian Election Study (AES) has tracked support for the alliance, and since it was introduced in 2005, the Lowy survey has done the same. Lowy uses simpler wording than the AES by omitting explicit mention of the ANZUS treaty, which is used in the AES question. The results in Table 3.1 show that this different wording produces broadly similar estimates, albeit with some decline in recent surveys. The AES, conducted after each federal election, shows little variation over the period. The Lowy surveys, conducted annually, show more fluctuation with a decline of about 10 percentage points since 2016. Nevertheless, both surveys confirm the strong and consistent public support that exists for the alliance.

Since 1993, then, the public has continued to demonstrate high support for the US alliance even while expressing concerns or doubt over the role played by the United States in world affairs. This is broadly consistent with past attitudinal patterns. Goot (2007: 287–9) observed that between 2001 and 2005, in which time Australian troops were sent to assist in Iraq with the US 'war on terror', 'some of the gloss had worn off the alliance, with respondents reporting strong support for ANZUS but ambivalence about the United States and its exercise of power internationally. The election of Trump had a tangible effect on Australian public opinion, but the changes observed in the surveys started from a high base, with a large majority taking an optimistic view of US relations, making the observed decline relative.

Over the longer period for which polling data on these issues is available, support for ANZUS has been relatively strong and consistent.[1] According to Chubb & McAllister (2021a), any observable changes have been in 'respondents moving between "very important" and "fairly important" in their responses rather than moving in the direction of seeing the alliance as unimportant. Moreover, the trends show that those taking a strong position in favour of ANZUS are proportionately greater than those who take a strong stance against it.' In many ways, then, the alliance is a valence issue, 'forming a stable and continuing backdrop to the public's views about foreign policy'. The role that the US alliance plays in Australian security thinking is at least partly related to concerns about China's behaviour in the region, which is discussed in the next section.

---

[1] 'Questions about US relations started to be asked in public opinion surveys from the 1950s. From 1993 a consistent trend question about the ANZUS alliance started to be asked, allowing for a rigorous tracking of attitudes' (see Chubb & McAllister, 2021a: 50–7).

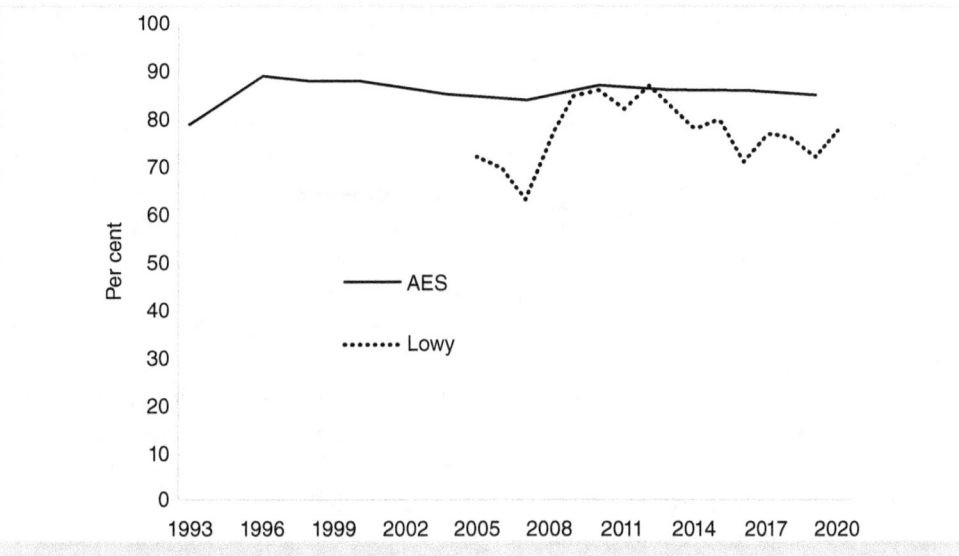

Figure 3.2 Support for the US alliance, 1993–2020

Notes:

» AES: 'How important do you think the Australian alliance with the United States under the ANZUS treaty is for protecting Australia's security?'

» Lowy: 'How important is our alliance relationship with the United States for Australia's security?' Estimates are the percentage who say 'very' and 'fairly' important.

Source: adapted from Chubb & McAllister (2021b). Based on data from AES (1993–2019); Lowy Institute Polls (2005–20).

PUBLIC CONCERNS ABOUT CHINA

Australia's trading and security relationship with Asia has undergone a gradual but significant transformation over the past three decades.[2] While most of this transformation has taken place within the foreign policy elite, the changing nature of the relationship has both been informed by public opinion and served to transform it. Attitudes towards migration and trade, as well as diplomatic and security relations, have changed significantly since the days of Australia's reliance on the British Commonwealth. These changes have, by and large, been steady and cautious, as has Australian policy.

During the period under review – notably 2018–20 – there was a sharp deviation from this cautious pattern of gradual change, with a sharp spike in concern around the role of China in Australia's internal affairs. Anxiety about China's economic and military rise and its implications for Australian interests increased considerably among the foreign policy elite. In turn, this anxiety was reflected in public debate about policy towards China, and this was evident in significant attitudinal shifts.

---

[2] This section is based on the authors' previous work: Chubb & McAllister (2021b) Fear and greed: Australian public opinion towards China's rise. *Australian Journal of Politics and History* 67(3–4): 439–53. © 2021 University of Queensland and John Wiley & Sons Australia. Reproduced with permission.

China's rise to global power status did not go unnoticed by the public. In parallel with its economic growth, China's military spending increased substantially, more than tripling since 2008 (Sandler & George, 2016). Tensions over freedom of navigation in the South China Sea, military exercises close to Taiwan, restrictions on personal freedoms in Hong Kong, and retaliation against the Australian economy in the form of trade bans and suspensions, all gave Chinese expansion a higher profile among the public than at any time in the past. The opacity of China's authoritarian political system, alongside its increasing disregard for international law and norms, fed into a rising vocal discourse around China as a potential (or actual) security threat.

Using three indicators that summarise public opinion towards China and a range of other countries, Table 3.1 shows that on all three, China was the country that the Australian public is most concerned about.[3] Almost one in three people surveyed after the 2019 federal election found that China was 'very likely' to pose a military threat to Australia in the future; the country that was ranked second as a threat was Indonesia, at only 12 per cent. These attitudes were also found in the 2020 Lowy survey, where 77 per cent said that they had 'not very much' or 'no' trust in China to act responsibly in the world, compared to 58 per cent for Russia and 49 per cent for Indonesia.[4] And on the third indicator, a 'feeling' thermometer in the 2020 Lowy Survey, sentiment towards China was among the 'coldest' of any of the 18 countries included in the question.[5]

Table 3.1 Views of China and other countries, 2019–20

Threat 'very likely' (2019)	Percentage	'Not very much' or 'no' trust (2020)	Percentage	Feeling 'cold' (2020)	Percentage
1. China	32	1. China	77	1. China	61
2. Indonesia	12	2. Russia	75	2. Russia	58
3. United States	7	3. Indonesia	65	3. Indonesia	49
4. Japan	4	4. US	49	4. Vietnam	42
5. Malaysia	4	5. India	55	5. US	38
6. Vietnam	3	6. Japan	19	6. Japan	31

Note: 'In your opinion, are any of the following countries likely to pose a threat to Australia's security?'; 'How much do you trust the following countries to act responsibly in the world? China'; 'Please rate your feelings towards some countries and territories, with 100 meaning a very warm, favourable feeling, zero meaning a very cold, unfavourable feeling, and 50 meaning not particularly warm or cold. You can use any number from zero to 100: the higher the number the more favourable your feelings are towards that country or territory. If you have no opinion or have never heard of that country or territory, please say so.'
Source: Chubb & McAllister (2021b). Based on data from AES (2019); Lowy Institute Poll (2020).

---

[3] Each of the questions contained different sets of countries. Those most relevant as comparators have been included in the table.

[4] The United Kingdom was also included in the battery of questions, with 3 per cent saying that they did not have any trust (Kassam, 2020: 6).

[5] The estimate for China was exceeded only by Iran (67 per cent) and Saudi Arabia (68 per cent). A total of 18 countries were included in the battery, as well as the United Nations and the European Union (Kassam, 2020: 41).

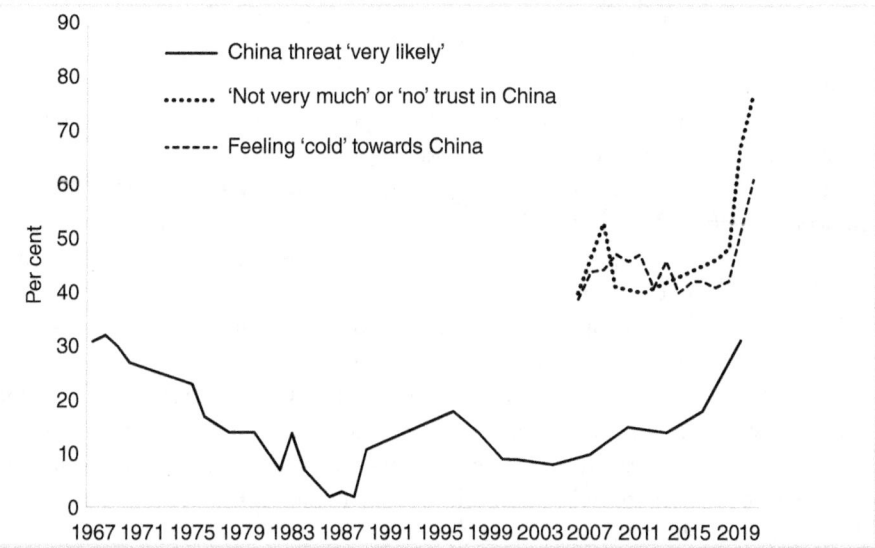

Figure 3.3 China as a threat, 1967–2020

Note: See Table 3.1 for question wordings. For 1967–88, exact question wordings and codes vary between surveys.
Source: Chubb & McAllister (2021b). Based on data from McAllister & Makkai (1991); AES (1987–2019); Lowy Institute Polls (2009–20).

On the questions of military threats and trust, the longitudinal data reveals that there was a substantial change in attitudes towards China from 2018. The data for China representing a military threat stretches back more than half a century, to the late 1960s (Figure 3.3). At the beginning of the time series, during the Vietnam War, almost one in three considered China to be a potential military threat. That proportion declined steadily following the end of the war in 1975, reaching its lowest point over the period in the late 1980s when just 2 per cent thought that China was a threat. This increased significantly after the 1989 Tiananmen Square protests and has risen steadily since, reaching a peak in 2019. As we saw in Table 3.1, almost one in three of the public thought it 'very likely' China represented a military threat, almost twice the comparable figure in 2016. This is a major change in public opinion in a short period.[6]

The two questions concerning trust in China and warmth towards China from the Lowy surveys have a shorter trend, from 2006 onwards, and are also represented in Figure 3.3. They show the same pattern as the military threat question. In 2006, 40 per cent of respondents said that they had 'not very much' trust or 'none at all' in China to act responsibly in the world. That figure increased to 48 per cent in 2018 but climbed substantially to 68 per cent in 2019, peaking at 77 per cent in 2020. Similarly, the warmth felt towards China using the thermometer question varied little between 2006 and as recently as 2018, with an average of 43 per cent feeling 'cold' (meaning that the majority felt 'warm'). In 2019 that increased to 51 per cent and increased again

---

[6] The Lowy Poll asked a similar question between 2009 and 2018, and its estimates track the AES findings closely. Lowy did not, however, ask the same question in 2019 or 2020.

to 61 per cent in 2020. These estimates – using different questions from another survey – confirm that there was a substantial change in public opinion towards China after 2018.

In parallel with fear of China as a military power were views about China's economic growth and its importance to the Australian economy. With China's ever-increasing economic power came large-scale investment in Australia. This investment was initially welcomed as it provided capital for industrial development, but as Chinese firms began to target electricity infrastructure, telecommunications, resources and agricultural land, public opposition to the purchases of these strategic assets became more vocal (Chubb & McAllister, 2021b).[7] Concern was heightened by revelations that Chinese businesses had made substantial donations to the major political parties before the 2016 election, and several politicians were embroiled in scandals involving links to Chinese interests.[8] In February 2018 the government announced restrictions on foreign ownership of agricultural land, measures that were strengthened in March 2020. Security concerns resulted in a Chinese telecommunications company, Huawei, being banned from building Australia's 5G network in 2018.

The debate about Chinese investment in Australia and its strategic implications was reflected in attitudinal changes. Since 2009 the Lowy surveys have asked respondents about the level of Chinese investment in Australia (Figure 3.4). In 2009 around half

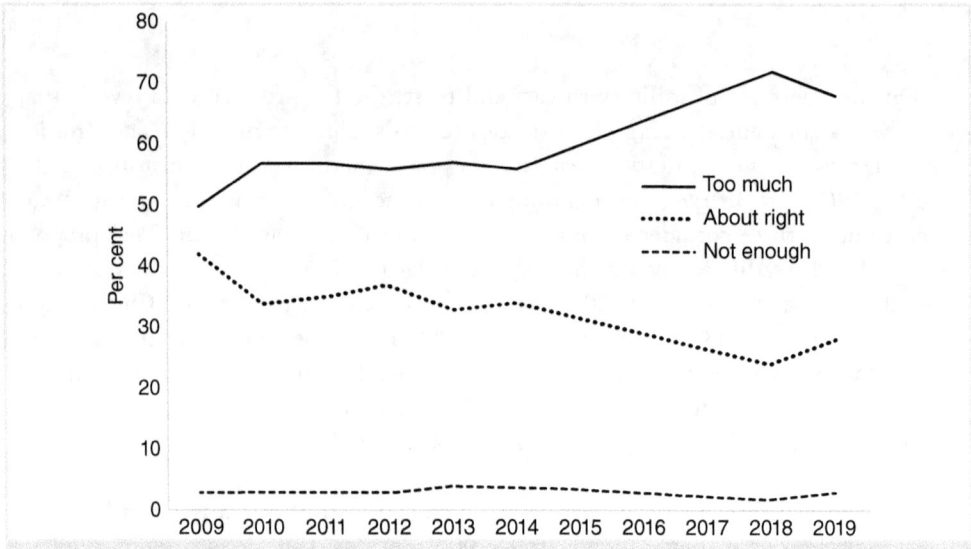

Figure 3.4 Levels of Chinese investment in Australia, 2009–19

Note: 'And now how about Chinese investment in Australia. Overall, do you think the Australian Government is ... allowing too much investment from China ... allowing about the right amount of investment from China ... not allowing enough investment from China?'

Source: Chubb & McAllister (2021b). Based on data from Lowy Institute Polls (2009–19).

---

[7] See the various reports by the Australian Strategic Policy Institute, available at https://www.aspi.org.au.

[8] In 2017 a Labor senator, Sam Dastyari, was forced to resign over links to a Chinese businessman, and in 2020 the home of a Labor NSW elected member, Shaoquett Moselmane, was raided following allegations that his office had been infiltrated by Chinese government agents.

Table 3.2 China as economic partner or security threat, 2015-20

	2015	2017	2018	2020	Change 2015-20
Economic partner	77	79	82	55	-22
Security threat	15	13	12	41	+26
Both equally	4	5	0	3	-1
Neither/don't know	4	3	6	1	-3
Total	100	100	100	100	
(N)	(1200)	(1200)	(1200)	(2448)	

Note: 'Thinking now about Australia and China. In your own view, is China more of an economic partner to Australia or more of a security threat to Australia?'
Source: Chubb & McAllister (2021b). Based on data from Lowy Institute Polls (2015-20).

thought that there was 'too much' Chinese investment, with 42 per cent taking the view that the current level was 'about right'. From 2009 to 2014 there was a slight increase in the proportion seeing the level of investment as 'too high', but it remained remarkably stable. From 2014 this figure started increasing, with a sharp uptick in 2018: to 72 per cent, with just one in four taking the view that the current level was 'about right'; it declined slightly to 68 per cent in 2019.[9] While we do not know exactly what caused these changes in opinion, it was almost certainly a response to widespread concern about the level of Chinese investment in Australia's strategic assets, notably agricultural land and telecommunications.

When it comes to managing Australia's relationship with China, the challenge for policy-makers has always been how to manage the economic benefits of China's rise alongside the political and security considerations. A question in the Lowy surveys from 2015 onwards has sought to capture attitudes towards this question, asking whether the public views China as more of an economic partner or more of a security threat. The question is important because respondents choose between the two images of China. Table 3.2 shows that until 2018 by far the predominant view of China was that of an economic partner; between 2015 and 2018 more than three in four of the survey respondents took this view. By 2020, however, these views had changed, with 55 per cent seeing China as an economic partner and 41 per cent as a security threat. This represents more than a threefold increase in the proportion seeing China as a threat between 2018 and 2020. Also notable is the relatively small proportion who either took an intermediate view or were unable or unwilling to answer the question. This suggests that most of the public had a firm view about China's role in Australia.

Drawing on a range of survey results and using multiple indicators, these findings show the paradoxical reaction of the public towards China's rise. While on the one hand most of the world has welcomed and accommodated the rise of China, the change has come with a concomitant fear of its ramifications: 'on one level accommodating and on another displaying an overwhelming sense of anxiety, a fear of being overtaken by China or of losing influence to a mysterious and potentially threatening China' (McCarthy &

---

[9] The question was not asked in the 2020 Lowy Survey.

Song, 2018: 323). There were major concerns about Chinese investment in Australia too, but until 2019 these were not matched by any significant increase in those viewing China as a military threat. That situation appeared to change in 2019 and 2020 when the proportion of respondents seeing China as a threat rose to equal the proportion who took the same view at the height of the Vietnam War (Chubb & McAllister, 2021a). In the absence of a war or a similar existential threat, such a rapid change in public opinion towards a single country is unprecedented.

CLIMATE CHANGE

Public opinion towards climate change and global warming has been remarkably stable since it first began to be measured consistently in surveys in the early 2000s. Internationally, people in European countries such as France, Spain and Sweden show the most concern about climate change, while those in less economically developed countries or those with major resource sectors (such as Australia, Canada and the United States) demonstrate the least concern.[10]

Opinions on climate change are sensitive to two factors. First, the economic impact of action to mitigate climate change influences public opinion: the more negative the economic effect, the less the public is concerned about the problem. Second, the level of political agreement on what action is required is important: the greater the political consensus, the higher the public concern. Both factors place Australia towards the bottom of the scale due to its economic reliance on the resources sector coupled with long-time partisan disagreement on the political response to the problem (Lewis, Palm & Feng, 2019; Tranter, 2011).

These patterns are evident in recent public opinion. Figure 3.5 shows concern about taking action on climate change from 2006 until 2020 using the Lowy surveys, together with evidence from the AES surveys of 2007–19 about the importance of global warming. The Lowy surveys show public support for taking action on climate change in the mid-2000s, but that concern declined significantly in the wake of the 2007–08 Global Financial Crisis, when economic security was a paramount consideration for many voters. From its lowest point, in 2012, public concerns about climate change again began to rise, in line with economic prosperity. In 2020, 56 per cent of the respondents to the survey said that action on climate change was a 'serious and pressing' problem that needed to be addressed.

While election campaigns are traditionally dominated by the issues of health, education and economic management, between one in 10 and one in 20 voters have seen the issues of climate change and global warming as either the most or second most important issue. The second line in Figure 3.5 shows that in the 2007 election 16 per cent of the respondents to the AES survey mentioned global warming as either the most or second most important election issue for them. In line with the pattern found in the Lowy surveys, this proportion declined to a low point of 8 per cent in 2013 in the wake of the Global Financial Crisis. However, by 2019 it had more than doubled to 20 per cent, ranking it fifth out of 10 issues, behind economic management, health and taxation, but ahead of education and immigration (Cameron & McAllister, 2020: table 1).

---

[10] See, for example, the most recent Pew surveys in https://www.pewresearch.org/fact-tank/2019/04/18/a-look-at-how-people-around-the-world-view-climate-change/.

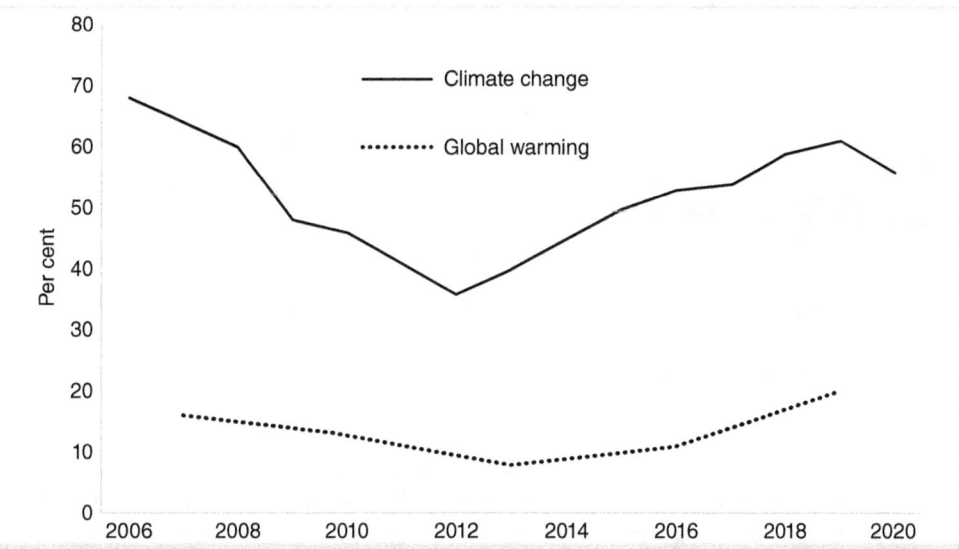

Figure 3.5 Public opinion towards climate change and global warming, 2006–20
Note: 'I'm going to read you three statements. Please tell me which statement comes closest to your own point of view ... "Global warming is a serious and pressing problem. We should begin taking steps now even if this involves significant costs." Thinking about these election issues, which of these issues has been most important to you and your family during the election campaign? And which was the second most important issue?'
Source: based on data from Lowy Institute Polls (2006–20); AES (2007–19).

The relatively low priority placed on climate change by the public might stem from the inability of both Liberal and Labor governments to present coherent narratives about multilateral action on climate change. In late 2016, the Turnbull government ratified the Paris Agreement, with Turnbull arguing that the agreement is a 'watershed [that] has galvanised the international community' and that Australia is 'playing our part with ambitious targets'. Just one week later, the Energy and Environment minister was criticised for lobbying in favour of the proposed – and highly controversial – Adani coal mine in Queensland (Parkinson, 2016).[11] The lack of any meaningful action on climate change by the Turnbull government, despite its advocacy for multilateral climate change action, reflects the highly politicised public discourse around climate change in Australia. In announcing his resignation in August 2018, Turnbull admitted that his government had been hamstrung by ideological and 'bitterly entrenched views' on climate and emissions policy (Hudson, 2019).

Turnbull resigned after a battle over climate policy within the government. In late 2017, the National Energy Guarantee (NEG) was introduced with the intention of providing certainty for investment in energy markets, as well as to provide a pathway for Australia to meet its commitments under the Paris Agreement. After Turnbull was replaced by Scott Morrison, the government reversed its commitment to multilateral

---

[11] The organisation Climate Action Network International awarded Australia the infamous 'fossil of the day' award for this behaviour (Slezak, 2016).

Table 3.3 Climate change and party support, 2020

	Coalition	Labor	Green	Other	None/DK
Critical threat	34	75	91	38	69
Important but not critical	49	22	8	37	25
Not important	17	3	1	25	6
Total	100	100	100	100	100
(N)	(781)	(610)	(262)	(166)	(547)

Note: See Figure 3.5 for question wording.
Source: based on data from Lowy Institute Poll (2020).

climate change action, dumped the NEG and announced that Australia would not join the Paris signatories in committing to emissions reduction targets. Divisions over climate change extended to the Labor opposition, which engaged in a public battle over the role that fossil fuels should play in its 2019 election platform. This reflected the tensions between its traditional, resource-intensive supporters and its urban, environmentally concerned base who wanted a firm commitment to zero emissions (Murphy, 2020).

The extent to which climate change was a party-political issue is demonstrated in Table 3.3, which shows the partisanship of those viewing climate change as a 'critical threat', as 'important but not critical' and as 'not important'. By any standards, the issue polarised the public along party lines: just one in three Coalition supporters saw it as a 'critical threat', but three-quarters of Labor voters and more than nine out of 10 Green supporters took the same view. The difference between Coalition and Labor supporters on viewing climate change as a 'critical threat' was a substantial 41 percentage points. By contrast, the next biggest divide between these sets of supporters was 'environmental disasters such as bushfires and floods', which had a difference of 17 percentage points, less than half that for climate change. The level of party polarisation on climate change was matched by few other issues in contemporary politics and demonstrates why the problem proved to be so intractable for politicians and policy-makers.

THE ROLE OF SOCIAL BACKGROUND

To what extent were these three concerns anchored in the social background of citizens? We would expect there to be a significant relationship since we know, for example, that younger generations are more concerned about global warming (Tranter, 2014) while older generations are more likely to express support for ANZUS and the United States (Miller, 2015). Similarly, education and higher social status generally result in greater concern about global warming. We also control for birthplace, divided between those born in Asia and those born in non-Asian countries, since we might expect these respondents to have differing views about the United States and China respectively.

To answer these questions, we estimate ordinary least squares regression models, predicting the three threats from gender, age, education, income and birthplace (Table 3.4). The dependent variables are scored from either one to four (trust in the United States) or one to three (China as a security threat and global warming). Since all

Table 3.4 Social background and attitudes towards the United States, China and global warming, 2020

	Trust in United States		China a security threat		Global warming	
	Est.	(SE)	Est.	(SE)	Est.	(SE)
Female	−.11**	(.04)	.05	(.04)	.09**	(.03)
Age (60 or over)						
18–29	−.51**	(.06)	−.28**	(.06)	.38**	(.04)
30–44	−.30**	(.05)	−.04	(.06)	.20**	(.04)
45–59	−.06	(.05)	.05	(.06)	.07	(.04)
University education	−.18**	(.04)	−.27**	(.05)	.27**	(.03)
Income (low)						
High	.00	(.05)	−.01	(.06)	−.05*	(.03)
Medium	−.08	(.05)	−.04	(.05)	−.03	(.03)
Birthplace (Australia)						
Asia	.15**	(.06)	−.03	(.06)	−.08	(.04)
Other than Asia	−.11*	(.05)	−.18**	(.05)	.04	(.04)
Constant	2.81	(.04)	2.01	(.04)	2.22	
Adj. R-squared	.06		.03		.08	

Note: Ordinary least squares regression results show partial regression coefficients (Est.) and standard errors (SE) predicting trust in the United States, China as a security threat and global warming, using listwise deletion. N = 2260. Trust in the United States is coded 4 = great deal, 3 = some, 2 = not very much, 1 = none; China as a security threat is coded 3 = threat, 2 = neither, 1 = partner; Global warming is coded 3 = more action, 2 = same as now, 1 = less action. The independent variables are coded zero or one, with the excluded category in parentheses. See text for coding of dependent variables.
Source: based on data from Lowy Institute Poll (2020).

the independent variables are scored zero or one, a one-unit change measures a change in the dependent variable. For example, in the first equation, being female rather than male results in being 0.11 less likely to trust the United States on the one to four scale, net of other things.

The results in Table 3.4 show that the major effects on attitudes towards the three issues were generational, closely followed by higher education. As foreshadowed earlier and in line with other research, older respondents are the most trusting of the United States, while the younger generation displays the least trust. The effect is substantial; the variables for age were greater than those of all the other independent variables in the model combined. It is those aged under 45, but most particularly those aged under 29, who are least trusting of the United States. Generation also plays a major role in predicting attitudes towards wanting more action on global warming, with younger generations most favouring more action while the two older generations largely opt for the status quo. Also notable is the fact that the younger generation (those younger than 30) is least likely to see China as a security threat.

Next in importance is having a university education, which 28 per cent of the survey reported as possessing. The largest impact for education is for wanting more action on global warming; in this case someone with a university education would be 0.27 more likely to want action (on a one to three scale). Those with a university education are also less likely to see China as a security threat and less likely to trust the United States. These are substantial effects and suggest that as the frequency of university education expands across the population, it will have gradual but still substantial effects on attitudes towards foreign affairs.

In comparison to generation and education, the other effects in the models in Table 3.4 are relatively modest. Women are substantially more likely to want action on global warming and less likely to trust the United States, but there is no effect on attitudes towards China. Income has virtually no influence on attitudes. There are some modest effects for birthplace: those born in Asian countries are more trusting of the United States, while those born in non-Asian countries are less trusting of the United States and less likely to see China as a security threat (see Chapter 6).

A variety of themes dominated debates in Australia about international politics after 2016, the most important of which were relations with the United States. This stemmed from the isolationism and protectionism of the Trump presidency as well as relations with China, especially in the wake of well-publicised attempts to influence Australian politics. In addition, the drought and the early 2020 bushfires focused attention on policies to combat climate change. As we have seen from the results in this section, each of these topics are driven in different ways by Australians' social backgrounds. Some of these attitudes could change, especially after the end of the Trump presidency, which might mitigate concerns about the United States. Others, however, might not, and it is unlikely that negative views of China will change, at least in the medium term.

CONCLUSION

Rather than the public being ill-informed and unpredictable, as earlier studies suggested (e.g. Stouffer, 1955; McCloskey, 1964), recent work on public opinion shows that the public can make sensible assessments about world affairs. The public can also evaluate how the international system influences their everyday lives. Such evaluations are guided by the information available to them, such as through the mass media, via social peers and by the cues provided by elites (Kertzer & Zeitzoff, 2017). During the period under review, the Australian public's capacity for judgement was well illustrated by trends in the three key areas of international politics that we have examined here.

With regard to the role played by the United States in the region and the importance of ANZUS, the public distinguished between short-term concerns about the Trump presidency and a long-term understanding that the US military alliance remained the bedrock of Australian defence. On the second concern – the international role China was seeking to play – the sharp change in public attitudes towards China was significant and had potentially lasting consequences for elite debate over this issue. Moreover, we would expect this substantial change in public opinion also to influence elite policy towards China. The third area of concern, the environment, remained a continuing and important backdrop to the drought and bushfires.

Public opinion polling tells us that Australians are interested and engaged in world affairs and hold strong and consistent opinions on Australia's national interests. Between 2016 and 2020, public attitudes towards international politics played a transformative role in the domestic political agenda. The end of Britain's membership in the European Union was the most dramatic example of this increase in populist politics. Along with other populist developments, it provided a background for Australian politics. The question of Chinese influence in Australia's social and political life was a challenge for politicians and policy-makers. They had on the one hand to protect democratic institutions from any real or imagined external threat while on the other safeguard the economic and political relationship with China in the face of a domestic debate that threatened to become ever more divisive and politically and racially charged.

Public opinion does not determine foreign policy, but it sets broad parameters within which it expects policy-makers to operate. Elites need to consider public opinion when they shape policy, particularly on salient issues such as the United States, China and climate change, which we have considered here.

References

Beeson, M. & Hamieri, S. (2016) Australian foreign policy and the new world disorder. In M. Beeson & S. Hamieri (eds), *Navigating the New International Disorder: Australia in World Affairs 2011–2015*, pp. 1–18. Melbourne: Oxford University Press

Bowen, J. (2017) Trump–Turnbull meet comes amid increasing debate over Australia's US ties. *Diplomat*, 5 May. https://thediplomat.com/2017/05/trump-turnbull-meet-comes-amid-increasing-debate-over-australias-us-ties/

Cameron, S. & McAllister, I. (2020) Policies and performance in the 2019 Australian federal election. *Australian Journal of Political Science* 55(3): 239–56

Carr, A. (2017) Is bipartisanship on national security beneficial? Australia's politics of defence and security. *Australian Journal of Politics and History* 63(2): 254–69

Chubb, D. & McAllister, I. (2021a) *Australian Public Opinion, Defence and Foreign Policy: Attitudes and Trends Since 1945*. Singapore: Palgrave Macmillan

——(2021b) Fear and greed: Australian public opinion towards China's rise. *Australian Journal of Politics and History* 67(3–4): 439–53

Goot, M. (2007) Neither entirely comfortable nor wholly relaxed: Public opinion, electoral politics, and foreign policy. In J. Cotton & J. Ravenhill (eds), *Trading on Alliance Security: Australia in World Affairs 2001–2005*, pp. 253–304. Melbourne: Oxford University Press

Hudson, M. (2019) A form of madness: Australian climate and energy policies, 2009–2018. *Environmental Politics* 28(3): 583–9

Kassam, N. (2020) *Lowy Institute Poll 2020*. Sydney: Lowy Institute

Kertzer, J. & Zeithoff, T. (2017) A bottom-up theory of public opinion about foreign policy. *American Journal of Political Science* 61(3): 543–58

Lewis, B.B., Palm, R. & Feng, B. (2019) Cross-national variation in determinants of climate change concern. *Environmental Politics* 28(5): 793–821

McAllister, I. & Makkai, T. (1991) Changing Australian opinion on defence: Trends, patterns, and explanations. *Small Wars and Insurgencies* 2(3): 195–235

McCarthy, G. & Song, X. (2018) China in Australia: The discourses of changst. *Asian Studies Review* 42(2): 323–41. https://doi.org/10.1080/10357823.2018.1440531

McClosky, H. (1964) Consensus and ideology in American politics. *American Political Science Review* 58(2): 361–82

Medcalf, R. (2017) The future of Australia's alliance with the United States. National Press Club speech, 21 February. https://www.anu.edu.au/news/all-news/speech-the-future-of-australia%E2%80%99s-alliance-with-the-united-states

Miller, C. (2015) Public support for ANZUS: Evidence of a generational shift? *Australian Journal of Political Science* 50(3): 442–61

Miller, G. & Rucker, P. (2017) Donald Trump blasted Malcolm Turnbull over refugee deal. *Australian Financial Review*, 2 February. https://www.afr.com/world/donald-trump-blasted-malcolm-turnbull-over-refugee-deal-20170202-gu3rxo

Murphy, K. (2020) Labor agrees to support new gas projects after public brawl sparked by Joel Fitzgibbon. *Guardian*, 29 October. https://www.theguardian.com/australia-news/2020/oct/29/labor-agrees-to-support-new-gas-projects-after-public-brawl-sparked-by-joel-fitzgibbon

Parkinson, G. (2016) Australia lobbies for Adani coal mine at climate talks. *Renew Economy*, 17 November

Sandler, T. & George, J. (2016) Military expenditure trends for 1960–2014 and what they reveal. *Global Policy* 7(2): 174–84

Slezak, M. (2016) Australia dubbed 'fossil of the day' after lobbying for coal mine at climate talks. *Guardian*, 17 November. https://www.theguardian.com/environment/2016/nov/17/australia-dubbed-fossil-of-the-day-after-lobbying-for-coal-mine-at-climate-talks.

Stouffer, S.A. (1955) *Communism, Conformity, and Civil Liberties: A Cross-section of the Nation Speaks Its Mind*. New Brunswick: Transaction Publishers

Tranter, B. (2011) Political divisions over climate change and environmental issues in Australia. *Environmental Politics* 20(1): 78–96

——(2014) Social and political influences on environmentalism in Australia. *Journal of Sociology* 50(3): 331–48

Zala, B. (2017) Issues in Australian Foreign Policy January to June 2017. *Australian Journal of Politics and History* 63(4): 610–23

Values, gender and foreign policy

Jacqui True and Tamara Ernest

Values and gender are an increasingly established part of Australian foreign policy, as was evident in the 2016–20 period. As stated in the Foreign Policy White Paper, the Australian Government believes that support for liberal institutions, universal values and human rights internationally advances Australia's national interests. Despite decades of Australian aid committed to promoting women's empowerment, however, gender equality only relatively recently emerged as a stand-alone attribute of Australian state identity and foreign policy. Indeed, it has meaningfully featured in this publication only since 2016, when one author (True, 2016) examined foreign policy from a gender perspective, discussed gender mainstreaming and the rise of women's leadership, as well as the global emergence of feminist principles in foreign policy. Between 2011 and 2015, Australia's approach to gendering foreign policy was representative of its overall principled but pragmatic bipartisan stance on both foreign policy and gender equality (True, 2016). This stance was underpinned by a rhetorical preference for open liberal democratic values that embraced gender equality and the rule of law, while also appreciating that every country in the world has different economic, social and political circumstances.

In 2010, Australia began to expand the role of gender in its foreign policy outcomes, fortified by its US alliance and encouraged by a global trend to promote gender equality in foreign policy and for the benefit of the international community (see Aggestam & True, 2020). Former US Secretary of State Hillary Clinton made the 'business case' for gender equality as smart diplomacy and economics during the first Obama administration when she argued that investing in women's economic empowerment would generate greater gains for development and security (US State Department, 2012). Australia began to mainstream gender programming in its foreign policy by investing in women's leadership in the Indo-Pacific region and launching a National Action Plan on Women, Peace and Security (2012–18) in 2012. That plan contributed to Australia's successful bid to secure a non-permanent seat on the UN Security Council in 2013–14. The Security Council election campaign emphasised Australia's commitment to progressing gender equality at home and abroad by recognising women as agents of change in achieving peace, security, economic stability and growth (Shepherd & True, 2014). As Foreign Minister from September 2013 to August 2018, Julie Bishop amplified and extended this approach. In 2016 she launched the first 'whole of foreign policy' gender strategy for Australia (Bishop, 2016; DFAT, 2016). Compared to the normative vision of more explicitly 'feminist' foreign policies in other countries like Sweden or Canada, where women's rights are centred and patriarchal power structures confronted through trade and defence policies, Australia adopted a more mild-mannered, diplomatic brand of foreign policy gender-mainstreaming (True, 2021).

In Australian politics, foreign policy tends to be bipartisan, with competitive politics playing out primarily in relation to domestic issues. Gender equality is also a bipartisan value within both domestic and foreign policy, promoting the extension of equal rights to all and aligning Australia's national and international identity as a liberal democratic state (Harris Rimmer & Sawer, 2016). Australia has redesigned its citizenship test to contain questions addressing our national values – including questions on gender equality and domestic and family violence against women – to reflect that citizenship is contingent on adherence to liberal democratic beliefs. Abroad, Australia has projected this identity to the world through its relationships with other states and its appointment of a Global Ambassador for Gender Equality, positioning Australia to lead by example in the Indo-Pacific region and align with other like-minded Western liberal democracies. As emphasised in the 2017 Foreign Policy White Paper:

> All government policies, including our foreign policy, must give expression to, and be formed on the basis of, the values of our community. Australia does not define its national identity by race or religion, but by shared values, including political, economic and religious freedom, liberal democracy, the rule of law, racial and gender equality and mutual respect ... Australia is pragmatic. We do not seek to impose values on others. We are however a determined advocate of liberal institutions, universal values and human rights. The Government believes that our support internationally for these values also serves to advance our national interests. (DFAT, 2017: 11)

Framing gender equality as a national and international value allows Australia to project its best face to the world, which distracts from other, more contentious human rights issues. Indeed, Australia's successful bid for UN Human Rights Council membership for 2018–20 was predicated on advancing gender equality as one of its main pillars. By emphasising what the government saw as the positive aspects of its engagement with the world, such as the promotion of gender equality at home and abroad, Australia attempted to deflect attention from the poor treatment of Aboriginal and Torres Strait Islander peoples and the detention of refugees. Indeed, there were claims of gender-based discrimination and violence against female asylum seekers in Australia's detention centres (Human Rights Law Centre, 2018). To focus solely on the positive aspects of Australia's record ignores the ongoing domestic debates regarding violence against women. In Australia, two in every five women (41 per cent) have experienced violence since the age of 15 (VicHealth, 2017), and on average, one woman is killed by male violence each week in Australia (Cussen & Bryant, 2015).

In the period under review, gender equality was also incorporated into Australia's security values. Former Defence Minister Linda Reynolds said that gender equality and women's empowerment were critical to national and global security, while Foreign Minister Marise Payne consistently spotlighted the role of women's leadership in achieving lasting peace agreements, greater gender equality and improved social and political outcomes. Their advocacy reflected strong government support for gendering foreign and security policy through a form of tacit 'militant liberalism': a commitment to protecting individual rights that align with Australian values at home and abroad and a preparedness to use aid and military capacities to secure these ideals (True, 2016). While a feature of past Australian foreign policy for other rights, the inclusion of gender equality and women's empowerment in this security approach was relatively recent.

This chapter interrogates the role of values and gender in Australian foreign policy from 2016 to 2020. We argue that gender equality continued to serve as a tangible expression of Australian identity and values in foreign policy, informing Australia's key international alliances and relationships and its foreign policy and security goals. The chapter begins by analysing the construction and expression of national identity through the values Australia projected in its foreign policy and international relations, and how these values changed during the five years under review. Next, we focus on who represented Australia and how Australia was represented in foreign policy through its diplomacy, security and development relationships, which we illustrate with reference to the Women, Peace and Security (WPS) agenda. The chapter also addresses the rise in women's representation in foreign policy and the extent to which an inclusive strategy for foreign policy leadership was realised. Third, the chapter critically examines the soft power aspect of Australia's foreign policy strategy and how values and gender equality principles were used to enhance Australia's reputation. The conclusion contemplates how values-driven foreign policy engagements, as evident in the global promotion of gender equality in realms of aid and security, contributed to the maintenance of a liberal international order and Australian foreign policy interests within that order.

AUSTRALIAN IDENTITY AND DIFFERENCE IN THE WORLD

The construction of Australia's (inter)national identity and the variance within it is critical to understanding Australia's national interest, its foreign policy decisions and its approach to international relations. Rather than viewing foreign policy as the external activity of a state with a fixed ideology, we interpret the decisions underpinning foreign policy as performative, boundary-producing acts that instantiate state identity (Campbell, 1992; Devetak & True, 2006). Consequently, shifts in expressions of identity over time tend to affect the framing of the national interest. This approach to understanding identity and difference in Australian foreign policy reflects the foundational constructivist tenet that identity forms the basis of interests (Jepperson, Wendt & Katzenstein, 1996; Wendt, 1992).

The increasing salience of gender equality in Australian foreign policy is the result of a gradual shift in values within Australia's historical policy positioning as a good international citizen. From the 1950s, values statements in Australian foreign policy largely addressed British interests: Australia was viewed as a willing agent of Commonwealth culture inclined towards the international liberal attitudes of leading global North powers. During the Cold War, this Western zeal was viewed as a point of contrast with Asian countries and used to explain Canberra's difficulties in establishing genuine regional rapport. When some semblance of distinctly Australian values became visible in foreign policy in the mid-1970s, its context was largely limited to Australia's flair for humanitarian activity in the South Pacific. There was some engagement with gender at the time, for instance in Australia's ratification of UN women's rights instruments and its engagement with International Women's Year (1975). However, these actions were largely performative in the wider context of an emerging global consciousness regarding gender discrimination and the need to address the roles of women and gender inequality in and through development policies (Sawer & Gray, 2014).

Any inkling of a specific gender focus was smothered by broad dialogue on human rights in Australian foreign policy in the 1990s. Given China's growing international influence, the Keating government drew upon human rights protections and liberal democratic institutionalism as distinct Australian values that impeded Asian engagement. In contrast, however, the Howard government capitalised on these values to promote regional activity; indeed, defending Australian values was a key justification for the 1999 intervention in East Timor (Milner, 2001). Unlike Keating, Howard's Foreign Policy White Paper contained a specific delineation of Australian values: the rule of law, freedom of press, responsible government and, given the post-Apartheid timeframe, racial equality. It suggested that '[n]ational interests cannot be pursued without regard to the values of the Australian community, including its support for fundamental human rights' (DFAT, 1997: iv). Not surprisingly, gender equality was absent from Howard's foreign policy considerations; instead it was considered to be best established through 'soft power' liberal institutionalism and economic growth.

Yet the growing recognition of human rights and humanitarianism as Australian foreign policy values at the turn of the 21st century helped to amplify gender equality and women's empowerment. Following UN Security Council Resolution (UNSCR) 1325 on WPS in 2000, community consciousness around gender equality and the rise of women's leadership led to a substantive focus on gender issues (set within liberal institutionalism) as crucial to Australia's national interest. A new ideal of what it meant to be a 'good international citizen' was emerging in Australia, one that not only encapsulated national security interests and the pursuit of multilateralism in foreign policy but also was meaningfully informed by community values (cf. Devetak, 2009; Abbondanza, 2020). As former Foreign Minister Gareth Evans (1990) first formulated:

> Good international citizenship is the area of foreign policy in which community values most influence the pursuit of national interests. Unlike a nation's strategic interests or commercial interests ... good international citizenship cannot be fully understood without reference to the community's self-image, and what it judges to be its guiding principles ... [G]ood international citizenship is no more – and no less – than the pursuit of enlightened self-interest.

Evans's enmeshing of state strategic and commercial interests with community values illustrated how state identity could be viewed as a composite of a nation's corporate and social 'international' identity (Reus-Smit, 2021). Corporate identity is reflected in the diverse struggles to define who and what constitutes national identity through claims on the state, whereas social identity is constructed through the state's self-understanding of its moral leanings and social norms that guide its relations with other states (Reus-Smit, 1999: 22). As this self-image is informed by conceptions of national identity – including, among other things, shared political and institutional values – social identity affects how states determine their national interests and subsequently foreign policy (Devetak & True, 2006).

Increasingly, gender equality and women's empowerment were integrated into both corporate and social aspects of Australian identity. Whereas Australia lacked explicit recognition of gender equality as a part of its foreign policy before 2011, thereafter it was openly used as a form of diplomacy and as a social values statement to bolster international relationships. For instance, the Gillard and Rudd Labor governments engineered an aid-based foreign policy underpinned by the empowerment of women and girls (True, 2016). As Foreign Minister, Julie Bishop 'placed the issue of gender empowerment at the heart of our foreign policy initiatives', with gender equality becoming a dominant form of Australian economic diplomacy (Bishop, 2018). Likewise, although cancelled in March 2020 due to COVID-19, the Australian Defence Force (ADF) organised a conference for its allies in the Indo-Pacific region, the United States and the Five Eyes group, focusing on closing gaps in WPS implementation.

Australian state identity and difference must also be positioned in its geopolitical context. The Foreign Policy White Paper established five priorities underpinning Australian international engagement from 2017 to 2027: increased foreign policy engagement in the Indo-Pacific; improved economic competition of Australian businesses in the international market; enhanced security via counterterrorism and foreign interference measures; strengthened rules-based international order; and renewed focus on Australia's aid commitments in the Pacific. In many ways, the White Paper operated more as a values statement conveying Australia's core liberal democratic identity traits than as a coherent foreign policy blueprint. As outlined in its introduction:

> Australia's values are a critical component of the foundation upon which we build our international engagement. Our support for political, economic, and religious freedoms, liberal democracy, the rule of law, racial and gender equality and mutual respect reflect who we are and how we approach the world. They underpin a strong, fair, and cohesive society at home and are a source of influence for Australia internationally. (DFAT, 2017: 3)

In the period under review this statement was highly relevant to Australian foreign policy and security strategy. In particular, Australia's 'Pacific Step-up' strategy (launched in 2017) to increase aid in the Pacific and better support small-island developing nations reflected an important shift from previous years.

First, as well as security concerns, the Step-up demonstrated the importance of human rights, including gender equality, in Australia's regional sphere of influence. Under this strategy, Australia consistently pursued development programming in the Indo-Pacific that supported women's leadership, women's economic empowerment and the elimination of violence against women. Examples included the A$320 million Pacific Women Shaping Pacific Development program (2010–22), the Investing in Women Initiative (2016–) to work with South-East Asian businesses to improve women's employment conditions and increase investment in women-led enterprises, and the Empowering Indonesian Women for Poverty Reduction Project (2012–20) to develop women's collective decision-making capacity.

Second, the prioritisation of aid-based Pacific engagement distinguished Australia in the context of Chinese competition for regional influence (see Chapter 12). Chinese aid to the Pacific did not include dedicated bilateral programmes to advance women's rights, which was consistent with a broader trend in Chinese foreign assistance to promote gender equality, which had been limited to multilateral support for the 1995 Beijing Platform for Action and implementing small-scale women's health projects (UN Women, 2016). In a speech discussing change and uncertainty in the Indo-Pacific, Bishop (2017) made clear that '[c]ompetition is ever-present and relentless' and '[w]hile non-democracies such as China can thrive when participating in the present system, an essential pillar of our preferred order is democratic community'. As such, Australia's Step-up integrated Pacific Island countries into the Australian economy and security institutions to achieve long-term stability and economic growth. It also established Australia's leadership prowess and capacity to partner widely and strongly with neighbours in distinctly liberal democratic unions.

Consequently, Australia's foreign policy regarding gender equality and women's empowerment adopted a more distinct Indo-Pacific flavour, which coincided with Australia's economic and security interests (see Chapter 11). However, this foreign policy approach was not internationally minded. In situating its values in this geographical context and underscoring the importance of regionalism, Australia sought to address common challenges, harness shared strengths, and deliver practical benefits to all Pacific nations. Australia attempted to position itself as a regional leader and counterpoint to China. In this sense, the liberal democratic values underpinning Australian identity were fundamental to its foreign policy undertakings. Many of these projected values accorded (albeit at different strengths) with Australia's domestic policies, such as improving gender equality and human rights protections, strengthening climate and disaster resilience, preventing violent extremism and supporting healthy, educated and inclusive populations.

INCLUSIVE LEADERSHIP AND STRATEGY

The incremental inclusion of a gender perspective in Australian foreign policy reflected a broader shift in *who* represented Australia and *how* Australia was represented in its diplomacy, security and development relationships. In 2016–20, a second successive female Foreign Minister was appointed under a Liberal government, with Defence Minister Marise Payne assuming the role of chief diplomat following Julie Bishop's retirement from politics in 2018. Given Payne's history of integrating gender into Defence operations, Bishop's legacy of a gender-sensitive foreign policy appeared to be in capable hands. Indeed, the collective leadership of Payne and Bishop in Defence and Foreign ministerships between 2016 and 2018 resulted in the pursuit of pro-gender norms across a range of diplomatic, aid, security and development policies, thus compelling real consideration of gender in top political decision-making circles for the first time.

Yet for all their collective power and even in the context of increasingly turbulent global affairs (Beeson & Hameiri, 2016), Australia's international representation remained relatively unchanged. Australia's foreign policy rhetoric reflected its positioning as a middle power committed to liberal democratic values and engagement with global institutions that supported a liberal approach to peace, security and trade. Unlike other global North middle powers, such as Canada and Sweden, Australia did not explicitly label its diplomatic, security and development strategies as 'feminist'. Gender equality was no doubt a core shared national value and driver of Australian foreign policy, but its strategic adoption occurred largely 'by stealth' (Lee-Koo, 2020).

As women's leadership of key Australian foreign and security positions expanded, it is worth revisiting the question asked in the previous edition of this volume: does the gender of the leader make a difference to the pursuit of a gender perspective in foreign policy? Certainly, Foreign Minister Bishop's strong leadership on gender equality and women's empowerment, in tandem with support by Defence Minister Payne, was successful in inculcating gender into Australia's diplomatic, security and development projects. Indeed, gender equality appeared at the heart of Australian foreign policy under Bishop, featuring 'wherever Australia is engaged' (Bishop, 2016).

To demonstrate this positioning, in 2016 DFAT established its *Gender Equality and Women's Empowerment Strategy*. At the launch, Bishop (2016) clearly expressed how this 'whole of foreign policy' strategy would be championed: 'We all know that women's empowerment, educating women, addressing women's health issues, women's economic issues, addressing domestic violence, these are all fundamental to sustainable economic growth, to prosperity, to ending poverty and ensuring that there's peace and stability.'

The strategy emphasised a gender perspective as a core priority in Australia's foreign and security policy, economic diplomacy and development programming. Arguably, it is as close as Australia has ever come to an explicitly 'feminist' foreign policy. Three priorities guided the strategy: promoting women's voices in decision-making, leadership and peace-building; stimulating women's economic empowerment; and ending violence against women and girls. In application, it offered a dual approach to gender equality: first, it defined gender equality and women's empowerment as a key priority in Australia's foreign policy, economic diplomacy and development programming; and second, it encouraged DFAT to integrate gender equality across all operations by requiring at least 80 per cent of investments to address gender equality issues in their implementation (DFAT, 2016). Consequently, gender shifted from being a siloed foreign policy consideration to being integral to overall foreign policy. As a mark of the seriousness with which gender considerations were required to occupy political thinking, strict accountability mechanisms were introduced. While DFAT's performance showed some improvement, it did not meet its 80 per cent target; in 2018–19, for instance, the achievement rate was 77 per cent across DFAT programming (DFAT, 2020a).

The promotion of gender equality was also a key part of Bishop's campaign for Australia's election to the UN Human Rights Council from 2018 to 2020. At the campaign launch, she lauded Australia as a 'pioneer of women's rights' and a place where gender equality is legally enshrined (Bishop, 2017). Australia was also celebrated as the first country in which women could simultaneously vote and be elected to parliament – an attractive statement that ignored Australia's racist exclusion of Aboriginal and Torres Strait Islander women from voting and the fact that it took 41 years for a woman actually to be elected, one of the greatest political lags across all Western democracies (Wilson & McKeown, 2003). Historical reticence aside, Australia used its three-year term on the Human Rights Council to integrate a gender perspective into human rights investigative mechanisms, releasing several statements addressing violence against women and girls, the rights of older women, and the role of women in peace-building and multilateralism.

The foundations of a gender-sensitive foreign policy were therefore well established by the time Marise Payne became Foreign Minister in August 2018. Payne declared to the UN General Assembly that 'Australia firmly believes that it is only through the inclusion of women in all aspects of peace and security initiatives, including negotiations, the design of peace processes, and the management and enforcement of peace programs, that lasting and resilient security can be achieved' (Payne, 2018). Her support for the WPS agenda followed naturally from the gender-mainstreaming she had pursued as Defence Minister (2015–18). Payne increased women's recruitment, addressed sexism in the ADF, implemented WPS frameworks in policy and operations, and established a 15 per cent minimum for female military members deployed on Australian peacekeeping mission teams. Moreover, the Defence Department's commitment to reporting and reflection on WPS implementation, including its 2018 self-review, was viewed positively on the global stage (Prescott, 2020; Wittwer, 2019). In 2019, Payne was also appointed as Minister for Women, the first person in Australia and possibly worldwide to hold these positions simultaneously. As a result, a gender lens became increasingly inextricable from Australian foreign policy; the view that gender equality and women's empowerment were essential to global security and within Australia's national interests had become mainstream.

Bishop and Payne artfully navigated domestic and international politics to lead on gender. In doing so, they challenged historical views that foreign and defence policy-making is in the realm of 'high politics' reserved for men. The unique positioning of foreign ministries – their international (rather than national) terrain and detachment from parliament – allowed these women to bolster the role of gender in Australian aid, humanitarian and security policy away from the often-puerile debates of domestic politics (Aggestam & True, 2020). Despite their leadership, Australian politics remained a highly masculinised domain (Ghazarian & Lee-Koo, 2021). As of December 2020, female politicians comprised just 31.1 per cent of the House of Representatives, which was the highest proportion in the history of Australia's lower house (Hough, 2020). Bishop and Payne's prioritisation of a pro-gender foreign policy in Australia therefore illustrated how they made strategic use of their appointments and was arguably a product of their wider roles as female leaders.

Unfortunately, Australia's pro-gender foreign policy stance was inhibited by persistent gender imbalances in diplomacy and security employment in the period under review. In 2019, the Lowy Institute found that 'Australia's international relations sector has a gender problem' (Cave et al., 2019: 2). Despite some notable leadership by women – for example Julie Bishop, Marise Payne and Linda Reynolds in Foreign Affairs and Defence, Frances Adamson as Secretary of DFAT, and Jan Adams as Ambassador to China and later Japan – the pace of change was slow and gender imbalances across the sector remained striking. Women had led Australia's 14 internationally focused public service departments and agencies only four times and were severely underrepresented in senior management in these organisations (approximately 14 per cent of department/agency heads) compared to the wider public service. Despite generating roughly 33 major white papers, reviews and inquiries to influence Australia's foreign and security policy architecture since 1966, not one major government policy-setting exercise had been headed by a woman. While the report contained notable exclusions from its dataset (e.g. international relations scholars), it nevertheless evidenced the fact that women were being overlooked as strategic leaders in international affairs. This was antithetical to the value of gender equality projected by Australia internationally. As Cave et al. noted, 'sending mostly men to the most important global positions and forums and to deal with complex intelligence and analytical issues is inimical to Australia's national interest and to the effective pursuit of Australia's foreign policy interests' (2019: 10).

However, some agencies and organisations defied this trend. For example, DFAT countered its shortcomings in women's senior leadership by implementing a Women in Leadership (WIL) strategy. It also embedded substantive equality measures and mainstreamed flexible work to dismantle career barriers to leadership (DFAT, 2015). Some evidence of this strategy's success emerged: as of October 2020, 43.6 per cent career-appointed head of mission/diplomatic post roles were held by women, and 48 per cent of departmental officials at the senior executive service band 2 level were women (Elmas, 2020). While Australia's literal face to the world was increasingly female – indeed, more women were taking leadership roles in diplomatic postings than ever before – gender hierarchies remained firmly in place for the most prestigious postings. By the end of 2020, women had yet to be appointed as ambassadors to four of the ten largest overseas posts: the United States, United Kingdom, Indonesia and Thailand.

The WIL strategy and broader foreign policy gender equality and women's empowerment strategy were significant legacies of Bishop's leadership, and later Payne's. Both women led these strategies not only because they were female political leaders but also because as female leaders they could see how 'gender inequality is holding us back in a globalised world' (Bishop, 2014) and especially in the Indo-Pacific region, where Australia's middle-power foreign policy was increasingly focused.

CRITICAL ASSESSMENT OF 'SOFT POWER'

The leadership shown by Julie Bishop and Marise Payne reflected a concerted move to build up Australia's foreign policy with regard to gender as a key 'soft power' resource. As a middle power, Australia does not wield great material (hard) power. In the period under review, it hovered around the 18th–19th most powerful state in military capability, had the 13th–14th largest economy by GDP and was the 12th–13th biggest aid donor (True, 2017; Global Firepower, 2020; Knoema, 2020; DonorTracker, 2021). Consequently, Australia's ability to harness soft power – such as its diplomatic networks, institutional reach, educational opportunities and development aid – was crucial to its global credibility. According to the Soft Power 30 Index, which ranks countries on the basis of enterprise, education, culture, engagement, government, polling and digital metrics, Australia was positioned 9th in the world in 2019 (Portland, 2019). Considering each country's UNDP-generated Gender Inequality Index score, this ranking spotlighted Sweden's explicitly feminist foreign policy as a soft power attraction.

In this context, Bishop and Payne's emphasis on gender equality and women's empowerment at home and abroad was a strategic soft power initiative. It was consistent with a middle power trend, wherein pro-gender foreign policy norms are adopted as soft power tools to promote national interests and 'to gain power and authority by manoeuvring among gendered leadership, institutions and structures in foreign policy' (Aggestam & True, 2021: 387).

Australia's spirited embrace of the WPS agenda reflected this trend. Since the passage of UNSCR 1325 in 2000, the WPS agenda has become a vital part of the normative international policy framework on conflict-related gendered violence, peace-building and women's participation in peace and security processes. The WPS agenda transcends the domestic/international divide by engaging policy-makers, institutions and feminist movements across defence, diplomacy, human rights and development. The result is a dynamic transnational feminist network that offers participating foreign leaders soft-power advantages. Policy-makers can harness the power of the WPS network to tackle common challenges in achieving gender equality and women's empowerment. For example, Australia has used its WPS agenda to promote conflict resolution through inclusive peace processes and to prevent violent extremism at the community level in South-East Asia. Furthermore, foreign leaders engage with WPS networks to legitimise their foreign policy pursuits among other liberal states and to distinguish themselves from non-democracies. For instance, Aggestam and True (2020) note how Australia draws upon its pro-gender foreign policy to engage in 'nation-branding' to foster greater regional and global influence. Foreign leaders can also use the network to forge and manage complex interstate relations, as reflected in Marise Payne's statement that her position as Foreign Minister gave her the 'unique advantage of being able ... to use women's empowerment as a way to strengthen relationships' (Payne, 2020). Between 2016 and 2020, the deepened WPS social networks pursued by Australia were an important course of action to generate greater regional stability and increase Australia's security without resorting to more coercive measures.

Beyond network benefits, the WPS agenda advanced Australia's soft power interests compared to other human rights initiatives. In particular, successive national action plans (NAPs) on WPS in 2012–18 and 2021–31 have established a comprehensive framework via 'whole of government' policies to institutionalise gender equality in peace and security operations. The first NAP was a potent catalyst for change, promoting greater women's peace-building agency in Australia's development policies and more gender-sensitive security policy and inclusive diplomacy in the Indo-Pacific (True, 2017). It encouraged deep shifts towards gender equality and gender leadership in the armed forces. In the period under review, mainstreaming WPS increased the number of ADF gender advisers, including ongoing placements in Afghanistan and Iraq, and the deployment of the first female gender adviser to the UN Mission in South Sudan in 2016 (Wittwer, 2019). Since 2017 the ADF has offered its own Operational Gender Adviser Course – the first of its kind in the southern hemisphere – to train ADF, DFAT and international armed forces staff on the incorporation of gender into military operations and planning processes (Department of Defence, 2017). Moreover, in June 2020 the ADF released its *Gender, Peace and Security Mandate 2020–30*, a long-term strategy to achieve key Defence goals on WPS, gender equality and human rights (Department of Defence, 2020).

Yet there were other instances where Australia's approach to advancing the WPS agenda faltered – and with it the nation's soft power status as a regional and global leader on gender. Most obviously, there was a significant delay in launching the second NAP to guide WPS practice in Australia. The two-year gap between plans raised concerns about how Australia would manage and meet its international commitments to the WPS agenda. While the disruption of COVID-19 was in part to blame for the delay, it also revealed that the WPS agenda was not essential to Australia's pandemic response. This marginalisation occurred despite UN recognition of the global shadow pandemic of gender-based violence (UN Women, 2020), the setbacks to gender equality caused by the pandemic (UN, 2020) and significant evidence that gender-sensitive health crisis responses result in more inclusive policies and better health, economic and social outcomes (True & Davies, 2020; Smith, 2019).

While waiting for the publication of the second NAP, other institutions attempted to maintain Australia's pro-gender soft power status and foreign policy. For example, the 2020 campaign for Natasha Stott Despoja's appointment to the Convention on the Elimination of Discrimination Against Women Committee projected Australia's pro-gender reputation to the world by marketing its 'proud record of international advocacy on ending violence against women and girls, promoting women's economic empowerment and enhancing women's leadership choices' (Department of the Prime Minister and Cabinet, 2020). Likewise, in early 2020, Foreign Minister Payne rebranded the Global Ambassador for Women and Girls as the Global Ambassador for Gender Equality, a key institution to demonstrate Australia's good international citizenship on gender. The position connected Australia to other countries and to the global agenda for the promotion of gender equality, women's human rights and women's equal participation in political, economic and social affairs.

A 'whole-of-government' policy on WPS, such as through NAPs, was a crucial soft power mechanism to connect multi-institutional endeavours on gender equality and women's empowerment. However, there was a risk that pro-gender policies and projects would be un(der)funded, inadequately resourced or insufficiently delivered. In October 2020 the Australian Government discontinued its Soft Power Review (launched in 2018 and which had received more than 130 submissions) on the basis that it was 'no longer as relevant to the significantly changed global environment' (DFAT, 2020b). Certainly, the period under review showed that the soft power of Australia's gender equality and women's empowerment programming remained acutely relevant to the form and substance of international relations during COVID-19 and beyond. A failure to recognise the powerful influence of gender as a soft power resource or competitive advantage in the Indo-Pacific region could hinder Australia's achievement of its foreign policy goals in the future.

CONCLUSION

Australian foreign policy has long reflected values and gender norms, but it is only recently that they have become an explicit part of foreign policy strategy and its measurable outcomes. While gender equality had previously been a significant lead indicator of broader liberal values at home, this chapter has illustrated how Australia also embraced such values in its foreign policy practice between 2016 and 2020. This shift was especially visible in Australia's policies towards the Indo-Pacific, where Australia was distinct for its professed commitment to gender-equal leadership and redressing gender inequities in economic and security spheres. Australian foreign policy-makers appeared to believe that a militant liberal commitment to human rights and gender equality was compatible with Australia's support for both a US-led global order and a rules-based international society. These values provided a certain coherence to Australia's strategy, despite the multiple agencies, allies and competing demands that had to be balanced in foreign and security policy.

Female Foreign Affairs and Defence ministers accomplished this balancing act well between 2016 and 2020. They practised soft and hard power politics convincingly, and their performance was celebrated by Australia's key allies and in international forums. Furthermore, the Women, Peace and Security agenda was a clear example of liberal values being advanced and good international citizenship being practised. Australia's pragmatic approach as a middle power involved balancing traditional national interest prerogatives associated with membership in security alliances with values-based foreign policy, which were vital to upholding the liberal international order and constructing a coherent and confident Australian identity in the world.

References

Abbondanza, G. (2020) Australia the 'good international citizen'? The limits of a traditional middle power. *Australian Journal of International Affairs* 75(2): 178–96

Aggestam, K. & True, J. (2020) Gendering foreign policy: Advancing a comparative framework for analysis. *Foreign Policy Analysis* 16(2): 143–62

——(2021) Political leadership and gendered multilevel games in foreign policy. *International Affairs* 97(2): 385–404

Beeson, M. & Hameiri, S. (2016) *Navigating the New International Disorder*. Melbourne: Oxford University Press

Bishop, J. (2014) Women in media – National Press Club address. Address by the Minister for Foreign Affairs, 29 October

——(2016) Launch of gender equality and women's empowerment strategy. Address by the Minister for Foreign Affairs, 29 February

——(2017) Human Rights Council campaign launch. Address by the Minister for Foreign Affairs, 18 May

——(2018) Keynote Address at the Opening Ceremony of the 2018 Global Summit of Women. Address by the Minister for Foreign Affairs, 26 April

Campbell, D. (1992) *Writing Security: United States Foreign Policy and the Politics of Identity*. Minneapolis: University of Minnesota Press

Cave, D., Oliver, A., Hayward-Jones, J., Munro, K. & Harris, E. (2019) *Foreign Territory: Women in International Relations*. Sydney: Lowy Institute

Cussen, T. & Bryant, W. (2015) *Domestic/Family Homicide in Australia*. Research in Practice No. 38. Canberra: Australian Institute of Criminology

Department of Defence (DOD) (2017) *Annual Report 16–17*. Canberra. https://www.defence.gov.au/sites/default/files/2021-10/AR-2016-17.pdf

——(2020) *Defence Gender, Peace and Security Mandate: From Rhetoric to Reality*. Canberra

Department of Foreign Affairs and Trade (DFAT) (1997) *In the National Interest: Australia's Foreign and Trade Policy White Paper*. Canberra

——(2015) *Women in Leadership Strategy*. Canberra

——(2016) *Gender Equality and Women's Empowerment Strategy*. Canberra

——(2017) *2017 Foreign Policy White Paper*. Canberra. www.fpwhitepaper.gov.au

——(2020a) *Performance of Australian Aid 2018–19*. October. Canberra. https://www.dfat.gov.au/sites/default/files/performance-of-australian-aid-2018-19.pdf

——(2020b) *Soft Power Review*. Canberra

Department of the Prime Minister and Cabinet (2020) Australia's candidate for the Committee on the Elimination of Discrimination against Women. https://www.pmc.gov.au/office-women/international-forums/convention-elimination-all-forms-discrimination-against-women/australias-candidate

Devetak, R. (2009) An Australian outlook on international affairs? The evolution of international relations theory in Australia. *Australian Journal of Politics and History* 55(3): 335–59

Devetak, R. & True, J. (2006) Diplomatic divergence in the Antipodes: Globalisation, foreign policy and state identity in Australia and New Zealand. *Australian Journal of Political Science* 41(2): 241–56

DonorTracker (2021) *Australia*. https://donortracker.org/country/australia

Elmas, M. (2020) How women in leadership are helping DFAT deal with the pandemic through a gendered lens. *Mandarin*, 26 October

Evans, G. (1990) Foreign policy and good international citizenship. Address by the Minister for Foreign Affairs, 6 March

Ghazarian, Z. & Lee-Koo, K. (eds) (2021) *Gender Politics: Navigating Political Leadership in Australia*. Sydney: New South Books

Global Firepower (2020) *GlobalFirepower.com Ranks*. https://www.globalfirepower.com/global-ranks-previous.php

Harris Rimmer, S. & Sawer, M. (2016) Neoliberalism and gender equality policy in Australia. *Australian Journal of Political Science* 51(4): 742–58

Hough, A. (2020) Composition of Australian parliaments by party and gender: A quick guide. Parliamentary Library, retrieved 30 November

Human Rights Law Centre (2018) Australia's record on women's rights to be scrutinised on the world stage. Media release, 2 July

Jepperson, R., Wendt, A. & Katzenstein, P. (1996) Norms, identity, and culture in national security. In P. Katzenstein (ed.), *The Culture of National Security: Norms and Identity in World Politics*, pp. 33–75. New York: Columbia University Press

Knoema (2020) *World GDP Rankings 2019*. https://knoema.com/nwnfkne/world-gdp-ranking-2019-gdp-by-country-data-and-charts

Lee-Koo, K. (2020) Pro-gender foreign policy by stealth: Navigating global and domestic politics in Australian foreign policy making. *Foreign Policy Analysis* 16(2): 236–49

Milner, A. (2001) Balancing 'Asia' against Australian values. In J. Cotton & J. Ravenhill (eds), *The National Interest in a Global Era: Australia in World Affairs 1996–2000*, pp. 31–52. Melbourne: Oxford University Press

Payne, M. (2018) National statement – United Nations General Assembly. Address by the Minister for Foreign Affairs, 28 September

——(2020) Statement on International Women's Day. Media release, 8 March

Portland (2019) *The Soft Power 30: A Global Ranking of Soft Power 2019*. https://softpower30.com/wp-content/uploads/2019/10/The-Soft-Power-30-Report-2019-1.pdf

Prescott, J. (2020) Moving from gender analysis to risk analysis of failing to consider gender. *RUSI Journal* 165(5): 46–56

Reus-Smit, C. (1999) *The Moral Purpose of the State: Culture, Social Identity, and Institutional Rationality in International Relations*. Princeton: Princeton University Press

——(2021) Constructivism. In R. Devetak & J. True (eds), *Theories of International Relations*, 6th edn. London: Palgrave Macmillan

Sawer, M. & Gray, S. (2014) The women's movement and government: Feminist fading? *Australian Feminist Studies* 29(82): 403–18

Shepherd, L. & True, J. (2014) The Women, Peace and Security Agenda and Australian leadership in the world: From rhetoric to commitment? *Australian Journal of International Affairs* 67(3): 257–84

Smith, J. (2019) Gender matters in responding to major disease outbreaks like Ebola. *Conversation*, 23 July

True, J. (2016) Gender and foreign policy. In S. Hamieri & M. Beeson (eds), *Navigating International Disorder: Australia in World Affairs 2011–2015*, pp. 224–41. Melbourne: Oxford University Press

——(2017) Soft power or smart power? Flipping Australia's White Paper. *Australian Institute of International Affairs*, 27 November

——(2021) Navigating change in international relations: Gendered games still. *Australian Journal of International Affairs* 75(6): 701–14

True, J. & Davies, S.E. (2020) The importance of gender inclusion in COVID-19 responses. *World Politics Review*, 5 June

United Nations (UN) (2020) Progress towards gender equality under threat, world leaders warn as General Assembly marks twenty-fifth anniversary of landmark women's rights conference. Press release, GA/12275, 1 October

UN Women (2016) China pledges USD 10 million commitment to UN Women, assistance for other developing countries to build 100 health projects for women and children

——(2020) Violence against women and girls: The shadow pandemic. 6 April

US State Department (2012) *Joint Statement on the Rarotonga Dialogue on Gender Equality*, 1 September

VicHealth (2017) *Violence against Women in Australia: An Overview of Research and Approaches to Primary Prevention*

Wendt, A. (1992) Anarchy is what states make of it. *International Organization* 46(2): 391–426

Wilson, J. & McKeown, D. (2003) Votes for women. Parliamentary Library, retrieved 30 November

Wittwer, J. (2019) Mainstreaming WPS in the armed forces: The case of Australia. In S.E. Davies & J. True (eds), *The Oxford Handbook of Women, Peace, and Security*, pp. 569–82. New York: Oxford University Press

Countering foreign interference

Domestic laws and international repercussions

Melissa Conley Tyler and Julian Dusting

From 2016 to 2020, Australia faced significant threats of espionage and foreign interference across several sectors. While threat data is not publicly available, we can accept statements by the Australian Security Intelligence Organisation (ASIO) in 2017 (Kendall, 2019) and 2020 (Grattan, 2020) that the espionage threat against Australia was unprecedented. Australia has long had to deal with the question of how to counteract foreign espionage, with previous volumes in this series charting the growth of Australia's intelligence community in the 20th century (Andrew, 1992) as well as intelligence coordination in national security policy (Wesley, 2011). In more recent years, the security environment has become complex and multifaceted, encompassing risks not just in the form of the gathering of classified intelligence by foreign agents.

The early decades of Chinese espionage and interference have been outlined in the official history of ASIO (Blaxland & Crawley, 2017: 225–33). In response, Australia put in place new legislation to counter these threats to Australia's security, including the *National Security (Espionage and Foreign Interference) Act 2018* (Cth) ('Foreign Interference Act'), *Foreign Influence Transparency Scheme Act 2018* (Cth) ('FITS') and *Australia's Foreign Relations (State and Territory Arrangements) Act 2020* (Cth) ('Foreign Relations Act'). These had a wide remit, covering international connections by individuals, organisations, state governments, local councils and universities.

In addition, Australia passed laws banning foreign political donations, tightening foreign investment rules and protecting critical infrastructure, thus presenting itself as 'a first mover' among Western democracies in using legislation to counter foreign interference (Medcalf, 2019). After Australia passed its laws, other similar countries appeared to be considering their own such legislation to prevent foreign interference (Shields, 2019; Kendall, 2019). This was part of a larger trend towards legislation on foreign interference and influence, including China's 2016 laws requiring foreign NGOs to register with the Ministry of Public Security to safeguard state security and provide protection from Western influence, and China's 2020 national security law, which included offences of colluding with foreign countries (Buckley, Bradsher & May, 2020).

These domestic laws, enforced by police and other security officials, were presented by the government and media as a response to foreign interference in Australian politics and democracy, especially by the People's Republic of China. During this period, Australia's relationship with China deteriorated markedly, including a freeze on high-level contacts and trade retaliation. This chapter focuses on the goals and effectiveness of these new domestic laws and their influence on Australia's international relations. It also assesses whether they were a significant factor in the worsening of Australia–China relations during this period.

FOREIGN INTERFERENCE LAWS

Foreign Interference Act

The *National Security (Espionage and Foreign Interference) Act 2018* (Cth) replaced four existing espionage offences with 27 new offences aimed at countering the threat of foreign states that exerted improper influence over Australia's system of government and politics through covert, coercive or corrupt means (Turnbull, 2017). The previous offences criminalised obtaining or communicating information regarding Australia's security and defence to another country or foreign organisation. The new offences were wider in scope, covering acting for a foreign principal and dealing with information that might damage Australia's national interests, broadly defined (Mack, 2020), as well as recruiting and preparing for espionage and actions outside Australia, such as cyberattacks (Kendall, 2019). The legislation represented a new approach: 'At least of the "Five Eyes" intelligence nations Australia has been the first country to enact such harsh and sweeping espionage legislation.' (Kendall, 2019: 159)

It arose from concerns that the existing offences would not cover 'espionage that, for example, intended to prejudice Australia's economic development, natural resource management strategies or vital infrastructure planning, or the trade secrets of Australian businesses, all of which are targeted by espionage today and can be used to compromise the country's national interests' (Kendall, 2019: 137). A further rationale for the legislation – that there had been very few espionage prosecutions under existing laws – can be explained by Australia's traditional preference for a 'catch and deport' system for foreign spies (Kendall, 2019: 140), which continued even after the new laws were passed (Grattan, 2020). Unstated was the inference that espionage might be conducted by people Australia could not easily deport, such as citizens and those citizens who held second passports.

The legislation was criticised for its broad intentions, the lack of sincere debate about it, and its underwhelming enforcement. The wide scope of the legislation – which criminalised conduct intended to prejudice almost any aspect of Australia's national security, not just the activities of intelligence or security agencies – led to concerns that it was a threat to civil liberties (Mack, 2020) that could be used to prosecute whistle-blowers and human-rights activists (Pearson, 2018) and undermine fundamental legal and democratic rights (Head, 2018). Following from experience with anti-terrorism laws, concerns were raised that the new offence of preparing for espionage could be used to prosecute mundane activities such as purchasing a laptop or phone (Kendall, 2019) or inadvertently connecting on LinkedIn with someone who turned out to be a foreign spy (Kendall, 2021). Additionally, with only three days between its second reading and enactment (Kendall, 2019: 159), the legislation was given little consideration by parliament. One international observer questioned whether 'paranoia and fear [had led] to impulsivity and hastiness' to garner electoral support (Mack, 2020: 367), while Indigenous leader Noel Pearson described it as 'reckless lawmaking for purely electoral gain' (2018). As of the end of 2020, there had been one prosecution under the new legislation, and a separate constitutional challenge was underway.

Foreign Influence Transparency Scheme

The *Foreign Influence Transparency Scheme Act 2018* (Cth) established a public register of activities taken on behalf of foreign principals, defined as foreign governments, political organisations, government-related entities or government-related individuals. The stated purpose of FITS was to ensure that Australia's democratic processes were more robust by providing visibility of the nature, level and extent of foreign influence in political and governmental processes. The focus of the legislation was on covert activity, with influence activity being not a crime if it was registered and conducted openly (Munro, 2018). Registrable activities included lobbying, communications and payments. The legislation was based on the United States *Foreign Agents Registration Act 1938* (FARA) (Draffen & Ng, 2020). It was criticised for criminalising a wide range of benign conduct involving international engagement, the uncertainty around what activities should be registered and its low level of efficacy, in that it had a high degree of non-compliance. The non-profit sector lobbied hard for amendments (Crosbie, 2018) and was eventually exempted amid a tightening of the legislation (Munro, 2018). Along with the Foreign Interference Act, FITS came into force in December 2018.

After its enactment, concerns were raised about the efficacy of the new law, given the relatively minimal information required to be registered (Krishnakumar, 2020). There was great uncertainty around what activities should be registered, with questions asked about former prime minister Tony Abbott's speeches at conservative conferences funded by the United States and Hungary (Hurst, 2020a) and former prime minister Kevin Rudd's role in the US-based Asia Society (Hurst, 2021). Both eventually registered: Rudd, for instance, was advised by the Attorney-General's Department that his interviews with state-owned broadcasters like the BBC and Radio NZ required him to register (Hurst, 2021).

By December 2020, FITS had a total of 82 registrants disclosing representation of foreign principals in 34 jurisdictions. This was a small proportion of the more than 500 organisations that were proactively contacted to encourage them to consider registering (Iggulden, 2019). There had been no prosecutions for non-registration. If former Cabinet ministers being interviewed by state-owned broadcasters was indeed registrable, this suggested a high degree of non-compliance.

Foreign Relations Act

Passed at the end of 2020, *Australia's Foreign Relations (State and Territory Arrangements) Act 2020* (Cth) gave the Australian Government the power to cancel international agreements made by other levels of government and by universities. The rationale for the legislation was the government's stated aim of having Australia 'speak with one voice' (Conley Tyler, 2020a). The government argued that the law would 'foster a systematic and consistent approach to foreign engagement across all levels of Australian government' (Parliament of the Commonwealth of Australia, 2019–20: 2). There did not appear to be any international precedents for this legislation, which required state governments, local councils and public universities to notify the Commonwealth of any arrangements they had with 'foreign entities', defined as foreign governments, departments, agencies, authorities and some universities. Corporations that operate on a commercial basis were excluded. Arrangements were recorded in an online public register, the same as for FITS. The Minister for Foreign Affairs could declare an arrangement invalid if it was considered likely to adversely affect Australia's foreign relations or be inconsistent with Australia's foreign policy, including retrospectively, and there was no appeal or review (Conley Tyler, 2020c).

The draft legislation was widely critiqued for overreach. A Senate inquiry received 33 submissions from the higher education sector outlining problems including compliance burdens, the risk of lost opportunities, and disincentives for international partners to engage with Australian universities. In response, the draft was amended so that arrangements between universities would have to be notified only if the non-Australian university lacked institutional autonomy. This significantly reduced the number of arrangements that had to be reviewed, although it was still likely to catch all Chinese and Vietnamese universities (Conley Tyler & Law, 2020). By the end of 2020, a Foreign Arrangements Taskforce had been established in the Department of Foreign Affairs and Trade and an online reporting system had been established. The sum of A$25 million was reallocated to this task at a time when DFAT's funding was the lowest in Australia's history (Conley Tyler, 2019).

Effectiveness and potential dangers

Looking at the overall pattern of the legislation, the rationale for these laws was that Australia's security faced a new threat: illegitimate interference by foreigners that, if not countered, would be successful. Unquestionably, there were real and significant espionage threats to Australia during this period, as there have been throughout its history, and these threats were particularly acute. At the same time, care must be taken when establishing new legislation, especially in an area like foreign interference, that can have significant flow-on effects. The question that must be asked therefore is whether the response is optimal: is it effective in addressing the risk and less costly than alternative means? Any new laws should therefore first be assessed on whether they are effective in countering foreign interference. They would fail this test if, for example, they insufficiently targeted illegitimate behaviour and criminalised benign activity. They would also be unjustified if the foreign attempts at interference were not likely to be successful or if the resources required to enforce the laws were out of proportion to the threat. Further, the legislation should be assessed on two additional criteria relating to potential dangers: on its influence on Australian civil liberties and any additional undesirable problems (Mack, 2020: 367–8). Negative consequences for civil liberties can include laws being used to stifle debate, stigmatise registrants and quell dissenting voices against the government (Draffen & Ng, 2020: 1102–3). An undesirable problem might be foreign interference laws preventing Australians from working with democracy activists abroad (Mack, 2020: 378).

The remainder of this chapter focuses on the potentially undesirable influence of the legislation on Australia's international relations. While the laws aimed to contribute to

Australian security, they might have been detrimental to Australia's prosperity and security if they damaged international relationships. To explore whether these new domestic laws had a negative effect on Australia's international relations, this chapter examines whether they were a significant factor in the worsening of Australia–China relations.

AUSTRALIA–CHINA RELATIONS

At the start of 2016, Australia–China relations were at something of a high point (Conley Tyler, 2020b). The China-Australia Free Trade Agreement (ChAFTA) had just entered into force, furthering an economic relationship that had seen Australia enjoy decades of uninterrupted economic growth. During President Xi Jinping's visit in 2014, he had addressed the Commonwealth parliament and toured Tasmania, which meant that he had personally visited every Australian state. He and Prime Minister Tony Abbott formally agreed to describe the Australia–China relationship as a 'comprehensive strategic partnership', the highest designation short of a formal alliance.

Fast forward to the end of 2020 and the relationship had hit its lowest point in decades (Raby, 2020). This was particularly evident in public opinion, where the Lowy Institute's annual poll found that those who saw China as more of a security threat than an economic partner jumped from 12 per cent to 41 per cent between 2018 and 2020 (Kassam, 2020) while the Pew Research Center found that unfavourable views of China rose from 32 per cent to 81 per cent between 2017 and 2020 (Silver et al., 2020). At the diplomatic level, Australia was regularly criticised by the Chinese foreign ministry's 'wolf warrior' diplomats, including with a highly offensive tweet (AAP, 2020), and a freeze was put on official and ministerial contact. Trade actions were taken on Australian products including barley, beef, wine and coal (Sullivan, 2020). What happened in these five years, and did the foreign interference legislation play a role in worsening relations?

Concerns surrounding Chinese interference grow

The first high-profile incident raising questions about foreign interference was the case of Labor Senator Sam Dastyari. After Dastyari gave a speech in June 2016 defending China's policy in the South China Sea, in direct conflict with his party's policy, allegations surfaced that he had accepted donations, hospitality and payment of legal bills from organisations headed by Chinese billionaire Huang Xiangmo (Garrick, 2019). Amid the 'Shanghai Sam' saga in June 2017, the ABC's investigative program *Four Corners* and Fairfax newspapers released *Power and Influence*, a report on Chinese infiltration and interference in Australian politics. The program covered several individual stories to create a narrative of a concerted effort by the Communist Party of China (CPC) to influence all levels of Australian society. The report was instrumental in taking issues of foreign interference into public discourse and produced immediate policy changes. Soon after, both major political parties stated that they would no longer accept donations from Huang and Chau Chak Wing, another ethnic Chinese businessman named in the program. The government also ordered an inquiry into Australia's espionage and foreign interference laws (Uhlmann & Gribbin, 2017). Huang's permanent residency in Australia was revoked (Garrick, 2019), but Chau was subsequently successful in his defamation case against the ABC for the program (McKinnell, 2021). Under continuing pressure, Senator

Dastyari announced his resignation in December 2017, just after draft foreign interference legislation was introduced to parliament (Sweeney, 2017).

Throughout 2016 and 2017, China rejected all reports of alleged interference efforts (Hua, 2017; Wang, 2016).

Australia puts up defences

In December 2017, Prime Minister Malcolm Turnbull announced a sweeping set of legislative changes, including the Foreign Interference and FITS Acts as well as a ban on foreign political donations (Belot, 2017). He asserted that these laws were not targeted at any one country, yet when introducing the legislation to parliament he noted, 'Media reports have suggested that the Chinese Communist Party has been working to covertly interfere with our media, our universities and even the decisions of elected representatives right here in this building. We take these reports very seriously.' (Reuters, 2017) Further illustrating the government's rationale behind the changes, just 90 minutes after the announcement, Turnbull used Parliamentary Question Time to attack Dastyari for his links to China. To remove any remaining doubt about the target of the laws, a few days later the Prime Minister made a statement on the proposed legislation where he said: 'Modern China was founded in 1949 with these words, "The Chinese people have stood up" ... And we stand up and so we say, the Australian people stand up.' (Gribbin, 2017)

China interpreted the anti-foreign interference laws as directed squarely at it (Raby, 2020: 5), with the Chinese Embassy saying it regretted 'irresponsible remarks to the detriment of political mutual trust between China and Australia' based on news reports 'made up out of thin air and filled with Cold War mentality and ideological bias' (2017). There were critics in Australia also, with former prime minister Rudd accusing the government of launching an 'anti-Chinese jihad' and describing the legislative package as 'neo-McCarthyism' (Karp, 2018).

In February 2018, academic Clive Hamilton released *Silent Invasion: China's Influence in Australia*, which received widespread media coverage and thereby further promoted the view among the public that Chinese interference was a threat to Australia. Hamilton painted a picture of systematic, coordinated, insidious and clandestine infiltration of Australian institutions, from universities to government, resulting in the 'erosion of Australian sovereignty' (Hamilton, 2018: 3). He claimed that through agents – from international students to members of parliament – China had amassed a network of thousands of spies intent on influencing Australian decision-making. The Chinese Embassy responded that his 'allegations, which are imbued with disinformation and racist bigotry, fully reveal his malicious anti-China mentality' (Hamilton, 2018).

Enforcement and worsening relations

Chinese foreign interference in Australia remained in the public consciousness throughout 2019 with a series of mysterious and sometimes bizarre incidents. In March, the body of car dealership owner Bo Zhao was found in a motel; it was later reported that he had approached ASIO claiming he had been offered A$1 million to be a Chinese plant in the Australian Government (Bucci & Hui, 2019). When two months later Hong Kong-born Gladys Liu became the first female MP of Chinese descent, she immediately faced scrutiny regarding her membership in several organisations with links to the CPC

(Harris, 2019). Then in November, Chinese defector Wang Liqiang was featured on the Nine Network's program *60 Minutes* claiming to have worked as a secret operative with involvement in international assassinations, kidnappings in Hong Kong and interference in Taiwan's elections (Greene, 2019).

The foreign interference legislation got its first workout in when, in June 2020, the joint ASIO–Australian Federal Police Counter Foreign Interference Taskforce conducted raids on New South Wales Labor MP Shaoquett Moselmane and his staffer John Zhang in relation to a private social media group that included a Chinese diplomat, journalists from state-owned media, and two academics (Rubinsztein-Dunlop, 2020). Moselmane was ruled out as a suspect, while Zhang challenged the validity of the search warrant and the constitutionality of the Foreign Interference Act in the High Court.

The investigation had flow-on effects. After two Chinese academics involved in Zhang's social media group had their visas cancelled by Australia, China responded in kind by banning two Australian researchers (Davidson, 2020). China reacted strongly to the raid on journalists, with its Ministry of Foreign Affairs calling this a blatant violation of the rights of Chinese journalists (Dziedzic & Rubinsztein-Dunlop, 2020) and the *Global Times* saying the incident had exposed 'Australia's hypocrisy in upholding so-called "freedom of the press"' (2020b). In quick succession, Australian journalist Cheng Lei was arrested in Beijing and two Australian journalists were rushed out of China after a five-day stand-off, marking the first time since the mid-1970s that no Australian media were reporting from China (Hurst, 2020b).

The last quarter of 2020 saw the introduction of the Foreign Relations Bill. A clear target was the ALP Victorian government's memorandum of understanding on the Belt and Road Initiative. Universities were a late addition to the legislation, perhaps as punishment for their getting too close to China (Tingle, 2020). Chinese officials reacted by saying 'Australia now seems to be in an abnormal state of political madness and paranoia' (Ruan, 2020), a charge seemingly borne out when Senator Eric Abetz asked three Chinese Australians at a Senate hearing to condemn the CPC, a demand not made of witnesses of other ethnicities (Jakobson, 2020). The *Global Times* accused Australia of letting its China policy be set by intelligence agencies and a group of anti-China parliamentarians who called themselves 'the Wolverines' (2020a).

In November 2020, the Foreign Interference Act saw its first prosecution when Duong Di Sanh was charged with preparing to commit an offence (Butler, 2020) after a year-long investigation by the ASIO–AFP Counter Foreign Interference Taskforce. China again made its displeasure with Australia clear, warning Chinese students to reconsider their studies in Australia (Kuo & Murphy, 2020) and imposing restrictions on Australian exports including barley, red meat, wine, cotton, lobsters, timber and coal (Sullivan, 2020). The year appeared to mark a shift in Chinese perceptions, with Australia increasingly framed as unfriendly and troublesome. *Global Times* editor Hu Xijin went as far as to describe Australia as 'a bit like chewing gum stuck on the sole of China's shoes' (Kuo, 2020).

ASSESSMENT

Correlation or causation?

To what extent did this domestic legislation contribute to the deterioration of Australia's ties to China from 2016 to 2020? The laws certainly correlated with worsening relations: for example, China imposed bans on Australian imports from seven sectors the same week the first person was charged under the Foreign Interference Act and the Opposition agreed to pass the Foreign Relations Bill. The question is whether these developments were related.

It is always difficult to determine a causal relationship in international relations. It is not often possible to test a hypothetical: in this case, what the relationship would have been like if foreign interference laws had not been passed. It is likely there would still have been tensions between Australia and China, for example over human rights and China's growing presence in the Pacific.

Unusually, in this case we have direct evidence in the form of a 14-point list of grievances released by the Chinese Embassy (Kearsley, Bagshaw & Galloway, 2020). Of the disputes explaining China's anger towards Australia, half related to foreign interference legislation and media coverage:

- » 'foreign interference legislation, viewed as targeting China'
- » 'politicization and stigmatization of the normal exchanges and cooperation between China and Australia ... including the revoke [sic] of visas for Chinese scholars'
- » 'the latest legislation to scrutinize agreements ... targeting towards China [sic] and aiming to torpedo the Victorian participation in B&R'
- » 'peddling lies around ... so-called China infiltration aimed at manipulating public opinion against China'
- » 'the early dawn search ... of Chinese journalists' homes'
- » 'allegations against China on cyberattacks'
- » 'unfriendly or antagonistic report on China by media, poisoning the atmosphere of bilateral relations' (Kearsley, Bagshaw & Galloway, 2020: 292)

The other half complain of negative foreign investment decisions; banning Huawei and ZTE from the 5G network; Australia's call for an inquiry into COVID-19 and spreading disinformation about China's efforts; condemnation by MPs and racist attacks on Chinese people; Australia's statement on the South China Sea; and interference in Xinjiang, Hong Kong and Taiwan affairs. This list shows that, while there were multiple factors in the downward spiral of Australia–China relations, the foreign interference legislation was a significant factor and China formed an impression of Australia as an unfriendly country.

Debate around the foreign interference legislation had other indirect effects on bilateral relations. For example, it meant that the 'China threat' narrative remained in the headlines and public consciousness for more than four years. This had a significant effect on public opinion, with a discernible increase since 2019 in the number of Australians who saw China as a military threat (Chubb & McAllister, 2021: 142–5). Further, by enacting domestic legislation, an element of relationship management was taken out of the diplomatic realm and put into the hands of security and intelligence agencies. This was a continuation of a longer-term trend of proliferation of the parts of government conducting some aspects of Australia's international policy (Wesley, 2011:

265). From the investigation into Moselmane, it is evident that law enforcement decisions had foreign policy consequences, leading directly to the expulsion of Australian journalists from China. Whether this was a successful transaction is debatable (Kelly, 2020b). As James Laurenceson (2020) puts it:

> Intelligence agencies may have incontrovertible evidence that Moselmane was a target of foreign interference. But what also seems incontrovertible is that his ability to influence political decisions in Australia in ways favourable to Beijing was marginal to non-existent. Answering the question of whether the benefits outweigh the costs of using intelligence and legal means to push back against PRC government interference is one that only political leaders can make.

The foreign interference laws meant that aspects of Australia's international relations were effectively outsourced to domestic law enforcement, with diplomats relegated to the role of 'complaints desk' (Gyngell & Lim, 2020). Once the laws were passed – and a 65-person enforcement unit established (McDonald, 2020a) – there would be pressure for successful prosecutions (Hartcher, 2019) even if this was not in Australia's foreign policy interests.

By the end of 2020 there were criticisms that Australia had reached a point where the security mindset was dominant, with the intelligence and security agencies viewed as having more influence than during the Cold War (Kelly, 2020b). No less a figure than Dennis Richardson, a former head of Foreign Affairs and Trade, Defence and ASIO, publicly warned that the 'national security cowboys' were running the show (Kelly, 2020a). Former prime minister Paul Keating opined that 'When the security agencies are running foreign policy, the nutters are in charge' (Wroe & McCauley, 2019).

Alternatives and design weaknesses

Given the reality of Chinese interference, the question is whether there were more effective ways for Australia to respond. This is difficult to assess, given that threat data is not available in the public domain and there is currently no mechanism to measure how well Australia's counter-interference laws are working (Van der Kley, 2020). It is possible that Australia could have counteracted China's most serious attempts even without such wide-ranging foreign interference legislation. For example, it appears that visa laws were sufficient for some 'catch and deport' espionage cases (Grattan, 2020). It may be that China's attempts were doomed to fail regardless of the new laws. Perhaps it could not help itself, given the CPC's approach to press outwards to pre-empt perceived threats to its security (Hartcher, 2019), but China's interference was spectacularly unsuccessful. Its efforts failed to persuade Australian elites or shape Australian public debate or federal government policy in its favour: 'Almost all major policy decisions at a federal level have gone against the PRC. Media reporting has become far more critical of the PRC. For a country that is so intrinsically linked to Australia's economic well-being, it has little policy influence.' (Van der Kley 2020) It is possible that structural problems restrict China's ability to project soft power and influence political opinion in Western countries (Raby, 2020). If so, Australia could have had more faith in its own resilience, argued Geoff Raby:

Above all, Australians need to be confident in the strength of their institutions – the rule of law, independence of the judiciary, accountability of security agencies to parliament, and independence of the media. Australia faces threats from all major powers in the new order, perhaps none more so than China, but it also has the resilience to resist and overcome. Political leaders in Australia should be building confidence among the public in the country's institutional strength, not spreading fear. (Raby, 2020: 183)

International observers agreed. The former head of Singapore's foreign ministry Bilahari Kausikan, for instance, said Australia's approach to China had swung from extreme complacency (such as allowing foreign political donations) to overreaction ('where almost everybody who looks vaguely Chinese may be suspect'). His advice to Australia was to 'Have a bit more confidence in yourselves' (McDonald, 2020b).

Arguably some of the problems created by the foreign interference legislation were built into its design, which targets links and connections. This was problematic as it meant the focus was not on improper conduct but on having connections with foreigners. It placed suspicion on, for example, attending a function or training course with 'connections' to China's United Front system (Jiang, 2020) or even just having contact on LinkedIn (Kendall, 2021). ASIO's public communications campaign focused on connections rather than on acts that are coercive, corrupt or covert, with the tagline 'think before you link' (Greene, 2020). Its advice was to be suspicious of foreigners who wanted to interact with Australians. Since it is not always possible to determine someone's citizenship, this amounted to telling Australians to be suspicious of anyone with a 'foreign' name. So when ASIO warned that 'almost every sector of Australian society is a potential target of foreign interference' (Butler, 2020), it was conflating international engagement with espionage.

This underscored the need to differentiate between foreign influence and interference. All governments, including Australia's, try to influence discussion and opinion. Whatever its stated intentions, it seems that in public debate there was a stigma attached to FITS registration. For example, just before FITS came into effect three former politicians – a trade minister, foreign minister and premier – all resigned from their roles in Chinese-owned business ventures, which could be interpreted as avoiding the need to register (Garrick, 2019).

The result of the legislation was an atmosphere in which there is nervousness about interacting with foreign countries. In this environment, having a meal with a Chinese diplomat could be painted as suspect, rather than a normal part of international relations (Gyngell & Richardson, 2020). Chinese Australians reported feeling that they were guilty until proven innocent (Jiang, 2020) and had to prove their loyalty (Gyngell & Richardson, 2020). This 'guilt by association' had real effects on whether Chinese Australians engage in politics and debate (Jakobson, 2020; see also Chapter 6). According to Rory Medcalf, the challenge for countries like Australia was: 'How can they protect democratic institutions from foreign influence and interference in ways consistent with both national interests and values, such as civil liberties, non-discrimination, and an inclusive society? How can they distinguish kinds and degrees of foreign involvement? In particular, how is interference distinct from mere influence, and how can suitable instruments of policy be designed in response?' (Medcalf, 2019: 109)

While there is no way to assess their positive effects, it could be said the foreign interference laws have caused demonstrable harm, particularly for Asian Australians. The legislation thereby had eroded the democratic freedoms that it was supposed to protect.

CONCLUSION

The passage of foreign interference legislation in 2018 and 2020 marked the moment when Australia began to see China as an adversary in the context of great-power rivalry. It was motivated by a perception of insecurity in the face of China's threat to Australian politics and society. There is no question that threats of interference and espionage during this period were significant and acute. What this chapter has questioned is whether the legislation that Australia implemented to combat these threats was effective in doing so.

The overall effect of these laws was to problematise international engagement, not just with China but across the board, given the country-neutral drafting of the legislation. Former race discrimination commissioner Tim Soutphommasane (2020) said a 'fortress Australia' mindset was emerging, whereby Australia was retreating inward and viewing everything outside as a threat. Advocating against the Foreign Interference Act, not-for-profit leader David Crosbie (2018) said: 'The Australia I want to live in is not a small-minded paranoid little country, seeking to close off our relationships with the rest of the world for fear of foreign influence. Surely, we want ... to learn from international experience, to collaborate, to develop more international partnerships. We should be promoting international relations, not seeking to restrict them.'

The consequence of Australia's foreign interference legislation is that what was previously a normal practice – forming international links – had been stigmatised as something that needed to be administered and regulated. Blanket suspicion of international engagement by individuals, organisations and universities is contrary to Australia's interests.

References

AAP (2020) Chinese diplomat says Scott Morrison overreacted to the 'repugnant' fake war crimes photo. *SBS News*, 4 December. https://www.sbs.com.au/news/chinese-diplomat-says-scott-morrison-overreacted-to-the-repugnant-fake-war-crimes-photo

Andrew, C. (1992) The growth of the Australian intelligence community and the Anglo-American connection. In P.J. Boyce & J.R. Angel (eds), *Diplomacy in the Marketplace: Australia in World Affairs 1981–1990*. Melbourne: Longman Cheshire for the Australian Institute of International Affairs

Belot, H. (2017) Malcolm Turnbull announces biggest overhaul of espionage, intelligence laws in decades. *ABC News*, 5 December. https://www.abc.net.au/news/2017-12-05/turnbull-announces-foreign-interference-laws/9227514

Blaxland, J. & Crawley, R. (2017) *The Secret Cold War: The Official History of ASIO, 1975–1989*. Sydney: Allen & Unwin

Bucci, N. & Hui, E. (2019) Bo 'Nick' Zhao was in a Melbourne jail awaiting a fraud trial during the Chisholm preselection. *ABC News*, 29 November. https://www.abc.net.au/news/2019-11-29/bo-nick-zhao-in-jail-at-time-of-chisholm-preselection/11746984

Buckley, C., Bradsher, K. & May, T. (2020) New security law gives China sweeping powers over Hong Kong. *New York Times*, 29 June. https://www.nytimes.com/2020/06/29/world/asia/china-hong-kong-security-law-rules.html

Butler, J. (2020) 'Multiple' foreign countries trying to bribe federal MPs, ASIO warns. *New Daily*, 10 November. https://thenewdaily.com.au/news/2020/11/10/foreign-countries-bribe-asio/

Chubb, D. & McAllister, I. (2021) *Australian Public Opinion, Defence and Foreign Policy: Attitudes and Trends Since 1945*. Singapore: Palgrave Macmillan

Conley Tyler, M. (2019) How to rebuild Australia's diplomatic capacity. *Australian Foreign Affairs* 10: 109–15

——(2020a) Morrison's foreign relations bill should not pass parliament. Here's why. *Conversation*, 7 September. https://theconversation.com/morrisons-foreign-relations-bill-should-not-pass-parliament-heres-why-145615

——(2020b) Australia–China relations: A downward spiral that can be reversed. *Pearls and Irritations*, 6 November. https://johnmenadue.com/australia-china-relations-a-downward-spiral-that-can-be-reversed/

——(2020c) What is the effect of Australia's new foreign relations law? *East Asia Forum*, 12 December. https://www.eastasiaforum.org/2020/12/12/what-is-the-effect-of-australias-new-foreign-relations-law/

Conley Tyler, M. & Fang Law, S. (2020) Why Australia's universities need to be free to engage globally. *Pursuit*, 27 November. https://pursuit.unimelb.edu.au/articles/australia-s-universities-need-to-be-free-to-engage-globally

Crosbie, D. (2018) 1938, foreign agents and government paranoia. *Pro Bono Australia*, 27 March. https://probonoaustralia.com.au/news/2018/03/1938-foreign-agents-government-paranoia/

Davidson, H. (2020) Australian academics Clive Hamilton and Alex Joske banned from entering China. *Guardian*, 8 January. https://www.theguardian.com/world/2020/sep/24/australian-academics-clive-hamilton-and-alex-joske-banned-from-entering-china

Draffen, C. & Ng, Y.F. (2020) Foreign agent registration schemes in Australia and the United States: The scope, risk and limitations of transparency. *University of New South Wales Law Journal* 43(4): 1101–36

Dziedzic, S. & Rubinsztein-Dunlop, S. (2020) China slams Australian Government for 'blatant irrational behaviour' over foreign interference investigation. *ABC News*, 10 September. https://www.abc.net.au/news/2020-09-10/chinese-government-slams-australia-blatant-irrational-over-raids/12647738

Embassy of the People's Republic of China in the Commonwealth of Australia (2017) Remarks of spokesperson of Chinese Embassy in Australia, 6 December. http://au.china-embassy.org/eng/gdxw/t1516965.htm

——(2018) Chinese Embassy spokesperson's remarks, 1 March. http://au.china-embassy.org/eng/gdxw/t1538617.htm

Garrick, J. (2019) Agents of foreign influence: With China it's a blurry line between corporate and state interests. *Conversation*, 27 February. https://theconversation.com/agents-of-foreign-influence-with-china-its-a-blurry-line-between-corporate-and-state-interests-112403

Global Times (2020a) Australian agents raid Chinese journalists' residences, seize computers 'in violation of legitimate rights'. *Global Times*, 8 September. https://www.globaltimes.cn/content/1200286.shtml

——(2020b) Australian intelligence community is manipulating its China policy in the shadows following the US steps. *Global Times*, 21 September. https://www.globaltimes.cn/content/1201504.shtml

Grattan, M. (2020) ASIO chief Mike Burgess says there are more spies in Australia 'than at the height of the cold war'. *Conversation*, 24 February. https://theconversation.com/asio-chief-mike-burgess-says-there-are-more-spies-in-australia-than-at-the-height-of-the-cold-war-132384

Greene, A. (2019) Chinese spy Wang Liqiang alleges Beijing ordered overseas murders, including in Australia. *ABC News*, 6 January. https://www.abc.net.au/news/2019-11-23/chinese-spy-wang-liqiang-seeks-political-asylum-australia-report/11732174

——(2020) ASIO launches first public awareness campaign to warn Australians of foreign spies on social media. *ABC News*, 17 November. https://www.abc.net.au/news/2020-11-17/asio-warns-foreign-spies-grooming-australians-on-social-media/12889228#

Gribbin, C. (2017) Malcolm Turnbull declares he will 'stand up' for Australia in response to China's criticism. *ABC News*, 9 December. https://www.abc.net.au/news/2017-12-09/malcolm-turnbull-says-he-will-stand-up-for-australia/9243274

Gyngell, A. & Lim, D. (2020) Foreign interference and the Australia–China relationship. *Australian Outlook*, 28 September. https://www.internationalaffairs.org.au/australianoutlook/episode-56-foreign-interference-the-australia-china-relationship/

Gyngell, A. & Richardson, D. (2020) The world in 2021. *Australian Outlook*, 30 October. https://www.internationalaffairs.org.au/australianoutlook/the-world-in-2021/

Hamilton, C. (2018) *Silent Invasion: China's influence in Australia*. Melbourne: Hardie Grant Publishing

Harris, R. (2019) Gladys Liu's Beijing confession deepens dispute over loyalty. *Sydney Morning Herald*, 5 January. https://www.smh.com.au/politics/federal/gladys-liu-s-beijing-confession-deepens-dispute-over-loyalty-20190911-p52qec.html

Hartcher, P. (2019) Power and paranoia: Why the Chinese government aggressively pushes beyond its borders. *Sydney Morning Herald*, 23 November. https://www.smh.com.au/national/peter-hartcher-on-china-s-infiltration-of-australia-20191118-p53bly.html

Head, M. (2018) Australia's anti-democratic 'foreign interference' bills. *Alternative Law Journal* 43(3): 160–5

Hua, C. (2017) Foreign Ministry spokesperson Hua Chunying's remarks on the Australian media's China-related reports. Embassy of the People's Republic of China in Australia, 8 February. http://au.china-embassy.org/eng/sghdxwfb_1/2017n/t1467996.htm

Hurst, D. (2020a) Tony Abbott registers as agent of foreign influence over UK trade adviser role. *Guardian*, 9 October. https://www.theguardian.com/australia-news/2020/oct/09/tony-abbott-registers-as-agent-of-foreign-influence-over-uk-trade-adviser-role

——(2020b) Australian journalists forced to flee China warn political situation in country is worst since 1970s. *Guardian*, 8 January. https://www.theguardian.com/australia-news/2020/sep/26/australian-journalists-forced-to-flee-china-warn-political-situation-in-country-is-worst-since-1970s

——(2021) Kevin Rudd registers interviews with BBC and Radio NZ but insists 'I am not a foreign agent'. *Guardian*, 21 January. https://www.theguardian.com/australia-news/2021/jan/21/kevin-rudd-registers-interviews-with-bbc-and-radio-nz-but-insists-i-am-not-a-foreign-agent

Iggulden, T. (2019) Australia's biggest companies asked to put themselves on Foreign Influence Transparency Register. *ABC News*, 25 September. https://www.abc.net.au/news/2019-09-25/australian-companies-asked-go-on-foreign-transparency-register/11545184

Jakobson, L. (2020) McCarthyism is now rampant in Australia. *Pearls and Irritations*, 26 October. https://johnmenadue.com/mccarthyism-is-now-rampant-in-australia/

Jiang, Y. (2020) Foreign interference and the Chinese diaspora: Guilty until proven innocent? *China Story*, 14 July. https://www.thechinastory.org/foreign-interference-and-the-chinese-diaspora-guilty-until-proven-innocent/

Karp, P. (2018) Kevin Rudd accuses Turnbull government of 'anti-Chinese jihad'. *Guardian*, 5 January. https://www.theguardian.com/australia-news/2018/feb/12/kevin-rudd-accuses-turnbull-government-of-anti-chinese-jihad

Kassam, N. (2020) *Lowy Institute Poll 2020*. Sydney: Lowy Institute for International Policy. https://poll.lowyinstitute.org/charts/china-economic-partner-or-security-threat

Kearsley, J., Bagshaw, E. & Galloway, A. (2020) 'If you make China the enemy, China will be the enemy': Beijing's fresh threat to Australia. *Age*, 18 November. https://www.smh.com.au/world/asia/if-you-make-china-the-enemy-china-will-be-the-enemy-beijing-s-fresh-threat-to-australia-20201118-p56fqs.html

Kelly, P. (2020a) China relations: 'National security cowboys' put nation's interests at unnecessary risk. *Australian*, 9 May. https://www.theaustralian.com.au/inquirer/china-relations-national-security-cowboys-put-nations-interests-at-unnecessary-risk/news-story/54eaac6914356341f54936eb401abca3

——(2020b) Our China relationship needs help before it's too late. *Australian*, 16 September. https://www.theaustralian.com.au/commentary/our-china-relationship-needs-help-before-its-too-late/news-story/0c37e5bb3480b0d48f55fc935491103b

Kendall, S. (2019) Australia's new espionage laws: Another case of hyper-legislation and over-criminalisation. *University of Queensland Law Journal* 38(1): 125

——(2021) You could break espionage laws on social media without realising it. *Conversation*, 13 January. https://theconversation.com/you-could-break-espionage-laws-on-social-media-without-realising-it-151665

Krishnakumar, T. (2020) FITS and starts. *Interpreter*, Lowy Institute, 3 September. https://www.lowyinstitute.org/the-interpreter/fits-and-starts

Kuo, L. (2020) Australia called 'gum stuck to China's shoe' by state media in coronavirus investigation stoush. *Guardian*, 28 April. https://www.theguardian.com/world/2020/apr/28/australia-called-gum-stuck-to-chinas-shoe-by-state-media-in-coronavirus-investigation-stoush

Kuo, L. & Murphy, K. (2020) China warns students to reconsider travel to Australia for study. *Guardian*, 11 February. https://www.theguardian.com/world/2020/jun/09/china-warns-students-to-reconsider-travel-to-australia-for-study

Laurenceson, J. (2020) Clear-eyed responses as well as assessments needed on the PRC. *Pearls and Irritations*, 5 October. https://johnmenadue.com/clear-eyed-responses-as-well-as-assessments-needed-on-the-prc/

Mack, D. (2020) An era of foreign political interference: Impulsive, overcompensation of Australia, and a comparison of legislative schemes with the United States. *Emory International Law Review* 34(1): 367–97

McDonald, H. (2020a) Australian media in the Asian century. *Pearls and Irritations*, 9 October. https://johnmenadue.com/hamish-mcdonald-australian-media-in-the-asian-century-2/

——(2020b) The Un-Australian Activities Committee and Eric Abetz. *Pearls and Irritations*, 23 October. https://johnmenadue.com/hamish-mcdonald-the-un-australian-activities-committee-and-eric-abetz-media-in-the-asian-century

McKinnell, J. (2021) Businessman Chau Chak Wing awarded $590,000 in defamation case against ABC. *ABC News*, 11 February. https://www.abc.net.au/news/2021-02-02/chau-chak-wing-wins-defamation-case-against-abc/13111934

Medcalf, R. (2019) Australia And China: Understanding the reality check. *Australian Journal of International Affairs* 73(2): 109–18

Munro, K. (2018) Australia's new foreign influence laws: Who is targeted? *Interpreter*, Lowy Institute, 5 December. https://www.lowyinstitute.org/the-interpreter/australia-new-foreign-influence-laws-who-targeted

Parliament of the Commonwealth of Australia, House of Representatives (2019–20) Australia's Foreign Relations (State and Territory Arrangements) Bill 2020. Explanatory memorandum. https://parlinfo.aph.gov.au/parlInfo/download/legislation/ems/r6596_ems_d3fd0486-c0d5-430e-83d7-5c2de5644e99/upload_pdf/747250.pdf;fileType=application%2Fpdf

Pearson, E. (2018) Australia's government must guard against foreign interference, but not by curbing our rights. *Pearls and Irritations*, 16 June. https://johnmenadue.com/elaine-pearson-australias-government-must-guard-against-foreign-interference-but-not-by-curbing-our-rights/

Pearson, N. (2018) Turnbull's foreign interference laws bad for Australian liberties. *Australian*, 28 July. https://www.theaustralian.com.au/nation/inquirer/turnbulls-foreign-interference-laws-bad-for-australian-liberties/news-story/efb27f68a54391c57441586f5aa3e026

Raby, G. (2020) *China's Grand Strategy and Australia's Future in the New Global Order*. Melbourne: Melbourne University Press

Reuters (2017) China complains to Australia over Turnbull comments on interference. *Reuters*, 17 December. https://www.reuters.com/article/us-china-australia-idUSKBN1E218S

Rubinsztein-Dunlop, S. (2020) Former Labor staffer John Zhang investigated for money laundering after Chinese foreign interference taskforce finds bundles of cash at Sydney home. *ABC News*, 7 January. https://www.abc.net.au/news/2020-11-18/investigation-finds-bundles-of-cash-at-ex-labor-staffers-home/12890806

Shields, B. (2019) Boris Johnson eyes Australia in biggest overhaul of foreign policy 'since the Cold War'. *Sydney Morning Herald*, 20 December. https://www.smh.com.au/world/europe/boris-johnson-eyes-australia-in-biggest-overhaul-of-foreign-policy-since-the-cold-war-20191219-p53loz.html

Silver, L., Devlin, K. & Huang, C. (2020) Unfavorable views of China reach historic highs in many countries. Washington: Pew Research Center, 6 October. https://www.pewresearch.org/global/2020/10/06/unfavorable-views-of-china-reach-historic-highs-in-many-countries/

Soutphommasane, T. (2020) Whither Australia–China relations? Alfred Deakin Institute Policy Forum, 29 October. https://www.youtube.com/watch?list=SRchina+york+times+tensions+rising&v=P5tnHPiBx7c

Sullivan, K. (2020) China's list of sanctions and tariffs on Australian trade is growing. Here's what has been hit so far. *ABC News*, 17 December. https://www.abc.net.au/news/2020-12-17/australian-trade-tension-sanctions-china-growing-commodities/12984218

Sweeney, L. (2017) Sam Dastyari resigns from Parliament, says he is 'detracting from Labor's mission' amid questions over Chinese links. *ABC News*, 5 February. https://www.abc.net.au/news/2017-12-12/sam-dastyari-resigns-from-parliament/9247390

Tingle, L. (2020) The government's plan for a veto over university agreements may have been a Baldrick moment. *ABC News*, 29 August. https://www.abc.net.au/news/2020-08-29/australia-plan-foreign-legislation-university-agreement/12606412

Turnbull, M. (2017) Speech introducing the National Security Legislation Amendment (Espionage and Foreign Interference) Bill 2017, 7 December. https://www.malcolmturnbull.com.au/media/speech-introducing-the-national-security-legislation-amendment-espionage-an

Uhlmann, C. & Gribbin, C. (2017) Malcolm Turnbull orders inquiry following revelations ASIO warned parties about Chinese donations. *ABC News*, 7 February. https://www.abc.net.au/news/2017-06-06/turnbull-orders-inquiry-following-revelation-asio-warned-parties/8592308

Van der Kley, D. (2020) What should Australia do about ... the influence of United Front work? *China Matters Explores*, September. http://chinamatters.org.au/policy-brief/policy-brief-september-2020/

Wang, X. (2016) Australian Labor Party senator accepts donations from Chinese companies and resign due to incorrect stance on China. *Guancha News*, 8 September. https://www.guancha.cn/Neighbors/2016_09_08_373777.shtml

Wesley, M. (2011) Australia's foreign policy machinery. In J. Cotton & J. Ravenhill (eds), *Middle Power Dreaming: Australia in World Affairs 2006–2010*. Melbourne: Oxford University Press

Wroe, D. & McCauley, D. (2019) Sack 'nutter' spy chiefs to fix relations with Beijing, Paul Keating urges. *Sydney Morning Herald*, 5 May. https://www.smh.com.au/federal-election-2019/sack-nutter-spy-chiefs-to-fix-relations-with-beijing-paul-keating-urges-20190505-p51k9p.html

Asian Australians, foreign policy and identity in Australia

Juliet Pietsch

Australia's engagement with Asia, and debates about whether Australian identity should be defined as part of or separate from the region, has had a long and fraught history.[1] Before the implementation of the White Australia policy in 1901, and especially until the 1850s, the British government virtually had an open-door policy, which included immigrants from such countries as China, India and Afghanistan. However, support for Asian immigrants deteriorated when there were large numbers of Chinese on the goldfields. The Chinese were the largest non-British group in the colonies and were subjected to widespread discrimination (Knott, 1988). In the period under review (2016 to 2020), Asian Australians again found themselves subject to suspicion and discrimination, albeit for different economic and security reasons. However, there has been a consistent pattern since the introduction of the White Australia policy that in times of high security threat, immigrants from Asia, even those who are Australian citizens, have struggled to find their place in Australia.

Unlike in earlier periods, in the five years under review Australia was home to an active Asian Australian citizenry in academia, politics and business, no longer content to be excluded from major policy- and law-making institutions. This cognitive dissonance between Australia's alleged support for multiculturalism and reports of Asian Australian exclusion was therefore jarring but perhaps not entirely surprising, given the growing body of research about racial and ethnic exclusion in Australia and in other immigrant countries such as the United States, Canada and New Zealand (Pietsch, 2018; Jupp & Pietsch, 2018). A report by the Lowy Institute, for instance, found that the lack of Asian Australian inclusion in senior executive levels of the public service meant that the government was potentially missing out on valuable advice during times of heightened security. This reached a new flashpoint between 2016 and 2020 when tensions between Australia and China hit a new low (Jiang, 2021).

---

[1] I would like to acknowledge and thank David Hundt, Baogang He, Kai Feng, Huiyun Feng and Ian McAllister for their many helpful comments and suggestions on this version of the chapter.

This chapter focuses on the tensions that emerged in Australian foreign policy towards Asia, and especially China, in the period under review, and how Asian Australians were implicated in these tensions. The commentary from academia and public policy think tanks, I show, was largely critical of Australia's approach. The chapter suggests that Asian Australians, particularly Australians of Chinese heritage, were fundamentally hamstrung in their capacity to shape Australian foreign policy towards Asia, and especially China. This was because of a widespread perception that no matter how innocent or benign, they might pose a threat to national security or, in the higher education and research sector, a risk of foreign interference. Rather than Asian Australians being a unique asset to Australia during a difficult period in foreign relations, this sizeable but growing segment of the population was instead marginalised and stigmatised.

THE RHETORIC OF ASIAN ENGAGEMENT VERSUS THE REALITY OF ASIAN AUSTRALIAN UNDER-REPRESENTATION

Australia has had a long-standing 'engagement' strategy and commitment to closer ties with Asia. This was acknowledged in 2012 with the release of the White Paper *Australia in the Asian Century*, which stated that 'we need to broaden and deepen our understanding of Asian cultures and languages, to become more Asia Literate. These capabilities are needed to build stronger connections and partnerships across the region' (Australian Government, 2012). However, there appears to be an unwillingness to live up to the commitment to fully reflect Australia's ethnic diversity and Asia literacy in the upper echelons of politics and policy-making.

By 2020, Asian Australians made up more than 14 per cent of the population, but their material contribution to the development and implementation of foreign policy was negligible, primarily because of their under-representation in the agencies responsible for foreign affairs. Similar arguments have been made for a lack of inclusion of women. According to a report published by the Lowy Institute, there is a severe gender imbalance in the government agencies responsible for foreign policy (Cave et al., 2019; see also Chapter 5). While this has led to calls for the sector to address its gender imbalance (e.g. Westendorf & Strating, 2020; Harris Rimmer & Stephenson, 2019), these efforts have not resulted in substantive change, and inequality in senior appointments persists. Similarly, solutions to racial or ethnic inequalities have not yet emerged to produce a workforce of foreign policy-makers that better reflect Australian society.

It makes strategic sense to address the lack of Asian Australian involvement in foreign policy, as this would result in a more ethical and inclusive policy process. There are good practical reasons for foreign policy-makers to draw on the expertise of those Australians who best understand Asia, including its people, languages, history, mindsets and politics. This is particularly so at a time when Australian academics with expertise in Asia are dwindling in number. Since the mid-1990s, Australia has lost most of its empirical research expertise on China, particularly in politics and security (Graham, 2019). With steady declines in student numbers, infrastructure and research funding, many Australians with Asia expertise have chosen to pursue careers elsewhere. In the case of independent Asian Australian thinkers, if they do not hold a policy position within government, they have little capacity to contribute.

In Australia, little research has been conducted into the participation of immigrants in foreign policy and world affairs even though first- and second-generation immigrants now account for 44 per cent of the population, making Australia one of the most diverse immigrant democracies in the world (Kwok & Pietsch, 2017; Pietsch, 2017; Pietsch, 2018). A comparatively large proportion of Australia's population, approximately 17 per cent, is from a 'non-white' immigrant or ethnic minority background. The largest group in this category are first- and second-generation immigrants from Asia ('Asian Australians'), who are also the fastest growing group among the pan-racial minority categories.

Despite Australia's large population of immigrants and ethnic minorities, minority under-representation in government and in political institutions, particularly from Asian Australians, persists. According to Kim (2005: 451), 'A diverse workforce with regard to race, ethnicity, national origin, or gender leads a bureaucracy to be not only internally democratic but also responsive to citizen needs.' Those with a relatively recent experience of migration or racism are more likely to make a stand on changes to legislation and policies that have a disproportionate impact on immigrants and ethnic communities (Pietsch, 2018; 2020). Having one or two voices in parliament is a step forward in making symbolic change. However, a stronger collective voice is required to address racism and promote diversity as a strength through substantive policy changes.

In non-white representation in the Australian Public Service (APS), there has been marginal improvement since the beginning of the millennium. The share of Asian Australians increased from 5 per cent in 1999 to 8 per cent in 2013. This improvement can be partly explained by section 18 of the Public Service Act of 1999, which required public service departments and agencies to implement cultural diversity programs. However, Asian Australians were under-represented in senior manager and senior executive levels of the APS (Pietsch, 2018). In terms of overall Asia capability, only 3 per cent of the APS had Chinese or Indian language skills and only 1 per cent had Indonesian language skills (APSC, 2013). This is a problem because it is only at these senior levels in government departments that important decision-making on major policies and public programs is approved.

THE LINGERING QUESTION OF IDENTITY AND ASIANS' PLACE IN AUSTRALIA

In Australia, the under-representation of Asian Australians in political institutions can be attributed to discriminatory practices and the lack of incentive to recruit 'non-white' immigrants and ethnic minorities. As a political representative of Asian background mentioned in relation to his desire to be promoted into a more senior role, 'The way I see it is they will be quite happy for you to be the chief engineer of the ship but not the captain of the ship' (cited in Pietsch, 2018: 2). The causes of under-representation at senior levels of the public service, however, are not easily explained, given the requirement for federal departments and agencies to increase the representation of ethnic minorities. There is evidence from the Australian Election Study (AES) that people from 'non-white' backgrounds are more than twice as likely as those of European origin to experience discrimination or racial prejudice, or both (AES, 2013; see also Markus, 2013). In other words, pervasive forms of discrimination and racial prejudice based on stereotypes may explain the participation gap of Asian Australians in government.

There are other factors, specific to Chinese Australians. In 2018 Clive Hamilton for instance raised fears that the Communist Party of China (CPC) was seeking to influence Australians of Chinese heritage (Hamilton, 2018), some of whom were descendants of goldminers who arrived in the mid-19th century. The depiction of Chinese Australians as a 'fifth column' for the CPC had parallels to the way Muslims in Australia were stigmatised following the 9/11 terrorist attacks in the United States (2001) and the Bali bombings in Indonesia (2002). This racialised tension peaked in 2005 when anti-Muslim riots broke out in Sydney's suburbs, Cronulla Beach being the epicenter. Thereafter Australians of Muslim background have reported a higher incidence of racial and ethnic prejudice in their daily lives (Dunn & Forrest, 2007; Forrest & Dunn, 2007; Dunn & Nelson, 2011; Dunn, Pelleri & Maeder-Han, 2011).

Australians of Chinese heritage, meanwhile, have long been the subject of racialised discrimination, starting in the 19th century. Anti-Chinese discrimination did not end with the cessation of the White Australia policy in 1973, as was demonstrated by the well-publicised instances of anti-Chinese racism that took place throughout Australia's 'first wave' of the COVID-19 pandemic in 2020.

When the outbreak was still centred in Wuhan, the Australian Human Rights Commission noted that about one in four people who lodged racial discrimination complaints during January and February 2020 were targeted because of the fear that the virus would spread to Australia (Pietsch, 2020). Mask-wearing Chinese and Hong Kong international students were particularly at risk because of their visible markers of difference. Besides their obvious Asian appearance, their prior experience of infectious diseases such as the SARS outbreak (2002–04) meant that they were much more likely to wear a face mask than most residents of Australia. This learned community practice, however, which had barely been seen in Australia since the influenza pandemic of 1919, became a marker of cultural difference that subjected many Asian Australians to stigmatisation or racial hostility. In 2020, a Lowy Institute Poll found that nearly one in five Chinese Australians felt threatened or were attacked owing to the indirect discriminatory effects of the pandemic and the deterioration of relations between China and Australia. One in three (31 per cent) had been called offensive names because of their Chinese heritage, and more than 37 per cent said that they had been treated differently or less favourably because of their background (Hurst, 2021).

The negative experience of Chinese Australians was no doubt emboldened by political leaders, such as US President Donald Trump, who regularly referred to coronavirus as the 'China virus' or the 'Wuhan virus' (Pietsch, 2020). The World Health Organization (WHO) had repeatedly advised political leaders not to target any nationality or ethnicity in references to the pandemic, as it could lead to racial profiling against Asians in immigrant-receiving countries around the world. Mike Ryan, executive director of the WHO's Emergencies Program, said that 'viruses know no borders and they don't care about your ethnicity, the colour of your skin or the money you have in the bank' (Gstalter, 2020). Pauline Hanson, Queensland Senator for One Nation, disregarded this advice, and instead suggested that 'China must be called out and any attempts to attack or criticise people for referring to COVID-19 as a "Chinese virus" should be pushed back on' (Hanson, 2020). This comment generated more than 3500 retweets and 9400 likes on Twitter (Pietsch, 2020).

The fear of the threat posed by a CPC-infiltrated Australian Chinese community (see Hamilton, 2018) undermined Chinese Australians' potential to play a constructive role in government and politics. The next section examines the US/China rivalry and the under-involvement of Asian Australians in managing the Australia–China bilateral relationship.

NAVIGATING CHINA/US RIVALRY – *SANS* CHINESE AUSTRALIANS

Between 2016 and 2020, the Australia–China bilateral relationship played out on several fronts: navigating a safe passage amid US/China rivalry; a polarised public debate on how best to respond to Chinese interference in Australian affairs; the emergence of legislation designed to counter foreign interference, which was widely perceived as being directed at China; disquiet over increased Chinese expansionism, coupled with China's poor human rights record; and, in the context of the pandemic, growing discomfort with China's increasingly assertive foreign policy stance in Hong Kong, the South China Sea and elsewhere, which coincided with Chinese trade bans on Australian goods and services. Bilateral relations reached a new low point in 2020. The context and events that led to it are discussed below.

From 2016 to 2020, Australia struggled to navigate a safe passage between the ongoing rivalry between the United States and China. Australian foreign policy-makers became concerned that they might be forced to choose one superpower over the other (Brophy, 2019). Australia's attempt to navigate a middle path between the United States and China did not proceed smoothly, as there was little consensus about the best approach to take. From about 2018 onwards, Australia's China experts, from both academia and the intelligence community, became embroiled in a new China debate. As Brophy (2019) put it, there was 'one side arguing that there is widespread Chinese party-state interference in Australian affairs; the other accusing the first of sensationalism, even racism'. This 'China debate' or 'China influence scare' (Brophy, 2018) was provoked by Australia's adoption of legislation aimed at combating foreign interference.

By 2018, growing fear of foreign interference in Australian domestic affairs led to the emergence of a package of new legislation designed to counter foreign interference, the *Foreign Espionage and Interference Act 2018* (Cth). This was accompanied by the Foreign Influence Transparency Scheme, which was designed to register individuals or organisations seeking to influence Australian affairs on behalf of a foreign principal (see Chapter 5). While not objecting to Australia's introduction of the new laws, Beijing objected to the perception that the Australian Government, through its public messaging on the Bills, was singling out China at the expense of other nations (Tillett, 2018).

By 2020, the Morrison government sought to expand this legislation by introducing a bill to allow the Commonwealth to cancel international arrangements by universities, state and territory governments, and local councils. Citing national security concerns as the need for a new Australia's Foreign Relations (State and Territory Arrangements) Bill 2020 (Cth), the government instigated the passage of the *Australia's Foreign Relations (State and Territory Arrangements) Act 2020* (Cth) ('the Act'). Morrison sought to better regulate activities between states and territories and foreign governments across education, culture, research and trade. The new legislation allowed, for example, the minister to veto or rescind the non-binding, symbolic memorandum of understanding between the State of Victoria and China on the Belt and Road Initiative (see Chapter 13), as well as other equally symbolic sister city agreements. The Act was criticised by the higher education sector, which complained of bureaucratic 'over-reach' (Tingle, 2020). Some state parliamentarians, meanwhile, criticised the Bill as 'overkill' for its thinly veiled targeting of China and its patronising attitude towards the states (Visontay, 2020). Conley Tyler (2020) suggested that passage of the Bill would discourage international collaboration and furthermore that thousands of non-controversial research and sister-city arrangements would need to be subjected to the scrutiny of DFAT staff, at a time when the department's resources were at record lows.

Beijing, meanwhile, was convinced that these new laws were directed at China and conveyed its displeasure in no uncertain terms. Australian wine, barley, lobster, coal and beef exports were subjected to retaliatory measures. In a further sign of the deteriorating relations, in early September 2020, Australia's last two China-based foreign correspondents were rushed out of China after a week of tense diplomatic negotiations, during which local police demanded interviews with both journalists. The incident came only days after the Chinese government arrested an Australian journalist working for China's state media, Cheng Lei.

Between 2016 and 2018, narratives of Chinese expansionism, led by the Australian Strategic Policy Institute (ASPI) in particular, coalesced with concerns about human rights in China and Hong Kong. By 2020, growing disquiet over these issues was afforded an additional overlay by the pandemic and China's increasingly assertive foreign policy (Nabbs-Keller, 2020). Australia took a more confrontational stance with China, beginning under Turnbull and more intensively under Morrison, resulting in an escalation of tensions, such as the economic measures noted above.

These issues, as well others such as the Sam Dastyari scandal (Hao Chai, 2020) and Gladys Liu's links with the CPC and the United Front, could have been more sensitively managed, or perhaps managed without giving so much offence, if there was more input from Chinese Australians. In such a fraught security context, 'securitised' Chinese Australians were reluctant to enter the political domain or work in government agencies where they might be viewed with suspicion. Chinese Australians were further hamstrung in what they could say publicly. This segment of the population found itself between a rock and a hard place: Chinese Australians were often regarded with distrust by both the Chinese and Australian governments, which affected their representation in Australian government and politics, especially on foreign policy matters. According to Baogang He (2018), the securitisation of Chinese Australians had a significant adverse influence on Australia's multicultural potential, especially in government, politics and foreign policy. The following section examines this notion in more detail, drawing on public attitudes towards China 'as a threat' and other foreign policy issues such as the ANZUS alliance and free trade.

AN ASIAN AUSTRALIAN PERSPECTIVE ON FOREIGN POLICY

Strengthening multiculturalism and drawing on Australia's Asia capability is important for making foreign policy, as already discussed. This is particularly relevant for the Commonwealth public service. The Australian Public Service Commission (APSC) notes that Australia's Asia capability is critical to our relations with Asia. In particular, Australia needs to have 'a sophisticated knowledge of Asian markets and/or environments, experience operating in Asia, long-term trust networks in the regions, the ability to adapt behaviour to Asian cultural contexts, and the capacity to deal with government and having a useful level of language proficiency' (APSC, 2020).

Asian Australians, especially those born in Asia, often have different views on foreign policy from those born in Australia. To understand these differences, the chapter draws on the 2019 Lowy Institute Poll on Australian attitudes towards the world. There are some limitations to the data, including ambiguity about the length of time that Asian respondents have lived in Australia and the collapsing of Asian immigrants into a single variable despite the heterogeneity of cultural and political experiences among these respondents. Nevertheless the findings show patterns of similarity on some foreign policy issues across the two groups. This has implications for foreign policy-making, suggesting that there needs to be more analysis of country-specific attitudes and perceptions that might not be fully represented within Australia's political system.

Tables 6.1 to 6.3 compare the Australian-born (not including second-generation Asians with a parent born in Asia) and Asia-born respondents and their attitudes on three key dimensions of foreign policy in Australia: threat perceptions, the ANZUS alliance, and free trade. Table 6.1 shows a list of possible threats to the vital interests of Australia. Lowy asked respondents whether they saw the issue as a critical threat, an important but not critical threat, or not an important threat at all. There were five issues on which Australians born in Asia had markedly different concerns from those born in Australia. The Asian-born respondents were 17 per cent more likely than their Australian-born counterparts to view international terrorism as a critical threat, perhaps because many might have lived experiences of terrorism in their country of birth. The Asian-born were also more fearful of the impact of climate change (+10.4), frequent changes in political leadership (+9.5), and a severe downturn in the global economy (+16.3). Some of these differences might have been expected, given that many

Table 6.1 Perceptions of foreign policy threats by birthplace, 2019

'A critical threat'	Asia-born %	Asia-born (n)	Australia-born %	Australia-born (n)	Difference
International terrorism	73.6	(92)	56.4	(888)	+17.2
North Korea's nuclear program	44.8	(56)	59.1	(930)	−14.3
Climate change	72.0	(90)	61.6	(970)	+10.4
Cyberattacks from other countries	68.8	(86)	63.0	(992)	+5.8
Large numbers of immigrants and refugees	27.2	(34)	32.8	(516)	−5.6
Foreign interference in Australian politics	52.0	(65)	49.4	(778)	+2.6
Frequent changes in Australia's political leadership	48.0	(60)	38.5	(606)	+9.5
If China opened military base in Pacific island country	54.4	(68)	57.1	(898)	−2.7
A severe downturn in the global economy	62.4	(78)	46.1	(726)	+16.3
Foreign investment in Australia	33.6	(42)	39.9	(628)	−6.3

Note: The question was: 'Here is a list of possible threats to the vital interests of Australia in the next ten years. For each one, please select whether you see this as a critical threat, an important but not critical threat, or not an important threat at all.'
Source: based on data from Lowy Institute Poll (2019), (N = 2130).

Table 6.2 Attitudes towards Australia's alliance with the United States by birthplace, 2019

	Asia-born		Australia-born		
'Very important'	%	(n)	%	(n)	**Difference**
Importance of alliance for Australia's security	26.4	(33)	42.6	(671)	−16.2
'Agree'					
Australians and Americans share values and ideals: a strong alliance is a natural extension of this	63.2	(79)	75.3	(1185)	−12.1
Alliance makes it more likely Australia will be drawn into war with Asia	66.4	(83)	67.3	(1060)	−0.9
Alliance makes Australia safer from attack or pressure from China	53.6	(67)	55.2	(869)	−1.6
The United States is in decline relative to China so the alliance is of decreasing importance	46.4	(58)	44.7	(704)	+1.7
Donald Trump has weakened alliance with the United States	66.4	(83)	68.1	(1072)	−1.7
The United States would come to Australia's defence if Australia was under threat	64.8	(81)	73.1	(1150)	−8.3

Note: The questions were: 'And now about Australia's alliance relationship with the United States. How important is our alliance relationship with the United States for Australia's security?' and 'Here are some different arguments about the alliance relationship with the United States. For each one, please indicate whether you personally agree or disagree.'
Source: based on data from Lowy Institute Poll (2019), (N = 2130).

immigrants have fled the effects of natural disasters, as well as political and financial instability. Migrants born in Asia were less concerned about North Korea's nuclear program (−14.3). Perhaps this reflected a high level of confidence that North Korea could be deterred from launching a nuclear war thanks to the collective desire to avoid such a scenario (Lee, 2007). While there were significant differences on these issues, there were also similarities such as in perceptions of threat related to foreign interference in Australian politics and foreign investment.

Table 6.2 focuses on the importance of the ANZUS alliance to Australia. The Lowy Institute Poll found that Australians born in Asia did not place as much importance on the alliance as those born in Australia (−16.2) and were less likely to feel that Australians shared much in common with Americans in their values and ideals (−12.1). This was consistent with previous findings on North Korea, which suggest that Australians born in Asia were less likely to feel dependent on the United States for protection and regional stability. This might have stemmed from the fact that Asian-born Australians were less confident that the United States would come to Australia's defence if Australia was threatened (−8.3).

Finally, on the issue of free trade, the findings in Table 6.3 show that Australians born in Asia were more likely than those born in Australia to believe that trade was good not only for their own standard of living but also for the economy and creating jobs. This would be expected given that Australians born in Asia might in many cases be the beneficiaries of free trade. For example, Chinese investment in Australia had

Table 6.3 Attitudes towards free trade by birthplace, 2019

'Free trade is good for ...'	Asia-born %	Asia-born (n)	Australia-born %	Australia-born (n)	Difference
... own standard of living	87.2	(109)	74.4	(1171)	+12.8
... the Australian economy	79.2	(99)	71.5	(1125)	+7.7
... Australian companies	70.4	(88)	64.0	(1008)	+6.4
... creating jobs in Australia	68.8	(86)	57.4	(904)	+11.4

Note: The question was: 'Overall, do you personally think free trade is good or bad for the following ...'
Source: based on data from Lowy Institute Poll (2019), (N = 2130).

reached A$65 billion by the end of 2015. The China-Australia Free Trade Agreement (ChAFTA), which entered into force in December 2015, benefited Chinese Australians and Australian exporters. In particular, the agreement reduced barriers to labour mobility and increased immigration and employment between China and Australia (DFAT, 2021).

These findings show that there were marked differences in views about foreign policy when comparing Australians born in Asia with those born in Australia. These differences underscore how important it is that political debates reflect the overall Australian community. Furthermore, having Asia capability would enhance Australia's standing in the region and produce greater policy quality that is more understanding and respectful of political, linguistic and cultural contexts, and less prone to bilateral disagreements that have unintended consequences for trade and some sectors of the economy such as higher education.

CONCLUSION

Political and diplomatic histories of Australian engagement with Asia, and especially ties with China, tend to describe the relationship in terms of economics and trade, contrasting geopolitical concerns and social and cultural links (e.g. Mackerras, 1985; Strahan, 1996; Thomas, 2004; Kendall, 2005). In the period under review, Australia's ties to Asia again centred on these issues. China was Australia's largest two-way trading partner in goods and services in 2020, but China's retaliatory measures sent the value of Australian trade in almost all sectors plummeting. The underlying cause of these measures was Chinese discontent about Australia's development and implementation of foreign interference legislation (see Chapters 5 and 13). Australia's security legislation, however, was not the only or even the primary reason, given that Australia was one of several countries to attract Beijing's wrath. China's increasing stridency towards Australia was an expression of a more assertive style of foreign diplomacy, which also targeted the United States, Canada and some South-East Asian countries.

In this context Australia could have benefited from its wealth of Asia expertise and, in particular, China literacy. As this chapter illustrated, Asian Australians were not well represented in the Australian Public Service. This was especially so in foreign affairs, which has not tended to draw on outside or non-governmental expertise (White, 2016). While Australians with Asian heritage might have expressed differences in attitudes and values towards key issues of foreign or international relations, the proportion of Asian Australians in the public service, as well as the federal and state parliaments, did not match their growing share of the population.

The dearth of Asia expertise was even more of a concern, given the broader discourse of Australia–China relations, which, while still dominated by trade and politics, was became increasingly overshadowed by national security. In earlier decades, the Chinese presence in Australia was governed by the policies and discourses of multiculturalism (Kendall, 2005). Between 2016 and 2020, however, attitudes towards Chinese Australians were overlaid with a growing sense of mistrust and suspicion, due to real or imagined links with the Communist Party of China. This 'securitisation' of Chinese Australians was reflected in the low numbers of Asian Australians working in government and politics. This was incompatible with Australia's long-professed goal of embracing its multicultural identity and drawing on the strength and diversity of its growing immigrant populations. It was also at odds with the aspiration of Australia to project a confident identity and engage productively and harmoniously with its Asian neighbours.

References

Australian Government (2012) *Australia in the Asian Century*. Canberra. https://www.defence.gov.au/whitepaper/2013/docs/australia_in_the_asian_century_white_paper.pdf

Australian Public Service Commission (2013) *State of the Service Report: The APS in the Asia Century*. Canberra. http://www.apsc.gov.au/_data/assets/pdf_file/0005/59387/SOSR-2012-13-chapter-8.pdf

——(2020) *Asia Capability of the Current APS Workforce*. Canberra. https://www.apsc.gov.au/asia-capability-current-aps-workforce

Brophy, D. (2018) *Silent Invasion: China's Influence in Australia* by Clive Hamilton. *Australian Book Review*, 400. https://www.australianbookreview.com.au/abr-online/archive/2018/218-april-2018-no-400/4663-david-brophy-reviews-silent-invasion-china-s-influence-in-australia-by-clive-hamilton

——(2019) Australia's China debate in 2018. In J. Golley, L. Jaivin, P.J. Farrelly with S. Strange (eds), *China Year Book: Power*, pp. 152–72. Canberra: ANU Press

Cave, D., Oliver, A., Hayward-Jones, J., Munro, K. & Harris, E. (2019) *Foreign Policy: Women in International Relations*. Lowy Institute. https://www.lowyinstitute.org/publications/gender-australia-ir-sector#sec37196

Conley Tyler, M. (2020) Morrison's Foreign Relations Bill should not pass Parliament. Here's why. *Conversation*. https://theconversation.com/morrisons-foreign-relations-bill-should-not-pass-parliament-heres-why-145615

Department of Foreign Affairs and Trade (DFAT) (2021) *China–Australia Free Trade Agreement: ChAFTA outcomes at a glance*. Canberra. https://www.dfat.gov.au/trade/agreements/in-force/chafta/fact-sheets/Pages/chafta-outcomes-at-a-glance

Dunn, K. & Forrest, J. (2007) Contemporary manifestations of racism in Australia. In N. Gopalkrishnan & B. Hurriyet (eds), *Racisms in the New World Order: Realities of Cultures, Colours, and Identity*, pp. 95–106. Newcastle, UK: Cambridge Scholars

Dunn, K. & Nelson, J. (2011) Challenging the public denial of racism for a deeper multiculturalism. *Journal of Intercultural Studies* 32(6): 587–602. https://doi.org/10.1080/07256868.2011.618105

Dunn, K., Pelleri, D. & Maeder-Han, K. (2011) Attacks on Indian students: The commerce of denial in Australia. *Race and Class* 52(4): 71–88

Forrest, J. & Dunn, K. (2007) Constructing racism in Sydney, Australia's largest ethnicity. *Urban Studies* 44(4): 699–721. https://doi.org/10.1080/00420980601185676

Graham, E. (2019) Australia has too few home-grown experts on the Chinese Communist Party. That's a problem. *Conversation*, 13 August. https://theconversation.com/australia-has-too-few-home-grown-experts-on-the-chinese-communist-party-thats-a-problem-121174

Gstalter, M. (2020) WHO official warns against calling it 'Chinese virus', says 'there is no blame in this'. *Hill*, 19 March. https://thehill.com/homenews/administration/488479-who-official-warns-against-calling-it-chinese-virus-says-there-is-no/

Hamilton, C. (2018) *Silent Invasion: China's Influence in Australia*. Richmond: Hardie Grant Publishing

Hanson, P. (2020) China must be held accountable for the coronavirus pandemic. Pauline Hanson's One Nation media release. https://www.senatorhanson.com.au/2020/03/24/china-must-be-held-accountable-for-the-coronavirus-pandemic/

Hao Chai, T.S. (2020) How China attempts to drive a wedge in the US–Australia alliance. *Australian Journal of International Affairs* 74(5): 511–31. https://doi.org/10.1080/10357718.2020.1721432

Harris Rimmer, S. & Stephenson, E. (2019) Diplomacy and defence remain a boys' club, but women are making inroads. *Conversation*, 9 July. https://theconversation.com/diplomacy-and-defence-remain-a-boys-club-but-women-are-making-inroads-119984

He, B. (2018) Diversity leadership multiculturalism: The challenge of the securitization of Chinese migrants in Australia. *International Social Science Journal* 68(227–228): 119–31. https://doi.org/10.1111/issj.12168

Hurst, D. (2021) Nearly one in five Chinese–Australians threatened or attacked in past year, survey finds. *Guardian*, 3 March. https://www.theguardian.com/australia-news/2021/mar/03/nearly-one-in-five-chinese-australians-threatened-or-attacked-in-past-year-survey-finds

Jiang, Y. (2021) *Chinese–Australians in the Australian Public Service*. https://www.lowyinstitute.org/sites/default/files/JIANG%2C%20Chinese-Australians%20in%20APS%2C%20Web_Print%20120421_0.pdf

Jupp, J. & Pietsch, J. (2018) A different dimension: Ethnic politics and the 2016 federal election. In A. Gauja, P. Chen, J. Curtin & J. Pietsch (eds), *Double Disillusion: Analysing the 2016 Australian Federal Election*. Canberra: ANU Press

Kendall, T. (2005) *Ways of Seeing China: From Yellow Peril to Shangrila*. Fremantle: Curtin University Books

Kim, C.K. (2005) Asian American employment in the federal Civil Service. *Public Administration Quarterly* 28(4): 430–59

Knott, J. (1988) Settlement 1851–1880. In J. Jupp (ed.), *The Australian People: An Encyclopedia of the Nation, Its People and their Origins*, pp. 48–54. North Ryde: Angus & Robertson

Kwok, J.T. & Pietsch, J. (2017) The political incorporation of Asian-Australian populations since the end of White Australia. *AAPI Nexus Journal* 15(1–2): 109–36

Lee, D.S. (2007) A nuclear North Korea and the stability of East Asia: A tsunami on the horizon? *Australian Journal of International Affairs* 61(4): 436–54

Lowy Institute Poll (2019) Understanding Australian attitudes towards the world. https://poll.lowyinstitute.org

Mackerras, C. (1985) *From Fear to Friendship: Australian Policies towards the People's Republic of China 1966–1982*. Brisbane: University of Queensland Press

Markus, A. (2013) *Mapping Social Cohesion: The Scanlon Foundation Surveys National Report*. Melbourne: Monash University

Nabbs-Keller, G. (2020) Can Indonesia lead? Maritime tensions with China escalate. *Interpreter*, Lowy Institute. https://lowyinstitute.org/the-interpreter/can-indonesia-lead-maritime-tensions-China-escalate

Pietsch, J. (2017) Trends in migrant and ethnic minority voting in Australia: Findings from the Australian Election Study. *Ethnic and Racial Studies* 40(14): 2463–80. https://doi.org/10.1080/01419870.2016.1250937

——(2018) *Race, Ethnicity, and the Participation Gap: Understanding Australia's Political Complexion*. Toronto: University of Toronto Press

——(2020) Australian ethnic change and political inclusion: Finding strength in diversity in responding to global crises. In S. Saggar & A. Zenz (eds), *Re-imagining Australia: Migration, Culture, Diversity*, pp. 57–63. Crawley: UWA Public Policy Institute

Strahan, L. (1996) *Australia's China: Changing Perceptions from the 1930s to the 1990s*. Melbourne: Cambridge University Press

Thomas, N. (ed.) (2004) *Re-orientating Australia–China Relations: 1972 to the Present*. Aldershot: Ashgate

Tillett, A. (2018) The Foreign Interference bill and the balance between security and transparency. *Australian Financial Review*, 13 June. https://www.afr.com/politics/the-foreign-interference-bill-and-the-balance-between-security-and-transparency-20180612-h11ad6

Tingle, L. (2020) The government's plan for a veto over university agreements may have been a Baldrick moment. *ABC News*, 29 August. https://www.abc.net.au/news/2020-08-29/australia-plan-foreign-legislation-university-agreement/12606412

Visontay, E. (2020) 'It is about China': Foreign Relations Bill lambasted as 'complete overkill' on Q+A. *Guardian*, 1 September. https://www.theguardian.com/australia-news/2020/sep/01/it-is-about-china-foreign-relations-bill-lambasted-as-complete-overkill-on-qa

Westendorf, J. & Strating, R. (2020) Women in Australian international affairs. *Australian Journal of International Affairs* 74(3): 213–27

White, H. (2016) ASPI at 15: Conception. *Strategist*, 23 August. https://www.aspistrategist.org.au/aspi-15-conception/

Part II
Global issues

7

Australian perspectives on the 'rules-based order'

Huiyun Feng and Kai He

In the five years after 2016, the world underwent profound economic and political change. Australia, for instance, took prudent action to minimise the relative economic and social damage caused by COVID-19. As a middle power, Australia faced hard strategic choices during this period of international transition. In the long run, Australia would need to decide what kind of world order it would embrace and support. As a close ally of the United States, Australia had found it easy to make security choices between its ally and China, despite US President Donald Trump's criticisms and questioning of alliances in general. However, China, as Australia's largest trading partner and biggest source of international tourists and foreign students, would be essential to the post-COVID recovery.

This chapter analyses Australia's perspectives on and strategies towards the rules-based order by focusing on three issues: how Australian policy-makers have viewed and conceptualised the international order, especially in the period under review; the most urgent challenges that they see in the current international order; and the strategies they have adopted in response to those challenges.

We address these issues by examining two types of sources. First, we consider official documents, including the 2016 Defence White Paper (DWP), the 2017 Foreign Policy White Paper (FPWP), the 2020 Defence Strategic Update and Force Structure Plan (DSUFSP), and other relevant statements and speeches by Australian policy-makers. Second, we review scholarly publications and commentaries, with a view to adding depth to our understanding of how Australian policy-makers perceive the world order and what they have done to defend the rules-based international order. The chapter ends with a discussion of the policy implications and risks that Australia will face in the future transition of the international order.

AUSTRALIA AND THE RULES-BASED ORDER

The 'rules-based' order became a buzzword in Australian policy discourse in the 2010s. Prime Minister Kevin Rudd first used the term in his 2008 National Security Speech, which promoted a 'global rules-based order' as one of Australia's five 'national security interests' (Rudd, 2008). In the 2009 Defence White Paper (DWP), the term appeared 10 times: 'a stable, rules-based global security order' was defined as one of four 'strategic interests' (DOD, 2009). In the 2013 DWP, the phrase 'rules-based order' was mentioned 11 times, and it remained part of Australia's declared strategic interest (DOD, 2013).

In 2016, the phrase peaked in one of Australia's official defence documents, appearing 56 times in the 2016 DWP. 'A stable Indo-Pacific region and a rules-based global order' was defined as one of three 'Strategic Defence interests', which Australia would use force to protect if needed (DOD, 2016; Bisley & Schreer, 2018: 306). The 2016 DWP provided a definition of the 'rules-based' order: 'A rules-based global order means a shared commitment by all countries to conduct their activities in accordance with agreed rules which evolve over time, such as international law and regional security arrangements. This shared commitment has become even more important with growing interconnectivity, which means that events across the world have the potential to affect Australia's security and prosperity.' (DOD, 2016: 15)

'Order' is a contested concept in international relations (see for example Tang, 2016; Feng & He, 2020). Henry Kissinger (2014: 9) defines 'international order' with two fundamental components: 'a set of commonly accepted rules that define the limits of permissible action and a balance of power that enforces restraint where rules break down, preventing one political unit from subjugating all others'. Here, Australia's understanding of 'rules-based' order was similar to Kissinger's conception of international order, with two key elements: power and rule.

In terms of power, Australian policy-makers highlighted the importance of US primacy in defining the rules-based order. US preponderant military power was seen as the key guarantee of the rules-based order (Bisley, 2017), meaning that Australia believed that US primacy was needed to maintain the balance of power in the world. Australia's understanding of 'balance' differed from a traditional definition of balance of power in the international relations (IR) literature, which refers to an equilibrium of great powers. According to IR theory, the US-led unipolar world signifies the most *unbalanced* power relations in world politics.

For Australian policy-makers, however, US primacy was *the* balance of power in the world. In other words, any challenge to US primacy threatened the balance of the international order. For example, the 2016 DWP stated that 'over the last 70 years that peace and stability has been underpinned by a strong United States presence in our region and globally as well as active engagement by regional states in building a rules-based order' (DOD, 2016: 14). This aspirational statement suggested that US-led unipolarity would last for a relatively long time in the foreseeable future.

With respect to rules, Australia emphasised both global institutions and regional arrangements, especially the UN-centred institutions (Bretton Woods) such as the World Bank, the International Monetary Fund (IMF) and the World Trade Organization (WTO). To a certain extent, these institutions were built on and maintained by US primacy after WWII. As Nick Bisley (2018) points out, '[I]n many ways the "rules-based international order" – understood as a shorthand for the UN-centred system that imposes limits on what states can do and which provides a wide array of rules governing international economic relations – is the only international environment Australia has known.'

As the only industrialised economy with uninterrupted economic growth during the 2008 Global Financial Crisis (GFC), Australia felt blessed by the existing rules and institutions. There was a public consensus that Australia's economic prosperity depended on multilateral institutions, especially bilateral and multilateral trade arrangements. Besides the UN-related institutions, Australia had participated in the G-20, the Trans-Pacific Partnership (the later Comprehensive and Progressive Agreement for Trans-Pacific Partnership (CPTPP)) and the Regional Comprehensive Economic Partnership (RCEP). These rules-based institutions that benefited Australia were understood to stem from US leadership directly or indirectly. This type of belief further reinforced the importance of US primacy to Australian views of the rules-based international order.

Australia's perceptions of the rules-based order, nonetheless, changed gradually during the period under review. First, the term 'rules-based' order slowly lost its popularity in Australia's official discourse after Trump came to power in 2017. In the 2017 Foreign Policy White Paper (FPWP), the term 'rules-based' order appeared only 15 times in various forms, such as rules-based global order or rules-based regional order. In the 2020 Defence Strategic Update, the term was mentioned only three times. This is not to suggest that Australian leaders had lost interest in defending the rules-based order *per se*: indeed, they continued to use the term in speeches and public statements.

However, the declining frequency of the term 'rules-based' order in official documents is puzzling (Scott, 2020) and deserves attention. It may reflect frustration and disappointment in the role of the United States in damaging existing institutions. If the 'rules' referred to the international institutions, international laws and multilateralism that Australia had cherished for decades, the Trump administration had become an apparent rule-breaker in the minds of Australian policy-makers. Trump, for instance, withdrew from several key international institutions, which Australians perceived to be the backbone of the rules-based international order.

As Allan Gyngell, a former diplomat and then National President of the Australian Institute of International Affairs, noted, the Trump administration was 'abandoning' the multilateral institutions the United States had built: 'Australians had to acknowledge that the global order that had shaped the world since the end of WWII was not challenged or changing, but over' (Gyngell, 2018). Putting aside frustrations and disappointments Australia might have towards the United States, it was understandable that Australia – a close US ally – would keep some distance from the term in its official statements if the United States had indeed given up the 'rules-based' order.

Between 2016 and 2020, a notable development of Australia's views on the rules-based order was the emergence of normative values in official discourse (see Chapter 4), especially democracy and liberalism. The 2013 DWP mentioned 'values' only once in reference to the North Atlantic Treaty Organization (NATO), but the word appeared seven times in 2016 (DOD, 2013; DOD, 2016). The 2016 DWP did not link values with liberalism or democracy explicitly. As Bisley and Schreer point out (2018: 312), Australia deliberately drew a distinction between the 'liberal' and 'rules-based order', a distinction that 'implicitly contain[ed] an offer of cooperation to non-democratic

Asia-Pacific countries'. Emphasising liberalism and democracy might alienate those Asian states that were not full democracies or did not embrace liberal norms and culture, especially Singapore and Vietnam.

This cautious and prudent attitude changed in 2017. In the 2017 FPWP, 'values had gone mainstream' (Reilly, 2020), being mentioned 31 times, including in a subsection entitled 'Australia's values'. This suggests that 'Australia does not define its national identity by race or religion, but by shared values, including political, economic and religious freedom, liberal democracy, the rule of law, racial and gender equality and mutual respect' (DFAT, 2017: 11).

As a liberal democracy, it is understandable that Australia is proud of its values, especially liberalism and democracy. However, the high-profile return to values in Australian foreign policy was more strategic than rhetorical. As Reilly (2020) suggests, Australia's embrace of 'values' mainly targeted China and especially the Communist Party of China (CPC). because China was seen to have become more authoritarian in domestic politics and more assertive in international affairs under Xi Jinping. China's negative reaction to the ruling of the Permanent Court of Arbitration in The Hague also convinced Australian leaders that China was a revisionist power challenging the liberal order. This values-based understanding of foreign policy became a bipartisan position between the Coalition and the Labor Party in Australia (Reilly, 2020). In other words, the 'rules-based' order became a term embedded with fewer 'rules' but more 'values' for Australian policy-makers.

Another feature of Australian views on international order was the change in Australia's political geography from the Asia Pacific to the Indo-Pacific (see Chapters 2 and 11). This change was rooted in Australia's strategic anxieties and concerns over China's rise (Pan, 2014; He & Li, 2020; He & Feng, 2020). By expanding its political geography to a broader Indo-Pacific, Australia intended to achieve two goals. On the one hand, it could embrace India – another rising power – to countervail China's influence. This was in keeping with the 'reliable ally' tradition of Australia's foreign policy (Taylor, 2020). On the other hand, expanding the strategic geography to the Indo-Pacific provided an opportunity for Australia to play an active and independent middle-power role in mediating and shaping great-power politics through multilateralism in the region (Carr, 2014).

CHALLENGES TO THE RULES-BASED ORDER

Some Australians might have wanted history to be frozen and US primacy to endure so that the existing international order could remain intact forever. In the period under review, however, Australian leaders began to realise that a transition or transformation in the international order was inevitable, given the changing balance between the great powers. China was seen as the main challenger to the rules-based order, in two ways.

First, China's rise changed the power configuration, unipolarity, in the international system. It also inevitably challenged US leadership, the key stabiliser of the international order in the view of Australian policy-makers. For example, the 2017 FPWP stated on page 1: 'The United States has been the dominant power in our region throughout Australia's post-Second World War history. Today, China is challenging America's position.' (DFAT, 2017) Since Australia's prosperity and security heavily relied on the US-led order, it was understandable that Australia attached a negative connotation to the mere notion of order transition. As the 2017 FPWP stated, 'powerful drivers of change are converging in a way that is re-shaping the international order and challenging Australian interests' (DFAT, 2017: 1). In particular, 'Navigating the decade ahead will be hard because, as China's power grows, our region is changing in ways without precedent in Australia's modern history.' (DFAT, 2017: 4)

Australian policy-makers also believed that China's rise, especially in an economic sense, was unstoppable. The FPWP cited economic forecasting by the Australian Treasury which suggested that China's GDP had become larger than that of the United States on a Purchasing Power Parity (PPP) basis in 2016. Moreover, China's GDP would become more than 1.5 times larger than that of the United States in 2030 (DFAT, 2017: 26). Therefore, the 2017 FPWP stated,

> by some measures China's economy is already the largest in the world. China is the most important trading partner for most of the region's economies and a major investor, including in infrastructure. China's military modernisation is rapidly improving the capability of its armed forces. It has the largest navy and air force in Asia and the largest coast guard in the world. It is a large aid donor and lender to the region. (DFAT, 2017: 25)

However, Australian policy-makers believed that 'the United States remains the most powerful country' even though 'the long [US] dominance of the international order is being challenged by other powers' (DFAT, 2017: 21), especially China. This seemingly contradictory statement indicated a psychological dilemma for Australian policy-makers in accepting the facts of China's rise and America's decline in the international system.

Besides official documents, Australian leaders spoke publicly about the rapid changes in the international order and the uncertainties surrounding a possible order transition. In 2016, Turnbull (2016) warned in his speech at the Lowy Institute that Australia was experiencing '[a] pace of transformation unknown, unprecedented in scale and pace in all of human history'. During the 2020 COVID pandemic, Morrison stated, '[W]e have not seen the conflation of global, economic and strategic uncertainty now being experienced here in Australia in our region since the existential threat we faced when the global and regional order collapsed in the 1930s and 1940s.' Morrison said Australia was at the epicentre of the rising strategic competition in the Indo-Pacific, which is 'under increasing – and ... almost irreversible – strain' (2020a).

Australian policy-makers had mixed feelings about China's booming economic power, given that its behaviour was seen as deleterious to the rules and values of the existing order. As noted, the rules-based order, for Australian policy-makers, specifically referred to the rules and norms embedded in UN-centred institutions and the Bretton Woods system, such as the United Nations Convention on the Law of the Sea (UNCLOS), the human rights declaration, and the open-market and free-trade regime.

Australian policy-makers regarded China's assertive behaviour in the South China Sea and the East China Sea after 2010 as revisionist behaviour against the UNCLOS. For example, the 2016 DWP said: 'Australia is particularly concerned by the unprecedented pace and scale of China's land reclamation activities' (DOD, 2016: 58). The DWP condemned China's 2013 unilateral declaration of an Air Defence Identification Zone in the East China Sea because it 'caused tensions to rise. Australia is opposed to any coercive or unilateral actions to change the status quo in the East China Sea' (DOD, 2016: 61). Similarly, the 2017 FPWP criticised China's assertiveness in the South China Sea, stating: 'Australia is particularly concerned by the unprecedented pace and scale of China's activities. Australia opposes the use of disputed features and artificial structures in the South China Sea for military purposes.' (DFAT, 2017: 46) Australia pushed China to abide by the ruling of the arbitral tribunal on the South China Sea dispute between the Philippines and China in 2016 (DFAT, 2017: 47).

In the 2020 Defence Strategic Update, China was again portrayed as a revisionist against the current rules-based order. It was the only country accused of being 'more assertive' in the Indo-Pacific: 'Since 2016, major powers have become more assertive in advancing their strategic preferences and seeking to exert influence, including China's active pursuit of greater influence in the Indo-Pacific. Australia is concerned by the potential for actions, such as the establishment of military bases, which could undermine stability in the Indo-Pacific and our immediate region.' (DOD, 2020a: 11) Besides official documents, Australian politicians used other occasions to raise their concerns about China. In the 2017 Shangri-La Dialogue, Turnbull (2017) warned:

> Some fear that China will seek to impose a latter-day Monroe Doctrine on this hemisphere in order to dominate the region, marginalising the role and contribution of other nations, in particular the United States. Such a dark view of our future would see China isolating those who stand in opposition to or are not aligned with its interests, while using its economic largesse to reward those toeing the line.

China was not only seen as a direct challenge to US primacy but also treated as a revisionist power against the whole rules-based order underpinned by US leadership. Australia, however, was uneasy about the hostile actions of the United States towards international institutions. In particular, Trump's bilateral trade war with China fundamentally challenged the multilateral trading regime that Australia had preferred and benefited from since World War II. In early 2020, the United States and China reached a truce in their two-year trade war by signing a 'phase one deal', but: 'The real danger of the new agreement, however, is that it replaces a trading system based largely on agreed rules with one based purely on negotiating muscle. The United States long championed a rules-based system, but is now discarding it in favour of a power-based system where the strong do what they can and the weak suffer what they must.' (Alden, 2020)

In other words, Australia, as a weaker power than the United States and China, might lose more in the future if the multilateral trading regime is crippled or even destroyed by the United States. However, Australian policy-makers refrained from publicly criticising the United States, their closest ally with a 'hundred years of mateship'. Instead, Australia explicitly praised US leadership in the region while being quietly disappointed and frustrated with the US role in the rules-based order. For example, in his Shangri-La speech, Turnbull (2017) highlighted US leadership, noting that 'the peace and stability of our region has been enabled by consistent US global leadership. That leadership, that commitment, those values are more important than ever.' He then said: 'Some have been concerned that the withdrawal from the TPP and now from the Paris Climate Change Agreement herald a US withdrawal from global leadership. While these decisions are disappointing, we should take care not to rush to interpret an intent to engage on different terms as one not to engage at all.' (Turnbull, 2017) While Turnbull's speech could be interpreted as a scolding of Trump and his inconsistent and weak leadership, there was a lingering hope in the speech that despite the damage, the United States would somehow reclaim its leadership role in global governance and multilateralism in the future.

Similarly, after Trump made his speech at the United Nations against globalisation, saying that 'the future does not belong to the globalists. The future belongs to patriots', Morrison delivered a speech at the Lowy Institute on 'negative globalism' (Galloway, 2020). Morrison (2019) stated that 'it also does not serve our national interests when international institutions demand conformity rather than independent cooperation on global issues'. To a certain extent, Morrison echoed Trump on the negative consequences of globalisation and globalism for national interests. However, in the same speech, Morrison (2019) reconfirmed that 'Australia does and must always seek to have a responsible and participative international agency in addressing global issues. This is positive and practical globalism. Our interests are not served by isolationism and protectionism.' Without mentioning names, Morrison disconfirmed the Trumpian views on globalism and multilateralism.

Moreover, in his 2020 Aspen speech, Morrison (2020b) said that 'an international society depends greatly on the leadership of the United States ... America has long been a major stabilising factor in the Indo-Pacific region, and its continued focus here and engagement is absolutely vital to the world.' He reminded his audience that '[together, China and] the United States have a special responsibility to uphold what [Hedley] Bull described as "the common set of rules" that build an international society' (see Bull 1977). It was understandable for Morrison to send a reminder to China, which has been labelled a revisionist state publicly by Australian leaders. Listing the United States and China together implied that both countries, especially the United States, should have done more because of their special responsibilities towards the rules-based international order.

AUSTRALIA'S RESPONSES: THREE BALANCING STRATEGIES

Although Australia was disappointed about Trump's inability to lead the defence of the existing order, it was more worried about the strength of China's rising power, which might be used to upend the rules and norms of the current order from which Australia had benefited and depended upon. How to counter China's growing influence, however, became a strategic choice. Australian leaders claimed that they did not need to choose between the United States and China, but in reality they had chosen to side with the United States to defend the existing order. Australia adopted three balancing strategies to 'take China down' and 'keep America up' in the region, especially since 2015.

The first balancing strategy was 'military balancing' with both internal and external efforts (Waltz, 1979). As an 'internal balancing' strategy against external threats, implicitly from revisionist powers like China, Australia continued to beef up its military capabilities through the defence budget. Before the Coalition came to power in 2013, the Labor government had kept the defence budget at a low level. In the 2016 DWP, the government introduced 'a new 10-year funding model for Defence which gives Defence the long-term funding certainty it needs'. More specifically, it would increase 'the defence budget to two per cent of Australia's GDP by 2020–21, providing an unprecedented investment in Australia's defence capability of approximately A$195 billion over ten years' (DOD, 2016). More specifically, Australia aimed to strengthen all aspects of its defence capabilities, through upskilling its personnel, modernising its platforms and systems, improving its information and communications technology, upgrading its infrastructure and making use of scientific and technological innovations.

It should be noted that Australia's 'internal balancing' effort was not only reflected in the increase of the military budget. It also made a long-term commitment to defence spending. The 2016 DWP exceeded the 2 per cent level of GDP: 'the 10-year funding model ... will not be subject to any further adjustments as a result of changes in Australia's GDP growth estimates' (Baldino & Carr, 2016). In other words, even though Australia's future GDP might decrease, the defence budget would continue to grow.

This commitment ran into a reality check during the COVID-19 pandemic that began in 2020. The Australian economy was hit by the pandemic, and accordingly it was expected to suffer its first recession in 28 years (Smyth, 2020). However, in July 2020, the Morrison government released a defence budget update, in which Australia pledged to increase its defence spending significantly. More specifically, Australia would increase its defence budget to A$73.7 billion over the ten years to 2029–30, with total funding of $575 billion over the decade, including 'approximately A$270 billion of investment in Defence capability, compared with approximately $195 billion for the decade to 2025–26 when the 2016 Defence White Paper was released' (DOD, 2020a: 7). In Morrison's words, the new budget model would go 'beyond our achievement of reaching two per cent of our economy of GDP this year' (Morrison, 2020a).

Why did Australia decide to increase its military budget significantly when the economy was hard hit by the pandemic? Morrison (2020a) explained that it was to prepare 'for a post-COVID world that is poorer, that is more dangerous, and that is more disorderly'. Although he did not explicitly mention any country in his speech, China was definitely the 'usual suspect' behind Australia's drastic military build-up during the pandemic. In explaining Australia's plans to purchase longer-range missiles, Defence Minister Reynolds said in July 2020 that 'it is essential that we have the capabilities that can hold forces and infrastructure at risk from a greater distance, to influence decision-making of those who may seek to threaten our national interests' (DOD, 2020b).

Through strengthening its own military capabilities, Australia could also increase its 'alliance value' and contribute to the US-led multilateral security systems in the Indo-Pacific. As Leahy (2020) points out, Morrison's new budget plan would transform the Australian Defence Force into 'a very different force' with much improved 'expeditionary capabilities and strike orientation'. However, 'this [transformation] can only be pointed in one direction: part of a US strategy towards China'. In other words, Australia's internal balancing (its military build-up) mainly aimed to better serve as a worthy ally for the United States in countering China's potential threats in the Indo-Pacific.

This internal balancing strategy was closely linked to Australia's external balancing, through strengthening the US-led security alliance system in the region. After World War II, the United States established the 'hub-and-spokes' alliance system to build a series of bilateral alliances with Japan, South Korea, the Philippines, Thailand, Australia and New Zealand. Besides buttressing its ties with the United States, Australia also actively advocated a minilateral security arrangement by reviving the Quadrilateral Security Dialogue – the so-called Quad 2.0 – in 2017 (Tow, 2019). Quad 1.0 was an informal security dialogue mechanism established by Australia, Japan, India and the United States in 2007. However, Australia unilaterally withdrew from the Quad under the Rudd government in 2008 out of concern for China's objection.

In 2017, senior security officials from the Quad countries reinvigorated the concept by meeting on the sidelines of the East Asia Summit. Australia played a proactive role in advocating security cooperation through the Quad 2.0 framework. In September 2019, the Quad was elevated from a senior officials gathering to a ministerial-level meeting in which the foreign ministers from the four nations met on the sidelines of the UN General Assembly. One week later, Morrison highly praised the upgrade of the Quad in his Lowy lecture by stating: 'it is a key forum for exchanging views on challenges facing the region, including taking forward practical cooperation on maritime, terrorism and cyber issues' (Morrison, 2019). Since the Quad 2.0 is a typical minilateral arrangement, focusing on regional security issues, it complements the US traditional bilateralism-based hub-and-spokes system in the regional security architecture (Tow, 2019).

The Quad 2.0 was a major venue for Australia as well as the United States to engage India – another rising power in the region, which was widely seen as a natural balancer against China. The Sino-Indian border dispute in early 2020 pushed India to tighten its security cooperation with the United States and Australia. In June 2020, Australia received a first-time invitation from India to join the Malabar naval exercise with India, the United States and Japan. In the eyes of Chinese strategists, the Quad 2.0 had the potential to become an 'Asian NATO' – a multilateral defence alliance – against China's rise in the future (Feng, 2020). If it succeeded, the Quad 2.0 would play a crucial role in 'taking China down', 'keeping America up' and defending the existing international order. During Morrison's visit to Japan in November 2020, Australia and Japan signed a reciprocal defence agreement, which aimed to 'elevate security and defence cooperation between Japan and Australia to a new level' (Takenaka & Park, 2020).

The second external balancing strategy that Australia adopted was 'institutional balancing', through which it intended to rely on multilateral institutions to constrain and shape China's assertive behaviour (He, 2008; 2009). There were two dimensions of Australia's institutional balancing against China. First, Australia actively supported ASEAN's leadership in regional multilateral institutions, such as the East Asia Summit as well as other institution-building efforts in the broader Indo-Pacific region. In the 1990s, ASEAN-oriented multilateralism played an important role in shaping China's behaviour in the South China Sea. Australia hoped that ASEAN could revive its institutional power to constrain China's assertiveness in the South China Sea, so Australia endorsed 'ASEAN centrality' as soon as ASEAN released its first official document on the Indo-Pacific entitled 'ASEAN Outlook on the Indo-Pacific' in mid-2019 (DFAT, 2019). At the ASEAN-Australia Foreign Ministers' Meeting on COVID-19 in 2019, Foreign Minister Payne announced that Australia would make a A$23 million commitment to 'help ASEAN bolster health security, economic recovery, and stability in our region' (DFAT, 2020).

Second, Australia actively cooperated with its Quad partners to establish an infrastructural coalition against China's Belt and Road Initiative (BRI), especially in the South Pacific. Australia saw China's BRI investment in the South Pacific as a penetration into its traditional 'sphere of influence' (White, 2019). Therefore, Australia actively applied institutional balancing by engaging other Quad countries, especially Japan and the United States, to counter China's BRI influence in the region.

In November 2018, Prime Minister Scott Morrison revealed a A$3 billion financial package to boost ties with Pacific Island nations (Pearlman, 2018a). The purpose of this financial aid was to curb China's growing influence in the South Pacific, which Morrison described as 'our patch ... our part of the world' (Pearlman, 2018b). In September 2019, the United States joined Australia's efforts in countering China's BRI influence in the South Pacific by announcing a US$100 million Pacific Pledge, which moved from other areas of the aid budget. This assistance was additional to the US$350 million annual US investment in the South Pacific (US State Department, 2019). In November 2019, the United States, Australia and Japan established a trilateral Blue Dot Network, which aimed to bring the public and private sectors together to 'promote high-quality, trusted standards for global infrastructure development in an open and inclusive framework' (ABC News, 2019).

Australia also adopted an 'ideological balancing' policy to target the CPC's sharp power, or political influence, in Australia. Australia was the first country to pass a foreign interference law implicitly to block the CPC's political influence in Australia (see Chapter 5). As noted, the Australian Government refused to endorse China's BRI projects, although some state governments, such as Victoria, signed infrastructure agreements as part of China's BRI. Australia was the first country to ban Huawei from participating in its 5G telecommunications system due to national security concerns. In addition, Australia actively campaigned against the wider use of Chinese technology (Gyngell, 2019; Bagshaw & Harris, 2019).

In her 2017 Fullerton lecture in Singapore, Foreign Minister Bishop targeted China's political system by highlighting the incompatibility between China's authoritarian rule and liberal democracy. Bishop (2017) asserted, '[T]he domestic political system and values of the United States reflect the liberal rules-based order that we seek to preserve and defend.' On the contrary, '[I]n more recent times, China is rising as an economic partner and geo-political and geo-strategic competitor with the United States and other nations. This brings with it its own challenges ... because China is disputing maritime boundaries in the East and South China Seas.'

In late 2019, Australia's Home Affairs Minister Peter Dutton publicly criticised the CPC, 'accusing it of conduct "inconsistent" with Australian values', as well as for 'cyberattacks, theft of intellectual property, and undue influence at universities'. The Chinese government was furious about Dutton's comments, calling them 'shocking and baseless' (Hunter, 2019).

However, Australian policy-makers seemed to ignore China's anger and fury by continuing their ideological balancing against the CPC, even during the COVID-19 pandemic. In April 2020, Foreign Minister Marise Payne publicly questioned China's transparency on the outbreak and announced that Australia would push for an investigation into the origins and spread of the coronavirus. China criticised 'Payne's comments as not based on facts' and treated Australia's call for an open investigation as a 'political attack' on the legitimacy of the CPC (Davidson, 2020). Hu Xijin, the chief editor of China's *Global Times*, attacked Australia as 'chewing gum stuck on the sole of China's shoes' because 'Australia is always there, making trouble' (Davidson, 2020).

In September 2020, during her speech to the United Nations Human Rights Council, Payne criticised the Chinese government for enforcing 'repressive measures' against Uighurs in Xinjiang province and for eroding rights and freedoms in Hong Kong. In the eyes of Chinese diplomats, Australia's accusations reflect its 'typical double standards' on human rights as well as a 'blatant smear against China' (Hurst, 2020). The bilateral relationship between Australia and China continued to deteriorate until the end of 2020.

CONCLUSION: ORDER, BALANCING AND RISK

In this chapter, we have reviewed how Australian policy-makers and academics understand the rules-based international order as well as how they responded to the potential challenges to it between 2016 and 2020. We suggest that Australia's understanding of the rules-based order was built on US supremacy as well as US-led multilateral institutions, such as the UN-centred system and the Bretton Woods institutions, like the World Bank, IMF and WTO.

The underlying ideology of the rules-based order, in Australian eyes, was based on liberalism and democracy. China's rise, however, posed serious challenges both to the power configuration and to the institutional foundation of that order. Australian leaders were aware that a rising China would eventually replace the United States as the largest economy in the world. However, they believed that the United States would enjoy a military advantage over China for decades. China's assertive diplomacy in the East China Sea and South China Sea was seen as an institutional and normative challenge to the existing rules and norms of international law. In addition, China's domestic authoritarianism was treated as a 'sharp power' threat, jeopardising the liberal and democratic values of Australia and other democracies (Fitzgerald, 2020). Therefore, Australia adopted a series of balancing strategies to cope with China's challenges by increasing its military budget, strengthening its security cooperation with the Quad countries, supporting ASEAN's centrality, coordinating an infrastructure coalition in the South Pacific, as well as campaigning against the sharp power of the CPC.

As a self-perceived middle power, Australian policy choices were constrained by its power capability as well as its geopolitical position in the world. Although there were major economic opportunities in the Indo-Pacific, it was also at the epicentre of strategic competition between the United States and China. Australian policy-makers understood that 'it is difficult for countries like Australia, even working with others, to influence an international system that is predominantly shaped by the actions of much larger nations' (DFAT, 2017: 6). They faced two strategic options in the context of this rivalry in a period of order transition: they could work with the United States to defend the existing order, or they could cooperate with China – a rising power – to upend that order.

Australian leaders made their 'China choice' to align with the United States, defending the existing order during the period under review. This choice was understandable, given that Australia had not only benefited from the existing US-led order for more than 70 years but also because it shared key values – democracy and liberalism – which underwrite that order. However, Australia's proactive balancing strategies against China in defending the existing order had risks for its national interests.

Australia's balancing strategies against China intensified bilateral trade tensions in 2020. In addition, Australia's democracy-driven and liberalism-based foreign policy alienates other non-democracies in the Indo-Pacific. As Gyngell (2019) suggests, 'History hasn't ended.' The future international order might or might not be liberal at all. There might be multiple or multiplex international orders coexisting in a pluralist international society (Acharya, 2017). How to cope with the dynamics and complexities of the international order transition will be one of the toughest tasks for Australian policy-makers in the coming decades.

References

ABC News (2019) China's 'Belt and Road' strategy has a new competitor – enter America's 'Blue Dot Network'. *ABC News*, 6 November. https://www.abc.net.au/news/2019-11-06/us-introduces-blue-dot-network-as-answer-to-belt-and-road/11675226

Acharya, A. (2017) After liberal hegemony: The advent of a multiplex world order. *Ethics and International Affairs* 31(3): 271–85

Alden, E. (2020) Smaller countries lose in the US–China trade deal. *East Asia Forum*, 9 February. https://www.eastasiaforum.org/2020/02/09/smaller-countries-lose-in-the-us-china-trade-deal/

Bagshaw, E. & Harris, R. (2019) China claims Australia the 'pioneer' of a global anti-China campaign. *Sydney Morning Herald*, 24 September. https://www.smh.com.au/politics/federal/china-claims-australia-the-pioneer-of-a-global-anti-china-campaign-20190924-p52ufk.html

Baldino, D. & Carr, A. (2016) The end of 2%: Australia gets serious about its defence budget. *Conversation*, 26 February. https://theconversation.com/the-end-of-2-australia-gets-serious-about-its-defence-budget-53554

Bishop, J. (2017) Change and uncertainty in the Indo-Pacific: Strategic challenges and opportunities. 28th IISS Fullerton Lecture, 13 March. https://www.foreignminister.gov.au/minister/julie-bishop/speech/change-and-uncertainty-indo-pacific-strategic-challenges-and-opportunities

Bisley, N. (2017) Australia and the evolving international order. In M. Beeson & S. Hameiri (eds), *Navigating the New International Disorder: Australia in the World Affairs, 2011–2015*. Oxford: Oxford University Press

——(2018) Australia's rules-based international order. Speech at Australian Institute of International Affairs, 27 July. http://www.internationalaffairs.org.au/australianoutlook/australias-rules-based-international-order/

Bisley, N. & Schreer, B. (2018) Australia and the rules-based order in Asia: Of principles and pragmatism. *Asian Survey* 58(2): 302–19

Bull, H. (1977) *The Anarchical Society: A Study of Order in World Politics*. London: Macmillan

Carr, A. (2014) Is Australia a middle power? A systemic impact approach. *Australian Journal of International Affairs* 68(1): 70–84

Davidson, H. (2020) Chewing gum stuck on the sole of our shoes: The China–Australia war of words – timeline. *Guardian*, 29 April. https://www.theguardian.com/world/2020/apr/29/chewing-gum-stuck-on-the-sole-of-our-shoes-the-china-australia-war-of-words-timeline

Department of Defence (DOD) (2009) *Defence White Paper 2009*. Canberra

——(2013) *Defence White Paper 2013*. Canberra

——(2016) *Defence White Paper 2016*. Canberra

——(2020a) *Strategic Update 2020*. Canberra

——(2020b) Long-range strike capabilities to maintain regional security. Media release, 1 July. https://www.pm.gov.au/media/long-range-strike-capabilities-maintain-regional-security

Department of Foreign Affairs and Trade (DFAT) (2017) *Foreign Policy White Paper*. Canberra

——(2019) Joint statement, Australia–US ministerial consultations (AUSMIN) 2019. Minister for Foreign Affairs. Media release, 4 August. https://www.foreignminister.gov.au/minister/marise-payne/media-release/joint-statement-australia-us-ministerial-consultations-ausmin-2019

——(2020) Special ASEAN–Australia Foreign Ministers' Meeting on COVID-19. Minister for Foreign Affairs. Media release, 30 June. https://www.foreignminister.gov.au/minister/marise-payne/media-release/special-asean-australia-foreign-ministers-meeting-COVID-19

Feng, H. & He, K. (eds) (2020) *China's Challenges and International Order Transition: Beyond 'Thucydides's Trap'*. Ann Arbor: University of Michigan Press

Feng, Q. (2020) India–Australia closeness draws attention. *Global Times*, 21 July

Fitzgerald, J. (2020) Soft power and sharp power: The view from Australia. *Asan Forum*, Special Forum, 6 June. http://www.theasanforum.org/soft-power-and-sharp-power-the-view-from-australia/

Galloway, A. (2020) PM warns of threats facing our region, revives criticism of negative globalism. *Sydney Morning Herald*, 4 August. https://www.smh.com.au/politics/federal/pm-warns-of-threats-facing-our-region-revives-criticism-of-negative-globalism-20200804-p55ij9.html

Gyngell, A. (2018) Australia's place in the new world order. *East Asian Forum*, 18 January

——(2019) History hasn't ended: How to handle China. *Australian Foreign Affairs* 7: 113–28

He, K. (2008) Institutional balancing and international relations theory: Economic interdependence and balance of power strategies in Southeast Asia. *European Journal of International Relations* 14(3): 489–518

——(2009) *Institutional Balancing in the Asia Pacific: Economic Interdependence and China's Rise*. London: Routledge

He, K. & Feng, H. (2020) The institutionalization of the Indo-Pacific: Problems and prospects. *International Affairs* 96(1): 149–68

He, K. & Li, M. (2020) Understanding the dynamics of the Indo-Pacific: US–China strategic competition, regional actors and beyond. *International Affairs* 96(1): 1–7

Hunter, F. (2019) Dutton takes aim at Chinese Communist Party for hostile conduct. *Sydney Morning Herald*, 11 October. https://www.smh.com.au/politics/federal/dutton-takes-aim-at-chinese-communist-party-for-hostile-conduct-20191011-p52zsm.html

Hurst, D. (2020) Australia criticises China over treatment of Uighurs and for eroding freedoms in Hong Kong. *Guardian*, 15 September. https://www.theguardian.com/australia-news/2020/sep/15/australia-criticises-china-over-treatment-of-uighurs-and-for-eroding-freedoms-in-hong-kong

Kissinger, H. (2014) *World Order: Reflections on the Character of Nations and the Course of History*. London: Allen Lane

Leahy, P. (2020) The latest defence plan is a robust pivot to our own backyard. *Australian Financial Review*, 3 July

Morrison, S. (2019) Speech – Lowy Lecture 'In our interest'. 3 October. https://www.pm.gov.au/media/speech-lowy-lecture-our-interest

——(2020a) Address – Launch of the *2020 Defence Strategic Update*. 1 July. https://www.pm.gov.au/media/address-launch-2020-defence-strategic-update

——(2020b) Address, Aspen Security Forum – 'Tomorrow in the Indo-Pacific'. 5 August. https://www.pm.gov.au/media/address-aspen-security-forum-tomorrow-indo-pacific

Pan, C. (2014) The Indo-Pacific and geopolitical anxieties about China's rise in the Asian regional order. *Australian Journal of International Affairs* 68(4): 453–69

Pearlman, J. (2018a) Australia boosts Pacific spending and pledges new commitment to 'our patch'. *Straits Times*, 8 November. https://www.straitstimes.com/asia/australianz/australia-boosts-pacific-spending-and-pledges-new-commitment-to-our-patch

——(2018b) Australia commits more funds to Pacific nations. *Straits Times*, 9 November. https://www.straitstimes.com/asia/australianz/australia-commits-more-funds-to-pacific-nations

Reilly, B. (2020) The return of values in Australian foreign policy. *Australian Journal of International Affairs* 74(2): 116–23

Rudd, K. (2008) National security speech. House of Representatives, Canberra, 4 December. https://parlinfo.aph.gov.au/parlInfo/genpdf/chamber/hansardr/2008-12-04/0045/hansard_frag.pdf;fileType=application%2Fpdf

Scott, B. (2020) Why Australia hasn't given up on a rules-based world order. *Australian Financial Review*, 27 July. https://www.afr.com/policy/economy/why-australia-hasn-t-given-up-on-a-rules-based-world-order-20200726-p55fht

Smyth, J. (2020) COVID-19 ends Australia's 28-year run without a recession. *Financial Times*, 2 September. https://www.ft.com/content/7057b5b2-01cf-4881-b40e-aa09035f1017

Takenaka, K. & Park, J.M. (2020) Japan, Australia reach security pact amid fears over disputed South China Sea. *Reuters*, 17 November. https://www.reuters.com/article/us-japan-australia-idUSKBN27X131

Tang, S. (2016) Order: A conceptual analysis. *Chinese Political Science Review* 1(1): 30–46

Taylor, B. (2020) Is Australia's Indo-Pacific strategy an illusion? *International Affairs* 96(1): 95–109

Tow, W.T. (2019) Minilateral security's relevance to US strategy in the Indo-Pacific: Challenges and prospects. *Pacific Review* 32(2): 232–44

Turnbull, M. (2016) Lowy Lecture. 23 March. https://www.malcolmturnbull.com.au/media/2016-lowy-lecture

——(2017) Keynote address at the 16th IISS Asia Security Summit. Shangri-La Dialogue, 3 June. https://www.malcolmturnbull.com.au/media/keynote-address-at-the-16th-iiss-asia-security-summit-shangri-la-dialogue

US State Department (2019) Indo-Pacific transparency initiative. Office of the Spokesperson, 3 November. https://www.state.gov/indo-pacific-transparency-initiative/

Waltz, K.N. (1979) *Theory of International Politics*. Reading: Addison-Wesley

White, H. (2019) In denial: Defending Australia as China looks south. *Australian Foreign Affairs* 6: 5–27

International security challenges

Sarah Percy and Rebecca Strating

Since the inaugural edition of *Australia in the World* in 1950, the main preoccupations of Australia's conventional security policy have been broadly static. The task for security planners has been to navigate a course for Australia while managing relations with the great powers that have had the ability to support Australian security interests while also placing obstacles and blandishments in its path. Over the years, the preoccupation with great powers, and especially with its long-term ally the United States, has changed very little. Indeed, in a previous iteration of this series, Boyce and Angel (1983: 36) wrote:

> The Australian policy line formulated in response to these perceived or assumed trends of events may reasonably be described as balance-of-power activism, of a traditional kind, rather than simply as an alliance policy ... the Prime Minister's policy response to the assumed darkening of the strategic landscape in Australia's vicinity was ... to suggest a wider and more coherent activist anti-hegemonial alliance.

This passage could well have described the challenge that faced Australian foreign policy from 2016 to 2020: its troubled relationship with the People's Republic of China and the changing regional landscape its rise had precipitated. It came, however, from the 1976–80 edition, and the potential hegemon in question was the Soviet Union. While the states might have changed, the need to pick and choose a course that balances Australia's interests and those of the great powers remains. As a middle power with regional ambitions, Australia's key security debates have centred upon how to develop an independent foreign policy to mitigate excessive dependence on the security alliance with the United States through regional cooperation, multilateralism and norm entrepreneurship (Bell, 1988; Tow, 2017).

The security picture for Australia is less historically consistent when we look beyond 'high politics' and focus on unconventional security challenges. Over the years, *Australia in World Affairs* has examined unconventional challenges ranging from nuclear testing in the Pacific, refugees, disarmament, climate change, smuggling and crime, and terrorism. The prominence of these challenges has varied over time, but

Australia has demonstrated a marked preference for dealing with unconventional challenges with conventional security tools, in a manner that blurs the lines between domestic and international.

The goal of this chapter is to examine security and Australian foreign policy in the period under review, using these two strands: the high politics that are the stuff of traditional Australian foreign policy, and the unconventional security challenges to which Australia has had to adapt. The first half of the chapter considers Australia's conventional security politics in the context of the strategic competition between the United States and China (see Chapter 1). Change and continuity is a dominant theme in security policy. Between 2016 and 2020, Australia's ongoing support for the US-led status quo sat uneasily in a region that had arguably already evolved well beyond that order.

We next assess 'unconventional' security issues and their impact on Australian national security. We reveal that the policy responses towards these threats were increasingly conventional and that Australia relied on domestic tools to solve international problems. We argue that some new threats brought international tools, like the military, to bear on domestic problems. Moreover, we demonstrate that the security environment was increasingly defined by the 'grey zone': acts that reside between war and peace and take on unconventional forms. Economic coercion, the use of foreign interference, hostage diplomacy, and the use of non-military tactics all formed part of the grey zone in the eyes of Australian foreign policy-makers. More broadly, the intensification of grey zone activity underlines that a conceptual split between conventional and non-conventional security threats was an increasingly prominent – and problematic – feature of contemporary international politics.

CONVENTIONAL SECURITY CHALLENGES: THE US ALLIANCE AND GREAT-POWER RIVALRY

Great-power rivalry is hardly a new issue for Australian foreign policy-makers. Between 1976 and 1980, for instance, superpower relations loomed large in *Australia in World Affairs*, with a prediction of 'deteriorating fortunes for the Western alliance and rising prospects for the Soviet Union' and a description of Australian policy, focused on 'balance of power activism, of a traditional kind' (Boyce & Angel, 1983: 36).

Similarities can be found in the 2016–20 period, which saw Australia attempting to manoeuvre through a landscape of superpowers while trying to retain regional influence. Previously, successive Australian governments had sought a pragmatic foreign policy orientation largely defined by engagement with both the United States (its security partner) and China (a key economic partner). While the US alliance might be interpreted as an act of taking sides, leaders insisted that Australia did not need to choose between its security and economic interests and could engage with both great powers. While China was still biding its time, this was a strategy that worked for Australia and allowed it to pursue prosperity and security simultaneously through engagement with those two powers (Tow, 2017). Yet Hugh White (2017) described this as Australia's inability to grapple with strategic rivalry and China's preparedness to contest US regional primacy. The emergent rivalry between the great powers put Australian policy-makers in an increasingly difficult position and made problematic the bipartisan preference for 'pragmatic' approaches towards the great powers.

Two examples from 2016 illustrate Australia's conundrum. First, the election of Donald Trump as President of the United States created a focus on allies as alleged free riders. Trump demanded that they 'burden share' and promised a more insular 'America First' posture in response to globalisation and the economic rise of China. This rhetoric was not limited to the election campaign: at a national security address in 2017, Trump argued that '[previous leaders] failed to insist that our often very wealthy allies pay their fair share for defence, putting a massive and unfair burden on the US taxpayer and our great US military' (Trump, 2017).

The second event was Beijing's rejection of the ruling by the Permanent Court of Arbitration in the Hague in 2016, which invalided its claims to historic rights to the islands and waters within the so-called nine-dash line in the South China Sea. During the Obama administration's second term, the Communist Party of China (CPC) had changed the status quo by creating and militarising artificial islands. For many in Australia, China's rejection of the international tribunal's findings was symbolic of the revisionist intentions of Xi Jinping's newly assertive China. With an entirely new model of leadership in the White House, the growing might of a potential regional hegemon put new pressures on Australia's capacity to navigate the emergent strategic competition.

These two events played into the dominant strategic anxiety tropes in Australia: that the dependability of the United States as an ally and security guarantor was not necessarily assured and that an increasingly confident and powerful Beijing would challenge US regional leadership and destabilise the region's existing security and economic order, which had served Australia's national interests so well.

The alliance between the United States and Australia – centred upon the 1951 ANZUS security treaty – had long been considered the central pillar of Australia's security policy, and it generally attracted strong public and bipartisan support (Chubb & McAllister, 2021). As such, the alliance was at the core of many Australian security discussions during this period, with the need to maintain the centrality of the alliance weighed against concerns that Australia lacked agency and independence. Leaders sought to assure international and domestic publics that the alliance reflected shared political interests and values and had 'never been a straitjacket for Australian policy-making' (Turnbull, 2017a). Indeed, previous editions of this series have emphasised the dilemmas of excessive strategic dependence: between 1996 and 2000, for example, the narrative that Australia was the United States' 'deputy sheriff in Asia' was viewed as damaging to Australia's regional credibility as an independent actor.

In the 2016–20 period, questions were raised about the reliability of the US, particularly after the election of Trump. In the context of conversations in Washington about 'alliance free-riding', the administration sought to reassure Australia that the alliance was 'unbreakable' (Pompeo, 2019), and in 2018, the US Congress passed a resolution recognising '100 years of the United States–Australia relationship' (US Senate, 2018). Yet, across the region, numerous diplomatic posts remained unfulfilled for several years, including the one in Canberra. The relationship between Australia and the United States had a tense beginning as Trump criticised an Obama-era agreement that Turnbull had negotiated on refugee resettlement. Australian leaders exchanged views in public and parliament about what Trump would mean for the security alliance, particularly given that the new President had upended established norms of US foreign policy and the global liberal order (see Chapter 7). This fuelled concerns about the US purpose and intentions as a leader and principal guarantor of regional stability. And while Trump's withdrawal from negotiations towards the Trans-Pacific Partnership (TPP) was primarily viewed through the lens of Australia's Asian trade strategy (Chubb, 2017), there were security implications insofar as it reinforced these broader concerns about the steadfastness of the US commitment to Asia. In time, these debates about US domestic politics and foreign policy under Trump faded into the background, and they had little influence on the centrality of the alliance to Australia's security.

The Coalition government reinforced Australia's commitment to the US alliance to Australian security interests, particularly in bilateral relations and defence cooperation. Prime Minister Scott Morrison in 2019 matched the US rhetoric by promising the United States 'another 100 years' mateship during a trip to Washington in which he was treated to a state dinner (Murphy, 2019). Defence cooperation was enhanced. In the maritime domain, for example, Australia and the United States increasingly coordinated naval activity in the Indo-Pacific, including integrating the participation of US forces in Australia's Indo-Pacific Endeavour. Australia's commitment to the Strait of Hormuz operation in 2019, ostensibly to protect freedom of navigation in the Gulf region, provided Australia with another opportunity to highlight its alliance dependability to the United States; only two other states (the United Kingdom and Bahrain) joined the coalition. Developments on the Korean peninsula led by North Korea's testing of Inter-Continental Ballistic Missiles (ICBM) compelled Prime Minister Turnbull to declare that Australia would join the conflict if North Korea attacked the United States as ANZUS would be invoked (Dziedzic, 2017). Australia remained engaged in US-led operations in Afghanistan, and in 2019 the number of US Marines in the Marine Rotation Force Darwin reached its full complement of 2500. The United States and Australia also reinforced their commitment to securing a stable Indo-Pacific region and deterring coercive acts and the use of force at the annual Australia-United States Ministerial Consultations (AUSMIN) meetings and in joint statements on such issues as Xinjiang, Hong Kong and the South China Sea.

The United States was a beneficiary of Australia's increased defence procurement, as it is one of the largest importers of American arms. The 2016 Australian Defence White Paper committed Australia to increasing defence spending to 2 per cent of GDP, a goal achieved in 2020. From 2017 to 2020, the Forum on the Arms Trade (2022) reported, Australia bought defence goods worth more than US$6 billion from the United States, including four modified Gulfstream G550 aircraft worth US$1.7 billion and long-range anti-ship missiles worth almost US$1 billion. The first of Australia's new maritime surveillance aircraft, the P-8A Poseidon, was welcomed to the Royal Australian Air Force in November 2016, following the 2016 Defence White Paper commitment to purchase 15 of the aircraft through the defence cooperation scheme. Twelve Boeing EA-18G 'Growler' airborne electronic attack aircraft acquired through the United States Navy under a Foreign Military Sales (FMS) agreement were delivered to Australia in 2017 (Department of Defence, 2022).

While Australia's belief in the endurance of a regional status quo led by US primacy eroded over time, this did not necessarily provoke doubts about Australia's dependence upon the United States or its commitment to the region. If anything, the 2020 Defence Strategic Update vision of a 'poorer, more dangerous, and more disorderly' world

(Roggeveen, 2020) led Australian leaders to recommit to the US alliance as the cornerstone of its security policy, rendering debates about choosing sides largely irrelevant.

In 2016 and 2017, some analysts were concerned that Australia was not doing enough to counter or negotiate China's aggressions at home and across the region. According to Chubb (2017: 277), the Turnbull government's 'cautiously calibrated' approach was characterised by critics in Washington as evidence of Canberra's 'strategic ambivalence'. The South China Sea issue demonstrated that despite Australia's commitment to the US alliance, it did not always toe the American line, even under intensifying great-power competition. In US strategic competition narratives, the South China Sea exemplified Chinese revisionism threatening the global rules-based order. The militarisation and artificial island-building between 2014 and 2016 had left the United States and its allies and partners, including in maritime South-East Asia, wondering what strategies they might undertake to reverse the PRC's gains, or at least maintain the status quo and prevent the South China Sea becoming a closed sea controlled by China. The Trump administration's response was to increase the regularity of Freedom of Navigation Operations (FONOPs) and encourage so-called 'likeminded' allies such as Australia to engage in US-style operations as well. While concerned about China's actions in the South China Sea, Australia avoided committing to FONOPs, not by directly saying 'no' to US officials but by reaffirming its unique approach to the problem, which was to conduct presence operations but avoid transiting within 12 nautical miles of land features claimed by China (Strating, 2020).

The South China Sea dispute was not the only matter between the great powers that complicated Australia's navigation of its major power relations, which followed a pattern of escalating tensions and strategic resets. Beijing increasingly used 'grey zone' tactics to assert its influence and create divisions between the United States and its allies, including through economic coercion and the use of foreign interference campaigns to influence political decision-making and democratic processes (see Chapter 5). The challenge for Australia was to address the security risks that proliferated outside traditional domains of defence and security, including in domestic politics and economics.

China's international activities, including the island-building and militarisation in the South China Sea, the Belt and Road Initiative, the mounting evidence of ethnic cleansing and cultural genocide in Xinjiang, and the erosion of democratic rights in Hong Kong, raised concerns among security planners in Australia. These officials became increasingly concerned that China was asserting its interests in ways that were inimical to Australia's strategic interests. An example was in the Pacific. One of the biggest developments in Australian foreign policy over this period was the Pacific 'Stepup', which was a response to China's activities and the implications of its Belt and Road Initiative to Australian interests in the South Pacific (see Chapter 12).

RESPONSES TO CONVENTIONAL SECURITY CHALLENGES

In 2016, the Turnbull government responded to China's rejection of the ruling by the Permanent Court of Arbitration by imploring Beijing to respect the rules-based order (Bishop, 2016), a concept that became increasingly dominant in Indo-Pacific discourses as a proxy term for a US-led regional order that reflected anxieties about the assertiveness and potential revisionism of a rising China (Bisley & Shreer, 2018). As part of the emerging Indo-Pacific concepts adopted by several states within and beyond Asia, the Quadrilateral Security Dialogue (the Quad) among the United States, Japan, India and Australia returned to prominence in 2017.

Australian strategists began to take seriously a region and/or world in which US primacy was no longer a feature (Dean, Freuhling & Taylor, 2014). The Defence of Australia (DoA) concept returned in the 2020 Strategic Defence Update, which made extensive investments in maritime long-range missiles and offensive cyber capabilities, aimed at improving Australia's offensive capabilities. The update highlighted concerns that an increasingly powerful and assertive China was destabilising the regional security order, which would imply that Australia needed to invest in defensive capabilities and become more self-reliant while also deepening its security cooperation with the United States. These concerns were also reflected in the reimagining of Australia's strategic neighbourhood as the Indo-Pacific (see Chapter 11). The update, which was described by one commentator as the 'most hawkish turn in Australia's defence policy' in two generations (Camilleri, 2020), justified higher levels of defence spending on the grounds of unprecedented strategic uncertainty.

Although it consistently referred to the rules-based order, the Morrison government's stance on multilateralism was less consistent. The appeal of multilateralism for Australia as a middle-sized country has long been evident in the *Australia in World Affairs* series, beginning with Australia's activities at the United Nations in the early 1950s. In the 1961–65 edition, for instance, Foreign Minister Paul Hasluck articulated principles of multilateralism that sound remarkably contemporary. He was quoted as saying that full international security 'could only be obtained when power was restrained by the acceptance of agreed principles of international conduct and when national states recognised that those in possession of power must pledge to restrict its use' (Greenwood & Harper, 1968: 35).

The so-called Morrison doctrine was guided by a 'sovereignty first' approach to international relations, and the Prime Minister criticised 'negative globalism' in a 2019 speech at the Lowy Institute. The rhetoric was partly a reflection of the need to shore up 'sovereign' resilience in the face of 'grey-zone' security threats presented by rising powers, particularly in the domestic political, economic and cyber realms. Yet it was also driven by the disjuncture between international rules-based rhetoric and domestic policy interests: negative globalism was negative because it criticised Australia's failure to fulfil its international responsibilities in such areas as climate change and asylum-seekers.

This emphasis on domestic sovereignty created its own problems, however, when the government was criticised for undermining multilateralism and the rules-based order. Foreign Minister Marise Payne issued a defence of multilateralism, arguing that 'at the heart of successful international cooperation is the concept that each country shares, rather than yields, a portion of its sovereign decision-making' (Payne, 2020). The mixed messaging highlighted the longer-term presence of distrust towards global institutions and multilateralism within the Coalition parties (Wesley, 2007). In the security realm, a preference for sidestepping traditional institutions, like the United Nations, emerged as novel forms of regional cooperation, such as the Quad-style 'minilaterals', became increasingly favoured.

Nevertheless, it was hardly feasible for a middle-sized state to abandon multilateralism. The desire to strengthen relations with the Association of South-East Asian Nations (ASEAN) was evident in the period under review. Indeed, 'ASEAN centrality' became an increasingly important diplomatic phrase, partly used to offset concerns about the new primacy of an 'Indo-Pacific' centred around the Quad. As a bloc, ASEAN was Australia's third-largest two-way trading partner after China and the European Union, representing more than 15 per cent of Australia's trade (DFAT, 2020a).

A significant landmark was the hosting of the ASEAN–Australia Special Summit in Sydney in early 2018. The summit was organised by the Prime Minister and Cabinet's office rather than DFAT, at a cost to Australia of A$56 million (Earl, 2017). This was the first time that the summit had met in Australia, and the resultant Sydney Declaration called for 'a new era in the increasingly close ASEAN–Australia relationship' (Department of Prime Minister and Cabinet, 2018). The summit, participants declared, had reaffirmed Australia and ASEAN as 'partners with a vital stake in a dynamic region undergoing major changes' committed to intensifying their 'shared work to shape a secure and prosperous region' (Department of Prime Minister and Cabinet, 2018). These efforts to engage ASEAN – including through the A$550 million COVID-19 relief funding for South-East Asia announced in 2020 – were presumably intended to counter China's growing influence in the region.

Great-power relations remained a challenge for Australia's security policy. On the one hand, the unpredictable Trump administration failed to shift Australia substantively away from the US alliance. On the other hand, non-military threats to security posed by bigger powers – particularly China – underscored the difficulties in distinguishing between conventional and non-conventional security challenges. The 'China challenge' moved Australia away from its 'pragmatic' policy settings as it recommitted to the US alliance, pursued stronger relations with other non-great powers via the Indo-Pacific concept, and reaffirmed its sovereignty.

UNCONVENTIONAL SECURITY THREATS: THE CASE OF THE PANDEMIC

In addition to its traditional security challenges, and the ongoing quest for balance between multilateral, bilateral and great-power relations, Australia faced a number of unconventional security challenges during the period under review. These challenges were unconventional in three senses: first, they stemmed from non-state actors; second, some of the challenges were caused by non-military and even non-political developments, such as climate and pandemic; and finally, they were 'grey zone' challenges, in that they took the form of something other than peaceful acts or acts of war. We argue that unconventional security threats became increasingly prominent in Australia's foreign policy and arguably should have attracted a commensurately higher degree of attention. In this section, we focus on the security impact of COVID-19.

The COVID-19 pandemic served as an important reminder of how unconventional security threats can swiftly become serious crises. Australia's response to COVID-19 illustrated that sometimes the most mundane aspects of economic life can result in serious security problems.

Before 2020, pandemics usually counted as one of many unconventional security threats about which states should be worried while not being a prominent inclusion on such lists. In the 2013 National Security Strategy, for instance, pandemics were not mentioned in the pillars of national security, nor did they qualify as a key national security risk. The strategy did, however, state that the government was 'preparing for pandemics and bio-threats by stockpiling vaccines' (Department of the Prime Minister and Cabinet, 2013: 21). In a 2019 speech, Home Affairs Secretary Michael Pezzullo warned of seven 'gathering storms' of the 2020s, which did not include pandemics. In 2020, by contrast, Australia saw first-hand the short-term security impacts of a pandemic, as well as several often-forgotten security vulnerabilities.

The pandemic revealed some vulnerabilities in Australian security. For example Australia's extensive dependency on maritime shipping increased substantially during the pandemic, rendering the preservation of shipping routes even more important (Hatch, 2020). COVID-19 was a useful reminder that Australia imports many of the raw materials used in fertiliser and that supply restrictions can damage the agricultural sector (Sim, 2020).

COVID-19 also highlighted how serious threats tend to defy conventional categorisations of foreign and domestic policy, and within these categories, the silos created by different policy departments. It altered, potentially permanently, how Australian political leaders marshal collective action through the creation of a National Cabinet of premiers and the Prime Minister, an institution created in March 2020 that was so effective that two months later Scott Morrison announced that 'COAG [Council of Australian Governments] is no more' (Menzies, 2020). COAG had been the main forum for coordination between the state and federal governments since 1992.

Finally, COVID also created another shift in Australian security policy: the use of the military to deal with unconventional threats within Australia. At its peak in September 2020, more than 3500 ADF personnel were deployed as part of Operation COVID-19 Assist, providing personnel for border control checkpoints, contact tracing, the support of quarantine arrangements and other logistical tasks (Department of Defence, 2020a).

UNCONVENTIONAL THREATS AND CONVENTIONAL RESPONSES

As Sara Davies (2017) argued in the previous volume of *Australia in World Affairs*, Australia has tended to respond to unconventional security threats, such as terrorism and migration, through a traditional security framework. Threats of this type are not state based, and migration at least does not have a military component. However, in the period under review they were increasingly managed in the same way as conventional security policy, relying on legislative tools and drawing on military and policing resources. These challenges were difficult to resolve. In the case of migration, the process began with events in other countries, over which Australia had limited control. Many of the root causes of terrorism likewise emanated from outside Australia, although home-grown terrorism emerged as a new cause of concern.

According to Davies, Australia 'has a tradition of locating the governance of people smuggling and people trafficking in traditional security areas such as border control, deterrence and immigration control' (2017: 148). The use of military and paramilitary means to control migration continued unabated between 2016 and 2020, and Australia's response to illegal migration was not significantly debated during the 2019 election.

Terrorism may be an unconventional security threat, in that terrorists are non-state actors who use a variety of unconventional methods, but it became a prominent feature of security policy in Australia after the September 11 attacks in 2001. Australia's anti-terrorist legislation has been adapted to deal with new variants of terrorist threat, including attempts to prevent the outflow of 'foreign fighters' to overseas conflicts and their subsequent return to Australia. By way of illustration, since 2006 more than 50 pieces of legislation related to terrorism have been presented to the Australian parliament, which is more than any other Western society (Billings & Ananian-Welsh, 2020: 176). However, Australia's policy on terrorism straddles both the domestic and foreign policy spheres, with implications for the conduct of both regular politics and the institutions responsible for public safety.

The phenomenon of Australian 'foreign fighters' joining conflicts in Syria and Iraq demonstrates the degree to which terrorism blurred the lines between the domestic and foreign policy realms. Approximately 250 Australians fought for ISIS, placing Australia among the biggest per capita suppliers of recruits to the movement (Safi & Evershed, 2014: 1; Angus, 2016). Security planners worried that if Australians joined terrorist movements overseas, they would return further radicalised and better equipped to plan attacks at home (Hegghammer, 2013; Klausen, 2014). According to the Victoria Police's (2018) *Counter Terrorism Strategy 2018–2021*, jihadist terrorism remained the primary threat.

A major consideration for security planners was how to prevent would-be fighters from radicalising and leaving Australia to take part in overseas conflicts. The government had to consider how to treat Australians detained overseas, how to prevent their return and how to reduce their influence if they did return. The Turnbull and Morrison governments leveraged the traditional response to terrorism, which was to rely on domestic legislation to deal with an overseas problem. They passed the *Foreign Fighters Act 2018* (Cth) and revised the *Australian Citizenship Amendment (Allegiance to Australia) Act 2015* (Cth), with the goal of revoking the citizenship of dual nationals who engaged in terrorism or who became foreign fighters (Moulds, 2020: 74).

This new approach, however, presumed that terrorism *would* blur the lines between the foreign and the domestic: that foreign influence might radicalise religiously inspired domestic jihadists or that terrorists would travel to Australia to conduct attacks. It also presumed that the primary terrorist threat to Australia remained an Islamist one. However, there were indications that terrorist threats could also spring from purely domestic sources.

The Christchurch terrorist attack, the deadliest in New Zealand history, was perpetrated by an Australian citizen in 2019. The incident underscored the rise of right-wing terrorism. ASIO called this threat a 'serious, increasing and evolving threat to security' (Basford Canales, 2020). As with all terrorist organisations, regardless of political or religious allegiance, right-wing terrorists drew support from across the world (United Nations Counter-Terrorism Committee Executive Directorate, 2020; Waldek, Ballsun-Stanton & Droogan, 2020). Nonetheless, it was unclear whether Australia's policy response would shift from its focus on Islamist groups to an expanded view that includes the radical right. Despite ASIO's announcement that up to 40 per cent of its caseload involved far-right activity (Karp, 2020), in February 2021, a Senate motion condemning far-right extremism in the wake of the US Capitol riots only passed after far-left extremists, communists and anarchists were included in the statement. Alex Hawke, the immigration minister, denied that right-wing extremism was growing in Australia (Karp, 2021).

There was also an increased focus on the possibility of cyberattacks, especially after a well-publicised denial of service attack hindered the conduct of the Australian census in 2016 (MacGibbon, 2016). In 2020, Defence Minister Linda Reynolds argued that the 'new normal' of cyberattacks 'really does blur what we previously understood to be peace and war, which is what we call that grey zone in between' (Probyn, 2020). Cyberattacks may emanate from state actors, which blurs the conventional lines between peace and war, but they also have a complex relationship with terrorism: the plotters of terrorist attacks may use cyber activities as a weapon and use sophisticated cyber encryption to hide their communications (Zammit, 2015: 16; Zerzri, 2017).

Most Australians were becoming increasingly aware of their personal cyber security, but the reality of cyberespionage became starkly apparent during the period under review. In September 2020, it was revealed that a Chinese company with links to the government had created a database of detailed information on 2.4 million people, including 35,000 Australians, from both open-source material and apparently some confidential records (Probyn & Doran, 2020).

Australia's responses to these unconventional threats resulted in significant institutional change. In July 2017, Prime Minister Turnbull announced the creation of a new Office for National Intelligence, which would incorporate the former Office for National Assessment and increase the coordination (and thereby the capacity of) Australia's security, intelligence and law-enforcement services (Turnbull, 2017b). The government also announced the creation of a new department and minister of Home Affairs, incorporating immigration, border protection, and domestic security and law-enforcement agencies. The new department was designed to respond to the increase in unconventional threats to Australia's domestic security, including those posed by foreign fighters, cyberattacks and foreign interference campaigns.

While these unconventional threats resulted in some institutional changes, in many ways the response to these threats remained resolutely conventional. Australia again created new legislation to deal with terrorism, a pattern that began in 2001; and it redrew the institutional and intelligence boundaries to bring together the relevant agencies into more efficient forms but without introducing any new players. These responses demonstrated that policy-makers were taking unconventional threats seriously, although it was arguable whether the threats should still be considered 'unconventional', given the time and attention they demanded from the government. That said, one difference in Australia's response to these threats was the crossover between domestic and foreign affairs, and the new institutional stature of Home Affairs, which was put in charge of formulating cross-governmental responses. It is unlikely that previous editions of *Australia in the World* would have needed to consider such an extensive role for domestic agencies in Australia's security outlook.

Australia continued to use its existing capacities in ways that blurred the lines between international and domestic spheres. The potential and realised impact of climate change, for instance, increasingly became part of the national security agenda. The Chief of Defence Force Angus Campbell argued in 2019 that 'Australia is the most natural disaster-prone region in the world' and that 'climate change is predicted to make disasters more extreme and more common', which would have a considerable impact on the ADF's commitment and capabilities (Clarke, 2019). In response to the severe bushfires during the summer of 2019–20, more than 6500 ADF personnel provided emergency relief, response and recovery as part of Operation Bushfire Assist (Department of Defence, 2020b). In late 2020, the government sought to make legislative changes giving the ADF more powers to respond to domestic emergencies, partly as a response to the Bushfire Royal Commission (Rimmer, 2020). The Australian military appears likely to play a role in domestic emergencies in the future.

An increased awareness of climate security was evidenced in the 2017 Foreign Policy White Paper, which outlined how climate change could lead to security challenges in the next decade (DFAT, 2017: 33). Despite such statements, as well as the lived reality of the bushfires, Australia was reluctant to change its climate policy, partly due to the shared scepticism of the Trump administration (see Chapter 9).

COVID-19 underscored that security challenges which are noted as real but distant prospects sometimes eventuate. It is therefore prudent to consider threats that have not yet caused serious problems or have not eventuated. An illustrative example was Australia's increasing focus on the security impact of telecommunications, especially the cabling needed for high-speed internet access in the Pacific Islands. The government agreed to pay for the Coral Sea Cable between Sydney and the Pacific Islands after it had banned Huawei from connecting the network to Australia's broadband system on the advice of ASIO (Loughran, 2018). Australia's decision (along with Japan and the United States) to finance an undersea cable to Palau (DFAT, 2020b) shored up Palau as a pro-Taiwan regional ally (Rej, 2020), while also ensuring the security of the cable.

Australia's international telecommunications were also vulnerable to challenge. The vast majority (97 per cent) of the world's internet and telecommunications data travels via undersea cables (Chew, 2018). Natural disasters have occasionally disrupted these connections, but human-induced disruptions have also caused significant damage. Between August 2006 and March 2007, 500 kilometres of Vietnamese underseas cable was stolen for its copper wiring, and 82 per cent of data traffic to Vietnam was lost for three months (Chew, 2018). Underseas cables could also be tapped, designed with backdoors to allow the theft of information, or severed to slow communications (Schadlow & Helwig, 2020).

Damage to undersea cables is not science fiction. Before its takeover in 2014, Russia cut all communications from Crimea and used mini-submersibles to sever or tap undersea cables (Sunak, 2017). There have also been reports that cables built by China's Huawei Marine had been accessed by the Chinese government (Schadlow & Helwig, 2020).

Security threats are not always predictable. Even when we are aware that a vulnerability exists, we might not have the mechanisms in place to counter threats when they arrive. COVID-19 revealed that despite repeated concerns over the impact of a pandemic, no state was truly prepared for what would happen. But if planners had not even considered the possibility of a pandemic, the outcome would have been far worse. Unconventional threats therefore need to remain a permanent feature of Australian security planning.

CONCLUSION

Australia's security landscape experienced both substantial continuity and significant change in the period under review. The strategic environment became increasingly defined by traditional realist balance-of-power preoccupations, precipitated by the rise of China. Australia's strategic preoccupations shifted from international terrorism back to more conventional concerns about the balance of power and strategic competition. The new rising hegemon, China, was firmly placed in the Asia Pacific, traditionally Australia's primary strategic theatre. The leadership commitments of the United States in this region were under great scrutiny, and China's rising confidence as a global power and the US domestic challenges intensified Australia's anxieties (see Chapter 6). Yet alongside the return of great-power politics, Australia managed other 'non-conventional' challenges. The defining characteristic of the period was increasing strategic uncertainty.

Our analysis has shown that Australia experiences significant challenges from unconventional security threats, but its response was mainly through conventional means. Some threats brought in different agencies or government departments, but responses tended to take a conventional government form once threats were challenging enough to be treated as matters of national security. The more serious the threat, the more likely it was that the government would bring in a variety of departments. In the case of terrorism, the threat spurred a reorganisation of the departments and processes involved in the policy process. Many of the unconventional threats outlined here straddled the international and domestic realms, a trend that seemed likely to accelerate. If the ADF, which is notionally responsible for the external aspects of Australian security, becomes increasingly involved in domestic emergencies, these lines are likely to blur further. In effect, considering 'Australia in the world' in terms of its security requires considering 'Australia at home'.

Another implication of our analysis is that while Australia faced an uncertain future in terms of the regional security challenges, and uncertainty about the unconventional threats that it might face, its responses continued to draw on defence, the military and the traditional security apparatus. This came at a time when the funding of the Department of Foreign Affairs, at 1.3 per cent of the federal budget, was at its lowest ever level (Tyler & Vandewerdt-Holman, 2019) and Australia's international aid program had experienced years of decline (Development Policy Centre, 2020). Australia's military and security institutions were undoubtedly part of the solution to conventional and unconventional threats alike, but it was unclear how Australia could ensure the long-term cooperation of its regional neighbours without a robust aid program to cope with challenges such as climate change. A functional diplomatic corps would seem essential to guiding Australia in its uncertain strategic future.

References

Angus, C. (2016) *Radicalisation and Violent Extremism: Causes and Responses* [e-brief]. NSW Parliamentary Research Service

Basford Canales, S. (2020) The 'increasing and evolving threat' taking up more of ASIO's time. *Canberra Times*, 16 October

Bell, C. (1988) *Dependent Ally: A Study in Australian Foreign Policy*. Oxford: Oxford University Press

Billings, P. & Ananian-Welsh, R. (2020) Counter-terrorism and the exclusion of refugees and refugee citizens from Australia. In J.C. Simeon (ed.), *Terrorism and Asylum*. Leiden: Brill

Bishop, J. (2016) *Australia supports peaceful dispute resolution in the South China Sea*. Press release, 12 July. https://www.foreignminister.gov.au/minister/julie-bishop/media-release/australia-supports-peaceful-dispute-resolution-south-china-sea

Bisley, N. & Shreer, B. (2018) Australia and the rules-based order in Asia. *Asian Survey* 58(2): 302–19

Boyce, P.J. & Angel, J.R. (1983) *Independence and Alliance: Australia in World Affairs 1976–80*. Sydney: George Allen & Unwin and Australian Institute for International Affairs

Camilleri, J. (2020) It's time to strip 'national security' of its sacred cow status. Part 1. *Pearls and Irritations*

Chew, A. (2018) *Protecting the Cloud Under the Sea: Submarine Cable Infrastructure*. Corrs Chambers Westgarth Insights

Chubb, D. (2017) Issues in Australian foreign policy, July to December 2016. *Australian Journal of Politics and History* 63(2): 270–83

Chubb, D. & McAllister, I. (2021) *Australian Public Opinion, Defence and Foreign Policy*. Singapore: Palgrave Macmillan

Clarke, M. (2019) Climate change could stretch our capabilities, Defence Force chief speech warns. *ABC News*, 25 September. https://www.abc.net.au/news/2019-09-25/australian-defence-force-angus-campbell-climate-change-speech/11543464

Davies, S.E. (2017) Asylum seekers and Australia's security. In M. Beeson & S. Hameiri (eds), *Navigating the New International Disorder: Australia in World Affairs 2011–2015*. Melbourne: Oxford University Press

Dean, P.J., Freuhling, S. & Taylor, B.(2014) *Australia's Defence: Towards a New Era?* Carlton: Melbourne University Press

Department of Defence (DOD) (2016) *Defence White Paper 2016*. Canberra

——(2020a) Latest updates – Operation COVID-19 Assist. https://www.defence.gov.au/operations/covid19-assist

——(2020b) Operation Bushfire Assist concludes. https://www.minister.defence.gov.au/media-releases/2020-03-26/operation-bushfire-assist-concludes

——(2022) Growler airborne electronic attack capability. https://www.defence.gov.au/project/growler-airborne-electronic-attack-capability

Department of Foreign Affairs and Trade (DFAT) (2017) *Foreign Policy White Paper*. https://www.dfat.gov.au/publications/minisite/2017-foreign-policy-white-paper/fpwhitepaper/index.html

——(2020a) *Trade and Investment at a Glance 2020*. https://www.dfat.gov.au/publications/trade-and-investment/trade-and-investment-glance-2020

——(2020b) Australia partnering with Japan and the United States to finance Palau undersea cable. https://www.dfat.gov.au/news/media-release/australia-partnering-japan-and-united-states-finance-palau-undersea-cable

Department of the Prime Minister and Cabinet (2013) *Strong and Secure: A Strategy for Australia's National Security*. https://apo.org.au/node/33996

——(2018) *Joint Statement of the ASEAN–Australia Special Summit: The Sydney Declaration*. Sydney. https://aseanaustralia.pmc.gov.au/Declaration.html

Development Policy Centre (2020) *Australian Aid Tracker Trends*. Canberra. https://devpolicy.org/aidtracker/trends/

Dziedzic, S. (2017) North Korea: Australia would support United States in conflict, Malcolm Turnbull says. *ABC News*, 11 August. https://www.abc.net.au/news/2017-08-11/australia-would-enter-conflict-with-north-korea/8796586

Earl, G. (2017) Economic diplomacy brief: Summit budges and mixed messages from Australia's foreign investment. *Interpreter*, Lowy Institute, 18 May. https://www.lowyinstitute.org/the-interpreter/economic-diplomacy-brief-summit-budgets-mixed-messages-australia-s-foreign

Forum on the Arms Trade (2022) Major arms sales (via FMS) notification tracker. https://www.forumarmstrade.org/major-arms-sales-notifications-tracker.html

Greenwood, G. & Harper, N. (1968) *Australia in World Affairs 1961–1965*. Melbourne: Cheshire for the Australian Institute of International Affairs

Hatch, P. (2020) Questions over exports as air cargo volumes nosedive. *Sydney Morning Herald*, 17 August. https://www.smh.com.au/business/companies/questions-over-exports-as-air-cargo-volumes-nosedive-20200816-p55m69.html

Hegghammer, T. (2013) Should I stay or should I go? Explaining variation in western jihadists' choice between domestic and foreign fighting. *American Political Science Review* 107(01): 1–15

Karp, P. (2020) ASIO reveals up to 40% of its counter-terrorism cases involve far-right violent extremism. *Guardian*, 22 September. https://www.theguardian.com/australia-news/2020/sep/22/asio-reveals-up-to-40-of-its-counter-terrorism-cases-involve-far-right-violent-extremism

——(2021) Coalition deletes references to far-right extremism in Senate motion. *Guardian*, 4 February. https://www.theguardian.com/australia-news/2021/feb/04/coalition-deletes-references-to-far-right-extremism-in-senate-motion

Klausen, J. (2014) They're coming. *Foreign Affairs*, 1 October. https://www.foreignaffairs.com/articles/iraq/2014-10-01/theyre-coming

Loughran, J. (2018) Huawei's undersea internet cable banned by Australia over spying fears. *E & T Magazine*, Institution of Engineering and Technology

MacGibbon, A. (2016) *Review of the Events Surrounding the 2016 eCensus*. Office of the Cyber Security Special Adviser. Canberra: Department of the Prime Minister and Cabinet

Menzies, J. (2020) Explainer: What is the national Cabinet and is it democratic? *Conversation*, 31 March. https://theconversation.com/explainer-what-is-the-national-cabinet-and-is-it-democratic-135036

Moulds, S. (2020) *Committees of Influence: Parliamentary Rights Scrutiny and Counter-Terrorism Lawmaking in Australia*. Singapore: Springer

Murphy, K. (2019) Scott Morrison lands in US promising 'another 100 years' of friendship. *Guardian*, 20 September. https://www.theguardian.com/australia-news/2019/sep/20/scott-morrison-lands-us-promising-another-100-years-friendship

Payne, M. (2020) Australia and the world in the time of COVID-19. Speech. Canberra: National Security College, Australian National University, 16 June

Pompeo, M. (2019) The US and Australia: The unbreakable alliance. Speech. State Library of NSW, 4 August. https://2017-2021.state.gov/the-u-s-and-australia-the-unbreakable-alliance/

Probyn, A. (2020) Cyber attacks on Australia blurring the lines between peace and war, Defence Minister says. *ABC News*, 4 September. https://www.abc.net.au/news/2020-09-04/cyber-attacks-on-australia-peace-war-defence-minister/12626396

Probyn, A. & Doran, M. (2020) China's 'hybrid war': Beijing's mass surveillance of Australia and the world for secrets and scandal. *ABC News*, 14 September. https://www.abc.net.au/news/2020-09-14/chinese-data-leak-linked-to-military-names-australians/12656668

Rej, A. (2020) Australia, Japan, US trilateral partnership to fund undersea cable for Palau. *Diplomat*, 31 October. https://thediplomat.com/2020/10/australia-japan-us-trilateral-partnership-to-fund-undersea-cable-for-palau/

Rimmer, S.H. (2020) Should the ADF take a bigger role in bushfires and other domestic emergencies? The answer isn't so easy. *Conversation*, 17 November. https://theconversation.com/should-the-adf-take-a-bigger-role-in-bushfires-and-other-domestic-emergencies-the-answer-isnt-so-easy-147188

Roggeveen, S. (2020) Morrison's defence reset. *Interpreter*, Lowy Institute, 1 July. https://www.lowyinstitute.org/the-interpreter/morrison-s-defence-reset

Safi, M. & Evershed, N. (2014) Australians fighting in Syria: How many have joined the conflict? *Guardian*, 9 April. https://www.theguardian.com/world/datablog/2014/apr/09/australians-fighting-in-syria-how-many-have-joined-the-conflict

Schadlow, N. & Helwig, B. (2020) Protecting undersea cables must be made a national security priority. *Defense News*, 2 July. https://www.defensenews.com/opinion/commentary/2020/07/01/protecting-undersea-cables-must-be-made-a-national-security-priority/

Sim, T. (2020) Fertiliser prices staying low, but COVID-19 supply warning. *Sheep Central*, 20 March. https://www.sheepcentral.com/coronavirus-global-concerns-hit-australian-lamb-seller-confidence/

Strating, B. (2020) Australia lays down the law in the South China Sea dispute. *Interpreter*, Lowy Institute, 25 July. https://www.lowyinstitute.org/the-interpreter/australia-lays-down-law-south-china-sea-dispute

Sunak, R. (2017) Undersea cables: Indispensable, insecure. *Policy Exchange*, 1 December

Tow, S. (2017) *Independent Ally: Australia in an Age of Power Transition*. Carlton: Melbourne University Press

Trump, D. (2017) National security strategy address. Washington: The White House. December. https://trumpwhitehouse.archives.gov/wp-content/uploads/2017/12/NSS-Final-12-18-2017-0905.pdf

Turnbull, M. (2017a) Press conference. Parliament House, Canberra

——(2017b) A strong and secure Australia. Media release, 18 July. Canberra: Department of the Prime Minister and Cabinet

Tyler, M.C. & Vandewerdt-Holman, M. (2019) Australia's incredible shrinking Department of Foreign Affairs and Trade. *Mandarin*, 28 October. https://www.themandarin.com.au/118942-australias-incredible-shrinking-department-of-foreign-affairs-and-trade/

United Nations Counter-Terrorism Committee Executive Directorate (2020) *Member States Concerned by the Growing and Increasingly Transnational Threat of Extreme Right-Wing Terrorism*. CTED Trends Alert, April. https://www.un.org/securitycouncil/ctc/sites/www.un.org.securitycouncil.ctc/files/files/documents/2021/Jan/cted_trends_alert_extreme_right-wing_terrorism.pdf

US Senate (2018) Resolution 324. Congressional Record – Senate

Victoria Police (2018) *Counter Terrorism Strategy 2018–2021*. Docklands

Waldek, L., Ballsun-Stanton, B. & Droogan, J. (2020) After Christchurch: Mapping online right-wing extremists. *Interpreter*, Lowy Institute, 24 November. https://www.lowyinstitute.org/the-interpreter/after-christchurch-mapping-online-right-wing-extremists

Wesley, M. (2007) *The Howard Paradox: Australian Diplomacy in Asia, 1996–2006*. Sydney: ABC Books

White, H. (2017) *Without America: Australia in the New Asia. Quarterly Essay 68*. Melbourne: Black Inc

Zammit, A. (2015) *Australian Foreign Fighters: Risks and Responses*. Sydney: Lowy Institute

Zerzri, M. (2017) *The Threat of Cyber Terrorism and Recommendations for Countermeasures*. CA·Perspectives on Tunisia, Center for Applied Policy Research

A perfect storm?

Climate change and Australian foreign policy

Matt McDonald

Wholly separating the domestic and the international in Australian foreign policy is difficult, if not impossible. Nowhere is this more immediately evident than with the issue of climate change, which is a genuinely global issue in scope and impact, even if that impact is uneven. It is also an issue that needs international cooperation if it is to be effectively addressed. Australia has regularly professed to be committed to playing a constructive and engaged role in the international climate regime, although it rarely claimed to be a 'good international citizen' in this issue area in the period under review in this volume. Instead, Australia's position on climate change was driven by domestic political considerations from 2016 to 2020. The conservative Turnbull and Morrison governments only committed to minimal emissions-reduction targets and limited policy instruments to realise these in the face of growing international pressure, and even in the face of damage to other foreign policy goals, such as expanding Australia's engagement with the Pacific Islands (see Chapter 12).

Australia's approach to climate change was not simply a story of the triumph of domestic over international considerations. Rather, a particular set of domestic considerations came to win out over other domestic *and* international concerns and interests, both in the period under review and in earlier times.

This is despite Australia being clearly vulnerable to climate change. This was evident in the immediate effects of higher temperatures on health, the implications of changing rainfall patterns for agriculture, and the increase in the frequency and severity of natural disasters. The catastrophic bushfires of 2019–20 demonstrated the scale of this vulnerability. Domestic support for climate action continued to grow, not least because of these bushfires (Lowy Institute, 2020). And the prospects for coal exports – lauded by Prime Minister Scott Morrison as a crucial driver of Australian economic growth – significantly deteriorated in the five years under review.

For these reasons, Australia's position on climate change was not simply the triumph of domestic considerations over international ones. National interests are not self-evident but are a site of significant and sustained contestation. This was true in the period under review, when the government began to feel the effects of international pressure on climate change and struggled to articulate a convincing case to the Australian public that its position was consistent with national interests and national values. How did the government come to view the national interests in this way, and how sustainable was its position in the face of growing domestic and international pressure to change its stance? Might a more enlightened position be possible?

This chapter reflects on these questions while examining Australia's approach to climate change, especially as a dimension of foreign policy. It first discusses Australia's approach to the international climate regime and the commitments made under the Paris Agreement, before examining the influence of changes in leadership from Turnbull to Morrison and election outcomes in the period under review. The third section examines the growth in domestic pressure for political action on climate change that stemmed from the 2019–20 bushfires and their aftermath, before shifting to the international pressure on Australia. The chapter concludes with a reflection on the state of climate politics and policy in Australia at the end of this period, and whether it might be possible to move beyond the 'toxic politics' of climate change that has long characterised Australia's engagement with this issue.

FROM RIO TO PARIS

Few countries have undergone greater shifts than Australia in their approach to the UN Framework Convention on Climate Change (UNFCCC), the central international instrument of the climate change regime (see McDonald, 2016a; Eckersley & McDonald, 2014; Parr, 2019). Before the UN Conference on Environment and Development (the 'Earth Summit') in 1992, when the UNFCCC was established, the Hawke Labor government had advocated binding emissions targets and committed itself to an interim planning target for greenhouse emissions reduction that was among the most significant in the world. At the Earth Summit itself, however, Australia's passion for climate activism had waned under the Keating government. But a broader commitment to 'good international citizenship' seemed to drive efforts to play a constructive role in addressing this transnational issue (McDonald, 2005).

Keating's ambivalence on climate action gave way to outright opposition to such action – and support for the rapid expansion of fossil fuels – under the Howard government. As was noted in Lorraine Elliott's (2001) chapter in the 1996–2000 iteration of *Australia in World Affairs*, Howard's approach to the Kyoto Protocol in 1997 was obstructionist. Australia secured generous concessions, including an 8 per cent *increase* in its emissions from 1990 levels by 2008–12, and the controversial inclusion of land-clearing rates in baseline emissions calculations, in response to its threat to walk away from the agreement (see Hamilton, 2001; McDonald, 2005). Howard's later, unsuccessful attempt to establish the Asia-Pacific Partnership on Clean Development and Climate was interpreted by many as a direct challenge to the Kyoto Protocol and the UNFCCC itself (McGee & Taplin, 2009).

The end of the Howard era in 2007 precipitated another sea change in Australian climate diplomacy. Obstructionism was replaced by outspoken climate activism, at least at the international level, by new Prime Minister Kevin Rudd. After winning what some commentators described as the 'world's first climate election' (Rootes, 2008) and declaring climate change the 'great moral challenge of our generation', Rudd took one of the largest national delegations to the Conference of the Parties (CoP) meeting in Bali in 2008. He also took on the role of 'friend of the chair' at the CoP meeting in Copenhagen in 2009 (see

McDonald, 2016a). His failure to pass climate legislation, in the form of the Carbon Pollution Emissions Reduction Scheme, contributed to his fall from power. Julia Gillard represented something of a mirror image of Rudd, in that she shied away from grandiose statements and the international limelight but oversaw the passage of the most significant piece of climate legislation passed in Australia to date: the *Clean Energy Act of 2011* (Cth).

Tony Abbott's election as prime minister in 2013 ushered in another major shift in climate politics with Abbott casting the election as a referendum on Gillard's 'carbon tax'. His government subsequently repealed the legislation. For the first time, Australia did not send a ministerial-level representative to the first CoP after he won power. Abbott's 'Direct Action Plan' legislation gave sizeable subsidies to companies that promised to reduce emissions, with only minimal effects on Australia's overall emissions. Emissions steadily increased following the repeal of the *Clean Energy Act 2011* (Cth). In mid-2015 and in response to the need for states to identify a national target before the Paris climate talks, Abbott announced a target for Australia of a 26–28 per cent reduction in greenhouse gas emissions by 2030 from 2005 levels, a target roundly criticised as inadequate. He was deposed by moderate Malcolm Turnbull in 2015, just months before the Paris Climate talks and soon after announcing Australia's emissions target. This was in part a response to the growing gap between Abbott's limited climate ambitions and the expectations of the Australian public (see McDonald, 2015).

Australia's position at the Paris climate talks was ambiguous. Prime Minister Turnbull offered the same targets and the same policy instruments, despite being much more concerned about the threat posed by climate change than his predecessor. Turnbull was also eager for Australia to take a constructive (even if not leading) role in the Paris negotiations. Australia was swept along with the momentum of global support for substantive action in Paris and agreed to support the goal of limiting global temperature rises to 1.5 degrees. Although initially not a member, Australia belatedly lobbied to become part of the 'Coalition of High Ambition', a group of states pushing for a strong Paris Agreement (Elliott, 2016).

The Paris Agreement came into force in November 2016, an event overshadowed by the results of the US presidential election earlier that month. Republican candidate Donald Trump had questioned climate science during his campaign and referred to climate change as a 'hoax'. He declared the Paris Agreement a 'bad deal' that would 'impose enormous costs on American households through higher electricity prices and higher taxes' (see Selby, 2019). In mid-2017 he announced that the United States would withdraw from the agreement altogether, a move that would take effect in November 2020, immediately after the next presidential election. As the world's second-largest emitter, and the country responsible for more than 15 per cent of global emissions, the US position had significant implications for the agreement itself and broader momentum for action on climate change. Trump's stance also reduced the pressure on Australia to adopt a meaningful position on this issue: conservatives could argue that Australia remained in the agreement, although there was minimal pressure to revise climate diplomacy.

FROM 'MODERATE MALCOLM' TO 'SCOTTY FROM MARKETING'

Prime Minister Turnbull was relatively progressive – at least compared to others in the Coalition parties – on the issue of climate change. As leader of the Opposition in 2008–09 he had attempted to persuade the Coalition to work with Prime Minister Rudd on the development of climate legislation, noting: 'I will not lead a party that is not as committed to effective action on climate change as I am' (ABC, 2020a). This position proved to be his downfall, precipitating a leadership spill triggered by Turnbull's announcement in late 2009 that he would support the Commonwealth Procurement Rules (CPRS) legislation. The initial insurrection was unsuccessful, but within a month Turnbull had lost the leadership to Tony Abbott, who promised to resist the passage of Rudd's climate legislation.

Turnbull's return to the leadership in 2015 was seen as a shift away from Abbott's adversarial stance on a range of issues, including climate change. But after regaining the leadership Turnbull appeared to be spooked by his own experience with climate politics. He announced no new target for emissions reduction, at Paris or subsequently, and the widely criticised Direct Action Plan remained the centrepiece of the Coalition's climate position ahead of the 2016 election (McDonald, 2016b).

The election was crucial for Turnbull and for the trajectory of climate policy. The Prime Minister hoped that victory would strengthen his mandate within the party room and allow him to pursue more ambitious policy on such issues as climate change. But Turnbull's victory was much closer than expected and did not provide the mandate he had hoped for. This undermined his capacity to push for significant climate action, even while he claimed to be personally committed to this goal (ABC, 2020a). Turnbull's experience in 2018 in trying to secure support for the National Energy Guarantee (NEG), an energy policy designed to address rising power prices, energy infrastructure and (indirectly) rising emissions, had parallels with his efforts to promote climate action in 2009. Even as he took direct responsibility for advancing the NEG in late 2018, rumblings within the government suggested a challenge was imminent.

The successful challenger – Scott Morrison – had a questionable background in respect to climate policy. Famously, in February 2017, as Treasurer, he had brandished a piece of coal in parliament during Question Time and held it aloft saying: 'This is coal. Don't be afraid. Don't be scared' (Murphy, 2017). But the moniker 'Scotty from Marketing', applied by the satirical news outlet *Betoota Advocate* in reference to the Prime Minister's previous vocation, captured the general sense that Morrison, while less progressive than Turnbull, was also less of an anti-climate ideologue than Tony Abbott. Morrison seemed to be a pragmatist within the party room and a master of spin outside it, securing his position as the middle ground between moderates like Turnbull and arch-conservatives such as the Home Affairs Minister, Peter Dutton.

In the lead-up to the 2019 election, however, the prospects for the Morrison government's re-election were not promising. Climate change loomed as an Achilles heel for the government. Australia's greenhouse gas emissions were continuing to increase, raising doubts about its capacity to reach even the modest Paris targets, while public support for stronger action continued to grow. Although relatively cautious in its climate position before the election, and eager to avoid accusations of introducing a 'carbon tax 2.0', the Labor opposition promised a more significant emissions target of 45 per cent and the introduction of the NEG that the Coalition had abandoned after Turnbull's demise.

Yet the climate election that had been mooted did not eventuate, and Morrison was re-elected. Climate policy did not win the election for the Coalition (Cameron & McAllister, 2020), but the anti-Adani coal mine convoy's trek to Queensland before the election encouraged the view that there was a climate policy schism between a poorer rural constituency and elite city-dwellers. The Prime Minister greeted his victory party by asking 'How good is Queensland?' (Tranter & Foxwell-Norton, 2019).

The second half of 2019 seemed to validate the concerns of advocates for climate action who had hoped for a change of government. With new modelling showing Australia on track to exceed its Paris targets significantly, the government said it would use 'carry-over credits' from the Kyoto Protocol period to let Australia reach its targets. Having secured generous concessions as part of Kyoto, the government had reduced emissions beyond these targets and wanted these surplus reductions (or 'credits') to be reflected in its new targets for the Paris Agreement. For advocates of climate action, this was a case of a government searching for loopholes rather than effective policy and practices aimed at emissions reduction (Morton, 2019). It appeared that problematic concessions were being used in the service of questionable legal arguments (see Foley, 2020).

Climate change also featured prominently in Australian foreign policy and diplomacy in 2019. Morrison's attendance at the Pacific Islands Forum in August 2019 – his first international trip since the election – saw the government criticised by Pacific Island states for its climate policy and targets, and specifically for the Prime Minister's watering down of a forum communiqué about the dangers of climate change to the region (see Handley, 2019). Even the announcement on the eve of the forum that Australia would commit $500 million to enhance climate resilience in the region did not assuage these concerns. Some noted the government's decision to cease funding for the Green Climate Fund, the central international financial mechanism for transferring resources to climate resilience and mitigation initiatives in developing states (Graue, 2019).

The Prime Minister was also criticised for his failure to attend the UN Climate Summit in New York only a few weeks later. It was particularly telling that this non-attendance was despite Morrison being in the United States at the time, where he found time to visit and attend rallies with President Trump (Probyn, 2019). Foreign Minister Marise Payne attended, but Australia was not among those countries invited to address the summit, which indicated that the UN Secretary General did not believe Australia had sufficient ambitions on the issue (Smoleniec, 2019).

Elections were significant for climate ambition and action in the period under review. Turnbull's narrow win in 2016 undermined the position of moderates on climate policy within the Coalition government, while the 2019 election kept progressive voices out of power.

AFTER THE FIRES?

For Australia, a key threat associated with climate change is the increase in the frequency and severity of natural disasters. In 2019 much of the country was declared to be in drought, with severe implications for plants, animals, agricultural output and the viability of rural communities. The Asia-Pacific region is also vulnerable to natural disasters. According to the Asian Development Bank, the Asia Pacific is home to 70 per cent of the world's countries that are most prone to climate change and natural disasters; more than 40 million people were displaced in 2010–11 alone (ADB, 2012: viii). There have been growing calls for Australia to undertake humanitarian assistance and disaster relief missions in the Pacific, especially in response to tropical cyclones (Bergin, Press & Garnsey, 2013).

Most Australians' concern about climate change has tended to be linked to natural disasters, especially drought, which has helped to overcome some of the traditional division between rural and urban citizens on this issue (Wahlquist, 2017). But the focus has usually been the more immediate (and dramatic) threat of bushfires. In Australia, higher temperatures and reduced rainfall associated with climate change mean an increasing number of high-risk fire days, increasing the quantum of dry fuels and soils, and limiting the time window for safely conducting fuel-reduction burning, or 'back-burning' (see Sharples et al., 2016). All these conditions were evident in the second half of 2019, when Australia suffered some of the worst bushfires in its history.

Every state in Australia was affected by bushfires in late 2019, but the worst were in Victoria and New South Wales. By the time the bushfires had subsided in early 2020, the scale of devastation was catastrophic. Close to 20 million hectares of forest had been burnt, and more than a billion animals perished. Whole communities were evacuated, more than 30 people lost their lives in the fires, and hundreds more died of respiratory illnesses linked to smoke haze in Sydney, Melbourne and Canberra (Pickrell, 2020). The fires made international headlines and underlined the relationship between these events and climate change (see McDonald, 2020b).

The response of the government was controversial. Morrison was criticised for taking a family holiday in Hawaii when the crisis was reaching its peak in December 2019. Upon his return Morrison announced the deployment of significant ADF resources and called up 3000 reservists to help with the recovery. He also announced that the government would commit $20 million to lease more firefighting aircraft (ABC, 2020b).

The leasing of the aircraft was significant. In 2018, the acquisition of a permanent national firefighting fleet had been specifically recommended by a Senate Inquiry into the National Security Implications of Climate Change. The recommendation was rejected by the government at the time, and again when it featured as a recommendation of the Royal Commission into the fires that Morrison commissioned in February 2020. The 2018 Senate Inquiry into the National Security implications of climate change also identified the threat posed by climate change in terms of natural disasters and rising sea levels, displaced populations in the Pacific, defence preparedness, and the capacity to undertake more humanitarian and disaster relief missions in Australia and elsewhere. The report recommended a White Paper on climate security, new senior positions in Defence and Home Affairs, and more ambitious mitigation efforts. None of these recommendations was accepted by the government (see McDonald, 2020b).

Morrison's response to the suggestion that the bushfires were linked to climate change was telling. Saying he had 'always acknowledged the connection between these weather events and these broader fire events and the impacts globally of climate change', the Prime Minister noted that climate change was 'one of many factors' contributing to the fires (in Dalzell, 2019). When asked whether the bushfires had exposed the limits of Australia's approach to climate change or suggested the need for more action, Morrison rejected any change to targets or broader mitigation policy, suggesting only a commitment to building adaptive capacity and resilience in the face of the fires (Martin, 2020).

Acknowledgment of a potential link between bushfires and climate change was a step further than Abbott had managed (Guardian, 2013) but was still short of public expectations. As national and international attention to the bushfires grew, so too did pressure on Australia to alter its climate policy. The 2019 Lowy Poll indicated continued growth in concern about climate change, but it also showed that climate change was *the* most pressing threat to Australia's vital interests (Baker, 2019). This concern only increased after the fires.

A PERFECT STORM? THE PRESSURE BUILDS

The Morrison government attempted to weather a storm of domestic pressure on climate change following the bushfires, but international pressure also increased significantly. In 2019, Australia was ranked the worst of 57 countries on climate policy and ambition (Martin, 2019). The international response to Australia's mooted use of Kyoto carryover credits was damning, with Pacific Island states in particular criticising the proposal. Pacific leaders signed a letter to the Prime Minister condemning this approach and urged Australia to adopt a target for achieving net-zero emissions. They described Australia's climate targets as 'one of the weakest' (see Doherty, 2020).

The pressure from Pacific nations was significant for Australia, and not only because the region has been viewed as the moral conscience of global climate change. For Australia, the central issue was the gap between its proposed commitment to regional engagement on the one hand and Pacific responses to Australian climate policy on the other (see SBS, 2019). The so-called Pacific Step-up, introduced by Turnbull in 2016 and upgraded by Morrison in 2018, was a commitment to increasing engagement with the region (see Chapter 11). It included $1.4 billion in development assistance to the Pacific in 2019–20, a $2 billion infrastructure financing facility, an expanded Pacific Labour Mobility Scheme and an upgrading of telecommunications infrastructure in Papua New Guinea and Solomon Islands (see Wall, 2020). Yet as Pacific critics of Australian climate policy noted, the government's commitment to the region looked partial or even disingenuous if it did not take seriously the issue most important to the region itself: climate change. In this sense, Australian climate policy at home actively undermined a stated foreign policy objective.

The role of China was significant in this context too. The Pacific Step-up was assumed to be at base a response to China's growing presence and influence in the Pacific, which Australian strategic planners deem to be Australia's backyard. Beijing's extension of aid and infrastructure programs to the region, and increasing diplomatic presence, stoked Australian concerns of a more interventionist Chinese presence on Australia's doorstep (see SBS, 2019). Viewed in this light, a case could be made that the period under review demonstrated a capacity for Australian climate policy to undermine bilateral relations with other states in the region and to complicate regional strategic considerations. Although China is still the world's largest emitter, its stated commitment to reach net-zero emissions by 2060 put further pressure on Australia. By the end of 2020, Prime Minister Morrison could only state a preference for realising the goal of net-zero emissions 'as soon as possible' and 'preferably by 2050' (Malos & Skarbek, 2021).

South Korea and Japan, two of Australia's key trading partners and allies, as well as key markets for coal exports, also announced their intention to achieve net-zero emissions by 2050. This had implications for Australia in reputational terms, highlighting the degree of the government's international isolation on this issue. More than 70 countries had committed to a net-zero target for emissions by the end of 2020, including most developed states. With the election in late 2020 of Joe Biden to the US presidency, partly on a platform of rejoining Paris and ramping up US diplomacy and policy responses on climate change, the extent of Australia's isolation was striking. It was becoming more and more difficult to avoid the impression that Australia was a climate laggard, and one unable to convince international and domestic audiences that it was playing a constructive role in the climate change regime.

Australia's minimal emissions target and refusal to commit to a net-zero target left the government isolated diplomatically. But increasing international efforts on addressing climate change also had financial implications for Australia, undermining the long-term prospects for the fossil fuel sector (see Smee & Butler, 2020). This was significant given the argument often invoked by Australian conservatives: that coal exports were too important to jeopardise through climate activism and constituted a key driver of economic growth (see Murphy, 2017). The effects of the commitments of other states were immediate in the pricing signals they sent regarding the future of fossil fuels. Financial institutions in Australia and beyond had already indicated that they would not invest in new projects, and even mining corporations such as BHP had encouraged the government to embrace a net-zero target (Fernyhough, 2020). Meanwhile post-Brexit trade negotiations with the United Kingdom and the European Union saw Australia pushed on the issue of its emissions reduction targets, again demonstrating the possibility that normative concerns with the effects of climate change could have tangible material implications for Australia (see Potter, 2019). Even before addressing China's decision in late 2020 to apply import restrictions on Australian coal (Karp, 2020), the future of the fossil fuel sector was looking increasingly bleak.

To some degree, the onset of the coronavirus pandemic eased the pressure on the Morrison government with respect to climate change, especially in the first half of 2020. As Australia and much of the world went into lockdown, the imperative of responding to COVID-19 took precedence over other policy issues. Changes in emissions associated with the response, such as a significant reduction in emissions by the transport sector due to lockdowns, also meant the government getting closer to realising its Paris targets without the use of Kyoto credits (McDonald, 2020b).

But the declarations of net-zero targets by South Korea, Japan and China, the election of Biden and its flow-on effects for fossil fuel markets and Australia's coal exports, continued criticism from the Pacific, and pressure in trade negotiations with key economic partners, all contributed to a perfect international storm for Morrison by the end of 2020, when Australia retreated from its plan to use the Kyoto carryover credits to meet its Paris targets (McDonald, 2020b). The triumphant declaration of this plan demonstrated the extent of pressure on the Morrison government, even though Australia's ability to meet its targets could be mainly attributed to the climate policies of the states and territories and the short-term reductions resulting from COVID-19. The Prime Minister turned his attention to convincing members of his own government of the merits of embracing a net-zero target, suggesting that he had belatedly understood that even this minimal level of action was necessary.

CONCLUSION

As in other aspects of foreign policy, the position of great powers was significant for Australia between 2016 and 2020 with respect to climate change. China's net-zero emissions target, its engagement with and in the Pacific, and its boycott of Australian coal in late 2020 all put significant pressure on Australia. Under the Trump administration, meanwhile, the United States abetted Australia in its unwillingness to take meaningful action on climate change. A change in US policy seemed likely under Biden. These two great powers are both crucial partners for Australia, being its most important trading partner and security ally respectively, and both are significant contributors to global greenhouse gas emissions. As with so many issues covered in this volume, the position of the great powers on climate change was hugely consequential for Australia.

In late 2020, the final year in the period under review, the COVID-19 pandemic prevented CoP 26 from being held as scheduled in Glasgow. Despite the postponement of the meeting until 2021, there was growing international pressure for climate action. Australia was marginalised from global climate events, faced criticism from the Pacific Island states, and found itself isolated in its unwillingness to commit to net-zero targets for emissions. Its economic prospects also worsened due to a decline in the value of bulk commodities such as coal and the threat that proposed trade deals might penalise Australia if it did not revise its climate policy. This external pressure calls for change within Australia, which began building after the repeal of the *Clean Energy Act 2011* (Cth) in 2013 and was accelerated by the devastating effects of the 2019–20 bushfires. Representatives of the resources, financial services and agricultural sectors, such as the National Farmers Federation in Australia, advocated for action on climate change (Sullivan, 2020), which suggests that a perfect storm was brewing.

None of this is to suggest that a significant policy shift was in the offing. In Australia, bipartisanship on the issue has often given way to acrimony, global climate activism has been replaced by diplomatic ambivalence, policy breakthroughs by repeal, and moderates by ideologues. And public opinion has rallied behind climate action when it has appeared that governments are doing nothing while collapsing when they genuinely pursuing policy change. In this context it would be understandable if political leaders were wary of the issue, not least given the role of climate change in toppling party leaders, including prime ministers, since 2007. But if conservative political leaders live up to their commitment to allow economic considerations to inform their policy on climate change, it will be increasingly difficult to justify continued support and subsidies for the fossil fuels sector.

Australia's engagement with climate change in the period under review had wider implications for its reputation and foreign policy. Australia's reputation was damaged due to its climate policy, with criticism from the Biden administration as well as the Pacific Islands, Europe and in the United Nations. The government's unwillingness to set meaningful targets, as well as its steadily increasing emissions and support for fossil fuels, undermined other foreign policy goals and were increasingly at odds with the expectations of the Australian public. By the end of 2020 there was little basis for claiming that Australia's position on climate change was consistent with the promotion and realisation of its national interests, whether defined in reputational or economic terms, or in terms of the representation of the values of the Australian people. Australian political leaders have continued to offer at least rhetorical support for climate change, which suggests that they at least recognise that it is in the national interest to play a constructive role in resolving this significant global threat. But Australia will need to resolve the toxic politics of climate change if a meaningful change is to take place.

References

ABC (2020a) Malcolm Turnbull on how the Liberal Party operates behind closed doors. *7.30 Report*, 20 April. https://www.abc.net.au/7.30/malcolm-turnbull-on-how-the-liberal-party-operates/12167030

——(2020b) Bushfire response to be boosted by deployment of 3000 ADF reservists, Prime Minister announces. *ABC News*, 5 January. https://www.abc.net.au/news/2020-01-04/australia-defence-reservists-to-help-in-bushfire-recovery/11840764

Asian Development Bank (2012) *Addressing Climate Change and Migration in Asia and the Pacific*. Manila: ADB

Baker, N. (2019) Australians rate climate change a bigger threat than terrorism. *SBS News*, 8 May. https://www.sbs.com.au/news/australians-rate-climate-change-a-bigger-threat-than-terrorism

Bergin, A., Press, A. & Garnsey, E. (2013) *Heavy Weather: Climate and the Australian Defence Force*. Special Report 49, Australian Strategic Policy Institute. https://www.aspi.org.au/report/special-report-issue-49-heavy-weather-climate-and-australian-defence-force

Cameron, S. & McAllister, I. (2020) Politics and performance in the 2019 Australian federal election. *Australia Journal of Political Science* 55(3): 239–56

Dalzell, S. (2019) Scott Morrison says he accepts criticism for Hawaii holiday during bushfires. *ABC News*, 22 December. https://www.abc.net.au/news/2019-12-22/prime-minister-scott-morrison-hawaii-holiday-bushfires/11821682

Doherty, B. (2020) Pacific leaders condemn Australia's 'weak' climate target in open letter to Scott Morrison. *Guardian*, 1 December. https://www.theguardian.com/world/2020/dec/01/pacific-leaders-condemn-australias-weak-climate-target-in-open-letter-to-scott-morrison

Eckersley, R. & McDonald, M. (2014) Australia and climate change. In D. Baldino, A. Carr & A. Langlois (eds), *Australian Foreign Policy: Controversies and Debates*. Melbourne: Oxford University Press

Elliott, L. (2001) Australia in world environmental affairs. In J. Cotton & J. Ravenhill (eds), *The National Interest in a Global Era: Australia in World Affairs 1996–2000*. Melbourne: Oxford University Press

——(2016) The environment in Australia's foreign policy. In M. Beeson & S. Hameiri (eds), *Navigating the New International Disorder: Australia in World Affairs 2011–2015*. Melbourne: Oxford University Press

Fernyhough, J. (2020) Qantas, BHP lead in global corporate push for net zero. *Australian Financial Review*, 17 December. https://www.theguardian.com/environment/2020/dec/13/the-end-of-coal-why-investors-arent-buying-the-myth-of-the-industrys-renaissance

Foley, M. (2020) Kyoto carry-over credits 'baseless' in international law, experts say. *Sydney Morning Herald*, 4 March. https://www.smh.com.au/politics/federal/kyoto-carry-over-credits-baseless-in-international-law-experts-say-20200304-p546rw.html

Graue, C. (2019) Disappointment as Australia ends Green Climate Fund contributions. *ABC*, 3 April. https://www.abc.net.au/radio-australia/programs/pacificbeat/pac-climate-change-group-disappointed-by-aus-gov-gcf-cut/10965488

Guardian (2013) Tony Abbott: Australia's bushfires not linked to climate change. *Guardian*, 23 October. https://www.theguardian.com/world/video/2013/oct/23/tony-abbott-australia-bushfires-climate-change-video

Hamilton, C. (2001) *Running from the Storm: The Development of Climate Change Policy in Australia*. Sydney: UNSW Press

Handley, E. (2019) Australia accused of putting coal before Pacific 'family' as region calls for climate change action. *ABC News*, 16 August. https://www.abc.net.au/news/2019-08-16/australia-slammed-watering-down-action-climate-change-pacific/11420986

Karp, P. (2020) China formalizes cut to Australian coal imports, state media reports. *Guardian*, 15 December. https://www.theguardian.com/australia-news/2020/dec/14/china-formalises-cut-to-australias-coal-imports-state-media-reports

Lowy Institute (2020) Attitudes to global warming. *Lowy Institute Poll, 2020*. https://poll.lowyinstitute.org/charts/attitudes-to-global-warming

Malos, A. & Skarbek, A. (2021) Scott Morrison has embraced net-zero emissions – now it's time to walk the talk. *Conversation*, 4 February. https://theconversation.com/scott-morrison-has-embraced-net-zero-emissions-now-its-time-to-walk-the-talk-154478

Martin, S. (2019) Australia ranked worst of 57 countries on climate change policy. *Guardian*, 11 December. https://www.theguardian.com/environment/2019/dec/11/australia-ranked-worst-of-57-countries-on-climate-change-policy

——(2020) Scott Morrison to focus on resilience and adaptation to address climate change. *Guardian*, 14 January. https://www.theguardian.com/environment/2020/jan/14/scott-morrison-to-focus-on-resilience-and-adaption-to-address-climate-change

McDonald, M. (2005) Fair weather friend? Ethics and Australia's approach to global climate change. *Australian Journal of Politics and History* 51(2): 216–34

——(2015) Australian foreign policy under the Abbott government: Foreign policy as domestic politics? *Australian Journal of International Affairs* 69(6): 651–69

——(2016a) 'Australia and global climate change. In S. Smith, A. Hadfield & T. Dunne (eds), *Foreign Policy: Theories, Actors, Cases*. 3rd edn. Oxford: Oxford University Press

——(2016b) Election 2016: Climate politics off to a chilly start, but could still heat up. *Conversation*, 20 May. https://theconversation.com/election-2016-climate-politics-off-to-a-chilly-start-but-could-still-heat-up-59660

——(2020a) 3 reasons meeting climate targets and dumping Kyoto credits won't salvage Australia's international reputation. *Conversation*, 10 December. https://www.theguardian.com/australia-news/2020/dec/14/china-formalises-cut-to-australias-coal-imports-state-media-reports

——(2020b) After the fires: Climate change and security in Australia. *Australian Journal of Political Science* 56(1): 1–18

McGee, J. & Taplin, R. (2009) The role of the Asia Pacific Partnership in discursive contestation of the international climate regime. *International Environmental Agreements* 9: 213–38

Morton, A. (2019) Australia's Kyoto loophole eight times larger than entire Pacific emissions. *Guardian*, 14 August. https://www.theguardian.com/world/2019/aug/14/australias-kyoto-loophole-eight-times-larger-than-entire-pacific-emissions

Murphy, K. (2017) Scott Morrison brings coal to question time: What fresh idiocy is this? *Guardian*, 9 February. https://www.theguardian.com/australia-news/2017/feb/09/scott-morrison-brings-coal-to-question-time-what-fresh-idiocy-is-this

Parr, B. (2019) *Australian Climate Policy and Diplomacy*. Abingdon: Routledge

Pickrell, J. (2020) Smoke from Australia's bushfires killed far more people than the fires did, study says. *Guardian*, 21 March. https://www.theguardian.com/australia-news/2020/mar/21/smoke-from-australias-bushfires-killed-far-more-people-than-the-fires-did-study-says

Potter, B. (2019) Australia faces free trade agreement pressure to cut emissions. *Australian Financial Review*, 25 March. https://www.afr.com/politics/australian-faces-increased-pressure-to-cut-carbon–french-officials-20190324-h1cq7a

Probyn, A. (2019) Scott Morrison sucked into Donald Trump's orbit as the President takes the Prime Minister hostage. *ABC News*, 28 September. https://www.abc.net.au/news/2019-09-28/analysis-scott-morrison-captive-in-donald-trumps-orbit/11551394

Rootes, C. (2008) The first climate change election? The Australian general election of 24 November 2007. *Environmental Politics* 17(3): 473–80

SBS (2019) Pacific leaders tell Australia its step-up policy will fail without strong climate change action. *SBS News*, 5 August. https://www.sbs.com.au/news/article/pacific-leaders-tell-australia-its-step-up-policy-will-fail-without-strong-climate-change-action/dds6i56dq

Selby, J. (2019) The Trump presidency, climate change and the prospect of a disorderly energy transition. *Review of International Studies* 45(3): 471–90

Sharples, J.J., Cary, G.J., Fox-Hughes, P. et al. (2016) Natural hazards in Australia: Extreme bushfire. *Climatic Change* 139: 85–99. https://doi.org/10.1007/s10584-016-1811-1

Smee, B. & Butler, B. (2020) The end of coal? *Guardian*, 13 December. https://www.theguardian.com/environment/2020/dec/13/the-end-of-coal-why-investors-arent-buying-the-myth-of-the-industrys-renaissance

Smoleniec, B. (2019) Australia banned from speaking at UN climate change summit in unprecedented rebuke. *SBS News*, 19 September. https://www.sbs.com.au/news/australia-banned-from-speaking-at-un-climate-change-summit-in-unprecedented-rebuke

Sullivan, K. (2020) National Farmers Federation calls for Australia to reduce net emissions to zero by 2050. *ABC News*, 20 August. https://www.abc.net.au/news/2020-08-20/farmers-back-zero-emissions/12576806

Tranter, B. & Foxwell-Norton, K. (2021) Only in Queensland? Coal mines and voting in the 2019 Australian federal election. *Environmental Sociology* 7(1): 90–101

Wahlquist, C. (2017) Climate change: 90% of rural Australians say their lives are already affected. *Guardian*, 16 January. https://www.theguardian.com/environment/2017/jan/16/climate-change-90-of-rural-australians-say-their-lives-are-already-affected

Wall, J. (2020) The importance of Australia's Pacific step-up in the post-virus environment. *Strategist*, 24 April. https://www.aspistrategist.org.au/the-importance-of-australias-pacific-step-up-in-the-post-virus-environment/

10

Health security and Australian foreign policy

Sara E. Davies

In the period under review (2016–20), the Australian Government's health security diplomacy had a strong regional focus and resulted in the creation of the Indo-Pacific Centre for Health Security, located in the Department of Foreign Affairs and Trade (DFAT). Given the outbreak of the COVID-19 pandemic in late 2019 and early 2020, this initiative looked prescient. Its origins, however, lay in Australia's pursuit of health security amid its broader foreign policy in the early 2000s. Since that time, health security has undergone phases of engagement, disengagement and, in the period under review, re-engagement.

This chapter traces the history of health security in Australia foreign policy in four parts. First, the tradition of 'non-traditional security' is examined with consideration of the placement of health security in this lexicon. From its inception, it shows, Australia's health and foreign policy engagement was primarily engaged in promoting health security in a regional context. The second part examines the decline of Australia's engagement in health security followed by the re-establishment of health and foreign policy as a core theme in DFAT's global challenges during the period under review. A core component of the government's strategy, the chapter shows, was to create the Indo-Pacific Centre for Health Security. Finally, the chapter examines how Australia conceptualised its health and foreign policy role during the first year of the COVID-19 pandemic and the challenges that lie ahead.

NON-TRADITIONAL SECURITY, HEALTH AND AUSTRALIAN FOREIGN POLICY

In the previous volume of *Australia in World Affairs*, I noted that Australia's primary reference to non-traditional security from 2011 to 2015 related to onshore asylum-seekers and people-trafficking (Davies, 2016). Prime Ministers Gillard, Rudd and Abbott identified Australia's territorial integrity, rather than the populations being trafficked, as the primary referent object to protect. Most of the focus for Australian policy – and other countries in the region – was on state-led deterrence measures. As such, traditional security tools – border control, deterrence and immigration control – were used to respond to this 'non-traditional' security threat.

A human-centred appreciation of security – coined 'human security' by the United Nations Development Program (UNDP)'s *Human Development Report* (see MacFarlane & Khong, 2006) – sought to redefine 'traditional' security and draw attention to the issues that fall under 'non-traditional' security (Acharya, 2001). The term 'non-traditional security' developed a theoretical and pragmatic purpose. Theoretically, 'non-traditional' served to identify *'global* challenges (resource scarcity, climate change, changing demographics, increasing urbanisation, and corruption and cyber insecurity) as *central* themes in the government's national security outlook' (Elliott, 2012: 4; emphasis added). Advocates of 'critical security' called for a shift from objectives that centred on securing the state to securing individuals from harm (Buzan & Hansen, 2009).

In Asia, non-traditional security became a popular lexicon in the late 1990s and 2000s. It enabled high-level political conversations about incidents that were creating regional disharmony but were not necessarily being instigated by a state actor, such as terrorism, human trafficking, piracy, haze pollution and disease. It was sometimes difficult to discuss these issues in regional dialogues because some states lacked the institutional capacity to prevent these threats from spreading (Goh, 2013: 185).

Identification of non-traditional security threats remained the remit of states, but regional conversations began about burdens and responsibilities. An example of this was 'illegal' border arrivals. Australia's political institutions, military forces and borders were never at risk of destabilisation due to the arrival of illegal migrants, but the identification of these arrivals as a threat enabled diplomats and policy-makers to formulate a response to the issue. No state within the region, including Australia, wanted to provide permanent resettlement to all the asylum-seekers seeking refuge. Threat identification enabled the investment of social capital in military expenditure, the creation of regional frameworks that spread the burden of illegal migrants, and cooperative governance arrangements to manage the threat (Booth, 2008; Hameiri & Jones, 2012; Davies, 2016).

In 2017 the Australian Government released a Foreign Policy White Paper, which identified specific 'threats and interests' under the umbrella term of 'security'. Health and disease, however, did not appear in the list of Australian security interests. Instead, the government's first duty was to protect domestic democratic institutions and thereby keep Australians safe, secure and free (Department of Foreign Affairs [DFAT], 2017a: 6). The White Paper identified domestic and international 'threats' from which Australia needs to be secured, namely: countering terrorism and violent extremism; securing Australia's borders (from illegal migrants); tackling transnational organised crime; open, free and secure cyberspace; guarding against foreign interference; and assisting Australians overseas. The White Paper referred to non-traditional security only once, in relation to 'transnational crime' (DFAT, 2017a: 73), amid a total of eight references to security, but climate change, natural disasters and pandemics were not mentioned as potential threats at all.

As the White Paper revealed, the previous separation of 'traditional' from 'non-traditional' security threats disappeared from the government's thinking about security and threats to Australia. The use of 'non-traditional' security language, however, did not indicate a rethinking of referent objects. Across the Asia-Pacific region it was the state, not individuals, that remained the primary actor to be protected. If the White Paper was any guide, security threats were identified according to their impact on Australia's physical security rather than who or where they came from. Acts of terror, foreign interference and the 'illegal' arrivals of asylum-seekers were grouped together as 'equal' threats to Australia's security interests. The response to all these security threats was 'mitigation'. In the discussion on 'securing our borders', the primary objective was to mitigate criminal activity. Regional cooperation sought to improve 'their' border management capacity and 'disrupt' people-smuggling, and humanitarian assistance was delivered to ensure that people remain 'as close to their homes as possible' (DFAT, 2017a: 72).

Unlike its policy on refugees and people trafficking, the government did not refer to health security as a 'non-traditional security' issue. In the first two decades of the 21st century, with the rise of economic and social stresses from infectious disease outbreaks such as the Severe Acute Respiratory Syndrome (SARS), influenza and the Ebola and Zika viruses, global health security was increasingly referred to in foreign policy or defence departments as traditional (McInnes & Lee, 2012). For Australia, health security was understood in terms of two complementary traditional security lenses.

Australian engagement in health as a foreign policy priority was motivated by its economic and geographic proximity to locations where disease outbreaks occurred, such as SARS in 2003 and H5N1 Avian Influenza in 2004. After SARS emerged in mainland China in 2002 and 2003, there were fears that further outbreaks of novel infectious diseases were inevitable. An article in *Nature* (Jones, Patel, Levy et al., 2008) identified a decade-by-decade rising trend in emerging infectious diseases (EIDs). Between 1990 and 2000, 60 per cent of EIDs had emerged from zoonotic pathogens, or non-human animal sources. Most of these pathogens (71.8 per cent) originated in wildlife. Asia, and the Indo-Pacific region more broadly, became the 'hot zone' and the locale for responses to EIDs. Before SARS (2003) and the H5N1 human and poultry influenza infections (2004), the region had endured the Nipah virus, a zoonotic virus that originated in Malaysia (1998), and the Hendra virus, which was discovered in Australia (1994). Vector-borne viral diseases had also spread across Asia and the Pacific, including Japanese encephalitis, Ross River fever, Chikungunya viruses, dengue and Zika (Mackenzie, 2005). Multi-drug-resistant tuberculosis had also increased in the Pacific, while the incidence of HIV infection rates in the Asia-Pacific region was also substantial (Hill-Cawthorne, Negin, Capon et al., 2019).

The Australian Government's domestic policy on health security was to prepare its health defences from threats that originated outside its borders. As far back as the 1990s, the government had developed contingency plans should an influenza virus with pandemic potential *arrive* (not *originate*) in Australia: the federal government and the states would prepare stockpiles and use response mechanisms through a whole-of-government approach (Kamradt-Scott, 2018). An Influenza Pandemic Planning Committee was established in 1997 by the Communicable Diseases Network Australia, a National Medical Stockpile was created in 2002, and the National Health Security Act was passed in 2007. These 'defences' would later prove vital in coordinating Australia's response to COVID-19. Domestically, at least, health security was therefore seen as a traditional security threat that required secure borders, protected infrastructure and a whole-of-government response.

Australia's traditional health security lens became outward focused. It shifted and coalesced with the priorities of regional and international partners. The health component of foreign policy adopted more flexible language, approaches and initiatives to achieve regional and global cooperation. In response to the outbreak of SARS and H5N1, the government had, under the former development agency AusAID, been a significant donor and diplomatic partner to various health security diplomacy initiatives across Asia and the Pacific. As Adam Kamradt-Scott (2018) argued:

> For its part, the Australian Government – led by then Prime Minister John Howard – placed a heightened emphasis on strengthening pandemic influenza preparedness (PIP), both at home and abroad. Of the government's overall AUD$599 million PIP (Pandemic Influenza Preparedness) spending package that was announced between 2003 and 2008, some $141 million was designated to assist neighbouring countries strengthen their preparedness and a further $44 million to preventing H5N1 entering Australia.

Australia invested in bilateral health security packages across the Asia Pacific to support countries that were seeking to strengthen their health systems in response to pandemics. It also invested in regional and multilateral health security initiatives, including the first phase of the World Health Organization (WHO)'s Asia-Pacific Strategy for Emerging Diseases (2005–10) and the ASEAN+3 Emerging Infectious Diseases Program (2006). Australia chaired an intergovernmental meeting organised by the WHO in 2007 and 2008, which led to the adoption of the Pandemic Influenza Preparedness Framework.[1]

In 2009, the outbreak of H1N1 (influenza) and the declaration by WHO that this was a global pandemic seemed to vindicate Australia's investment in national and regional health security. Australia, however, soon diverted its attention to the rising number of asylum-seekers arriving in its waters between 2009 and 2012. Australia's commitment to its aid program weakened from 2012, and health security gradually receded as a foreign policy and aid priority. Australia continued to support regional health security initiatives, but there was not the same level of funding and diplomatic commitment as had existed under the Howard government.

AUSTRALIA'S RETURN TO HEALTH DIPLOMACY

Under the leadership of Foreign Minister Julie Bishop (2013–18), health security was again identified as a regional and global challenge that could align goodwill and strategic interests across Asia and the Pacific. The steps towards this return of interest seemed to be motivated by a combination of events and politics.

First, events. Bishop took up her position in 2013. In 2014, the Ebola virus spread across Guinea, Liberia and Sierra Leone, and soon threatened to reach the United States,

---

[1] The Pandemic Influenza Preparedness (PIP) Framework promotes virus sample sharing among WHO member states through the creation of a transparent standard material transfer agreement.

Singapore and the United Kingdom. Fearing that it too might become vulnerable, Australia adopted the *Health for Development Strategy 2015–2020* (Hill-Cawthorne, Negin, Capon et al., 2019; Kamradt-Scott, 2018).

In the aftermath of the Ebola outbreak, the Australian Government began to re-establish health as a priority for aid to Asia and the Pacific. In 2015, the government identified five 'investment pathways' to 'collectively address the region's health security challenges' (DFAT, 2015: 8). The concept of health security it developed was expansive. Some programs focused on specific infectious disease threats while others focused on strengthening health systems, universal access to health care, and cross-issue links, especially gender equality, disability, water and sanitation.

The 'Core public health systems and capacities in key partner countries' program, for instance, concentrated on funding public and private health systems. This program adopted an explicitly pro-gender, pro-poor and pro-disability focus to promote access to essential health services. In addition to supporting service delivery through training and capacity development, the program also aimed to strengthen civil society organisations to become active partners in health-care advocacy (DFAT, 2015: 9).

The second program, 'Combatting health threats that cross national borders', explicitly engaged with regional health 'risks' and 'threats'; 'namely, the spread of infectious disease outbreaks due to a combination of factors associated with weak governance and health system capacity' (Davies, 2018: 526). The program focused specifically on 'rapid urbanisation, the movement of people across and within borders, conflict, sub-standard medicines, unregulated health markets, and natural disasters. The highest priority disease threats are those that cross borders and potentially affect whole populations. They include preventable infectious diseases such as measles, TB, malaria, HIV, and human and animal-to-human influenzas in the Pacific and Asia.' (DFAT, 2015: 9)

The outbreak of Ebola in 2014–15 was referred to in the program, with specific mention of the humanitarian assistance provided to Guinea, Liberia and Sierra Leone. Nonetheless, the program was specifically focused on the Indo-Pacific region to harness 'political leadership, technical support, and financing mechanisms needed to address regional and cross-border infectious disease threats' (DFAT, 2015: 11).

The third program, 'A more effective global health response', was dedicated to funding the UN system, development banks and health funds like the Global Alliance for Vaccination and Immunisation (GAVI). The goal was to ensure that investments delivered on Australia's aid-effectiveness test.

The fourth program, 'Access to clean water, sanitation, hygiene, and good nutrition as pre-conditions for good health', was dedicated to improving water, sanitation and hygiene (WASH) and nutrition. It explicitly focused on addressing gender inequality, and sought to address the prenatal and postnatal risks stemming from insufficient access to safe water, the risks of infection and personal violence due to lack of access to sanitation, and the high burden of care that stems from a lack of access to water and sanitation (DFAT, 2015: 12–13). In the 2017–18 budget, the government announced that $100 million from the health budget would be used over five years for a 'Water for Women' initiative in the Pacific and South-East Asian regions. With a particular focus on disabled women, the initiative committed Australia to work with non-government organisations on 'innovative ways to improve water, sanitation, and hygiene services, focusing on women, girls and people with disabilities in the poorest communities' (DFAT, 2017a: 68).

The final program, 'health innovation, and new approaches and solutions that benefit our region', included $100 million over four years for a public–private partnership with Bloomberg Philanthropy Data for Health initiative. This program was focused on improving data-collection processes in developing countries and establishing the causal links between morbidity and mortality on the one hand and service delivery and resourcing on the other.

Despite these investments in health security and diplomacy, it remained unclear how much of a priority health security was in foreign policy. Some clues were provided in statements by such people as Robin Davies, who was then associate director of the ANU Development Policy Centre and later director of the Australian Government Indo-Pacific Centre for Health Security. According to Davies, the government was not doing enough to support its 'global challenge' programs, including climate change, refugees and health. The incorporation of the former aid agency AusAID into the Department of Foreign Affairs and Trade had hollowed out the technical program expertise and knowledge that had existed in AusAID. The health sector was especially weakened by the merger. Since 2012, successive governments had reduced the aid budget (Bruere & Hill, 2016). During Bishop's term in office, the struggle to secure funding and prevent budget cuts for DFAT intensified (Howes, 2018). Bishop latched on to challenges and themes to invigorate DFAT's appeal and sought to promote Australian research and investment opportunities that aligned with foreign policy goals (Howes, 2018; Kamradt-Scott, 2018). Bishop identified investment in research and capacity-building as diplomatic priorities, and by 2017 health security was slowly becoming a priority in the aid budget (Howes, 2018).

As noted earlier in the chapter, climate change and pandemics were mentioned in the 2017 Foreign Policy White Paper *but not as potential threats* to Australia's security and safety. Instead, the government referred to these issues as 'global challenges' (DFAT, 2017a: 3). The White Paper said Australia could offer 'solutions' to the region's technical and prosperity challenges (DFAT, 2017a: 5), but at the same time as the government announced the founding of the Indo-Pacific Centre for Health Security, health was not a spending priority. In the 2017–18 aid budget of A$3.9 billion, health came fifth out of seven sectors: 13.3 per cent of the budget was spent on health, compared to 22 per cent on governance, 18 per cent on education, 16.6 per cent on building resilience and 14.6 per cent on infrastructure and trade (DFAT, 2017b: vi). In the 2019–20 budget, health again ranked fifth in spending priorities (DFAT, 2019: 6). Moreover, there was a slight reduction in investment in global health programs, such as the World Health Organization and global health programs including GAVI, the Vaccine Alliance and Joint United Nations Programme on HIV/AIDS (UNAIDS), between 2016–17 and 2019–20.

The Pacific region received the largest contribution of bilateral aid followed by South-East Asia (DFAT, 2017b: 7–8; 2019: 6), but health in these regions was not a high investment priority: Before the outbreak of the COVID-19 pandemic in the Pacific, the health sector was fourth out of the seven priority areas (DFAT, 2017b: 12; 2019: 10). In South-East Asia, investment in health was sixth out of the seven priority investment areas (DFAT, 2017b: 28; 2019: 34). In other words, health security was still a niche area for Australian diplomacy. Despite the government's stated aim of strengthening technical engagement and investment in health security, the issue received little funding.

In 2017, Bishop announced the largest strategic health funding investment by her government to date, with a A$300 million investment over five years in the Health Security Initiative for the Indo-Pacific (Minister for Foreign Affairs, 2017). As noted above, this investment was not additional aid money. The Health Security Initiative was funded from the existing aid budget, thereby diverting funds from other initiatives (Howes, 2017). DFAT signalled its intent for the Health Security Initiative to receive most of the health aid funding and a high level of diplomatic and programmatic support in Asia and the Pacific. The signature feature of the new strategy was the Indo-Pacific Centre for Regional Health Security. Bishop stated that the purpose of the initiative and the centre was to 'strengthen health systems and invest in research and partnerships to mitigate the social and economic risks of a major disease outbreak' (Minister for Foreign Affairs, 2017). Upon its launch, four investment priorities were listed: promoting global and regional cooperation; catalysing international support; capitalising on Australia's strengths; and accelerating access to new products (Indo-Pacific Centre for Health Security, 2018; Davies, 2018).

The centre's primary geographical focus was the Pacific and South-East Asia, and it had a budget of $300 million over five years from 2017 (Indo-Pacific Centre for Health Security, 2018). It prioritised 'expanding partnerships at the national, regional and global level to strengthen human and animal health systems, and deepening people-to-people linkages that build national and regional health security capacity' (DFAT, n.d.b). In 2019–20, the centre's priorities were redesigned to encompass:

» **Anticipate:** To help countries assess their infectious disease threats and capacity deficits, and equip themselves with appropriate policy and regulatory arrangements, particularly with respect to access to medicines and vector control technologies.

» **Avert:** To mitigate infectious disease threats through support for improved infection prevention and control; vector control; and surveillance with respect to infectious diseases, immunisation coverage and treatment-resistance in pathogens and vectors.

» **Arrest:** To build capacity to detect and respond to infectious disease outbreaks through laboratory strengthening; targeted public health workforce development; and support for improved outbreak detection and management. (Indo-Pacific Centre for Health Security, n.d.: 2)

The challenges identified for the 2019–20 strategic framework were: Climate Change; People with Disability; Gender Inequality; and One Health. The priorities before the outbreak of COVID-19 were investment in research and development partnerships in the Pacific and South-East Asia, with the centre financing research in Systems for Health Security, Pacific Infectious Diseases Prevention, and ASEAN–Pacific Infectious Diseases Detection and Responses. These regional partnerships became the centre's focus for aid and diplomacy after the outbreak of COVID-19.

COVID-19, HEALTH DIPLOMACY AND AUSTRALIA'S REGIONAL ROLE

In 2020, DFAT released the *Partnership for Recovery: Australia's COVID-19 Response*, which detailed how the government would prioritise its development and diplomatic response during the crisis. Australia's priority focus was on the Pacific, Timor-Leste and Indonesia (DFAT, 2020: 7–8), and the three 'core action' areas would be Health Security, Stability and Economic Recovery. The Indo-Pacific Centre for Health Security would play 'a central role in the region's COVID-19 response' (DFAT, 2020: 9).

Beyond DFAT, the Department of Defence's 2020 Defence Strategic Update identified the long-term security implications of the COVID-19 pandemic and predicted its 'impact on regional growth, trade and societies will have lasting consequences' (DFAT, 2020c: para 1.14). There was a growing concern that pre-existing political fragility would hinder the surveillance and detection of disease outbreaks. Surveillance, detection and risk communication during disease outbreaks might be compromised in political environments with trust and transparency deficits (Davies, 2020). How to support neighbouring civilian governments during outbreak emergencies, without compromising the rule of law, was a growing concern for Australia (Australian National Audit Office, 2014).

In 2020, the government played an active international role in responding to COVID-19. Australia was one of the leading states in the May 2020 World Health Assembly (WHA) that called for the creation of an Independent Panel for Pandemic Preparedness and Response (IPPR) to review the international response to the COVID-19 outbreak. Australia joined the COVAX vaccine facility, a global vaccine cooperation initiative that was intended to secure equitable vaccine production and supply across low-, middle- and high-income countries through an advance market commitment. When announcing the creation of the IPPR in July 2020, the WHO's director general stated:

> The greatest threat we face now is not the virus itself. Rather, it is the lack of leadership and solidarity at the global and national levels. That is why I said each and every individual should reflect. This is a tragedy that is forcing us to miss many of our friends and lose many lives. And we cannot defeat this pandemic as a divided world. (WHO, 2020)

Australia supported the creation of the independent review. Prime Minister Morrison and his Cabinet questioned whether the WHO had acted fast enough to alert the international community to the virus. Diplomatic tensions between Australia and China escalated as the virus spread. By May 2020, at the WHA, Australia was less vociferous in its criticism of the WHO but supported the European Union's diplomatic effort to adopt a WHA resolution to create the IPPR. In September, Morrison voiced support for the WHO in his address to the UN General Assembly and emphasised the need to ensure global cooperation and equal distribution in the event of a COVID-19 vaccine discovery.

However, Australia's approach to the pandemic stood in contrast to its health security in the Asia Pacific since 2017. In devising international cooperation mechanisms in response to COVID-19, Australia was a joiner rather than a leader. Despite the ongoing cuts to its aid budget, Australia made new contributions to multilateral initiatives. In the October 2020 budget, after eight years of reduced contributions, the government maintained its contributions to UN organisations and agencies, including the WHO (Cornish, 2020).

Australia joined the COVAX vaccine facility in September 2020, three months after the announcement of the new vaccine initiative. The UN–WHO–GAVI COVAX facility was intended to secure vaccine production and supply at affordable prices and to guarantee a 20 per cent supply for all signatory countries. Across South-East Asia and the Pacific, most countries joined COVAX. There were 'real concerns', however, that the COVAX mechanism would not be able to purchase and secure enough vaccines to meet the 20 per cent coverage target by the end of 2021. Countries – including Australia – were going outside COVAX to secure their own supplies of vaccines from pharmaceutical companies. This, in turn, undermined the COVAX purchasing agreements with the same pharmaceutical companies. However, Australia also committed to donate vaccine purchases to the Pacific and South-East Asia, as 'part of a shared recovery for our region from the pandemic'. This was in addition to $80 million that the government invested in COVAX and $363 million investment in COVID-related vaccine and therapeutic research in Australia and overseas. It was estimated that Australia would need to invest approximately $200 million to support COVAX's goal of vaccinating 30 per cent of lower-income countries by the end of 2022.

Another proposed solution was to allow low- and middle-income countries to issue compulsory licences that would permit their own vaccine production. Australia did not initially support the India–South Africa joint submission, in October 2020, to waive temporarily the intellectual property rights on vaccines and other treatments protected under the World Trade Organization (WTO) Trade Related Intellectual Property Rights (TRIPs) agreement. By the end of 2020, there was growing support for the India–South African joint submission to the WTO among Asia-Pacific countries, with Australia and New Zealand being the outliers in not committing to support the submission.

Australia committed to making a substantial financial contribution to international efforts to respond to COVID-19. During the pandemic, and despite its earlier criticism of the WHO, Australia maintained its contribution to UN agencies and slightly increased its contributions to humanitarian organizations, including the International Committee of the Red Cross. The medium-to-long-term challenge for Australia would be to maintain political interest and budget support for investing in health diplomacy and cooperation.

Australia's earlier disengagement from health diplomacy was caused by a failure to sustain investment after changes of government. Investment in health diplomacy and technical cooperation through multilateral international (WHO) and regional organisations (ASEAN) significantly slowed, and emerging infectious disease programs did not maintain their momentum (Davies, 2019). Boat arrivals and the global financial crisis precluded sustained health diplomacy. Bishop's support for health diplomacy was motivated, in part, by a desire to ensure that Australia maintained a regional advantage in health partnerships and research in South-East Asia and the Pacific (Horton, 2017). Health was a low-risk strategic investment for a government that had been decreasing its aid budget. Again, the strategic turn to health in 2017 did not deliver more money but rather redirected it from other areas within DFAT. However, the government's COVID-19 recovery response clearly identified its interest – perhaps leadership – in health diplomacy in South-East Asia and the Pacific.

In March 2020, the government announced a $304 million 'Pacific Step-up' COVID-19 recovery package, and in September 2020 Australia announced a $60 million package of COVID-19 response and recovery initiatives to be run by ASEAN (DFAT, n.d.a; Minister for Foreign Affairs, 2020). The focus of diplomatic and development activity increasingly turned to health security. In contrast with the Howard era, the Morrison government signalled that the Pacific was a site of principal investment, and its diplomacy centred on sharing technical skills, logistics, and research geared towards response and recovery, in the form of personal protective equipment (PPE), polymerase chain reaction (PCR) tests and vaccines.

Technical-centred diplomacy continued the investments that were initiated as part of the Indo-Pacific Centre for Health Security. Before COVID-19, the centre had mainly facilitated technical and bilateral – rather than diplomatic and multilateral – partnerships. The emphasis was on promoting 'value for money' programs: distribution of personal protective equipment, research partnerships, and health scholarship exchanges between Australian experts and their counterparts in South-East Asia and the Pacific. The government, and the Centre itself, seemed to be comfortable with health diplomacy that delivered immediate and tangible results, such as deliveries of PPE and assistance with administering PCR tests in Timor-Leste. The lessons Australia gleaned from its regional engagement after SARS were that multilateral cooperation was too slow and that technical health investments would deliver the best results (Davies, 2019).

An opportunity, however, might have been lost. A collective regional response to COVID-19 would be more effective through the development of shared norms on health security. Some gaps emerged in the regional response where governments were uncertain of the respective economic and health gains in addressing COVID-19, and where marginalised populations, such as low-income earners, ethnic minorities and the poor, faced higher risks of infection or were unfairly affected by public health responses. COVID-19 revealed the cost of failing to ensure that rights-based approaches were included in health emergency preparedness planning and equitable access to vaccine development technology (Global Preparedness Board, 2020). In Australia and across the region, there was an opportunity to learn from these experiences and build a regional health challenge recovery plan that was inclusive and responsive.

The pandemic also pointed to a potential ongoing role for Australia in supporting regional health diplomacy. In the most affected South-East Asian countries, such as Indonesia and the Philippines, improving the capacity of health systems to cope with COVID-19 while also delivering primary health care and managing the economic fallout of the virus was politically and socially contentious (UNDP, 2020). Before the pandemic, South-East Asia seemed set for an intergenerational change that would lift most of the population out of extreme poverty. There was a risk that this would be reversed due to the pandemic. These political and social changes could drastically alter the economic trajectory for the region.

Australia's developmental diplomacy focused on sustaining the capacity of the region's health systems in response to the humanitarian crisis that some countries could face if COVID-19 cases continued to soar. Across the region there were vast discrepancies within countries in the availability of trained health-care workers, the production and supply of COVID-19 testing kits, the supply of vital medical equipment and the capacity to administer vaccines. Australian foreign policy could supply the logistical skills, materials and research to address these COVID-related challenges in the region. This was an ideal opportunity for Australia to cooperate with its counterparts in the Pacific and South-East Asia to better prepare for the next outbreak and within these technical preparations to ensure that a rights-based recovery and response system is built into programs.

CONCLUSION

The strategic turn to health in the period under review did not deliver significantly more money to this aspect of Australian foreign policy, but it did enable Australia to develop technical (especially research and development) partnerships across the region. DFAT's identification of health as a global challenge led to the development of five health security programs that sought to connect Australian research and development initiatives with regional partners. The Pacific and South-East Asia increasingly became partners rather than recipients of technical solutions. The challenge that remained, however, was sustaining Australia's political interest and long-term investment in these partnerships. Australia's pattern of engagement then disengagement in health security was a cautionary tale in this respect.

Despite the creation of the Indo-Pacific Centre for Health Security in 2017, health remained a low priority in Australia's aid budget. The challenges posed by the COVID-19 pandemic notwithstanding, Australia risked creating a diplomatic gap between rhetoric, policy and practice in the region. The centre allowed the government to self-promote its role in addressing health security, but Australia would be expected to deliver on its claims in the years to come.

In the period under review, Australia demonstrated its credibility and goodwill in health diplomacy in the Indo-Pacific region. Before the pandemic, Australia had sought to strengthen health security, health preparedness *and* health systems as part of its regional aid strategy. The test for future governments would be to maintain that interest and capitalise on the investment – and goodwill – in the long term.

References

Acharya, A. (2001). Human security: East versus West. *International Journal* 56(3): 442–60

Australian National Audit Office (2014) *Emergency Defence Assistance to the Civil Community*. Department of Defence. 16 April. https://www.anao.gov.au/work/performance-audit/emergency-defence-assistance-civil-community

Booth, K. (2008) *Theory of World Security*. Cambridge: Cambridge University Press

Bruere, W. & Hill, C. (2016) Changes to Australia's overseas aid program under the Abbott and Turnbull governments 2013–2016: Key policies and responses. Research Paper Series, 2016–17. Canberra: Parliamentary Library. http://parlinfo.aph.gov.au/parlInfo/download/library/prspub/4832715/upload_binary/4832715.pdf;fileType=application/pdf

Buzan, B. & Hansen, L. (2009) *The Evolution of International Security Studies*. Cambridge: Cambridge University Press

Cornish, L. (2020) The winners and losers in Australia's 2020 aid budget. Devex. 6 October. https://www.devex.com/news/the-winners-and-losers-in-australia-s-2020-aid-budget-98255

Davies, S.E. (2016) Asylum seekers and Australia's security. In M. Beeson & S. Hameiri (eds), *Navigating the New International Disorder: Australia in World Affairs 2011–2015*. Melbourne: Oxford University Press

——(2018) Gender empowerment in the health aid sector: Locating best practice in the Australian context. *Australian Journal of International Affairs* 72(6): 520–34

——(2019) *Containing Contagion: The Politics of Disease Outbreaks in Southeast Asia*. Baltimore: Johns Hopkins University Press

——(2020) A role for defence in accelerating regional health security. In S. Harris Rimmer, *How to Defend Australians: A Heterodox Approach*. Strategic and Defence Studies Centre, Australian National University. http://sdsc.bellschool.anu.edu.au/experts-publications/publications/7518/fresh-perspectives-security

Department of Defence (DOD) (2020) Department of Defence 2020 Strategic Update. https://www.defence.gov.au/about/strategic-planning/2020-defence-strategic-update

Department of Foreign Affairs and Trade (DFAT) (2015) *Health for Development Strategy 2015–2020*. Canberra

——(2017a) *Foreign Policy White Paper*. Canberra. www.fpwhitepaper.gov.au

——(2017b) Australian Aid Budget Summary 2017–18. https://www.dfat.gov.au/sites/default/files/2017-18-australian-aid-budget-summary.pdf

——(2019) Australian Aid Budget Summary 2019–2020. https://www.dfat.gov.au/sites/default/files/2019-20-australian-aid-budget-summary.pdf

——(2020) *Partnerships For Recovery: Australia's COVID-19 Development Response*. https://www.dfat.gov.au/sites/default/files/partnerships-for-recovery-australias-COVID-19-development-response.pdf

——(n.d.a) Australia stepping up to address COVID-19 in the Pacific. https://www.dfat.gov.au/geo/pacific/australia-stepping-up-to-address-COVID-19-in-the-pacific

——(n.d.b) *Health Security Initiative: 2017–2022*. https://indopacifichealthsecurity.dfat.gov.au/health-security-initiative-2017-2022

Elliott, L. (2012) *The Alliance and Non-Traditional Security*. United States Studies Centre. http://www.alliance.ussc.edu.au/wp-content/uploads/2015/07/alliance-21-report-united-states-elliott.pdf

Global Preparedness Board (2020) *A World in Disorder: Global Preparedness Monitoring Board Annual Report 2020*. Geneva: World Health Organization

Goh, E. (2013) 'Hierarchy and Great Power cooperation in the East Asian security order', in J. Prantl (ed.), *Effective Multilateralism: Through the Looking Glass of East Asia*, pp. 177–95. Basingstoke: Palgrave Macmillan

Hameiri, S. & Jones, L. (2012) The politics and governance of non-traditional security. *International Studies Quarterly* 57(3): 462–73

Hill-Cawthorne, G., Negin, J., Capon, T. et al. (2019) Advancing planetary health in Australia: Focus on emerging infections and antimicrobial resistance. *BMJ Global Health* 2019(4): e001283

Horton, R. (2017) Offline: Are China's global ambitions good for global health? *Lancet*, 23 December. https://doi.org/10.1016/S0140-6736(17)33355-X

Howes, S. (2017) Health security: Part one. *Devpolicy*, 26 October. http://www.devpolicy.org/health-security-20171026/

——(2018) Julie Bishop's aid and development legacy. *Devpolicy*, 4 September. https://asiapacific.anu.edu.au/news-events/all-stories/julie-bishops-aid-and-development-legacy

Indo-Pacific Centre for Health Security (2018) About Us. https://indopacifichealthsecurity.dfat.gov.au/about-us

——(n.d.) *Health Security Initiative for the Indo-Pacific Region: Provisional Strategic Framework 2019–22*. https://indopacifichealthsecurity.dfat.gov.au/sites/default/files/2022-08/20191209%20Health%20Security%20Initiative_Strategic%20Framework.pdf

Jones, K.E., Patel, N., Levy, M. et al. (2008) Global trends in emerging infectious diseases. *Nature* 451: 990–3. https://doi.org/10.1038/nature06536

Kamradt-Scott, A. (2018) Securing Indo-Pacific health security. *Australian Journal of International Affairs* 72(6)

Macfarlane, S.N. & Khong, Y.F. (2006) *Human Security and the UN: A Critical History*. Indianapolis: Indiana University Press

Mackenzie, J.S. (2005) Emerging zoonotic encephalitis viruses: Lessons from Southeast Asia and Oceania. *Journal of NeuroVirology* 11: 434–40. https://doi.org/10.1080/13550280591002487

McInnes, C. & Lee, K. (2012) *Global Health and International Relations*. Cambridge: Polity Press

Minister for Foreign Affairs (2017) Indo-Pacific health security initiative. Media release. 7 October

——(2020) Australia's support for South-East Asia's COVID-19 recovery. 20 September. https://www.foreignminister.gov.au/minister/marise-payne/media-release/australias-support-southeast-asias-COVID-19-recovery

UNDP (2020) *The social and economic impact of COVID-19 in the Asia-Pacific region. Position note prepared by UNDP Regional Bureau for Asia and the Pacific*. Bangkok: United Nations Development Programme

World Health Organization (WHO) (2020) WHO Director-General opening remarks at the Member State Briefing on the COVID-19 pandemic evaluation. 9 July. https://www.who.int/dg/speeches/detail/who-director-general-opening-remarks-at-the-member-state-briefing-on-the-COVID-19-pandemic-evaluation—9-july-2020

Part III

Regional issues

Reimagining Australia's regional security for the Indo-Pacific century

Thomas Wilkins

The 'Indo-Pacific' concept emerged as perhaps the defining leitmotif for Australian foreign and security policy between 2016 and 2020, leading to a sweeping shift in the country's 'geopolitical vocabulary' (Nieuwenhuis, 2016: 114). This descriptor largely displaced the term 'Asia Pacific' and was commonly used by policy-makers, strategic analysts and scholars in Australia and overseas to express the view that the area spanning the Indian and Pacific oceans had come to be 'the engine of global growth' (DFAT, 2018). This was reflected in the proliferation of economic institutions and initiatives, such as the Comprehensive and Progressive Agreement for Trans-Pacific Partnership (CPTPP) and Regional Comprehensive Economic Partnership (RCEP), as well as China's ambitious Belt and Road Initiative (BRI), all of which were reconfiguring the geo-economic landscape of this pivotal region.

While ostensibly serving as a neutral geographic descriptor, the Indo-Pacific was also a new arena for superpower rivalry. The 2020 Australian Strategic Defence Update (SDU) said: 'The Indo-Pacific is at the centre of greater strategic competition', which was not confined to traditional geopolitical rivalries but encompassed 'geo-economics' and therefore heightened economic security concerns, alongside more traditional military–security risks. Hence Australia's traditional emphasis on prosperity as an element of regional engagement became strongly tempered by fears of a deteriorating security environment. The resultant security–economy nexus further complicated Australian efforts to navigate the increasingly fraught regional environment. By 2020, Australia was beginning to learn the painful lesson that its commitment to its alliance with the United States on the security front would antagonise its primary trading partner China and that the latter would try to use directed economic pressure to bring Australia to heel. The delusion that trade and security could be compartmentalised was cruelly exposed for the fallacy it always was (see Chapter 14).

To address these issues, this chapter first provides some background on how the Indo-Pacific concept became the dominant regional frame of reference for Australia. It then presents an analysis of how Australia's Indo-Pacific strategy unfolded through new policy initiatives towards the region's major powers as well as the key subregions of South-East Asia and the South Pacific.

RECONCEPTUALISING AUSTRALIA'S REGION THROUGH THE INDO-PACIFIC LENS

The term 'Indo-Pacific' had quietly languished in the background of Australian strategic debates since the mid-1960s but resurfaced in the mid-2000s (see Medcalf, 2020). In the previous volume of *Australia in World Affairs*, only one chapter (He, 2016) made extensive reference to the Indo-Pacific concept. Between 2016 and 2020, however, it assumed a pivotal place in Australian discourse on regional policy. According to Dobell (2016: 5), 'In the second decade of the twenty-first century, the Indo-Pacific has replaced the Asia Pacific as the reigning geographic construct of Australian Defence policy.'

This strategic reorientation away from the Asia Pacific to a wider Indo-Pacific geopolitical construct began as early as the 2000s, but this prolonged process reached fruition in the period under review. This mirrored the earlier efforts, instigated by Prime Minister Paul Keating and Foreign Minister Gareth Evans, to forge consensus on the Asia Pacific as *Australia's* region (Cotton & Ravenhill, 1997). Although the creation of this new narrative involved a multitude of actors, such as think tanks, scholars and political constituencies, the fervent adoption of the term by political leaders put the seal on this new national conception of 'region-ness'. In 2017, Prime Minister Malcolm Turnbull declared Australia to be 'focused on *our region*, determined to realise a secure, open and prosperous *Indo-Pacific*' (DFAT, 2017; emphasis added). Turnbull's successor, Scott Morrison, went even further with such 'speech acts', claiming that 'The Indo-Pacific is where we live' before proceeding the codify its import to Australia (Prime Minister of Australia, 2019a). He encouraged Australians to recognise their Indo-Pacific identity, saying, 'We are an Indo-Pacific nation' (Prime Minister of Australia, 2019b). Morrison thereby sought to propel the country into the Indo-Pacific century. This rhetoric trickled down to the bureaucratic organs of state that were tasked with implementing the change in Australia's regional policies. The *Defence White Paper* (2016), *Foreign Policy White Paper* (2017) and *Defence Strategic Update* (2020) used the term prolifically, consummating the process of entrenching it in the new policy lexicon. The DFAT *Annual Report 2018–19* echoed the political discourse by enunciating that 'The Indo-Pacific is our home and the region that will have the greatest impact on Australia's future prosperity and security'.

Australia now (re)identified its geographic region as follows: 'the region ranging from the eastern Indian Ocean to the Pacific Ocean connected by South-East Asia, including India, North Asia and the United States' (DFAT, 2017: 1). In this respect it served simply as a neutral and objective cartographic descriptor. As Medcalf (2020: 3) attests, 'At a descriptive level, the Indo-Pacific is just a neutral name for a new and expansive map centered on maritime Asia.' Serious doubts were expressed about its genuine coherence as a region (like for instance Europe, North America or even the Asia Pacific), especially given its lack of codification through regional institutionalism. The new definition, however, was adopted with a specific strategic purpose in mind. To this end, it quickly morphed from a pure geographic descriptor into a 'mental map' (Brewster, 2014: 164).

The Indo-Pacific became characterised as a 'single strategic system' (Medcalf, 2014b: 47) through which it assumed the form of a geospatial arena in which policy would be conceived and enacted. To wit, in a rescaled Indo-Pacific region, several Australian geopolitical aims were facilitated: India's influence was increased while China's was diluted, more middle powers were brought into the regional orbit, the United States was kept engaged, the region's maritime emphasis was codified, and Australia was accorded a central position (Wilson, 2018: 178).

The last of these was notable, as Beeson identifies: 'Australia is literally and metaphorically at the centre of the putative region' (2018: 93). This repositioning allowed Australia to overcome its 'liminality' in the Asian region by reimagining (and expanding) the conception of the region itself – as it had previously with the Asia Pacific (Higgott & Nossal, 1997).

Consequently, the Indo-Pacific concept assumed 'a practical, strategic reality that has to be addressed' (cited in Pan, 2016: 9), according to the former Defence Minister and Ambassador to the United States, Kim Beazley. Canberra retained a certain amount of strategic ambiguity in its national agenda for the Indo-Pacific (unlike the United States, where it was explicitly defined), but Australia's putative Indo-Pacific strategy began to emerge in official statements such as the Defence White Paper (2016), Defence Strategic Update (2020) and the Foreign Policy White Paper (2017) (see Wilkins, 2019a).

This strategy aimed to advance the three main pillars of Australian foreign and security policy: upholding a rules-based order (RBO), the US alliance, and deepening regional engagement (Gyngell, 2017). As a middle power, much of Australia's strategy was designed to be compliant with that of its closest Indo-Pacific partners: Australia lacked the resources and capacity to implement a 'grand strategy' independently (Abbondanza, 2020). As Patience notes, the Australian enterprise was at least partially 'reflected influence', or 'influence that comes from affiliations with other states' (2018: 32). Thus, to '[p]romote a stable and prosperous Indo-Pacific' (DFAT, 2018: n.p.), Australia attempted to connect its national objectives to those of the major powers that had also adopted their own versions of the Indo-Pacific concept as a region or mental map (Wilkins & Kim, 2020). These interactions shaped Australia's role in regional security affairs in the period under review.

REGIONAL SECURITY RELATIONS IN THE INDO-PACIFIC

The Indo-Pacific concept and the policies attached to it shaped Australian relations with the region's major powers. The selection of states examined here reflects the 2017 Foreign Policy White Paper's identification that 'The future balance of power in the Indo-Pacific will largely depend on the actions of the United States, China and major powers such as Japan and India' (DFAT, 2017: 25). The section ends with a discussion of two important subregions: South-East Asia and the South Pacific, which were also integral to Australia's Indo-Pacific approach (see Chapters 12 and 13).

The United States

The period under review started poorly for Australia–US relations, as embodied by a fractious phone call between incoming President Donald Trump and Prime Minister Malcolm Turnbull in 2017 about an agreement on refugee resettlement. The initial phase of Trump's presidency was marked by chaos and disorganisation as he fumbled to translate his 'American First' rhetoric into policies that would lessen US commitment to global governance in favour of more nationalist and isolationist sentiments (Beeson & Bloomfield, 2019). The reassuring 'Pacific Century' vision espoused by the former Secretary of State Hillary Clinton was discarded.

More worryingly for Canberra was the jettisoning of the formal policy strategy, the 'Pivot/Rebalance', which had been designed to implement this vision (Campbell, 2016). This included withdrawal from the Trans-Pacific Partnership (TPP) in 2016, the centrepiece of US claims to regional geo-economic leadership, which left US economic engagement with the region adrift. This was particularly worrying for Australia since the US abandonment of TPP appeared to cede the primary role in regional economic governance to Beijing, a situation that did not bode well for the rules-based order, given China's economic might and willingness to engage in sharp economic practices.

Worse still, Trump called into question US security guarantees for its treaty allies in the region, disparaging their value and contributions as part of his 'transactional' approach. Australia, for instance, was fortunate to escape US tariffs when these were applied to steel and aluminium imports from a range of countries in 2018. Such deprecative actions undermined not only US credibility among allies such as Australia but also the basis of its own claim to regional primacy (White, 2017).

This sparked a recurrent domestic debate about the reliability and desirability of the US alliance, in which former leaders such as Bob Carr, Paul Keating and Gareth Evans criticised Australia's strategic dependence on a Trump-led America. Turnbull's unfettered support for the United States during Trump's talks with North Korea over denuclearisation, when he claimed that the allies were 'joined at the hip', also attracted criticism for Australia's seemingly unreflective subservience to Washington.

Yet, around 2017, official US embrace of the Indo-Pacific concept improved the situation for Canberra. Behind the *Sturm und Drang* of the White House, the 'deep state' began to reassert itself and provide welcome assurance for allies such as Australia, through the publication of the National Security Strategy (Trump, 2017) and National Defence Strategy (Mattis, 2018). These documents also testified to the diffusion of the Indo-Pacific concept among the policy establishment, and the official adoption of the nomenclature was reflected in the renaming of America's Pacific Command (PACOM) to INDO-PACOM, an important symbolic shift in 2018. These positive developments were sealed by the long-awaited successor to the abandoned Pivot strategy, as outlined in the Indo-Pacific Strategy Report (IPSR) prepared by the US Department of Defense (2019a). This was accompanied by the State Department's Free and Open Indo-Pacific (FOIP) vision (US Department of State, 2019), which formed a key platform for this broader Indo-Pacific strategy.

US adoption of the Indo-Pacific concept boosted Australia's regional interests and aspirations, and potentially reinforced its associated policies. The US Indo-Pacific Strategy focused on three pillars: security, economics and governance, and dovetailed seamlessly with Australia's loosely defined 'Indo-Pacific strategy' (Wilkins, 2019a; Taylor, 2020). This was a vital element of Australia's approach to the region, with DFAT proclaiming: 'Our alliance with the United States is central to Australia's approach to the Indo-Pacific.' To ensure that Washington was aware of its burden-sharing contribution to the alliance, Canberra increased defence spending to 2 per cent of GDP, in part thanks to major purchases of US military hardware. It also assiduously promoted its credentials as a faithful ally through a campaign in the United States entitled '100 Years of Mateship' in 2018 (Wilkins, 2019b). Although the relationship gradually stabilised thanks to these recalibrations, and Australian politicians learned the art of 'managing Trump', Canberra's hope that Washington would take a stronger lead in economic leadership and multilateral engagement went unfulfilled.

In addition to underlining US commitment to the region, the FOIP contains several principles that resonated with Australian security interests. These included respect for sovereignty; peaceful resolution of disputes; free, fair and reciprocal trade; and adhesion to international rules and norms (US DOD, 2019a: 4). The US approach emphasised the maintenance of the 'rules-based order' (RBO). As noted, this had long been a core element of Australia's approach, and it was validated by DFAT's stated determination to 'strengthen the rules-based international order' (DFAT, 2017: v). Although Trump could not be persuaded to rejoin the TPP, some efforts to cooperate on economic and governance issues emerged through the Trilateral Investment Fund (with Japan), which aimed at improving governance and economic connectivity in the South Pacific. Most of the key elements in the US Indo-Pacific Strategy served to reinforce the credibility and capabilities of Australian approaches to the region through the Indo-Pacific concept. The belated adoption of the concept by the United States therefore bolstered Australia's ability to pursue its regional security interests. As the 70th anniversary of the ANZUS Treaty loomed, and with Trump leaving office in early 2021, alliance relations had recovered their poise, with both partners as committed as ever to cooperating in the Indo-Pacific.

Japan

In the period under review, Australia's 'Special Strategic Partnership' with Japan took on increasing significance and, with their shared adhesion to the Indo-Pacific concept, became an important fixture in advancing Australian regional security interests. In 2019, Defence ministers Linda Reynolds and Taro Kono noted that, 'as Indo-Pacific security dynamics became more challenging, the strategic logic underpinning Japan–Australia cooperation was only getting stronger' (Japanese MOD, 2020: 346). Indeed, 'Japan was an early proponent of the "Indo-Pacific" concept' (He & Li, 2020: 3). In 2007, Prime Minister Shinzo Abe had unveiled his vision of a 'confluence of two great oceans', and this concept shaped Australia's perspective on the issue. Reflecting the agreed change in 'geopolitical vocabulary', the strategic partners discontinued the use of 'Asia Pacific' in their joint statements in favour of 'Indo-Pacific' in 2017. They repeatedly declared their 'shared strategic interests in the security, stability and prosperity of the Indo-Pacific region' (e.g. Prime Minister of Australia, 2020).

Founded in 2007, with the Joint Declaration on Security Cooperation, the bilateral relationship with Tokyo continued to broaden and deepen, continuing the momentum built up under the Abbott government, which completed a 'Special Strategic Partnership' in 2014 (Wilkins, 2018). It survived what many presumed would amount to a major setback in relations when Canberra selected a French contractor to build its new submarine flotilla in preference to the Japanese bid in 2016, and continued to further layer its institutional apparatus through upgrades in its logistical agreements. As part of its approach to the Indo-Pacific, Canberra supported Japan's progressive security reforms towards 'normalisation', such as the 2015 Peace and Security Legislation, and encouraged Tokyo to play a larger role in regional security (DFAT, 2017). The warm atmospherics of the relationship were evinced through efforts at historical reconciliation such as Abe's visit to Darwin in 2018, the first time a serving Japanese leader had visited the port, which was devastated by Japanese air raids in 1942. The two countries engaged in regular bilateral military exercises, such as *Nichi-Gō* Trident (2016; 2019) and *Bushidō*-Guardian (2019), aimed at improving interoperability, as well as addressing Humanitarian Assistance/Disaster Relief (HA/DR) contingencies.

Although it became most associated with the United States, Japan was the progenitor of the FOIP vision, and Australia's approach was closely aligned with this vision (Japanese Ministry of Foreign Affairs, 2020). According to Tokyo, 'The core idea of the Free and Open Indo-Pacific (FOIP) concept is to establish a rules-based international order and consolidate principles such as free trade, freedom of navigation, and the rule of law, which are essential for the stability and prosperity of the region.' (Japanese Ministry of Foreign Affairs, 2020: 8)

In 2020 Australia and Japan released a mission statement for their partnership, expressing their joint 'determination to deepen cooperation to promote a free, open, inclusive and prosperous Indo-Pacific region' (Prime Minister of Australia, 2020). To this purpose they reiterated their opposition to provocative Chinese actions in the South China and East China seas, which they said defied international law (according to the United Nations Convention on the Law of the Sea [UNCLOS]), and China's use of 'maritime militia' to exploit 'grey zones' in maritime sovereignty. As geo-economics came to the fore, the two countries shared concerns over China's use of economic statecraft to pressure small states into projects that lack economic viability through 'debt trap diplomacy'. Working through Official Development Assistance (ODA) and the Trilateral Investment Fund, Australia and Japan sought to provide quality-assured infrastructure projects to the region. Hence, their 2020 leaders' summit 'confirmed that a key element of bilateral security cooperation is to promote coordination in the area of economic security' (Prime Minister of Australia, 2020). Australia and Japan were both subjected to economic coercion by Beijing and sought to resist it through bilateral and minilateral economic cooperation and diversification, including supply chains and access to critical minerals. They jointly affirmed that 'trade should never be used as a tool to apply political pressure. To do so undermines trust and prosperity' (Prime Minister of Australia, 2020).

This mutual advancement of shared interests under the Indo-Pacific banner and through the strategic partnership constituted a major platform of Australia's middle-power diplomacy. Outside their alliances with the United States, Australia and Japan emerged as the spearheads of middle-power cooperation to uphold the RBO.

Having in earlier decades cooperated to establish Asia-Pacific Economic Cooperation (APEC), Canberra and Tokyo united again in 2018 to preserve the TPP as an alternative to Chinese-led efforts at economic regionalism, through the CPTPP. The CPTPP had 11 member countries, including Japan, although not all had ratified the agreement by the end of 2020. Australia and Japan wanted the United States to reconsider joining, in part to offset the regional economic dominance that Beijing was exercising through the US decision to withdraw from the talks.

In November 2020, Canberra, alongside Japan and 14 other countries (including China), signed the RCEP, a trade agreement backed by China but nominally led by ASEAN, designed to reduce barriers and stimulate regional economic growth. Australia supported the pact in an attempt to promote ASEAN-led regional multilateral architecture in the broader Indo-Pacific concept and to bolster cooperation with Japan in the vital subregions of South-East Asia and the Pacific Island countries. This cooperation also entailed joint capacity-building and ODA coordination, including a joint Strategy for Cooperation in the Pacific (2016). In addition, they championed 'value-based diplomacy' as part of the FOIP. The 2020 Joint Statement cited 'a commitment to democracy, human rights, free trade' as 'shared values' (Prime Minister of Australia, 2020). The two countries repeatedly denounced Chinese actions in Xinjiang and Hong Kong, for example.

Canberra sought to expand and deepen cooperation with Tokyo with a view to jointly preserving aspects of the RBO and to respond to the erratic policies of the Trump administration, which upset the strategic equilibrium. The strategic partnership provided the venue for discrete consultations on these issues and the best practice for 'managing Trump' diplomatically. It also involved discussion of how to prepare for a 'Plan B' in the event of US withdrawal from the region, and the potential promulgation of an Australian–Japanese alliance treaty (Jennings, 2018). The partners also began to engage in trilateral discussions with New Delhi, without the United States. However, once Washington fully embraced the Indo-Pacific concept, a degree of equilibrium returned, and US–Japan–Australia Trilateral Strategic Dialogues (TSD) were held in 2018 and 2019, with a view to coordinating Indo-Pacific approaches. This return to 'normality' came as a welcome relief to policy-makers in Australia and Japan as the role of the United States in providing alliance security and leadership of the RBO was vital to both countries' Indo-Pacific strategies.

India

Australia used the Indo-Pacific concept to catalyse its bilateral and minilateral relations with India, since it provided 'Australia further discursive grounds to construct India as a "natural partner"' (Barthwal-Datta & Chacko, 2020: 258). A key rationale of the concept was to create a regional construct that accorded a more central role for India than the former 'Asia–Pacific', which sometimes appeared to confine India to the margins. Instead, Jaishankar (2020: 24) notes, 'the Indo-Pacific is about bringing India into a broader strategic space'. Advocacy for the Indo-Pacific concept in its discursive phase therefore contained a strong emphasis on India as a rising power and the extension of Australia's strategic outlook to the Indian Ocean. The economic potential of India and bilateral/minilateral investment or infrastructure collaboration provided motivation for the business community, as former diplomat Peter Varghese noted (DFAT, 2018). Moreover, India's democratic credentials and shared British Commonwealth past, it was argued, would ensure smooth cooperation in upholding shared values, including a commitment to the RBO. By accommodating Indian initiatives such as its 'Act East' program, connectivity with Australian policy in South-East Asia could be also achieved. Thus New Delhi became central to the Indo-Pacific framework since 'There are obvious commonalities in the Indian and Australian perceptions of the Indo-Pacific' (Jaishankar, 2020: 21).

Therefore Australia substantially augmented its 2009 strategic partnership with India by formally establishing '2+2' Foreign and Defence ministers annual meetings in 2017 and upgrading the relationship to a Comprehensive Strategic Partnership in 2020. Further institutional architecture was introduced, such as the Mutual Logistics Support Agreement. Given the oceanic nature of the Indo-Pacific, Australia and India announced a Joint Declaration on a Shared Vision for Maritime Cooperation in the Indo-Pacific in 2020. They engaged in joint army manoeuvres (Exercise AUSTRAHIND in 2017 and 2018) and bilateral naval exercises (AUSINDEX maritime warfare exercises in 2015, 2017 and 2019). The Australian navy was also readmitted to the multilateral Malabar exercises in 2020. According to Jaishankar (2020: 2), there was 'close cooperation on Indian Ocean security, sophisticated bilateral naval exercises, high-level strategic dialogues, military exchanges and training, and some nascent defence technology cooperation' between Australia and India. As with Japan, a variation of the FOIP bound the strategic partners together through the Indo-Pacific concept in which 'Both India and Australia share a vision of a free, open, inclusive and rules-based Indo-Pacific region' (DFAT, 2020).

The expansion of trilateral Australia–US–Japan cooperation into a quadrilateral format that included India was a key element in Australia's efforts to enhance ties. This expansion had its antecedents in former Japanese Prime Minister Abe's 'democratic diamond', which resulted in the first Quadrilateral Strategic Dialogue in 2007. The Quad minilateral quickly unravelled after Australia's abrupt withdrawal, but these arrangements were revitalised in 2017 and began to bind India to some elements of Australia's Indo-Pacific strategy. Indeed, as Huong Le Thu (2019: 2) notes, 'A key to the success of the Quad is its relationship with the Indo-Pacific concept.' The Quad members all subscribed to some variant of the concept as a 'region' or 'mental map', and they were loosely united around the core principles of the FOIP, although the Quad was not a vehicle for directly implementing the FOIP. While emphasising 'inclusivity' to differing degrees, the Quad members were concerned about Chinese actions that undermined the RBO.

Like the Indo-Pacific itself, the Quad remained somewhat ambiguous and was subject to multiple interpretations. There was much speculation about the Quad being an incipient 'anti-China alliance', but instead it represented something quite different: a network of strategic partnerships between the four member states in minilateral institutional formats were being replaced by ministerial-level meetings (Wilkins, 2019b). As the most prominent institution related to the Indo-Pacific concept, the Quad also facilitated the incorporation of extra-regional powers, such as the United Kingdom, France and Germany (sometimes in tandem with the FOIP), and some South-East Asian states, into relatively informal but collective talks with the Quad members ('Quad-plus'). This accorded with the strategic intent behind Australia's Indo-Pacific concept and reflected how it has been put into policy practice. In the words of one observer, Australia did not want to be 'a major focus of Chinese displeasure', so '[w]orking with other Quad countries on economic initiatives and diplomatic positions where common values are threatened [was] preferable to Canberra than acting alone' (Lee, 2020: 17).

China

China may have been 'the quintessential Indo-Pacific power' (Medcalf, 2014a: 472), but the Indo-Pacific concept had anti-China connotations for many Chinese analysts. For this reason, Australia's enthusiasm for the concept as a means of advancing its interests in tandem with the United States, Japan and India contributed to a marked deterioration of relations with China. By the end of 2020, bilateral relations had reached their lowest-ever ebb, with polls showing 81 per cent 'unfavourable' perceptions of China among the Australian public (Silver, Devlin & Huang, 2020; see also Chapter 3). Much of the discord either directly or indirectly resulted from Australia's prosecution of its national interests and values through its Indo-Pacific strategy.

First, Beijing responded to the concept with hostility and declared it would 'dissipate like foam' (Chinese Ministry of Foreign Affairs, 2018). China remained wedded to the term 'Asia–Pacific' as its preferred geographical descriptor, and even the more narrowly cast 'East Asia', which would potentially exclude Australia, the United States and even India.

By adopting the new Indo-Pacific mental map, Canberra put itself directly at odds with Chinese conceptions of regionalism. In recent decades China had established institutions associated with this conception, such as the Belt and Road Initiative (BRI), Shanghai Cooperation Organization (SCO) and Asian Infrastructure Investment Bank (AIIB), which undergirded its 'Silk Road mental map' in direct contradistinction to the Indo-Pacific concept. As Medcalf (2019: 80) noted, 'The Indo-Pacific is being posited as a counter to a China-centric view of regional order under the Belt and Road Initiative.' Beijing particularly opposed the use of the Indo-Pacific concept as an umbrella for combining regional constellations, such as the FOIP and Quad, which it viewed as inherently tied to the concept itself. For Beijing, these arrangements were tantamount to anti-China containment.

China's hostility to the Indo-Pacific concept created dilemmas and disputes between Canberra and Beijing. First, China was implicitly identified as one of the biggest challenges to the RBO, which was central to the Australian Indo-Pacific strategy and to the FOIP in particular. Canberra viewed Chinese assertive behaviour in the region, such as its continued militarisation of the South China Sea, its refusal to abide by the ruling by the Permanent Court of Arbitration in 2016 on its maritime territorial claims, its use of 'maritime militias' to encroach on territory held by other states in the South China Sea and East China Sea, and the use of the BRI to practice 'debt trap diplomacy', as contrary to the principles of the RBO.

Furthermore, China's political and economic influence was increasing in the South Pacific (see Chapter 12), undermining Australian national interests directly. The federal government challenged the State of Victoria's accession to the BRI and eventually ripped up the agreement. Canberra's emphasis on the 'inclusive' nature of the Indo-Pacific and its version of the FOIP did not placate Beijing: 'While the strategy does not exclude China explicitly, the expression of the Indo-Pacific principles aforementioned will not be accepted in toto by China' (Choong, 2019: 416). Each in their own way, the two sides appeared to conclude that the Indo-Pacific strategy was incompatible with China's alternative vision for the region.

Previous editions of *Australia in World Affairs* identified the complex policy dilemmas faced between the divergence of Australia's security and economic interests. In the period under review, this was revealed far more starkly. The 'security/economic disconnect', or the cleavage between Australian security interests (support for its US ally) and its economic interests (desire to profit from Chinese trade), became ever more apparent (Wilkins, 2023). The previously confident assertion that Australia 'did not have to choose' became impossible to sustain. Even as bilateral trade flourished and Australia continued to benefit from the Asian Century, Canberra was embroiled in a series of disputes with China, its major trading partner (see Chapter 14). Australia's call for an international enquiry into the origins of the COVID-19 virus emanating from Henan Province was met with vitriolic denunciations from Beijing, as well as travel bans and the retaliatory measures against Australian beef, barley, wine and coal, among other products. These measures were accompanied by a list of '14 grievances' that Beijing expressed against Australia (Kearsley, Bagshaw & Galloway, 2020). For Australia, economics could no longer be viewed solely through the lens of prosperity: economic interdependence explicitly entered the security equation (see Chapter 1).

Since the Indo-Pacific concept was a cypher for the values that Australia and its fellow Quad members sought to uphold (such as democracy, human rights and free trade), China's departures from these values underscored the growing discord between Canberra and Beijing. According to Pan (2014: 462), 'As the "Indo-Pacific" takes on a value-based quality, China now emerges effectively as the new "odd man out" of Asia.' The hardening of techno-authoritarianism and nationalism in China, as exemplified by 'Xi Jinping thought', was antithetical to Australia's value system. The quashing of democracy in Hong Kong through the National Security Law, increased pressure on democratic Taiwan, and reports of alleged abuses against the Uighur peoples of Xinjiang, all created friction in bilateral relations. Furthermore, revelations of extensive Chinese influence operations within Australia, including cyberattacks on critical infrastructure and organisations, media organisations and universities, compelled Australia to pass 'foreign interference' legislation in 2018 (see Chapter 5). The exclusion of Chinese tech giant Huawei from the construction of Australia's 5G communications network, and increased scrutiny of Chinese investment in critical infrastructure through tighter regulations via the Foreign Investment Review Board, drew predictable ire from Beijing (see Chapter 14). In recognition of the difficulties of managing bilateral relations in such a context, Australia announced the formation of the National Foundation for Australia–China Relations in March 2019. Nevertheless, the Indo-Pacific concept, and the values and policies flowing from it, generated serious bilateral discord that the new foundation would be unlikely to repair on its own.

South-East Asia and the South Pacific

South-East Asia's vital strategic importance for Australia was reflected by the subregion's salience in the Indo-Pacific concept. A DFAT official, for instance, described the region as 'the nexus of major power competition in the Indo-Pacific' (Adamson, 2019). Most South-East Asian states, however, were tepid in their support for the concept, which they largely viewed as too confrontational towards China, and preferred to retain the less contentious 'Asia-Pacific' descriptor (see Chapter 13). Initial conceptualisations of the Indo-Pacific by Australia and other proponents inadvertently gave the impression that the new region was primarily an oceanic one, which bypassed South-East Asia. This was maladroit given how sensitive the Association of South-East Asian Nations (ASEAN) was to perceptions of its regional 'centrality'. Defence Minister Reynolds (2019) confirmed that the Indo-Pacific had 'ASEAN at its heart', but this was insufficient to overcome scepticism towards the concept. Australia thus made the case that the expansive suite of regional security architecture centring on ASEAN would be a core element of the Indo-Pacific concept in practice. To this end Canberra hosted the 2018 ASEAN–Australia special summit in Sydney and made South-East Asia and the Indian Ocean the centrepieces of its naval diplomacy, known as 'Indo-Pacific Endeavour', from 2017 to 2019.

ASEAN was necessarily a key interlocutor in the promulgation of Australia's Indo-Pacific policy, given its prominence in regional security architecture. According to Taylor (2020: 102), 'The EAS [East Asian Summit] is generally regarded as the organization that first gave institutional expression to the Indo-Pacific concept.' Some form of institutionalisation of the Indo-Pacific concept therefore would be required if it was to be sustainable (He & Li, 2020). Proponents of the concept, including Australia, highlighted the EAS above other alternatives such as the ASEAN+3 (which China preferred), because of its inclusivity and its being the closest match with the Indo-Pacific's geographical scope. Institutions that focused on the Indian Ocean, such as the Indian Ocean Regional Association (IORA) or Indian Ocean Naval Symposium (IONS), were not serious contenders. No country, meanwhile, was willing to suggest the creation of a new pan-regional institution for the Indo-Pacific from scratch, in light of the failure of Rudd's 'Asia-Pacific community' in 2009. As the Indo-Pacific became further entrenched in the regional policies of the United States in particular, ASEAN responded collectively through its 'Outlook on the Indo-Pacific' (Wilkins, 2020). This rather banal document simply restated ASEAN's institutional centrality and stressed non-confrontation while noting how existing bodies could be made to fit the new concept (Choong, 2019).

The South Pacific was another subregion that featured heavily in Australia's Indo-Pacific strategy. The South Pacific had long been viewed as an Australian sphere of influence and variously described as 'our patch' (see Chapter 12), due to its centrality to the defence of Australia and the disbursement of Australia's aid budget. Although the Pacific Island states were not evidently enthusiastic about the abstract regional concept of the Indo-Pacific, they were keen to benefit from the increased attention they received as part of the new strategy.

A crucial part of Australia's Indo-Pacific strategy was the Pacific Step-up, announced in 2016. Prompted by fears that China was augmenting its economic and political influence in the Pacific, Australia 're-doubled efforts to promote itself as a historical friend and partner to Pacific Island nations, basing the relationship on "respect, equality, and openness"' (Lee, 2020: 15). To lend substance to this aspiration, a dedicated Office of the Pacific was established within DFAT in 2019, as well as the Australian Pacific Security College in Canberra and a Pacific Fusion Centre in Vanuatu. These mechanisms were designed to assist the Pacific states in defending their maritime sovereignty and resources from incursions into their exclusive economic zones (EEZs) by capacity-building activities, including training and the provision of coastal patrol craft. It also resulted in plans for a naval base in Manus (Lombrum), designed to signal to Beijing that Chinese naval facilities in the area would be unwelcome. Increased funds were made available through a $2 billion Australian Infrastructure Financing Facility for the Pacific (AIFFP) and an extra $1 billion to the Australian Export Financing Agency to support economic development in the Pacific. In partnership with the United States and Japan, Australia also provided undersea telecommunications cables to Papua New Guinea, Solomon Islands and Palau, in line with the standards of economic development and good governance outlined in the FOIP.

CONCLUSION: MORE 'CONCEPT' THAN 'STRATEGY'?

The Indo-Pacific concept achieved near-universal currency in the Australian strategic consciousness in the period under review. It featured prominently in the rhetoric of policy-makers, and it became thoroughly embedded in associated policy documents. In the process, there was a discernible shift from previous regional conceptions such as the Asia–Pacific, which had concentrated on economic regionalism and therefore such themes as 'prosperity', towards and a heavier focus on security as part of the Indo-Pacific (i.e. security regionalism).

Policy-makers continued to talk about prosperity, but it was qualified by a recognition of heightened 'strategic competition' and regional rivalry. In this sense, the Indo-Pacific, stripped of its conceptual finessing, was largely a response to the rise of China and its more assertive regional agenda. Hence, Beeson (2018: 96) argues, the 'Indo-Pacific idea is as a strategic vehicle that can be used to rally countries concerned about the implications of China's rise'. This did not go unnoticed in Beijing, and therefore Australia's adoption of the concept appeared likely to further heighten divisions and complicate its future policy options in respect to China. For all its fanfare, critics of the Indo-Pacific such as Phillips (2016: 5) remained convinced that it was 'a bold but flawed regional template for Australian foreign and defence policy-makers'.

References

Abbondanza, G. (2020) Australia the 'good international citizen'? The limits of a traditional middle power. *Australian Journal of International Affairs* 75(2): 178–96

Adamson, F. (2019) *The Indo-Pacific: Australia's Perspective*. Australian High Commission, Kuala Lumpur, 29 April. https://www.dfat.gov.au/news/speeches/Pages/the-indo-pacific-australias-perspective

Barthwal-Datta, M. & Chacko, P. (2020) The politics of strategic narratives of regional order in the Indo-Pacific: Free, open, prosperous, inclusive? *Australian Journal of International Affairs* 74(3): 244–63

Beeson, M. (2018) Institutionalizing the Indo-Pacific: The challenges of regional cooperation. *East Asia* 35(2): 85–98

Beeson, M. & Bloomfield, A. (2019) The Trump effect downunder: US allies, Australian strategic culture, and the politics of path dependence. *Contemporary Security Policy* 40(3): 335–61

Brewster, D. (2014) Dividing lines: Evolving mental maps of the Bay of Bengal. *Asian Security* 210(2): 151–67

Campbell, K. (2016) *The Pivot: The Future of American Statecraft in Asia*. Hachette UK

Chinese Ministry of Foreign Affairs (2018) Foreign Minister Wang Yi meets the press. https://www.fmprc.gov.cn/mfa_eng/zxxx_662805/t1540928.shtml

Choong, W. (2019) The return of the Indo-Pacific strategy: An assessment. *Australian Journal of International Affairs* 73(5): 415–30

Cotton, J. & Ravenhill, J. (1997) *Seeking Asian Engagement: Australia in World Affairs 1991–1995*. Melbourne: Oxford University Press

Department of Defence (DOD) (2016) *Defence White Paper*. Canberra

——(2020) *Defence Strategic Update*. Canberra

Department of Foreign Affairs and Trade (DFAT) (2017) *Foreign Policy White Paper*. Canberra

——(2018) *Annual Report 2018–19*. Canberra

——(2020) Joint Statement on a Comprehensive Strategic Partnership between Republic of India and Australia. https://www.dfat.gov.au/geo/india/Pages/joint-statement-comprehensive-strategic-partnership-between-republic-india-and-australia

Dobell, G. (2016) Australia's Defence White Papers by the numbers. *Security Challenges* 12(2): 1–8

Gyngell, A. (2017) *Fear of Abandonment: Australia in the World since 1942*. Melbourne: La Trobe University Press

He, B. (2016) Australian ideas of regionalism. In M. Beeson & S. Hameiri (eds), *Navigating the New International Disorder: Australia in World Affairs 2011–2015*, pp. 75–92. Melbourne: Oxford University Press

He, K. & Li, M. (2020) Understanding the dynamics of the Indo-Pacific: US–China strategic competition, regional actors, and beyond. *International Affairs* 96(1): 1–7

Higgott, R.A. & Nossal, K.R. (1997) The international politics of liminality: Relocating Australia in the Asia Pacific. *Australian Journal of Political Science* 32(2): 169–86

Jaishankar, D. (2020) *The Australia–India Strategic Partnership: Accelerating Security Cooperation in the Indo-Pacific*. Lowy Institute Analyses, 17 September. https://www.lowyinstitute.org/publications/australia-india-strategic-partnership-security-cooperation-indo-pacific

Japanese Ministry of Defense (2020) *Defense of Japan 2020*. Tokyo

Japanese Ministry of Foreign Affairs (2020) *Diplomatic Bluebook 2020*. Tokyo

Jennings, P. (2018) Trump means we need a 'Plan B' for defence. *ASPI Opinion*, 21 July. https://www.aspi.org.au/opinion/trump-means-we-need-plan-b-defence

Kearsley, J., Bagshaw, E. & Galloway, A. (2020) 'If you make China the enemy, China will be the enemy': Beijing's fresh threat to Australia. *Sydney Morning Herald*, 18 November. https://www.smh.com.au/world/asia/if-you-make-china-the-enemy-china-will-be-the-enemy-beijing-s-fresh-threat-to-australia-20201118-p56fqs.html

Le Thu, H. (2019) New perspectives for the revived quad. *ASPI Strategist*, 14 February. https://www.aspistrategist.org.au/new-perspectives-for-the-revived-quad

Lee, L. (2020) *Assessing the Quad: Prospects and Limitations of Quadrilateral Cooperation for Advancing Australia's Interests*. Lowy Institute Analyses, 19 May. https://www.lowyinstitute.org/publications/assessing-quad-prospects-and-limitations-quadrilateral-cooperation-advancing-australia

Mattis, J. (2018) 'Summary of the US Defense Strategy', US Department of Defense, Washington. https://dod.defense.gov/Portals/1/Documents/pubs/2018-National-Defense-Strategy-Summary.pdf

Medcalf, R. (2014a) In defence of the Indo-Pacific: Australia's new strategic map. *Australian Journal of International Affairs* 68(4): 470–83

——(2014b) Mapping the Indo-Pacific: China, India, and the United States. In M. Malik (ed.), *Maritime Security in the Indo-Pacific: Perspectives from China, India, and the United States*. Lanham: Rowman & Littlefield

——(2019) Indo-Pacific visions: Giving solidarity a chance. *Asia Policy* 26(3): 79–95

——(2020) *Indo-Pacific Empire: China, America, and the Contest for the World's Pivotal Region*. Manchester: Manchester University Press

Nieuwenhuis, M. (2016) Imagining the Indo-Pacific region. In P. Chacko (ed.), *New Regional Geopolitics in the Indo-Pacific: Drivers, Dynamics, and Consequences*, pp. 114–30. Abingdon: Routledge

Pan, C. (2014) The 'Indo-Pacific' and geopolitical anxieties about China's rise in the Asian regional order. *Australian Journal of International Affairs* 68(4): 453–69

——(2016) China anxieties in the geopolitical cartographies of the Indo-Pacific. In P. Chacko (ed.), *New Regional Geopolitics in the Indo-Pacific: Drivers, Dynamics, and Consequences*, pp. 97–113. Abingdon: Routledge

Patience, A. (2018) *Australian Foreign Policy in Asia: Middle Power or Awkward Partner?* Cham: Springer

Phillips, A. (2016) *From Hollywood to Bollywood: Recasting Australia's Indo/Pacific Strategic Geography*. Canberra: ASPI

Prime Minister of Australia (2019a) Where we live. Speech presented at Asialink and Bloomberg. Sydney, 26 June

——(2019b) In our interest. Speech presented at Sydney Town Hall, NSW, 3 October

——(2020) Japan–Australia Leaders' Meeting Joint Statement. https://www.mofa.go.jp/files/100116180.pdf

Reynolds, L. (2019) Shangri-La Dialogue 2019. https://www.minister.defence.gov.au/minister/lreynolds/speeches/shangri-la-dialogue-2019

Silver, L., Devlin, K. & Huang, C. (2020) Unfavorable views of China reach historic highs in many countries. Washington: Pew Research Center, 6 October. https://www.pewresearch.org/global/2020/10/06/unfavorable-views-of-china-reach-historic-highs-in-many-countries

Taylor, B. (2020) Is Australia's Indo-Pacific strategy an illusion? *International Affairs* 96(1): 95–109

Trump, D.J. (2017) *National Security Strategy of the United States of America*. Executive Office of the President, Washington, DC

US Department of Defense (2019) *Indo-Pacific Strategy Report*. Washington, DC

US Department of State (2019) *A Free and Open Indo-Pacific: Advancing a Shared Vision*. Washington, DC

White, H. (2017) Without America: Australia in the New Asia. *Quarterly Essay* 68

Wilkins, T. (2018) After a decade of strategic partnership: Japan and Australia 'decentering' from the US alliance? *Pacific Review* 31(4): 498–514

——(2019a) Does Australia have an 'Indo-Pacific strategy'? JIIA Policy Brief. Tokyo: Japan Institute of International Affairs

——(2019b) Re-assessing Australia's intra-alliance bargaining power in the age of Trump. *Security Challenges* 15(1): 9–32

——(2020) *Searching for a Middle Path: ASEAN and the 'Indo-Pacific'*. Tokyo: Japan Institute of International Affairs

——(2023). Middle power hedging in the era of security/economic disconnect: Australia, Japan, and the 'Special Strategic Partnership'. *International Relations of the Asia–Pacific* 23(1): 93–127

Wilkins, T. & Kim, J. (2020) Adoption, accommodation or opposition? Regional powers respond to American-led Indo-Pacific strategy. *Pacific Review* 35(3): 1–31

Wilson, J.D. (2018) Rescaling to the Indo-Pacific: From economic to security-driven regionalism in Asia. *East Asia* 35(2): 177–96

Australia's security interests in South-East Asia and the Pacific

Joanne Wallis and Huong Le Thu

South-East Asia and the Pacific Islands have long been central to Australia's security imaginary: successive Defence White Papers have identified that the defence of the Pacific is second only to that of the Australian mainland in the hierarchy of Australia's strategic interests. In the 2016 Defence White Paper, the security of South-East Asia was elevated to equal importance as part of Australia's 'nearer region' (DOD, 2016: 68). Australia expressed its concern about 'the threat of a foreign military power seeking influence in ways that could challenge the security of our maritime approaches' through the Pacific Islands, and about its 'reliance on maritime trade with and through South-East Asia', which prompted the authors of the White Paper to argue that 'the security of our maritime approaches and trade routes within South-East Asia must be protected, as must freedom of navigation' (DOD, 2016: 69). With tensions rising in the broader Indo-Pacific (see Chapter 11), the 2020 Defence Strategic Update reiterated that 'defence planning will focus on our immediate region: ranging from the north-eastern Indian Ocean, through maritime and mainland South-East Asia to Papua New Guinea and the South West Pacific' (DOD, 2020: 6). As part of Australia's growing focus on the Indo-Pacific, it reiterated that South-East Asia and the Pacific Islands were priority subregions. Foreign and strategic policy, including Australia's force structure, were aligned accordingly.

In the period under review, Australian leaders began to articulate their concern about the current 'era of great power competition' (Morrison, 2019b). Prime Minister Scott Morrison (2019b) argued that 'Australia does not have to choose between the United States and China' in this competition, as 'it is in no one's interest in the Indo-Pacific to see an inevitably more competitive US–China relationship become adversarial' (Morrison, 2019a). However, the 2017 Foreign Policy White Paper warned that 'China is challenging America's position' and that 'the stability of the Indo-Pacific region ... cannot be assumed' (DFAT, 2017: 1). Australia avoided explicitly labelling China as a threat to its security, but the government was concerned about the increased Chinese presence in the Pacific Islands, with a perception that China was exercising a potentially malign influence in the region. Australia also expressed concerns about increased Chinese activism in South-East Asia, particularly in the context of contested claims to maritime territory in the South China Sea. The Australian Government therefore began to assume that China's presence in South-East Asia and the Pacific equated to greater Chinese influence. While this assumption influenced Australia's strategic and foreign policy choices, it was largely untested.

As we outline below, Australia responded by increasing its engagement in both subregions to consolidate its relationships, bolster its influence and reassure its regional partners of Australia's continued commitment. South-East Asian and Pacific Island states generally welcomed Australia's increased diplomatic and developmental focus, but they were more cautious about its emphasis on geostrategic competition. This reflected their concerns about how they would be affected by geostrategic competition and their determination to exercise agency and chart their own courses. That is, Australia did not sufficiently recognise that it had different geostrategic perceptions and interests from South-East Asian and Pacific Island states, nor did Australia sufficiently understand the agency of these neighbours. This sometimes led to Australia making counterproductive, or mutually conflicting, strategic and foreign policy decisions.

SOUTH-EAST ASIA AND THE PACIFIC IN AUSTRALIA'S WORLDVIEW

Australia has had a longstanding interest in being the pre-eminent power in the Pacific Islands and in being an influential player in South-East Asia. Starting in the first decade of the 21st century, however, Australia was becoming concerned about the possibility of China emerging as a new source of competition for influence in these subregions. The Australian Government's reprioritisation of these subregions began between 2006 and 2010 (Firth, 2011), specifically in response to China's growing influence.

At first blush, South-East Asia and the Pacific Islands do not share many similarities, particularly if judged in terms of size. In 2020 the most populous Pacific Islands state, Papua New Guinea, had a population of 8.6 million people, while the most populous country in South-East Asia, Indonesia, had 267.7 million people. The gap in the relative size of their economies is also large, and while levels of development varied across the two subregions, South-East Asian states tend to have more developed economies and be less dependent on aid. South-East Asia also has significantly more strategic weight and capacity, and is recognised as the centre, rather than the periphery, of great-power competition. Some countries in South-East Asia, like Indonesia (a fast-growing middle power) and Vietnam (an increasingly consequential player in regional strategic matters, including the South China Sea disputes), have global significance. Both collectively and individually, South-East Asian states are likely to play an important role in the future of great-power politics and influence the emerging regional order. Indeed, South-East Asia has played host to more interstate conflict than the Pacific Islands, although both have the experience – and memory – of being battlegrounds during World War II. Consequently, both regions are wary of being treated again as pawns in wider geopolitical conflicts that may emerge between the United States and China.

South-East Asia and the Pacific Islands have traditions of regionalism, under the auspices of the Association of South-East Asian Nations (ASEAN) and the Pacific

Islands Forum (PIF) respectively. There are similarities between the way both regional institutions operate, with the practice of consensual decision-making being common between them, as well as strong respect for the sovereignty of member states and consequently a preference for non-intervention in their affairs. These institutions offer means of engaging with major powers, especially in response to growing tensions in both regions, but these powers have generally engaged with countries in these regions on a bilateral basis rather than multilaterally through ASEAN and the PIF.

During the five years under review, Australian policy-makers referred to South-East Asia and the Pacific Islands as 'our near region' (DOD, 2020; DFAT, 2017). The near region's stability, prosperity and political development were deemed to be particularly relevant to Australia's national interests, and for this reason Canberra felt particularly responsible for it. In the broader Indo-Pacific strategies that Australia, Japan, the United States, India and several European countries were crystallising (see Chapter 11), South-East Asia and the Pacific Islands were part of Australia's main regions of interest. While there were good reasons for Canberra's strategy towards South-East Asia and the Pacific Islands to acknowledge the differences between these subregions, in practice Australian policy tended to bundle them together. For example, when announcing Australia's COVID-19 vaccine assistance strategy, Foreign Minister Marise Payne (2020a) said: 'We're investing in people, in economies, in security and systems, to help to keep our region strong. We are doing so through policies such as our COVID-19 vaccine program for the Pacific and South-East Asia, our Pacific economic recovery package and our additional South-East Asia initiatives recently announced.'

ENTER CHINA

The main reason why Australia refocused its foreign and strategic policy on South-East Asia and the Pacific Islands was in response to China's increased presence in both regions. While the Chinese state and Chinese firms had undoubtedly been increasing their *presence* in these regions, this did not necessarily translate into increased Chinese *influence*. When that influence did increase, it tended to be in respect of discrete matters and was unpredictable. Relatedly, China's growing presence sometimes backfired on Chinese interests, leading to resentment and a deterioration of relations with some countries in these regions. For example, in the Pacific Islands the dominance of Chinese firms in some sectors of the economy generated anti-China sentiment and sometimes violence.

This underscored the fact that the terms 'China' or 'the Chinese' were not unitary. Chinese immigrants had been present in South-East Asia for centuries and the Pacific Islands for more than a century. Often Chinese people who had lived in these regions for generations had little in common with, and indeed could be resentful of, more recent Chinese immigrants.

Moreover, while much focus was on the strategic implications of China's presence, this presence was mainly economic in nature: Chinese state-owned enterprises began to contract for Chinese-funded aid projects and bid for commercial contracts. These corporations were assisted by Chinese soft loans, which funded much of their work, and which increased thanks to the Belt and Road Initiative (BRI). From the vantage point of Australia and other countries, it was not easy to tell whether these loans were intended to enhance China's influence or to create economic opportunities for Chinese companies amid oversupply and economic stagnation at home.

The persistence of the Chinese presence in South-East Asia

Proximity, history and even shared natural resources had long bonded China with South-East Asia, and especially with the mainland states. Historical complexities added to China's strategy towards its South-East Asian neighbours, and there was no unified blueprint for exerting influence in the region. Economic engagement, however, was the primary tool of Beijing's global policy and proved successful.

Decades before the BRI was launched in 2014, China had built roads and bridges, assisted in the extraction and transportation of energy and natural resources, and invested in infrastructure in Vietnam, Laos, Cambodia, Myanmar and even Thailand, which had been America's ally. Even before its economic miracle, China assisted fellow communist states: the friendship bridges from that era are still visible in provinces that border China. In the 1990s, China showed South-East Asians a benign image and, guided by its 'good neighbourliness policy', looked for opportunities to cooperate.

These attempts to cooperate with South-East Asia were replicated as part of the BRI and expanded globally. During the period under review, mainland South-East Asia was the testing ground for China's BRI. South-East Asia received a massive boost in plans and pledges of investment from Beijing. Implementation of those pledges in individual countries, however, was not just a matter of feasibility and commercial assessments, but also contingent on political factors. For example, BRI projects in the Philippines were limited when President Benigno Aquino III took China to the International Tribunal on the Law of the Sea against its nine-dashed claims in the South China Sea. But President Rodrigo Duterte, who vowed not to observe the 2016 verdict (PCA, 2016), which denied the legality of Beijing's historical claims, won new pledges of economic support from China through the BRI (De Castro, 2019).

Beijing's political calculations when deciding on economic engagement with the neighbours were largely characterised as either inducement or punishment (Le Thu, 2018). Vietnam, another active claimant in the South China Sea, was an example of punishment as it was repeatedly either subjected to economic discrimination or bypassed for large investment projects. On the other hand, under President Joko Widodo, who showed less interest in diplomatic and strategic regional matters compared to his predecessors and had a quieter voice on Natuna disputes, Indonesia benefited from China's inducement strategy. Indonesia became one of the biggest recipients of BRI-pledged projects, which aligned with its economic and infrastructure ambitions (Negara & Suryadinata, 2018).

China's investments in South-East Asia might have influenced some leaders in the region in the period under review, including Duterte, Jokowi and Cambodia's Hun Sen, but they did not necessarily enhance Chinese soft power. As in the Pacific Islands, the presence of Chinese workers who accompanied BRI projects often caused social discontent or tension when there were pre-existing racial prejudices, as in Indonesia. This large influx also caused problems with housing, brought Chinese businesses to cater for the workers, and generated illicit activities (Felbab-Brown, 2013). Gambling, prostitution, crime and an increase in casino-building projects were also related to increased Chinese investments, fuelling social discontent and negative perceptions of China. For example, Chinese resorts and casino projects remade one of Cambodia's coastal cities, Sihanoukville, to the extent that it appeared Chinese, with Chinese workers, Chinese shopfronts and Chinese language being spoken, and use of the Renminbi currency being commonplace. This prompted many locals to worry that there was no room for Khmer workers (Chheang, 2017).

While the political and strategic aspects of the Sino-South-East Asian relations were complex and did not always concern the South China Sea disputes, they did not completely overshadow economic ties. South-East Asians were aware of the Chinese strategy of inducement and coercion, but they also had massive infrastructure needs and an appetite for trade. A baseline estimation was that the region needed nearly US$3 trillion worth of infrastructure investment between 2016 and 2030 (Asian Development Bank, 2017), and the COVID-19 pandemic threatened to multiply those needs. Unlike other major powers, however, China was willing and able to satisfy some of these needs (albeit at a price). South-East Asia therefore knowingly accepted some political risks associated with Beijing's economic influence, even if Australian policy-makers struggled to understand why.

The COVID-19 pandemic was an opportunity for Australia to strengthen its alliance with the United States, which had implications for Australian engagement with South-East Asia and the Pacific. The Trump administration referred to COVID-19 as the 'China virus', accused Beijing of deliberately releasing the pandemic, and demanded that China take responsibility for its spread around the world. Australia supported an independent inquiry into the origins of the virus (Payne, 2020b).

While it was legitimate to seek a scientific understanding of the origins of COVID-19, Australia's diplomatic messaging was often conflated with Trump-style accusations. This was not well received in South-East Asia. The deterioration of Australia's relations with China in 2020 and its close alignment with the United States were the primary motivation for it to call for an inquiry.[1] While the inquiry was an international collective effort brought into the multilateral arena of the World Health Assembly (WHA) and involving the World Health Organization (WHO), Canberra's advocacy reinforced the perception in South-East Asia that Australia had become increasingly hostile to China. To paraphrase an Indonesian policy-maker: 'It seems that in the eyes of Australia, there is nothing that China does that would not be criticised. China can do no good, not any more.'[2]

Australia was one of the most vocal critics of China's human rights abuses towards its Muslim minority Uyghurs; it openly supported the protests in Hong Kong in 2019; and it improved its non-official ties to Taiwan. Australia was also one of the first states to ban Huawei from its 5G market and to raise security concerns about China's malign use of technology. South-East Asian countries, despite their many disputes and long-standing animosities, did not openly criticise China. Not even Indonesia, the world's largest Muslim country, made as explicit a reference to the plight of the Uyghurs as Australia did. South-East Asian states did not proclaim a values-based foreign policy like Canberra. Some might have quietly cheered on Australia's stance, but none were willing to openly support its condemnation of China. Canberra's over-emphasis on an alliance of democracies to stand up to China was not well received in South-East Asia. Misunderstanding the regional mood and nuances was not conducive to Australian national interests, its relationships in the region or the promotion of its agenda.

---

[1] Confidential briefing with the authors, July 2021.
[2] Confidential briefing with the authors.

Australia considered South-East Asia one of the most significant theatres of great-power competition and tried to maintain and deepen relationships in the region. It invested in key bilateral partnerships, such as with Indonesia, Malaysia, Vietnam and Singapore (see Chapter 13), and participated in and supported the ASEAN-centred regional architecture. Canberra signalled, along with the United States and Japan, its commitment to provide a balance and 'an alternative' for infrastructure, aid and other assistance to China in South-East Asia. As Foreign Minister Payne (2020a) said: 'The Indo-Pacific is in a period of strategic competition. As that competition evolves, we have agency and influence to contribute to shaping our region through the decisions we make, and the actions that we take ... Australia will compete constructively.'

South-East Asia is populous, economically uneven and politically diverse, making its needs challenging to meet. Canberra's ambition to be a 'provider of public goods' in the region was positive, especially when the great powers were lagging. But Australia's capacity was limited, and far behind that of Japan and some European states. Canberra's policies failed to acknowledge that gap, particularly in the wake of cuts to Australia's budget for development aid.

The growth of Chinese influence in the Pacific

Similar dynamics were evident in the Pacific Islands, where China helped to meet the development needs of the subregion. Its economic presence translated into a certain degree of political influence, as seen in the decisions of Kiribati and Solomon Islands to switch their diplomatic recognition from Taiwan to China in 2019. However, some decisions by Pacific leaders that appeared political, such as whether to recognise Taiwan or China, were driven by local social and economic motivations, such as securing the support of local socio-political elites and other constituents. Australian commentary often overlooked this when analysing the strategic consequences of these decisions and tended to overstate the presence and influence of China in the Pacific.

Some Pacific leaders expressed concern about Australia and its allies and partners 'recasting of geostrategic competition and cooperation under the rubric of the "Indo-Pacific"' (Taylor, 2018). Samoan Prime Minister Tuilaepa Sailele Malielegaoi described this as a 'form of strategic manipulation' because '[t]he big powers are doggedly pursuing strategies to widen and extend their reach and inculcating a far-reaching sense of insecurity' (Malielegaoi, 2018). Some said that the Indo-Pacific framing implied that Pacific Island states would inevitably need to make a strategic choice, but PIF Secretary-General Dame Meg Taylor 'reject[ed] the terms of the dilemma in which the Pacific is given a choice between a "China alternative" and our traditional partners' (Taylor, 2019a). Implicitly admonishing Australia and other states that were seeking bilateral security partnerships, Taylor said that Pacific states needed 'to maintain our solidarity in the face of those who seek to divide us, particularly through the aggressive pursuit of bilateral relations' (Taylor, 2018; see also Wallis, 2021).

Australian leaders and officials expressed concern about geostrategic competition, but many in the Pacific did not have the same perception, which heightened their insecurity. In other words, Pacific Island states did not share Australia's geostrategic perspective (Naupa, 2017). Pacific leaders did not necessarily see China's increased presence in negative terms. According to Taylor (2019a), 'If there is one word that might resonate among all Forum members when it comes to China, that word is access.

Access to markets, technology, financing, infrastructure. Access to a viable future.' In a barely veiled reference to Australia's 'Step-Up' (see next section), Taylor (2019a) noted that 'China's presence has meant that other actors, new and old, are resettling their priorities and stepping up engagement in the Pacific'.

AUSTRALIA STEPS UP

In the context of rising tensions in the broader Indo-Pacific, Australia sought to reassure South-East Asia and the Pacific Islands that it would remain committed to, and a credible actor in, both regions. Australia's renewed engagement with South-East Asia had been preceded by declining aid budgets. For example, the budget allocation for South-East Asia was $385 million less in the 2019/20 financial year than five years previously. This raised concerns that the Pacific Step-Up was coming at the expense of South-East Asia.

Australian development assistance was shrinking, but its diplomatic engagement, both bilaterally with selective South-East Asian states and multilaterally with ASEAN, was more consistent. A highlight was the first Special Australia–ASEAN Summit in Sydney in 2018. It created a momentum – which arguably was wasted because of the Pacific Step-up – to foster neighbourly relationships on many functional levels, including cooperation in such initiatives like smart cities, cyber-security and technological cooperation.

Canberra elevated its engagement in terms of scope and quality, as well as frequency and quantity, to assert its presence in and contribution to the region. The Morrison government promoted the concept of the Indo-Pacific – or at least Australia's understanding of it – in South-East Asia. Australia encouraged and supported ASEAN's efforts to achieve a collective approach to the new construct, in the form of the ASEAN 'Outlook on the Indo-Pacific' (see Chapter 11). Recognising the region's demand for infrastructure, Australia also increased its role by partnering with the United States and Japan, particularly in relation to 'hard' infrastructure, to provide a sustainable and transparent alternative to China's BRI.

Australia also responded to the COVID-19 pandemic in South-East Asia. In May 2020 the government announced the 'Partnerships for Recovery', an initiative through which Australia worked globally to respond to the pandemic but with particular focus on South-East Asia and the Pacific. Canberra committed to redirecting $280 million from existing development programs to support critical medical assistance, including protective personal equipment (DFAT, 2020a). In November 2020, at the virtual East Asia Summit, Morrison committed another $500 million to support COVID-19 vaccinations in South-East Asia and the Pacific. In addition, almost $500 million was budgeted to assist South-East Asia with the consequences of the pandemic. This was hailed as the largest financial commitment to the region since the 2004 Indian Ocean tsunami (see Chapter 4).

Australian efforts to support South-East Asians were not recognised by regional partners. In a regional opinion survey conducted in late 2020, representatives from all ten ASEAN member states were asked which state among the ASEAN Dialogue Partners had provided the most help for the region for COVID-19. Of the roughly 1000 respondents in the survey, only 4.3 per cent pointed to Australia (ISEAS, 2021: 43). Most instead nominated China (44.2 per cent), Japan (18.2 per cent), the European

Union (10.3 per cent), the United States (9.6 per cent), the Republic of Korea (5.4 per cent) and New Zealand (4.7 per cent) (ISEAS, 2021: 15). On a question about geostrategic partners beyond the United States and China, Australia (7.5 per cent) was a distant third, behind the European Union (40.8 per cent) and Japan (39.3 per cent). If these quantitative opinions were any indication, Australia was far from becoming 'a partner of choice' to the region.

Australia made a more explicit attempt to enhance its engagement in the Pacific. At the 2017 PIF leaders' meeting, Prime Minister Malcolm Turnbull (2017) made a 'commitment to "step-up" Australia's engagement in the Pacific'. The 2017 *Foreign Policy White Paper* said that the Step-Up would include 'promoting economic cooperation and greater integration within the Pacific and with the Australian and New Zealand economies', 'tackling security challenges' and 'strengthening people-to-people links, skills and leadership' (DFAT, 2017: 99). In a speech at Lavarack Barracks in November 2018, Prime Minister Morrison (2018a) launched numerous initiatives. The Step-Up was overseen by a dedicated cross-agency Office of the Pacific within the Department of Foreign Affairs and Trade. Australia's commitment to the region was reiterated in its 2020 *Defence Strategic Update* and its COVID-19 *Development Response* (DOD, 2020: 6; DFAT, 2020a). However, as Stewart Firth observed in a previous edition of *Australia in World Affairs*, 'these developments, though branded as new, were refinements and reiterations of Australia's existing policy of deepening engagement with the region'.

The first aspect of the Step-up was economic development, which included a $2 billion Australian Infrastructure Financing Facility for the Pacific (AIFFP), enhanced labour mobility opportunities for Pacific islanders via the Seasonal Worker Scheme and Pacific Labour Mobility Scheme, and the Coral Sea Cable project, a submarine cable system connecting Papua New Guinea and Solomon Islands to Sydney. In keeping with its long-standing approach, Australia remained the largest aid donor to the region, providing $1.4 billion in development assistance to the Pacific in the 2019/20 financial year (DFAT, 2020b).

A second aspect was diplomatic and people-to-people links. This included efforts to enhance sports, education, media and church partnerships. Australia also undertook to open diplomatic missions in all Pacific states.

The third aspect, security, attracted the most attention. Initially there appeared to be a focus on the traditional security concerns prioritised by Australia, particularly advancing its interest in countering perceived Chinese influence. In 2018 Australia outbid China to fund the upgrade of Fiji's Blackrock Peacekeeping and Humanitarian and Disaster Relief Camp. It was also reported that Australia was in talks with Papua New Guinea about redeveloping a joint naval base on Manus Island in partnership with the United States (Dziedzic, 2018). Australia announced its intention to create an Australian Defence Force Pacific Mobile Training Team and a Pacific Faculty of Policing at the Australian Institute of Police Management.

This emphasis on traditional Australian security concerns in the Step-up was received cautiously in the Pacific, particularly the redevelopment of the Lombrum naval base. Vanuatu's former Foreign Minister Ralph Regenvanu said that 'we are not interested in militarisation' (Pacific Beat, 2018), a sentiment repeated by Dame Meg Taylor (2019b). Samoan Prime Minister Tuilaepa Sailele Malielegaoi (2018) similarly expressed concern about potential militarisation: 'As Pacific leaders we strongly believe in being ... free from military competition.'

Controversy over the redevelopment of the Lombrum base highlighted the risks relating to Australia's Pacific Step-up. Morrison said that Australia and the region were 'connected as members of a Pacific family', with their relationship based on 'respect, equality and openness' (Morrison, 2018a). There was a rhetorical emphasis on listening to Pacific priorities (Morrison, Payne & Reynolds, 2018), with the head of the Office of the Pacific, Ewen McDonald (2019), saying that 'our Step-up is taking place in consultation with our Pacific partners, in response to Pacific priorities'.

However, Morrison's (2018a) initial Pacific family framing was delivered in a speech at a military barracks during which he described at length an increased role for the Australian Defence Force, which highlighted the security concerns underpinning the Step-up. Morrison presumably assumed that the perceived security imperative would be needed to justify its cost to Australian taxpayers. But this had counterproductive consequences and cast doubt on the sincerity of the Step-up and claimed familial affection for the region.

Given that foreign policy is largely bipartisan and that the Australian electorate seldom removes governments because of foreign policy choices, the government could arguably have framed the Step-up in a less securitised way. The redevelopment of the Lombrum naval base exemplified this dynamic. While framed by the media as a response to the rising Chinese presence, the redevelopment was a routine part of Australia's long-standing Pacific Maritime Security Program (previously the Pacific Patrol Boat Program), with improvements to the base needed to accommodate the Guardian-class patrol boats being put into operation under the revitalised program. Although the program faced challenges, it was overwhelmingly appreciated by Pacific states because it addressed their priority of helping to police their exclusive economic zones (Wallis, 2017).

The Australian Government seemed to realise that its messaging was important. In 2020 it began to reframe the security aspects of the Step-Up in terms of meeting the priorities of Pacific Island states, as identified in the Boe Declaration on Regional Security at the 2018 PIF leaders' meeting. This declaration enshrined an 'expanded concept of security inclusive of human security, humanitarian assistance, prioritising environmental security, and regional cooperation in building resilience to disasters and climate change'. Australia reframed the security aspect of its Step-Up to emphasise its commitment to implementing the Boe Declaration, including through the creation in 2019 of the Pacific Fusion Centre to help share security-related information between Pacific Island states, and the Australia Pacific Security College to train and enhance cooperation between Pacific Islands security agencies.

Australia also emphasised its commitment to addressing climate change, which the Boe Declaration said 'remains the single greatest threat to the livelihoods, security and well-being of the peoples of the Pacific'. According to Collin Beck (2020: 15), Permanent Secretary of the Solomon Islands Ministry of Foreign Affairs and External Trade, climate change was a 'death sentence for the Pacific'. As a signatory to the declaration and in public statements, Australia recognised that 'here in the Pacific ... the impact of climate change, the impact of rising sea levels, it's not a theory. It's real ... And so the actions and directions that are set out in [the PIF communiqué] ... speak about our collective commitment to continue to address those issues' (Morrison, 2019c).

For these reasons Australia's renewed engagement included the 'Stepping up Climate Resilience in the Pacific' package (Morrison, Payne & Hawke, 2019).

This package did not represent new funding, instead drawing $500 million from existing aid funds. Pacific leaders were disappointed that Australia emphasised spending overseas rather than domestic action (see Chapter 9) in addressing climate change. Tuvalu's Prime Minister, Enele Sopoaga, responded to the 2019 announcement by saying: 'No matter how much money you put on the table, it doesn't give you the excuse ... not to do the right thing' (quoted in Clarke, 2019). Australia's climate change assistance also emphasised 'supporting our Pacific family's own efforts to respond to climate change and to build disaster resilience' (Payne, 2019). This focus on adaptation and resilience – which implicitly accepted the inevitability of climate change and preparing communities to adapt to it – frustrated the Pacific, which favoured mitigation (Wallis, 2021).

Beyond the Step-up, Australia continued to conduct development, governance and policing programs across the region with the aim of addressing the perceived vulnerabilities of Pacific Island states. The region had remained largely peaceful since the instability in Solomon Islands, Tonga and Fiji in 2006 (Firth, 2011), which had justified Australia's drawdown of the Regional Assistance Mission to Solomon Islands in 2013 after ten years of policing and governance intervention. In the period under review Australia kept a watching brief on instability in the region, with potential future redeployment to Solomon Islands facilitated by the Australia–Solomon Islands Bilateral Security Treaty signed in 2017. Australia and Papua New Guinea agreed to a Comprehensive Strategic and Economic Partnership in August 2020, which committed them to developing a bilateral security treaty. Australia and Vanuatu similarly agreed to negotiate a bilateral security treaty (Morrison, 2018b). Australia also signed the Fiji–Australia Vuvale Partnership, which although more effusive in its language of family, contained weaker commitments to advance security cooperation.

Most Pacific states prevented entry of COVID-19 or eliminated it, but the indirect consequences of the pandemic were considerable. It acted as a threat multiplier for existing and emerging challenges, such as climate change, the uneven nature of economic development, the porous nature of trade and tourism-dependent economies, the underdevelopment of public services, unequal gender relations, transnational crime, and unrest at mine sites in Papua New Guinea and elsewhere.

Reflecting this, Pacific Island states were among recipients of the $280 million Australia devoted to COVID-19 responses under its 'Partnerships for Recovery'. The government also undertook to consider the potential for economic growth, employment and health when assessing projects funded under the AIFFP (Clarke, 2020). Australia's response to COVID-19 was influenced by its geostrategic concerns. The perception that Australia was competing with other donors – primarily China – was enhanced in April 2020, when a Royal Australian Air Force plane arrived in Vanuatu with humanitarian supplies. Although the crew were given approval to land by the Vanuatu authorities, they could not do so because a plane chartered by a Chinese firm that had also donated supplies to Vanuatu was on the runway already. The Australian plane returned to Australia before heading back to Vanuatu the next day. The Australian media reported that there was 'growing concern within Defence about whether the hold-up was intentional to delay the Australian plane from landing' (Galloway, 2020). Foreign Minister Payne (2020b) described the incident as 'absolutely regrettable' and raised her concerns with the governments of Vanuatu and China, but refused to say whether the incident was deliberate.

CONCLUSION

This chapter has illustrated how and why Australia became more anxious about its security interests in South-East Asia and the Pacific Islands in the five years beginning in 2016. That concern was not new and reflected Australia's long-standing view that the geographic proximity of these two regions was central to its security. Australia's concern about China's growing presence in these regions was also not new but instead continued a preoccupation that had developed since 2010.

Australian security planners assumed that China's presence in these subregions equated to greater Chinese influence. This assumption influenced Australia's strategic and foreign policy choices – particularly its Step-Up in the Pacific and increased aid to South-East Asia, but it was largely untested. The assumption also limited the government's ability to recognise that it had different geostrategic perceptions and interests to South-East Asian and Pacific Island states, particularly regarding China's role. This led Australia to underestimate the agency of its South-East Asian and Pacific Islands neighbours, including their ability to forge their own relationships with China. This was particularly the case in South-East Asia, where states generally have a higher degree of capacity than those in the Pacific, have more experience in dealing with China, and are therefore better at resisting Australia's efforts to dictate the terms of their engagement with China.

Although Australia made a significant investment in the Pacific Islands, it underestimated the policy focus and spending commitment that was required to bolster its relationships in South-East Asia, which was closer to the front line of the emerging geostrategic competition. Therefore, by the end of 2020, Australia also faced the need to 'Step-Up' in South-East Asia in a way that would reflect the circumstances and scale of its engagement in the subregion. Indeed, while the Pacific Step-up was welcomed, Pacific Island states remained wary of Australia, particularly given its reluctance to commit to domestic action to combat climate change. South-East Asian states were even more ambivalent about Australia. They had some negative perceptions due to Australia's tendency to frame its engagement in South-East Asia and the Pacific in terms of its perception that China's presence in both regions had generated influence and that it needed to compete with China in response. For South-East Asians in particular, their historical experience with China led them to think they had developed a strategy to co-exist with China (Le Thu, 2020). Australia had come to resemble a neighbour that had forgotten that its proximity to South-East Asia and the Pacific Islands meant that it needed to navigate challenging circumstances with a mindset of building long-standing and beneficial relationships.

References

Asian Development Bank (2017) *Meeting Asia's Infrastructure Needs*. https://www.adb.org/publications/asia-infrastructure-needs

Beck, C. (2020) How should the Pacific Islands states advance their strategic and security interests? *Security Challenges* 16(1): 11–16

Chheang, V. (2017) *The Political Economy of Chinese Investment in Cambodia*. Singapore: ISEAS – Yusof Ishak Institute

Clarke, M. (2019) Tuvalu's PM says Australia's climate funding for Pacific 'not an excuse' to avoid emissions cuts'. *ABC News*, 13 August. https://www.abc.net.au/news/2019-08-13/australias-climate-funding-pacific-islands-forum-tuvalu/11408930

——(2020) Australia spends $100m in 'quick financial support' for Pacific countries hit by cyclone and pandemic. *ABC News*, 20 May. https://www.abc.net.au/news/2020-05-20/australia-financial-support-pacific-governments-cyclone-pandemic/12262328

De Castro, R. (2019) China's Belt and Road Initiative (BRI) and the Duterte administration's appeasement policy: Examining the connection between the two national strategies. *East Asia* 36: 205–27

Department of Defence (DOD) (2016) *2016 Defence White Paper*. Canberra: Commonwealth of Australia

——(2020) *2020 Defence Strategic Update*. Canberra: Commonwealth of Australia

Department of Foreign Affairs and Trade (DFAT) (2017) *2017 Foreign Policy White Paper*. Canberra. www.fpwhitepaper.gov.au

——(2020a) *Partnerships for Recovery: Australia's COVID-19 Development Response*. Canberra

——(2020b) *2019–2020 Australian Aid Budget Summary*. https://www.dfat.gov.au/sites/default/files/2019-20-australian-aid-budget-summary-pacific.pdf

Dziedzic, S. (2018) US to partner with Australia, Papua New Guinea on Manus Island naval base. *ABC News*, 17 November. https://www.abc.net.au/news/2018-11-17/us-to-partner-with-australia-and-png-on-manus-island-naval-base/10507658

Felbab-Brown, V. (2013) Illegal trade in Southeast Asia and its East Asian markets. Brookings Institution. https://www.brookings.edu/articles/the-illegal-trade-in-wildlife-in-southeast-asia-and-its-links-to-east-asian-markets/

Firth, S. (2011) Australia, the Pacific Islands and Timor-Leste. In J. Cotton & J. Ravenhill (eds), *Middle Power Dreaming: Australia in World Affairs 2006–2010*. Melbourne: Oxford University Press

Galloway, A. (2020) Defence looks at Chinese plane blocking Australian aid plane in Vanuatu. *Sydney Morning Herald*, 15 April. https://www.smh.com.au/politics/federal/defence-looks-at-chinese-plane-blocking-australian-aid-plane-in-vanuatu-20200415-p54k5i.html

ISEAS – Yusof Ishak Institute (2021) *State of Southeast Asia: 2021 Survey Report*. Singapore. https://www.iseas.edu.sg/wp-content/uploads/2021/01/The-State-of-SEA-2021-v2.pdf

Le Thu, H. (2018) China's dual strategy of coercion and inducement towards ASEAN. *Pacific Review* 32(1): 20–36

——(2020) Post-COVID-19 Australia and South-east Asia: Aligning more closely or drifting further apart? In M. Shoebridge & L. Sharland (eds), *After Covid-19: Australia, the Region and Multilateralism*, Vol. 2. Canberra: ASPI

Malielegaoi, T.S. (2018) Speech on Pacific perspectives on the new geostrategic landscape. Sydney: Lowy Institute, 30 August. https://www.lowyinstitute.org/publications/speech-hon-prime-minister-tuilaepa-sailele-malielegaoi-pacific-perspectives-new

McDonald, E. (2019) Realising the Pacific's vision for stability, security and prosperity. Speech, Canberra, 7 June. https://www.dfat.gov.au/news/speeches/Pages/realising-the-pacifics-vision-for-stability-security-and-prosperity

Morrison, S. (2018a) Australia and the Pacific: A new chapter. Townsville: Lavarack Barracks, 8 November. https://www.pm.gov.au/media/address-australia-and-pacific-new-chapter

——(2018b) Enhanced security cooperation with Vanuatu. Media release, 18 November. https://www.pm.gov.au/media/enhanced-security-cooperation-vanuatu

——(2019a) Where we live. Address to Asialink. Sydney, 26 June. https://www.pm.gov.au/media/where-we-live-asialink-bloomberg-address

——(2019b) In our interest. 2019 Lowy lecture. Sydney, 3 October. https://www.lowyinstitute.org/publications/2019-lowy-lecture-prime-minister-scott-morrison

——(2019c) Doorstop – Funafuti, Tuvalu. Funafuti, 15 August. https://www.pm.gov.au/media/doorstop-funafuti-tuvalu

Morrison, S., Payne, M. & Hawke, A. (2019) Stepping up climate resilience in the Pacific. 13 August. https://www.pm.gov.au/media/stepping-climate-resilience-pacific#:~:text=Prime%20Minister%20Scott%20Morrison%20said,change%20challenges%20the%20Pacific%20faced.&text=%E2%80%9CThe%20%24500%20million%20we're,%24300%20million%20for%202016%2D2020

Morrison, S., Payne, M. & Reynolds, L. (2018) Strengthening Australia's commitment to the Pacific. Media release. Canberra, 8 November. https://www.pm.gov.au/media/strengthening-australias-commitment-pacific

Naupa, A. (2017) Indo-Pacific diplomacy: A view from the Pacific Islands. *Politics and Policy* 45(5): 902–17

Negara, S.D. & Suryadinata, L. (2018) *Indonesia and China's Belt and Road Initiatives: Perspectives, Issues and Prospects*. Singapore: ISEAS – Yusof Ishak Institute

Pacific Beat (2018) Chinese military base in Pacific would be of 'great concern', Turnbull tells Vanuatu. *ABC News*, 10 April. https://www.abc.net.au/news/2018-04-10/china-military-base-in-vanuatu-report-of-concern-turnbull-says/9635742

Pacific Islands Forum (2018) Boe Declaration on Regional Security. https://www.forumsec.org/2018/09/05/boe-declaration-on-regional-security

Payne, M. (2019) Speech to the Fijian Press Club Lunch. Suva, 5 June. https://www.foreignminister.gov.au/minister/marise-payne/speech/speech-fijian-press-club-lunch

——(2020a) Building a cohesive Indo-Pacific. Speech at DFAT, Canberra, 4 December. https://www.foreignminister.gov.au/minister/marise-payne/speech/building-cohesive-indo-pacific

——(2020b) Interview with David Speers. *ABC Insiders*, 19 April. https://www.foreignminister.gov.au/minister/marise-payne/transcript/interview-david-speers-abc-insiders

Permanent Court of Arbitration (2016) *The South China Sea Arbitration (Philippines vs The People's Republic of China)*. https://pca-cpa.org/en/cases/7/

Taylor, M. (2018) Address by PIFS Secretary General Dame Meg Taylor – 2018 State of the Pacific Conference. Canberra: Australian National University, 8 October. https://www.forumsec.org/keynote-address-by-dame-meg-taylor-secretary-general-the-china-alternative-changing-regional-order-in-the-pacific-islands/

——(2019a) The China alternative: Changing regional order in the Pacific Islands. Speech, University of the South Pacific, Port Vila, Vanuatu, 8 February. https://www.forumsec.org/keynote-address-by-dame-meg-taylor-secretary-general-the-china-alternative-changing-regional-order-in-the-pacific-islands/

——(2019b) Griffith Asia Lecture 2019. Brisbane: Griffith University, 11 November. https://www.forumsec.org/griffith-asia-lecture-2019-delivered-by-the-secretary-general-of-the-pacific-islands-forum-dame-meg-taylor/

Turnbull, M. (2017) Pacific Islands Forum in Samoa. Media release, 6 September. https://pmtranscripts.pmc.gov.au/release/transcript-41165

Wallis, J. (2017) *Pacific Power? Australia's Strategy in the Pacific Islands*. Melbourne: Melbourne University Press

——(2021) Contradictions in Australia's Pacific Islands discourse. *Australian Journal of International Affairs* 75(5): 487–506

13

Australia's engagement with ASEAN

Singapore as a conduit

See Seng Tan

A longstanding but under-realised aim of Australian foreign policy has been to strengthen its ties with South-East Asia (Huong, 2018; Lemahieu, 2020; Maude, 2020). The Department of Foreign Affairs and Trade identified this aspiration in the 2017 White Paper on foreign policy (DFAT, 2017: 43–4), which was timely given the increasing strains that were emerging in Australia's ties with China.

Australians have historically regarded Indonesia as the most important South-East Asian country with which they ought most to engage.[1] That said, both countries continue to harbour a deep distrust of one another, leading an Indonesian news editorial to describe ties with Australia as a 'love–hate relationship' (Purba, 2020).

By contrast, despite their considerable cultural, political and physical differences (Meyrick, 2016), the commonalities between Australia and Singapore – their international activism and robust support for multilateralism and a rules-based order, and their conundrum of having the United States as their top security partner and China as their leading trade partner in an era of US/China rivalry, *inter alia* – arguably renders Singapore a logical and reliable partner. Through Singapore, Australia can access and engage more extensively and deeply with the rest of South-East Asia and the Association of South-East Asian Nations (ASEAN).

Beginning with an assessment of present-day bilateral ties, the chapter looks at how Australia and Singapore overcame drawbacks in their relationship and examines their growing strategic and normative congruence as part of the foundation on which their evolving partnership rests. It argues that the partnership reached new heights in the period under review. There are, to be sure, areas of potential disagreement within that general pattern of congruence, most acutely over how best to manage China's strategic

---

[1] Beyond their security agreement of 1995, Canberra and Jakarta successfully inked a comprehensive strategic partnership in 2018 and finalised a 'comprehensive economic partnership agreement' in 2020 that spanned not only economics, education and development but defence and security cooperation too (Lemahieu, 2020; Wibawa, 2020).

intentions and rising assertiveness in the region. This was evident between 2016 and 2020, when both Australia and Singapore were guilty of sending mixed messages on and towards China. This highlighted the common challenges both countries confront in their complex relations with China. Finally, the chapter makes a case for the Australia–Singapore partnership as a foundation and catalyst on and through which Canberra's aspiration to engage more deeply with South-East Asia can be more fully realised.

ENGAGING SOUTH-EAST ASIA: AN ENDURING THEME IN AUSTRALIAN FOREIGN POLICY

The engagement of South-East Asia has been an enduring theme in Australia's foreign policy, albeit one serially overpromised but underdelivered due to limitations on both the Australian and South-East Asian sides (Evans, 2017; Rodan, 2012; Wesley, 2007). When the Gillard government proclaimed the so-called Asian century as an Australian opportunity in its 2012 White Paper – a direction welcomed by those who argued its necessity in the interest of Australia's economic survival (McGregor, 2013; Thakur, 2013) – it quickly became obvious to most Australian and other regional observers that 'Asia', for Canberra, really meant China and considerably less so South-East Asia and ASEAN (Cook, 2018; Evans, 2014; Milner, 2012; Zhang, 2007; Zhang, 2012). The lacuna seemed odd, given that Australia was the very first dialogue partner of ASEAN, a relationship dating back to 1974. Together with its ASEAN counterparts, Australia played key roles in the formation of Asia-Pacific Economic Cooperation (APEC) and the ASEAN Regional Forum (ARF). Indeed, it could be argued that through its participation in ASEAN's regional institutions, Australia has had far more opportunities to engage with the world's major powers than it could do on its own (Tan, 2014a). Nor does this imply that Australia has done little over the years to engage with the region. South-East Asia is Australia's second-largest trading partner with Thailand, Malaysia, Vietnam and Singapore as the key markets; between 2017 and 2018, Australia's two-way trade with ASEAN countries was A$110 billion, with Indonesia, Malaysia, Singapore and Vietnam accounting for 77.2 per cent of total Australian exports of goods to South-East Asia (Cook, 2018; Sainsbury, 2019). There was robust collaboration between Australia and South-East Asia in security, counterterrorism and humanitarian relief. In response to the Indian Ocean tsunami in December 2004, for instance, the Australian Government and public provided well over A$1 billion in humanitarian assistance for the affected South-East Asian countries (DFAT, 2014).

In light of Australia's difficulties with China in the period under review, South-East Asia and ASEAN, understandably if somewhat belatedly, regained a measure of significance for Canberra (Lemahieu, 2020; Roughneen, 2019). Indeed, Australia's efforts to re-engage with South-East Asia did not go unnoticed by China's state-sponsored media (Power, 2020; Quiggin, 2020). For example, the *Global Times* urged (or, if you like, warned) that Australia's deepening engagement with South-East Asia was for economic reasons, not political ones (Qu, 2020). But that engagement did not amount to much relative to Canberra's outreach to the South Pacific via its 'Pacific Step-Up' (see Chapter 12), a mismatch on which even the US ambassador to Australia urged the need for readjustment (Greene, 2020; Lemahieu, 2020; Wyeth, 2020). Indeed, it could be argued that ASEAN was simply ignored in a lot of Australian foreign policy analysis. For instance, one study urged Australia to pursue a more concerted effort at strategic hedging through 'enmeshing' regional powers and partners other than the United States and China, but not ASEAN (Chan, 2020). Likewise, a leading analyst of Australian foreign policy implored Canberra to continue its 'incremental' hedging by maintaining strong, positive relations with all of Asia's major powers – again, with no mention of ASEAN (Bisley, 2020). If anything, the relentless focus on China by Australia arguably rendered economic-cum-strategic collaboration and convergence with South-East Asia appear myopic and misguided in its unexploited opportunities (Evans, 2014). Granted, the prospect of Australian membership in ASEAN, raised in the wake of the first ASEAN–Australia Special Summit in Sydney in 2018, was probably ill-conceived, but there was much more that could be done to enhance trade, security and diplomatic cooperation between Australia and South-East Asia (Cook, 2018; Tan, 2014b).

The Australia–Singapore partnership was something that Canberra could leverage to extend and deepen its engagement with South-East Asia and ASEAN. As alluded to earlier in the chapter, the prospect for a pragmatic convergence on support for a rules-based order in the Indo-Pacific – one in which liberal values, although important, are no longer the dominant element in Canberra's approach – implied that Singapore might have an indirect role to play in Australia's reset of its relations with China by helping Canberra to understand better the Chinese disposition and shaping responses that permit the Australian position to be stated without needlessly provoking apoplectic reactions from Beijing. Arguably, such pragmatic convergence could even pave the way for Australia to play a constructive role, in conjunction with ASEAN, in managing the delicate politics of South-East Asia. If Australia was intent on becoming an incremental strategic hedger (Bisley, 2020; Chan, 2020), it would need to pursue relations with ASEAN and other regional actors in ways that eschewed looking at and defining such engagements solely via the prism of the US/China rivalry, as the 2017 DFAT White Paper appeared to suggest.

With its partnership with Singapore as a basis, Australia could look at engagement with South-East Asia as a good in itself. The case of Japan's relations with South-East Asia is instructive in this respect. Despite the propensity of Prime Minister Abe to treat foreign aid to South-East Asia as tied to the perceived need to balance China, Japan nonetheless successfully engaged with ASEAN on its own terms (Tan, 2015: 75–6). According to an opinion poll conducted by a leading Singapore-based think tank in 2020, a majority of South-East Asian respondents picked Japan as their preferred strategic partner in the event of the United States' continued downward slide from global prominence and relevance (ISEAS, 2020). Fairly or otherwise, many of those respondents were confident that Japan would do the right thing when it came to providing global public goods because Japan had proved its worth as a responsible stakeholder in South-East Asia (Glosserman, 2020). Developing a track record of engagement with South-East Asia that brings Australia closer to that of Japan could prove immensely helpful to Australian foreign policy in future.

SINGAPORE AS A CONDUIT

The 'longstanding, deep and mutual' relationship (WPR, 2016) that Australia and Singapore shared during the period under review was not always so sturdy or amicable. Singapore's founding father Lee Kuan Yew famously warned in 1980 that Australia was destined to become the 'poor white trash of Asia' if it continued to resist opening its economy. Notwithstanding its impolitic nature, Lee's putdown indirectly prompted the Hawke–Keating reforms of the 1980s. Counterintuitively perhaps, the comment occupies 'a position of respect in Australia's political psyche today' (Kerin, 2015). After that awkward moment, bilateral relations endured several low points. In 2001, the Singaporean telecommunications giant SingTel's bid for Australia's Optus in 2001 floundered in the wake of Australian allegations, including those made by the respected Australian National University academics Ross Babbage and the late Des Ball, regarding the Singaporean government's history of spying on Australia (McGrath, 2001). Ironically, a decade later in 2013, SingTel made the news again, except this time for reportedly facilitating efforts by the Five Eyes alliance (Australia, Canada, New Zealand, the United Kingdom and the United States) to conduct electronic surveillance on certain South-East Asian leaders. Included in SingTel's efforts was its purported enabling of Australia's monitoring of Indonesian president Susilo Bambang Yudhoyono's personal mobile phone (Tan, 2015: 45).

Another historical drawback involved the vehement disagreement over Prime Minister Rudd's proposed 'Asia-Pacific community' (APc) in the late 2000s, which South-East Asians judged as inimical to the centrality of ASEAN in the institutional architecture of the Asia Pacific (Rodan, 2012). Rudd's disenchantment with the perceived lack of progress made by the ARF since its inception in 1994 led him to propose his APc as an alternative arrangement for the region (Woolcott, 2009). Reportedly, an early effort by Rudd – via his envoy, Richard Woolcott – to consult ASEAN leaders engendered the conclusion that the South-East Asians had no appetite for a new institution, and certainly not the proposed APc (Koh, 2009). However, at a subsequent meeting convened to discuss the APc proposal in Sydney in December 2009, the veteran Singapore diplomat Tommy Koh went so far as to accuse his hosts of attempting to force the contrary view that the ASEAN states had agreed to Australia's claim that existing regional institutions were inadequate and ineffective – a view that Koh flatly denied (Koh, 2009). The ASEAN delegates also took umbrage at their Australian colleagues' insinuation that South-East Asia had supported the notion of a 'group of eight' comprising the world's major powers and Asia-Pacific regional powers – including Australia and Indonesia, but crucially not ASEAN itself – that presumably would co-manage Rudd's APc and underwrite the regional order, much as a concert of powers might (Tan, 2015: 51). If anything, Australia's advocacy of a 'G8' *sans* ASEAN was consistent with the perception held by some Australian analysts that South-East Asia was never really significant in Canberra's outreach to Asia (Evans, 2014, 2017; Milner, 2012).

A development that paved the way towards the subsequent healing of the bilateral rift over the APc was a WikiLeaks exposé regarding Rudd's aspiration for the APc as a plausible regional platform for balancing China institutionally. At the time, China's growing power and influence was a concern shared by Rudd and many other regional countries, including Singapore (Asia Sentinel, 2011).[2] Reportedly, Rudd's efforts were subsequently, if belatedly, acknowledged by Singapore's foreign minister at the East Asia Summit (EAS) meeting in July 2011, where the latter praised Rudd's 'original

---

[2] For an analysis of the workings and impact of institutional balancing within and across regional institutional arrangements in the post–Cold War Asia Pacific, see He (2020).

thought [and] leadership', which, indirectly or otherwise, led to the enlargement of the EAS membership to include Russia and, more critically, the United States (Flitton, 2011).

Between 2016 and 2020, the most significant and emblematic development in bilateral relations between Singapore and Australia was the signing of the Comprehensive Strategic Partnership (CSP), which was formally completed on 29 June 2016, precisely 50 years after they established diplomatic relations. A broad agreement that spans defence, foreign policy, trade and investment, and people-to-people links, Prime Ministers Malcolm Turnbull and Lee Hsien Loong referred to the CSP as a 'massive upgrade' and a 'landmark agreement', respectively, in bilateral ties. The two countries sought to transform their 'longstanding friendship into a dynamic, innovative and truly strategic partnership' and to become what Turnbull called 'natural partners' (Parameswaran, 2016).

In December 2017, the enhanced version of the Singapore–Australia Free Trade Agreement (SAFTA), originally established in 2003, entered into force upon ratification by both sides. In July 2020, Turnbull's successor Scott Morrison and Lee jointly referenced the CSP and reaffirmed the 'excellent relations between Singapore and Australia and looked forward to working together to advance bilateral cooperation' (CNA, 2020). The CSP did not engender so much as to reflect and leverage economic and security facts on the ground in the ongoing integration between the two partners. It referenced the successful conclusion in May 2016 of the Third Review of the SAFTA to reflect changing conditions in global and regional trade. In addition to tariff elimination, the reinforced SAFTA improved 'market access for Australian exports of services, particularly education, environmental, telecommunications, and professional services. It also provides a more open and predictable business environment across a range of areas, including competition policy, government procurement, intellectual property, e-commerce, customs procedures, and business travel' (DFAT, n.d.; see also Lim, 2020). It created the potential to expand and deepen even further bilateral trade and investment. By this time Singapore was Australia's largest two-way trade and investment partner in South-East Asia and its second-largest source of new investment flows, behind only the United States (Cook, 2018; Graham, 2016; Murphy, 2016).

SECURITY TIES AND THE ENABLING OF THE UNITED STATES' STRATEGIC PRESENCE

Australia and Singapore share broad agreement in terms of their respective security perspectives and policies where the wider Asia Pacific is concerned, and their shared perspective was evident in the period under review. The two countries shared a litany of concerns ranging from Islamic terrorism and cyber-related vulnerabilities to the management of big-power rivalry and discord. Both also remained members of the Five Power Defence Arrangements (FPDA), the world's second-oldest military partnership after the North Atlantic Treaty Organization (NATO), although a crucial difference was that the FPDA was a 'suballiance pact' that allowed for consultation among its parties (which also include Malaysia, New Zealand and the United Kingdom) in the event of an external attack occurring on the Malay Peninsula (Graham, 2016: 4).

The CSP further consolidated bilateral security cooperation. It committed both countries to a broad range of measures designed to enhance their already close ties, including elevating Exercise Trident (a signature joint bilateral military exercise), enhancing personnel exchanges, boosting intelligence and information-sharing, and launching a 'Track 1.5' dialogue involving government officials and academic practitioners from both sides (Department of the Prime Minister and Cabinet, 2016). The CSP's *pièce de résistance* was a multibillion-dollar agreement to develop jointly military training areas and facilities in Queensland, known as the Australia–Singapore Military Training Initiative. These facilities were fully funded by Singapore via a A$2.25 billion investment in the expansion of existing facilities in Shoalwater Bay in Central Queensland and the establishment of a new facility in Greenvale in North Queensland. This expansion granted the Singaporean armed forces increased access to much-needed training space. Projected to handle up to 14 000 military personnel for 18 weeks a year, when fully operational, the facilities would allow Singapore, whose small land size cannot accommodate all its military training needs, to exercise its troops in a tropical zone (Turnbull, 2016).

In October 2018, both countries inaugurated Exercise Crescent Star involving 220 participants from Singapore's Army Deployment Force and the Australian Army's Rifle Company Butterworth in Singapore. The coronavirus pandemic prevented Singapore from conducting its annual Exercise Wallaby in 2020, which would have involved the short-term deployment of up to 4000 troops to Shoalwater Bay (Yeo, 2020). Beyond military training, the Republic of Singapore Navy and Australia's Maritime Border Command, a multi-agency task force within the Australian Border Force, inked a pact in September 2019 on 'white' (as opposed to 'grey') shipping, which facilitates mutual information-sharing on maritime traffic that would enable both services to better secure their countries' respective waters (Parameswaran, 2019).

A commonality between Australia and Singapore is that they are committed to extensive economic engagement with China and support a greater Chinese role in regional leadership, while they also harbour concern over its strategic intentions. As Scott Morrison noted in the 2020 Defence Strategic Update and Force Structure Plan, the Asia-Pacific region is 'in the midst of the most consequential strategic realignment since the Second World War' – with China's power and influence the key driver behind it all (Cooper & Edel, 2020). While Singapore Premier Lee Hsien Loong warned the United States against 'colliding with China' or conversely quitting the region (Werner, 2020), there was no denying that since the passing of Lee Kuan Yew in March 2015, the city-state no longer seemed to enjoy the special standing it once had with China (Chang, 2019; Tan, 2019; 2020a).

In terms of policy congruence, however, the most evident feature was the robust support for and active facilitation that Australia and Singapore have offered for the US military presence in Asia, which both believe is critical to their security, stability and prosperity. In an interview on ABC Radio in June 2017, Lee noted the commonality in interests between the two countries. The Prime Minister observed that one such enduring interest, in view of the Trump administration that had just taken office in Washington, was to ensure that

> the US continues to have a major role to play and that the US continues to see itself as fully engaged in the region ... We should work with it and hope that they will be able to work something out which will be in the long-term interests of the US and of the region, which will mean is good for Singapore and I think will be good for Australia. (PMO, 2017)

Australia and Singapore rarely wavered in their public support for the US strategic presence in Asia, despite the private reservations they might have held about former President Trump's views and policy conduct. This included his withdrawal from the original Trans-Pacific Partnership (which both Australia and Singapore strongly favoured), his opposition to Canberra's refugee deal struck with the Obama administration, and his unfounded allegation that Singapore was cheating on trade against the United States.[3]

At some level, this loyalty and solidarity was recognised even by the famously sceptical Trump administration. At the 2018 G20 summit, Trump described the Australia–US alliance as 'one of [America's] oldest and one of our best' (Parmer, 2019). Australian forces have fought alongside their US counterparts in nearly every war the United States has entered since World War I and, along with its fellow Quad members (India, Japan and the United States), Australia has promoted the 'free and open Indo-Pacific' strategy that the United States and Japan initiated in 2017 and 2016 respectively (see Chapter 11).

For its part, Singapore reportedly declined President George W. Bush's offer to be a non-NATO major ally due to its wariness about *de jure* alliances (Graham, 2016: 5). For all intents and purposes, however, Singapore was the United States' strongest and most reliable security partner in South-East Asia (Graham & Huxley, 2015). Its relations with the United States, in turn, were hailed by various US leaders in the strongest and most positive terms (Tan, 2016: 33).

Both Australia and Singapore participated in the US-led coalitions in Iraq and/or Afghanistan and facilitated rotational deployments of US forces, with US Marines in Darwin and US Navy littoral combat ships and P-8A maritime surveillance aircraft in Singapore, for example. Steadfast support for their common ally was the hallmark of Australian and Singaporean foreign policy between 2016 and 2020, further solidifying their capacity to reach a common perspective on the region.

SECURING THE INDO-PACIFIC

Arguably, in an Indo-Pacific region chockful of both traditional and non-traditional security challenges, the most vexing regional concern for both Australia and Singapore in the period under review was China's strategic intentions and the military assertiveness it was displaying in the South China Sea.

Crucially, both Australia and Singapore were on the receiving end of Chinese influence operations, including cyberattacks (Hsiao, 2019; Searight, 2020). While it was the Morrison government's call for an independent global investigation into the origins and early handling of the COVID pandemic – a motion that Beijing supported, following intense negotiations with the involvement of the European Union – that sparked Chinese outrage, it bears reminding that his initial optimism with China notwithstanding, Malcolm Turnbull's assessment of China changed subsequently in the light of what he later saw as glaring evidence of China's cyber espionage against Australia (Turnbull, 2020). Moreover, Australia had to deal with China's efforts to influence Australian domestic politics and civil society debate (Cave & Tarabay, 2019; see also Chapter 5).

---

[3] Singapore was the only ASEAN state not to have a trade surplus with the United States (Guilford, 2018).

Singapore had its own set of difficulties with China. Widely known for its leading role in the United Nations process that eventually delivered the 1982 Law of the Sea Convention, Singapore's support for the 2016 Arbitral Tribunal's decision to deny Chinese claims to huge swathes of the South China Sea significantly complicated its relations with China (Tan, 2020a). Whatever their respective perspectives and strategies on the Indo-Pacific might be, their approaches to China suggested a pattern of congruent disposition and conduct that reflected the shared dilemma of managing an assertive China, on which their economic wellness depends.

That said, there were some differences, or nuances perhaps, in their respective approaches. In 2017, the Australian Department of Foreign Affairs and Trade (DFAT) published a White Paper with the express aim to 'support a balance in the Indo-Pacific favourable to [Australia's] interests and promote an open, inclusive, and rules-based region' (DFAT, 2017: 3). According to Hervé Lemahieu, Australia's Indo-Pacific strategy as presented by DFAT could be understood in terms of three 'geographic rings': an inner ring focused on the South Pacific region, Australia's so-called sphere of influence, where it is the preponderant resident power; a middle ring focused on the South-East Asian/ASEAN region, with which Australia seeks to work in the common quest for regional order; and an outer ring focused on the Quad powers with which Australia aims to establish jointly a strategic-cum-military counterweight to an increasingly assertive China (Lemahieu, 2020).

The White Paper made clear that Australia's alliance with the United States was central to Canberra's approach to the Indo-Pacific (DFAT, 2017: 4). As Nick Bisley put it, 'Australia has made up its mind about its strategic policy: it has bound itself to the United States and will do all it can to support America's conception of regional and global order' (Bisley, 2012). On the other hand, Australia's penchant for middle-power diplomacy was also evident in the document. Australia's differences with its ally's strategy were clear in the way Australia, together with like-minded regional states, forged ahead with strengthening the regional architecture through, among other things, enacting the Comprehensive and Progressive Agreement for Trans-Pacific Partnership without the United States and, along with 14 other countries including China, establishing the Regional Comprehensive Economic Partnership.

Despite having taken the lead in resisting China – Australia was the first country to ban Huawei's 5G technology, to pass foreign interference laws aimed at addressing Chinese influence, and to call for an international inquiry into the source of the coronavirus pandemic – Canberra also sought a reset in its ties with Beijing, having endured economic retaliation by China against its exports (Cave, 2020). As argued in a recent assessment of Australia's Indo-Pacific strategy, Canberra's implementation of its strategy was much less consistent than its very vocal support would appear to suggest (Taylor, 2020).

Singapore had its own perspective on the Indo-Pacific: that it remained a region where principles like freedom of navigation, rule of law, respect for sovereignty, and open markets were observed (Tan, 2020b). Singapore assiduously eschewed backing the respective Indo-Pacific strategies advanced by the Quad countries, including Australia. But apart from its obvious support for ASEAN's 'Outlook on the Indo-Pacific', Singapore had no specific strategy of which to speak – no public articulation of any such, at least – other than a generalised preference for a stable balance of power in the region that favoured its interests (Koh, 2019). To that end, Singapore persisted in the belief in the United States' 'indispensability' as the region's quintessential balancer – not as an extra-regional actor but as a residential pillar and guarantor of regional stability and order (Goh, 2008; Tan, 2011).

Yet it was fair to say that this belief was tested like never before in the five years under review, not simply by Trump's hard-line approach to China but also by the growth of Chinese power and assertiveness under President Xi Jinping. It was against this backdrop that Singapore's Lee Hsien Loong warned, in his 2019 Shangri La Dialogue address, against what he felt was unhelpful talk by Americans of 'containing China'. His warning left American attendees fuming and their Chinese counterparts cheering (CNA, 2019). A year later, in an article written for *Foreign Affairs* on the ongoing power transition and the impact evolving US–China ties would have on the regional status quo, Lee contended that Washington and Beijing 'must work out a *modus vivendi* that will be competitive in some areas without allowing rivalry to poison cooperation in others' (Lee, 2020). With respect to Indo-Pacific strategies, Singapore's concern was to do with what it saw as the potential undesirable formation of 'rival blocs' to manage China's rise. For that reason, Lee proposed that the Quad evolve into part of 'an inclusive and open regional architecture' (Tan, 2020b: 141).

The question that Singaporeans presumably had for their Australian friends was whether Canberra's goal to establish 'an open, inclusive and rules-based region', which Singapore shared, could only be achieved by means of the Quad as a rival bloc to China. Thus understood, to the extent that a Biden administration would be prepared and willing to consult ASEAN with respect to the future of Sino-American relations (Cooper, 2020), a plausible outcome that Singapore and its fellow ASEAN members might wish to see was a smoothing of the Quad's sharp edges.

Finally, it is worth noting that apart from US allies like Japan and South Korea, the Asian region for the most part was ambivalent about Canberra's advocacy of the liberal rules-based order for the Indo-Pacific (Medcalf, 2018; Taylor, 2020). In its dealings with Asia, Australia was guided and defined by its liberal values (Bisley, 2017). Yet it was not just in China but also throughout much of South-East Asia where non-liberal values of one type or another were increasingly advocated (Milner, 2019). It was in this vein that Richard Woolcott, whose imprint was on some of the post–Cold War Asia-Pacific's key regional initiatives, insisted that Australia was best served by an Asia policy that was not guided solely by liberal principles. Calling on Canberra to focus its engagement efforts on South-East Asia, North Asia and the South-West Pacific, Woolcott advocated more effective, better balanced and updated policies as opposed to merely reinforcing longstanding, outdated solutions (Woolcott, n.d.).

Similarly, Singapore had long been and remained a firm supporter of a rules-based order. At the United Nations in September 2018, Foreign Minister Vivian Balakrishnan urged his fellow leaders not to abandon the rules-based world order amid the worldwide rise of anti-globalisation (United Nations, 2018). But Singapore's and South-East Asia's conceptions of a rules-based order differed from that of Australia in that it lacked the latter's ideological focus (Ng, 2019). Hence, despite the likelihood of disagreement over the use of political ideology to define the rules-based order, both countries were in close concurrence with respect to the place of international law and the perceived need to preserve rationality, consistency and predictability in world affairs. Moreover, in the light of the Trump administration's recusal from the international leadership role the United States had played since the end of War World II, Australia and Singapore sought to keep it engaged and committed to Asia as best they could (Bloomberg, 2021; Jackson, 2018).

CONCLUSION

This chapter has argued that Australia's partnership with Singapore was a valuable conduit towards enhancing Canberra's relations with South-East Asia in the period under review. As one analyst suggested, the most important attributes of their partnership were non-material, namely, 'a shared mindset and a willingness to commit for the long term' (Graham, 2016: 1). Their partnership mattered in the context of Australia's envisaged engagement with South-East Asia, especially given that Australia's relations with its near-neighbour Indonesia have included periods of turmoil – often due to Australian missteps. Much as the respective destinies of Australia and Singapore were tied inextricably to their politically fragile region – one made worse by the growing rivalry and discord among the great powers – their enduring partnership underscored their codetermination to transgress those limitations where possible and to redefine the region's future. This was a goal that would only be achieved, if at all, collectively. As Singapore's Lee said in affirming Canberra's turn towards Asia, 'You have had to re-orientate yourself from Britain in the old days, now to Asia and to this part of the world and to be wholly this part of the world. I think your leaders are fully engaged in this, they fully understand this.' (PMO, 2017)

Each in their own way, the region's major powers made international diplomacy a purely transactional and self-centred affair in the period under review – the United States via Trump's professed 'art of the quid pro quo' and China via its no less transactional brand of diplomacy and *fait accompli* approach to the South China Sea under Xi Jinping's leadership (Bernstein, 2020; Mendis, 2017). In such a region, the Australia–Singapore partnership stood as a testament to their unremitting pursuit of amity and collaboration against the odds.

While the incoming Biden administration brought relief to an international community rocked by the highly transactional and protectionist style of Trump's 'America First' approach, the Indo-Pacific region was looking for reassurance from the new president, whose ability to deliver on his promise to restore US international leadership and to return the United States to the multilateral fold, although welcomed, would invariably need to compete with domestic consideration for Biden's time and attention. Less in doubt was the commitment of Australia and Singapore, in their roles as ally and security partner respectively of the United States, to the ongoing enablement of the US strategic and military presence in the region. During the transition period the Biden administration signalled its intention to consult deeply with ASEAN where the former's strategy on China and the Indo-Pacific region broadly was concerned (Liow, 2020). Here too, an Australia that was deeply engaged with South-East Asia and ASEAN – aided by its partnership with Singapore – would certainly prove immensely useful to helping the United States find a surer footing in the region following the tumultuous four years under Trump.

References

Asia Sentinel (2011) Singapore, Malaysia and the WikiLeaks. *Asia Sentinel*, 20 January. www.asiasentinel.com/politics/singapore-malaysia-and-the-wikileaks/

Bernstein, A. (2020) Where Trump learned the art of the quid pro quo. *Atlantic*, 20 January. https://www.theatlantic.com/ideas/archive/2020/01/trumps-brand-of-transactional-politics/604978/

Bisley, N. (2012) No hedging in Canberra: The Australia–US alliance in the 'Asian Century'. *Asia-Pacific Bulletin* 157, 3 April: 1–2. Honolulu: East-West Center

——(2017) Bishop puts the 'liberal' into 'liberal international order'. *Interpreter*, Lowy Institute, 15 March. https://www.lowyinstitute.org/the-interpreter/bishop-puts-liberal-liberal-international-order

——(2020) Australia's incrementalist hedging in a fractured order. *East Asia Forum*, 4 May. https://www.eastasiaforum.org/2020/05/04/australias-incrementalist-hedging-in-a-fractured-order/

Bloomberg (2021) Singapore optimistic US will stay engaged with Asia: Chan. *Bloomberg*, 21 January. https://www.bloomberg.com/news/videos/2021-01-22/singapore-optimistic-u-s-will-stay-engaged-with-asia-chan-video

Cave, D. (2020) The world in a vise: Sounding the alarm on China, then running for shelter. *New York Times*, 7 December. https://www.nytimes.com/2020/12/01/world/australia/china-australia-morrison-tweet.html

Cave, D. & Tarabay, J. (2019) Espionage and interference? Australia grapples with its China relationship. *New York Times*, 29 November. https://www.nytimes.com/2019/11/29/world/australia/china-espionage-interference.html

Chan, L.H. (2020) Strategic hedging: A 'third way' for Australian foreign policy in the Indo-Pacific. *Asia Policy* 15(3)

Chang, F.K. (2019) The odd couple: Singapore's relations with China. Foreign Policy Research Institute, 3 December. https://www.fpri.org/article/2019/12/the-odd-couple-singapores-relations-with-china/

Channel News Asia (2019) In full: PM Lee Hsien Loong's speech at the 2019 Shangri-La Dialogue. *Channel News Asia*, 31 May. https://www.channelnewsasia.com/news/singapore/lee-hsien-loong-speech-2019-shangri-la-dialogue-11585954

——(2020) GE2020: Australia's PM Morrison congratulates Singapore's PM Lee on election results. *Channel News Asia*, 16 July. https://www.channelnewsasia.com/news/singapore/ge2020-australian-pm-congratulates-pm-lee-12938896

Cook, M. (2018) ASEAN–Australia Relations: The Suitable Status Quo. *Lowy Analyses*, 6 August. https://www.lowyinstitute.org/publications/asean-australia-relations-suitable-status-quo

Cooper, Z. (2020) Back to the future: Will Biden's Asia policy come full circle? *Interpreter,* Lowy Institute, 20 November. https://www.lowyinstitute.org/the-interpreter/back-future-will-biden-s-asia-policy-come-full-circle

Cooper, Z. & Edel, C. (2020) Australia is having a strategic revolution, and it's all about China. *Foreign Policy*, 22 July. https://foreignpolicy.com/2020/07/22/australia-military-strategy-regional-policy-china/

Department of Foreign Affairs and Trade (DFAT) (2014) Indian Ocean tsunami. Canberra, 19 December. https://www.dfat.gov.au/news/news/Pages/indian-ocean-tsunami

——(2017) *2017 Foreign Policy White Paper*. Canberra, November. https://www.dfat.gov.au/sites/default/files/2017-foreign-policy-white-paper.pdf

——(n.d.) Singapore–Australia FTA. Canberra. https://www.dfat.gov.au/trade/agreements/in-force/safta/singapore-australia-fta

Department of the Prime Minister and Cabinet (2016) Joint communiqué by the prime ministers of Australia and Singapore on the state of bilateral relations. https://pmtranscripts.pmc.gov.au/release/transcript-40502

Evans, G. (2014) Australia needs to refocus on ASEAN. *East Asia Forum*, 17 December. https://www.eastasiaforum.org/2014/12/17/australia-needs-to-refocus-on-asean/

——(2017) ASEAN at 50: Reflections from Australia. *ASEAN @ 50 Volume 1: The ASEAN Journey: Reflections of ASEAN Leaders and Officials*. Jakarta: Economic Research Institute for ASEAN and East Asia, 227–30

Flitton, D. (2011) My dream of Asia is here now, says Rudd. *Sydney Morning Herald*, 24 July. https://www.smh.com.au/world/my-dream-of-asia-is-here-now-says-rudd-20110723-1hu3i.html

Glosserman, B. (2020) In the competition for Southeast Asia influence, Japan is the sleeper. *Japan Times*, 22 January. https://www.japantimes.co.jp/opinion/2020/01/22/commentary/japan-commentary/competition-southeast-asia-influence-japan-sleeper/

Goh, E. (2008) Hierarchy and the role of the United States in the East Asian security order. *International Relations of the Asia-Pacific* 8(3): 353–77

Graham, E. (2016) *The Lion and the Kangaroo: Australia's Strategic Partnership with Singapore*. Lowy Analysis, May. Sydney: Lowy Institute for International Policy

Graham, E. & Huxley, T. (2015) The US–Singapore enhanced defence agreement: A third upgrade for bilateral collaboration. *Interpreter*, Lowy Institute, 10 December. https://www.lowyinstitute.org/the-interpreter/us-singapore-enhanced-defence-agreement-third-upgrade-bilateral-collaboration

Greene, A. (2020) US urges Australia to expand Pacific push to South-East Asia to counter China's expansion. *ABC News*, 11 March. https://www.abc.net.au/news/2020-03-12/us-ambassador-pacific-step-up-us-china-battle/12048780

Guilford, G. (2018) Singapore's prime minister schools Trump on how trade actually works. *Quartz*, 20 April. https://qz.com/1257865/singapore-prime-minister-lee-hsien-loong-schooled-trump-on-trade/

He, K. (ed.) (2020) *Contested Multilateralism 2.0 and Asian Security Dynamics*. London: Routledge

Hsiao, R. (2019) A preliminary survey of CCP influence operations in Singapore. *China Brief*, 16 July. https://jamestown.org/program/a-preliminary-survey-of-ccp-influence-operations-in-singapore/

Huong, L.T. (2018) Australia and ASEAN: Together for the sake of a new multipolar world order. *Security Challenges* 14(1): 26–32

ISEAS – Yusof-Ishak Institute (2020) *The State of Southeast Asia: 2020 Survey Report*. Singapore: ISEAS Yusof-Ishak Institute

Jackson, S. (2018) What does Australia need from Trump's US? *BBC News*, 21 February. https://www.bbc.com/news/world-australia-43109231

Kerin, J. (2015) The poor white trash of Asia: A phrase that changed an economy. *Australian Financial Review*, 24 March. https://www.afr.com/politics/the-poor-white-trash-of-asia-a-phrase-that-changed-an-economy-20150323-1m5mzm

Koh, S.L.C. (2019) Singapore and the Indo-Pacific: The relentless quest for balance. In S. Nagao (ed.), *Strategies for the Indo-Pacific: Perceptions of the US and Like-Minded Countries*, pp. 26–9. Washington: Hudson Institute

Koh, T. (2009) Rudd's reckless regional rush. *Australian*, 18 December. www.theaustralian.com.au/opinion/rudds-reckless-regional-rush/story-e6frg6zo-1225811530050

Lee, H.L. (2020) The endangered Asian century: America, China, and the perils of confrontation. *Foreign Affairs*, 4 June. https://www.foreignaffairs.com/articles/asia/2020-06-04/lee-hsien-loong-endangered-asian-century

Lemahieu, H. (2020) The case for Australia to step up in South-east Asia. *Foreign Policy at Brookings*, October. https://www.brookings.edu/wp-content/uploads/2020/10/FP_20201022_australia_se_asia_lemahieu_v2.pdf

Lim, Y.L. (2020) Singapore and Australia deepen bilateral ties with raft of new agreements. *Straits Times*, 24 March. https://www.straitstimes.com/politics/singapore-and-australia-deepen-bilateral-ties-with-raft-of-new-agreements

Liow, J.C. (2020) Biden and South-east Asia: When foreign policy begins at home. *ISEAS Commentary*, 2020/186, 24 November. https://www.iseas.edu.sg/media/commentaries/biden-and-southeast-asia-when-foreign-policy-begins-at-home/

Maude, R. (2020) Australia gets more diplomatic firepower in South-east Asia. *Asia Society*, 16 November. https://asiasociety.org/australia/australia-gets-more-diplomatic-firepower-southeast-asia

McGrath, C. (2001) Claims Singapore is spying on Australia. *PM, ABC News*, 9 August. http://www.abc.net.au/pm/stories/s343929.htm

McGregor, J. (2013) An 'Asia capable' Australia for the coming century. *Melbourne Review*, March. www.melbournereview.com.au/features/article/an-asia-capable-australia-for-the-coming-century-2012

Medcalf, R. (2018) Australia's Foreign Policy White Paper: Navigating uncertainty in the Indo-Pacific. *Security Challenges* 14(1): 33–9

Mendis, P. (2017) Trump's 'America first' and Xi Jinping's 'China first': How different are they? *South China Morning Post*, 14 April. https://www.scmp.com/comment/insight-opinion/article/2087354/trumps-america-first-and-xi-jinpings-china-first-how

Meyrick, J. (2016) In a glass clearly: Singapore and Australia compared. *Conversation*, 26 July. https://theconversation.com/in-a-glass-clearly-singapore-and-australia-compared-63045

Milner, A. (2012) Think again about ASEAN. *Asialink Essays 2012* 4(2): 1–4

——(2019) Australia does face a foreign relations crisis. *Pearls and Irritations*, 5 June. https://johnmenadue.com/anthony-milner-australia-does-face-a-foreign-relations-crisis/

Murphy, K. (2016) Australia–Singapore free trade pact expands to embrace services. *Guardian*, 12 October. https://www.theguardian.com/australia-news/2016/oct/13/australia-singapore-free-trade-pact-expands-to-embrace-services

Ng, J. (2019) Unpacking the 'rules-based order'. *RSIS Commentaries* CO19043, 12 March. https://www.rsis.edu.sg/rsis-publication/cms/unpacking-the-rules-based-order/#.X3ZATC9h3Sw

Parameswaran, P. (2016) Singapore, Australia deepen comprehensive strategic partnership with new deal. *Diplomat*, 10 May. https://thediplomat.com/2016/05/singapore-australia-deepen-comprehensive-strategic-partnership-with-new-deal/

——(2019) What's in the new Australia–Singapore white shipping pact? *Diplomat*, 7 October. https://thediplomat.com/2019/10/whats-in-the-new-australia-singapore-white-shipping-pact/

Parmer, S. (2019) The US–Australia alliance: What to know. *Council on Foreign Relations*, 13 September. https://www.cfr.org/in-brief/us-australia-alliance-what-know

Prime Minister's Office (2017) PM Lee Hsien Loong's interview with ABC Radio, 3 June. PMO. https://www.pmo.gov.sg/Newsroom/pm-lee-hsien-loongs-interview-abc-radio

Power, J. (2020) As Australia–China ties spiral downward, why is Lee Kuan Yew's warning a talking point? *South China Morning Post*, 5 September. https://www.scmp.com/week-asia/explained/article/3100323/australia-china-ties-spiral-downwards-why-lee-kuan-yews-warning

Purba, K. (2020) Indonesia–Australia ties: The more you know, the less you love. *Jakarta Post*, 9 July. https://www.thejakartapost.com/academia/2020/07/09/indonesia-australia-ties-the-more-you-know-the-less-you-love.html

Qu, C. (2020) Australia needs South-east Asia for market, not politics. *Global Times*, 15 October. https://www.globaltimes.cn/content/1203633.shtml

Quiggin, J. (2020) Relax, losing access to China won't make us the 'poor white trash of Asia'. *Conversation*, 10 September. https://theconversation.com/relax-losing-access-to-china-wont-make-us-the-poor-white-trash-of-asia-145442

Rodan, G. (2012) Progress and limits in regional cooperation: Australia and South-east Asia. In J. Cotton & J. Ravenhill (eds), *Middle Power Dreaming: Australia in World Affairs 2006–2010*, pp. 165–84. Melbourne: Oxford University Press

Roughneen, S. (2019) Why Australia desperately needs ASEAN allies. *South-east Asia Globe*, 11 September. https://southeastasiaglobe.com/why-australia-desperately-needs-asean-allies/

Sainsbury, M. (2019) ASEAN countries emerge as our second-largest trading bloc. *Australian Financial Review*, 12 September. https://www.afr.com/companies/financial-services/asean-countries-emerge-as-our-second-largest-trading-bloc-20190911-p52q90

Searight, A. (2020) Countering China's influence operations: Lessons from Australia. *CSIS*, 8 May. https://www.csis.org/analysis/countering-chinas-influence-operations-lessons-australia

Tan, S.S. (2011) America the indispensable: Singapore's view of the United States' engagement in the Asia Pacific. *Asian Affairs: An American Review* 38(3): 156–71

——(2014a) Hobnobbing with giants: Australia's approach to Asian regionalism. In S. Percival Wood & B. He (eds), *The Australia–ASEAN Dialogue: Tracing 40 Years of Partnership*, pp. 33–48. New York: Palgrave Macmillan

——(2014b) Digging in Its Backyard: Why Australia should Deepen Engagement with South-east Asia, pp. 18–21. Centre of Gravity Series 17. Canberra: Strategic and Defence Studies Centre, Australian National University

——(2015) *Multilateral Asian Security Architecture: Non-ASEAN Stakeholders*. London: Routledge

——(2016) Facilitating the US rebalance: Challenges and prospects for Singapore as America's security partner. *Security Challenges* 12(3): 20–33

——(2019) Crossing the Rubicon: Singapore's evolving relations with China in the context of the 2016 arbitral award. In D. Letts & D. Rothwell (eds), *Law of the Sea in South East Asia Environmental, Navigational and Security Challenges*, pp. 193–209. London: Routledge

—— (2020a) Coping with the dragon: Vulnerability and engagement in Singapore–China relations. In D.K. Emmerson (ed.), *The Deer and the Dragon: Southeast Asia and China in the 21st Century*, pp. 197–220. Palo Alto: Walter H. Shorenstein Asia-Pacific Research Center, Stanford University

—— (2020b) Consigned to hedge: Southeast Asia and America's 'free and open Indo-Pacific' strategy. *International Affairs* 96(1): 131–48

Taylor, B. (2020) Is Australia's Indo-Pacific strategy an illusion? *International Affairs* 96(1): 95–109

Thakur, R. (2013) Is Australia serious about Asia? *Global Brief*, 5 March, pp. 1–6. http://globalbrief.ca/blog/2013/03/05/is-australia-serious-about-asia/print/

Turnbull, M. (2016) Australia–Singapore comprehensive strategic partnership announcement. 6 May. https://www.malcolmturnbull.com.au/media/australia-singapore-comprehensive-strategic-partnership-announcement

—— (2020) *A Bigger Picture*. Melbourne: Hardie Grant

United Nations (UN) (2018) 'We cannot abandon' rules-based world order, Singapore urges in UN speech. *UN News*, 28 September. https://news.un.org/en/story/2018/09/1021682

Werner, D.A. (2020) Singapore's prime minister has a message for the US: Don't choose China confrontation or Asia withdrawal. *New Atlanticist*, 28 July. https://www.atlanticcouncil.org/blogs/new-atlanticist/singapores-prime-minister-has-a-message-for-the-us-dont-choose-china-confrontation-or-asia-withdrawal/

Wesley, M. (2007) Australia and Southeast Asia. In J. Cotton & J. Ravenhill (eds), *Trading on Alliance Security: Australia in World Affairs 2001–2005*. Melbourne: Oxford University Press

Wibawa, T. (2020) Indonesia and Australia at a 'strategic turning point' as relationship reaches 70-year milestone. *ABC News*, 3 January. https://www.abc.net.au/news/2020-01-04/indonesia-australia-reaches-70-years-diplomatic-relations/11825010

Woolcott, R. (2009) Towards an Asia Pacific community. *Asialink Essays* 9(3)

—— (2017) An Asia policy for Australia in the Trump era. *Disruptive Asia: Asia's Rise and Australia's Future*, Asia Society. https://asiasociety.org/australia/asia-policy-australia-trump-era

World Politics Review (2016) Defense deal shows strength of ties between Singapore and Australia. *WPR*, 18 May. https://www.worldpoliticsreview.com/trend-lines/18816/defense-deal-shows-strength-of-ties-between-singapore-and-australia

Wyeth, G. (2020) Australia's South-east Asian step down. *Diplomat*, 17 March. https://thediplomat.com/2020/03/australias-southeast-asian-step-down/

Yeo, M. (2020) Annual large-scale Singaporean military exercise in Queensland cancelled. *Asia-Pacific Defence Reporter*, 12 May. https://asiapacificdefencereporter.com/large-scale-singaporean-military-exercise-in-queensland-canceled/

Zhang, J. (2007) Australia and China: Towards a strategic partnership? In J. Cotton & J. Ravenhill (eds), *Trading on Alliance Security: Australia in World Affairs 2001–2005*, pp. 89–111. Melbourne: Oxford University Press

—— (2012) Australia and China: The challenges to forging a 'true friendship'. In J. Cotton & J. Ravenhill (eds), *Middle Power Dreaming: Australia in World Affairs 2006–2010*, pp. 71–93. Oxford: Oxford University Press

Australian foreign economic policy and the Belt and Road controversy

Baogang He, Geoffrey Stokes and David Hundt

Since the 1980s, a major objective of Australia's foreign economic policy has been to strengthen links with the global economy. Previously, national and state governments promoted global integration largely through 'industry policy' or 'strategic trade policy' as practised in East Asia and northern Europe (see Fenna, 2016; Thurbon, 2016). In line with growing pressures for economic globalisation, however, Australian governments shifted their approach to overseas markets. With the goal of reducing barriers to trade, Australia's strategy was to encourage and secure multilateral, regional and bilateral trade agreements. Australia aimed thereby to reap the benefits of growing economic engagement with East Asia and especially with China, without compromising its security relations with the United States (see e.g. Keating, 2000). As Hugh White (2016) observed in the previous volume of *Australia in World Affairs*, successive governments claimed, dubiously, that 'we don't have to choose' between closer economic relations with China and the US alliance.

Australia's approach to the Belt and Road Initiative (BRI), however, brought a host of challenges for external affairs. It is beyond the scope of this chapter to analyse all aspects of Australian foreign economic policy between 2016 and 2020, but we illustrate how the BRI presented Australia with a set of inter-related foreign policy, trade and security problems. Indeed, the politics of the BRI suggested that the economic and security aspects of Australia's foreign policy could no longer be compartmentalised as had been claimed (see Chapters 2 and 11).

In managing these various policy issues, Australia's position on the BRI became problematic. It changed from offering support to giving lukewarm acceptance, to criticism and something resembling outright opposition, then offering alternatives. There was no such wavering on security policy. Culminating in 2020, Australia tightened nearly every aspect of its internal security, defence and intelligence apparatus, among which were stronger controls upon subnational foreign agreements, foreign investment, and ownership of critical infrastructure (Hundt, 2020). Externally, it also strengthened defence ties with India and Japan. All these initiatives had a negative influence on relations with China.

Diplomatic tensions were aggravated by the government's call for an international inquiry into the origins of COVID-19 in China, which resulted in economic retaliation against some Australian exports. Consequently, most aspects of Australia's relations with China deteriorated rapidly. The climax was the Chinese embassy's publication of a list of 14 grievances against Australia (Kearsley, Bagshaw & Galloway, 2020).

This chapter examines Australia's policy predicament on the BRI between 2016 and 2020. It establishes the political and economic context for the controversy, traces the government's contradictory positions, and explains its inconsistent messaging. The chapter critically analyses the specific but overlapping explanations offered for Australia's rejection of the BRI. In addition to problems specific to the BRI, the government's perception of regional insecurity, as well as increasing domestic security threats, contributed to its decision. For the first time since the Cold War, we contend, the effects of great-power rivalry in the Indo-Pacific region extended beyond security to influence Australian foreign economic policy and harm trade relations.

THE BRI IN POLITICAL AND ECONOMIC CONTEXT

After its launch in 2013, the BRI became the centrepiece of China's foreign and trade policy. The BRI encompassed a series of bold economic and diplomatic initiatives intended to address domestic issues, such as overcapacity in key sectors and inequality between provinces, and to assert greater international leadership. The BRI was also a way of exporting China's state-led economic development model (Fukuyama, 2016). China envisaged the BRI offering significant business opportunities for developing countries and industrialised ones alike, including Australia, through a network of land and maritime infrastructure projects stretching from East Asia to Europe (Cai, 2017). The BRI was the type of regional economic initiative that Australia had tended to see as favourable to its interests, insofar as it had the potential to increase trade.

China became Australia's largest trading partner in 2007 and its largest export market two years later (Australian Embassy, China, 2012). By 2014, the two countries had completed a free trade agreement and were among the parties negotiating the Regional Comprehensive Economic Partnership (RCEP), an agreement that excluded the United States. In the 2019/20 financial year, two-way trade with China amounted to $251 billion, or 29 per cent of Australia's international trade (DFAT, 2020a). In 2020, Chinese investment in Australia amounted to $46 billion, or 4.5 per cent of all foreign direct investment (DFAT, 2020a). Given China's status as Australia's main economic partner, it might reasonably be expected that joining the BRI would be another evolutionary step – albeit a symbolic one – towards strengthening a complementary and mutually beneficial relationship. But that did not occur. Instead, the BRI became a source of tension with China and of controversy in Australian domestic politics.

A crucial contextual development was that the election of Donald Trump to the presidency of the United States created uncertainty about the US role in the world. One of Trump's first acts on taking office in early 2017 was to withdraw the United States from negotiations towards another significant regional trade agreement, the proposed

Trans-Pacific Partnership (TPP). This proposed agreement had been particularly attractive to Australia: the United States was a party to its negotiation, but China was not (Duffy, 2017). From the perspective of Australia–US relations, however, the decision signalled a potential retreat by the United States from the Indo-Pacific and reduced the value of the TPP as a hedge against the growing economic weight of China. Trump also seemed to be reappraising the utility of defence alliances. Both the willingness and capacity of the United States to remain Australia's security guarantor were thus thrown into doubt. The government feared that engaging officially with the BRI might send the wrong signal to the United States about Australia's commitment to the ANZUS alliance.

In addition, China had been extending its military reach by stealth in the East China and South China seas, as well as taking more aggressive action over Hong Kong, Taiwan and China's border with India. In asserting its territorial claims in the South China Sea, China had refused to accept a ruling against it in 2016 by the Permanent Court of Arbitration convened under the United Nations Convention on the Law of the Sea. It demonstrated scant regard for the rules-based order (see Chapter 6), which was central to Australia's global trade policies. Australia therefore had to proceed carefully in any criticism of China. The government worried that a failure to engage with the BRI would antagonise China.

The domestic security environment was also changing. In 2017, concern about agents of influence – some with links to China's security services – resulted in the introduction of new laws to curb foreign interference in Australian politics (Maley & Berkovic, 2017; see also Chapter 5). In 2018 and 2019, cyber espionage attacks on Australian governmental, corporate and higher education institutions were conducted by 'sophisticated state actors', who were suspected of being based in countries including China and Russia (see Brangwin & Portillo-Castro, 2020). In 2020, several Chinese journalists were forced to leave Australia and others had their visas cancelled due to concerns about foreign interference (Benson & Packham, 2020).

On this account, both the United States and China were generating uncertainty in the Indo-Pacific region. Maintaining domestic security in Australia had also become a priority. The BRI controversy unfolded alongside efforts to address serious security problems.

AUSTRALIA'S SHIFTING POSITION

At first, Australia indicated a strong interest in the BRI. In 2014, Prime Minister Tony Abbott and President Xi Jinping described the bilateral relationship as a 'comprehensive strategic partnership' (Abbott, 2014), and the two sides signed a Free Trade Agreement. In an address to the Australian parliament, Xi welcomed 'Australia's participation in the 21st century Maritime Silk Road' (Commonwealth of Australia, 2014: 12725).

In June 2015, Abbott released the White Paper on Developing Northern Australia, which aspired to link Australia more closely with the 'economic powerhouse' of the Asia–Pacific region (Thurbon, 2016: 154). The BRI was not mentioned in the White Paper, but the government encouraged Australian firms to participate in the initiative. Abbott's successor, Malcolm Turnbull, led a business delegation to China in April 2016, indicating further interest in the BRI. Xi again invited Australia to align its

'Northern Development' plan with the BRI, but Turnbull seemed reluctant to sign on formally (Collinson, 2017: 2).

In June 2016, Turnbull committed Australia to joining the Asian Infrastructure Investment Bank (AIIB), a multilateral agency established by China to finance BRI projects (White, 2016: 103). The decision was taken despite pressure from the United States, which feared that the AIIB would strengthen China's regional leadership. Later that year, the government provided funding for the Australia–China One Belt One Road Initiative, chaired by a former Trade Minister, Andrew Robb (Australia–China OBOR Initiative, 2016). The government appeared confident that these forms of engagement with China would deliver diplomatic and economic benefits without damaging relations with the United States.

In September 2016, Xi issued a third invitation for Australia to link the Northern Development strategy to the BRI, but Turnbull made no reply (Collinson, 2017: 2). At the Australia–China Foreign and Strategic Dialogue in February 2017, Foreign Minister Wang Yi repeated the call for Australia to 'align' the two schemes. At their joint media conference, however, Wang's counterpart Julie Bishop reported that they had 'talked about the need for greater infrastructure' (Bishop & Wang, 2017) and mentioned the BRI and the Northern Australia initiative only in passing. It soon became apparent that Australia had no intention of joining the BRI.

The turning point came in March 2017, when the Australian National Security Committee of Cabinet (NSC) decided not to sign a memorandum of understanding (MOU) that would link the BRI with the Northern Development Strategy (Greene & Probyn, 2017). Bishop's 'upbeat' arguments for engagement were rejected (Kelly, 2017), but there were no official announcements. On 13 March, Australia's tone towards China sharpened when Bishop (2017) gave a speech in Singapore that promoted the virtues of liberal democracy and a rules-based international order, and indirectly criticised China.

There was no public reference to the BRI when Chinese Premier Li Keqiang visited Canberra on 24 March to discuss trade and security (Turnbull, 2017a). Turnbull later reported, however, that he had personally informed Li that Australia would not join the BRI (Kelly, 2020a). To complicate the message, Trade Minister Steve Ciobo attended the Belt and Road Forum for International Cooperation in Beijing in May 2017. Ciobo said that the Northern Australian Initiative was complementary to the BRI but warned that 'we take decisions about initiatives in Australia on the basis of what is in Australia's national interest' (cited in ABC/Reuters, 2017). As if to confirm this complementarity and alignment with the national interest, in September, Ciobo signed a confidential MOU to cooperate in 'third-party countries' on BRI initiatives (Kelly, 2020c: 17). Ciobo thus contributed to a perception that Australia intended to engage with the BRI, albeit at the margins.

By November 2017, the public discourse had shifted further, and the government began to formalise principles for Australian participation in the BRI. First, DFAT Secretary Frances Adamson (2017) noted that the BRI was 'an ambitious undertaking', so Australia should 'think constructively yet clearly about the principles, rules and institutions that underpin [such] an initiative'. A few days later Turnbull (2017c) acknowledged the BRI had a role to play in regional infrastructure development but said it needed to meet the criteria of 'transparency, fairness, accountability and market need'. The 2017 Foreign Policy White Paper also made reference to principles:

Australia, it said, 'favour[ed] infrastructure that has robust social and environmental safeguards and avoids unsustainable debt burdens' (Australian Government, 2017: 45). In this way, the government cast doubt on the motivations underlying the BRI and how it might operate.

Ministers used effusive rhetoric to obscure the hard reality of rejection. In November 2017 Ciobo said 'we see great chances for collaboration and cooperation' (cited in Turnbull, 2017d), and Turnbull (2018) claimed in August 2018 that Australia 'look[s] forward to working with China on Belt and Road Initiative projects'. In May 2019, Turnbull's successor as Prime Minister, Scott Morrison, declined to commit to joining the BRI, saying: '... we have a neutral [*sic*] position on that. We don't sign up to it. We don't participate in it – that's the position of the Australian Government' (Morrison, 2019b). In June, Morrison professed to welcome the BRI's contribution to 'regional infrastructure investment and to regional development', repeating the criteria that would need to be met (Morrison, 2019c).

The government's public communications on the BRI were thus contradictory and misleading. Although the public message to China was somewhat positive, the personal message to Li was unequivocally negative. Domestically, however, the government was ambiguous. It did not prohibit Australian firms from joining the BRI as long they abided by prescribed principles.

The government had difficulty tailoring its communications for two different audiences, international and domestic. It seemed oblivious to the fact that speeches intended for a Chinese audience would be heard and interpreted differently by its domestic audience and vice versa. Businesses and state governments therefore could be forgiven for thinking that they were being encouraged to participate, or at least that Canberra would not stand in their way. The federal government's incoherent messages inexorably led to conflict with Victoria, whose government sought to engage with the BRI.

DOMESTIC DISCORD

Australia's state and territory governments generally deferred to Canberra on the BRI. In April 2018, for instance, Queensland Premier Anastacia Palaszczuk said that 'One Belt One Road and the relationships between China and the Australian Government should be at the (national) government-to-government level' (cited in Collinson, 2019: 4; parentheses in original). The Premier of New South Wales, Gladys Berejiklian, expressed a similar view, as did Western Australia's Mark McGowan, although the latter also advised the federal government to improve its relationship with China (Butterly, 2019).

In the Northern Territory, there was bipartisan support for the BRI and for deeper engagement with China. Part of former Chief Minister Adam Giles's justification for leasing the Port of Darwin to China's Landbridge in 2015 was that it would 'secure our place on China's Maritime Silk Road trade route' (Giles, 2016). Michael Gunner, who became Chief Minister after the 2016 election, was similarly optimistic about the BRI: the Territory, he said, 'welcomes Chinese investment in line with Australia's rules and regulations' (Gunner, 2018).

Victoria was an outlier among the subnational governments and became entangled in a dispute with the Morrison government. In October 2018, in line with commonly accepted practices (see Stokes, 1994; Carr, 2020), the Victorian government signed an MOU with China's National Development and Reform Commission to explore collaboration on the BRI (Harrison, 2018). Morrison expressed surprise that Victoria had not consulted his government on the matter (Karp, 2018), but the state government claimed that it *had* consulted with the relevant federal agency, DFAT (ABC, 2018).

The Trade Minister, Simon Birmingham (2018), continued to encourage 'engagement by Australian companies' in the BRI, but said such engagement 'ought to be consistent with our clearly stated foreign policy priorities', which were unspecified. Birmingham added: 'I can't say whether or not Victoria should have signed it.' The Foreign Minister, Marise Payne (2018), acknowledged that Australian 'states and territories ... make arrangements of this nature, at this level, regularly with other countries, in this region and more broadly'. She added, 'We obviously seek opportunities to strengthen engagement with China ... and that includes the BRI where those align with international best practice.'

Undeterred by the federal government's criticisms, Victorian Premier Daniel Andrews signed a second MOU with China in October 2019 that aimed to 'deepen cooperation' in the areas of 'infrastructure, innovation, ageing and trade development' (Government of Victoria, 2019). Andrews claimed that the agreement would increase the role of Chinese firms in infrastructure projects in Victoria and create employment and business opportunities (Murray-Atfield, 2020). This time, however, Victoria did not consult DFAT and attracted criticism from the federal government. This criticism, however, did not address the content of the MOUs (which were uncontroversial) nor how binding they were on the parties (which they were not), but simply that the agreements (which were not treaties) had been reached by a state government.

In May 2020 Sky News brought Victoria's agreement to the attention of the US Secretary of State Mike Pompeo. The outcome, however, was not as dramatic as might have been envisaged. Pompeo admitted to knowing little about the matter but recognised its security implications: 'To the extent [Victoria-based BRI projects] have an adverse impact on our ability to protect telecommunications from [*sic*] our private citizens, or security networks for our defence and intelligence communities – we simply disconnect, we will simply separate' (cited in Ferguson, 2020). The US ambassador in Canberra clarified that Pompeo was responding to a 'very remote hypothetical' (cited in Murray-Atfield, 2020), and the Victorian government said that no telecommunications projects were being considered under the BRI. Nonetheless, the Home Affairs Minister Peter Dutton (2020) was adamant: '[W]e don't support the agreement that the Victorian Government's entered into. I don't think it's in our national interest. It's against our foreign policy.'

Victoria's apparent defiance of federal views prompted the Morrison government to consider how to control such arrangements. Using the rhetoric of the 'national interest' and 'sovereignty', in August 2020 the government introduced legislation to monitor, review, approve and nullify international agreements made at the subnational level (see Chapter 5). The federal government thereby sought to prevent further subnational participation in the BRI.

Victoria's enthusiasm for the BRI brought it into conflict with the federal government, which was of a different party-political persuasion and which had not articulated a coherent policy. Although joining the BRI was not considered to be in the Morrison government's version of the national interest, nor by implication in the interests of state governments, it *was* considered to be in the interest of Australian business. In addition to its disagreement with the United States over the AIIB, and sending mixed messages to China, the government had provoked controversy within Australia. We examine why this occurred.

JUSTIFYING THE BRI DECISION

The public rationale for rejecting the BRI evolved over time. Initially, the government alluded to issues of economics, overseas development, governance and values, while avoiding discussion of security. But silence on security did not mean that it was irrelevant; it was simply a pragmatic strategy to avoid making relations with China more difficult. Evidence for the salience of security can be found in the government's decisive actions at home and abroad that were taken alongside debate over the BRI, and in indirect and direct reference to it by ministers. We review these justifications.

Economics: foreign investment

The government first justified its non-participation in the BRI with the claim that Australia would glean no extra economic benefit, such as greater Chinese investment (Kelly, 2017). When asked directly why Australia had not committed to joining the BRI, Turnbull (2017b) said that there was 'massive Chinese investment in Australia', which was not entirely accurate. Turnbull also said that the 'delay' in joining the BRI was due to 'economic and business concerns' (SBS, 2017). Since Australia already attracted substantial foreign investment from many sources, the government claimed there was little to be gained from joining the BRI. If this were the case, then there would be little risk in joining the BRI, especially where the diplomatic and symbolic benefits were significant. Other, more plausible reasons emerged.

Overseas development

Another explanation was that there were unacceptable economic and political risks associated with joining the BRI. But this was argued primarily with reference to developing countries. According to Bishop, the BRI could create 'unsustainable debt burdens' (Wroe, 2018a) for the small island countries of the Pacific, and a loss of sovereignty. Birmingham (2018) echoed these sentiments, which became a recurring theme. For some critics such as Clive Hamilton, the BRI was a form of 'debt trap diplomacy' (Galloway, 2020).

A common claim was that many BRI projects were unviable, except where recipient governments agreed to financial terms favourable to Chinese banks. Bishop raised the spectre of BRI participants being unable to repay their loans and having to surrender strategic assets to Chinese interests (Wroe, 2018a), as had happened with the Hambantota port facility in Sri Lanka. If Australia's neighbours in South-East Asia or the Pacific entered such debt traps, the strategic consequences could be significant. For this reason, in September 2016 Australia announced its 'Pacific Step-up' program, which aimed to enhance the region's 'sovereignty, stability, security and prosperity' (DFAT, 2019). In November 2018, Morrison committed to increasing development and defence assistance to Pacific nations, through initiatives such as the Australian Infrastructure Financing Facility for the Pacific and the Australia Pacific Security College.

Governance

Australian officials criticised the substance of the BRI by questioning how it was governed (He, 2019). Unlike multilateral banks, they argued, the BRI consisted of a series of bilateral and corporate arrangements that were dominated by one country: China. There was no clearly identifiable body governed by specific principles or processes with which foreign governments could interact. According to Turnbull (2017b), the BRI was 'an agenda' of the Chinese government, and its governance was problematic. A report of the Joint Standing Committee on Foreign Affairs, Defence and Trade (2019: 18) raised concerns about the BRI's transparency and how disputes would be resolved in projects funded through it, as well as the possible 'exclusion of local suppliers and services'.

Accordingly, Australian officials claimed that the BRI did not meet the criteria it expected of international infrastructure development programs. Policy-makers formed the view that Australia should consider partnering on Chinese infrastructure projects that served its economic interests, but 'it can't involve bribing local officials, unnecessarily damaging the environment, or leaving the host nation heavily indebted and therefore vulnerable to coercion' (Wroe, 2018b).

Australia addressed such concerns by collaborating with Japan and the United States on new infrastructure development initiatives. To provide an alternative to the BRI that met sound development principles, in 2018 these countries established the Trilateral Partnership to 'invest in projects in the Indo-Pacific region that would build infrastructure, address development challenges, increase connectivity, and promote economic growth' (Bishop, 2018). The following year, Australia joined Japan in supporting the Trump administration's Blue Dot Network, which aimed to 'promote high-quality, trusted standards for global infrastructure development' (US Department of State, 2019). The United States committed US$17 billion to the program, to foster better investment decisions by countries contemplating BRI projects, especially in the Asia-Pacific region. Australia thus not only conveyed its reservations about the BRI in the language of development efficiency, financial transparency and probity but also contributed to modest institutional alternatives.

Values

The BRI was also portrayed as a question of competing values. Australian ministers emphasised that China's polity was different from Australia and its major security ally, the United States, which shared Australia's commitment to democracy, markets and a rules-based international order (Bishop, 2017; Payne & Reynolds, 2020; see also Chapter 4). A former Ambassador to China, Geoff Raby (2017), summarised the prevailing view among policy-makers: the BRI was 'an attempt by China to impose a "Sino-centric" order on the world'. Hamilton gave a more alarmist assessment, saying that the BRI fostered a form of 'discourse control', whereby participants 'unconsciously reproduce[d] the language and the concepts that have been implanted in them' (Galloway, 2020) by the Chinese Communist Party. In effect, joining the BRI would aid the global ambitions of a rising communist state.

The government argued that a rules-based international system aligned with Australia's liberal values of democracy, human rights, open markets and free trade.

By implication, China's rise and its illiberal government threatened that system. As Bishop (2017) stated, 'While non-democracies such as China can thrive when participating in the present system, an essential pillar of our preferred order is democratic community.' John Lee (2020), one of Bishop's advisers from 2016 to 2018, depicted the BRI as a strategic process of authoritarian, non-market predation upon weak states.

Critics of the BRI emphasised the leading role played by Chinese state-owned banks and state-owned enterprises (e.g. Cai, 2017). This model of development, they claimed, was at odds with Australia's support for liberal economic institutions, based on free markets. Australian leaders presented their preferred mode of infrastructure development, with Bishop (2018) citing such factors as 'transparency, open competition, sustainability, adhering to robust global standards, employing the local workforce, and avoiding unsustainable debt burdens'. By proclaiming Australia's values, preferred process of development and outcomes, the government ruled out joining the BRI. Yet there was one other issue: security.

Security

Originally, the government tried to maintain its public silence on the security implications of the BRI and to keep trade and development issues to the fore. Indeed, at the release of the Defence White Paper in 2016, Turnbull spoke positively about the rise of China and security: 'We welcome China's rise and its greater capacity to share responsibility for supporting regional and global security' (Turnbull, 2016). When asked in October 2017 if the BRI raised any national security concerns, Turnbull (2017d) avoided giving a direct reply.

It was evident, however, that the government had revised its assessments about the BRI and its risk to national security. Heads of the Defence and Immigration departments, for example, had warned against joining the BRI because of 'strategic concerns' (Greene & Probyn, 2017). Geoff Wade (2016: 151) summarised the broader security perspective, declaring that 'the BRI agenda is aimed at creating a Eurasia-wide, China-led bloc to counter the US'.

When the government directly addressed the issue of security in trade and investment matters, this took the form of more rigorous scrutiny of foreign investment. It cited security concerns when rejecting Shanghai Pengxin's bid for the Kidman property empire in 2016, and the Chinese-owned State Grid's bid for Ausgrid, the New South Wales-based electricity generator and distributor (Courtenay, 2018). In 2018 the government banned Chinese telco Huawei from participating in building Australia's 5G telecommunications network (Biggs & Duke, 2018). If Australia could reject links with Chinese firms such as Huawei on security grounds, then it could also apply this strategy to the BRI.

In this context of heightened external and internal insecurity, Australia responded by transforming its security agencies. It created the Critical Infrastructure Centre in January 2017, with the goal of assessing applications for foreign investment in 'sensitive federal-owned, state-owned and privately owned assets' (Yang & Brennan, 2017: 99). In December 2017, Home Affairs became a new mega-department that brought the Australian Federal Police, the Australian Border Force and the Australian Security Intelligence Organisation into one portfolio. In addition, a new Defence Intelligence Group integrated previously separate agencies in the Australian Defence Force, thus contributing to a new National Intelligence Community in June 2020.

The creation of new agencies was accompanied by major reforms, bureaucratic initiatives and laws to address weaknesses in national security, intelligence, defence strategy, and foreign investment. These included new security-related legislation, such as the *Security of Critical Infrastructure Act 2018* (Cth) and the Australian Foreign Relations (State and Territory Arrangements) Bill 2020 (Cth). The latter was intended to block efforts, such as Victoria's, to join programs initiated by foreign governments.

The drive to increase controls over investment culminated in March 2020 with the announcement of 'temporary' regulatory changes that would require approval of *all* foreign investment (Frydenberg, 2020a). In December 2020, the government revised the *Foreign Acquisitions and Takeovers Act 1975* (Cth) to take account of national security. This enabled the Foreign Investment Review Board to consider national security businesses or land, all of which would need approval regardless of value (Frydenberg, 2020b). The fixation on security was evident in the publication of reports and reviews, including the 2017 Independent Intelligence Review, the 2020 Strategic Defence Update and the declassified Report of the Comprehensive Review of the Legal Framework of the National Intelligence Community (the Richardson Review), and the government's official response in December 2020.

By these means, Australia closed off all obvious loopholes in the regulation of foreign trade and investment. Few of these initiatives explicitly and directly referred to China, but it was hard to escape the conclusion that this was their focus. The government also took external measures in 2020 to address security concerns about China. It signed a new defence pact with Japan and renewed its participation in the Quad grouping, which brought Australia into closer defence coordination with the United States, Japan and India (see Chapter 11). It thereby shared a growing consensus of concern across the region about China's activities in Asia and the Pacific.

TRADE AND AUSTRALIA'S INTERNATIONAL 'LEADERSHIP' ON COVID-19

The BRI controversy was a reminder of Australia's dependence on China for its prosperity. Although Australia's iron ore and coal were vital to the Chinese iron and steel industry, they were also critical for Australian government revenues and achieving a trade surplus. This co-dependency provided a strong rationale for compartmentalising trade and security and for keeping Australia–China relations cordial.

Despite the contradictory messages and formal rebuffs on the BRI, its public criticisms and the above-mentioned strategic initiatives, China had primarily responded with words: that is, diplomatic complaints and aggressive rhetoric in its state media, notably the *Global Times*. But this changed in 2020 when Australia initiated calls for an international inquiry into the origins of the global COVID-19 pandemic (see Payne, 2020a). This became the trigger not only for an escalation in hostile language but also economic retaliation – 'coercive diplomacy' – of the kind applied previously against US-aligned states such as the Philippines and South Korea (Hanson, Currey & Beattie, 2020).

In May 2020, China began imposing trade sanctions – delays, anti-dumping and quarantine measures, and punitive tariffs – on Australian barley, cotton, timber, wine, beef and seafood. There were threats to direct Chinese tourists and students to countries other than Australia. Even the handling of shipments of Australian iron ore and coal were delayed. The government, however, seemed to have no sense of the role it had played in bringing about these threats to Australian economic interests. Instead, it represented its 'leadership' on the COVID-19 inquiry as a diplomatic victory (Payne, 2020b).

The consequences of Australia's call for an inquiry into the origins of COVID-19 should have been foreseeable. China could tolerate what it saw as conflicts, rejections and slights in its bilateral relations, but it could hardly ignore a 'comprehensive strategic partner' leading the charge for global intervention in Chinese affairs. The Australian Government seemed neither to understand the significance of its actions nor care about the possible outcomes of such actions. To present the decision to hold an international inquiry as a vindication suggests that the government had lost touch with the exigencies of foreign economic policy. That China's actions were arbitrary and disproportionate does not absolve the government from its responsibility for damaging Australian economic interests. It was a testament to diplomatic persistence and acumen that Australia (along with other countries) completed the Regional Comprehensive Economic Partnership in November 2020 (DFAT, 2020b) while also being a party to the TPP.

The BRI controversy, the security challenges and the COVID-19 pandemic stimulated a rethinking of foreign economic and industry policies. China's economic retaliation, along with the disruption to global supply chains due to the pandemic, brought a keener awareness among government, business and citizens of Australia's vulnerability. The risks of Australia relying heavily on overseas suppliers for a large share of manufactured goods, especially defence materials, became actual problems needing attention. Accordingly, the government began exploring how Australia might revitalise its manufacturing industry and reduce its vulnerability to supply shocks (Aedy, 2020). Only a few years after abandoning industry policy and allowing some of its largest manufacturing industries to close, the Morrison government was reconsidering its steadfast commitment to free markets.

This shifting stance on the efficacy of markets appeared to stem from Prime Minister Morrison's puzzling reference to the concept of 'negative globalism' in late 2019 when he suggested that Australia's national interests were not best served 'when international institutions demand conformity rather than independent cooperation on global issues' (Morrison, 2019a). He warned against 'unaccountable international institutions' seeking to impose a 'mandate from an often ill-defined borderless global community ... Globalism must facilitate, align, and engage, rather than direct and centralise. As such an approach [negative globalism] can corrode support for joint international action.' (Morrison, 2019a)

This mysterious version of globalism that Morrison opposed was presumed both to require conformity and to undermine collective action among the international community. In its place, Morrison appeared to be proposing a highly selective approach to collective action: he would presumably support international collaboration for issues such as responding to pandemics, promoting free trade, and organising security, while returning greater authority to national governments for other issues, such as averting climate change (see Chapter 9). But without sufficient elaboration from the government, such an incoherent approach risked eroding the generally accepted principles of internationalism that have been vital to Australian interests and practice as a middle power.

CONCLUSION

The period under review was not the first time that tensions emerged between Australia's economic and security interests, but the BRI controversy destabilised numerous aspects of Australian foreign economic policy. Prevarication over the BRI, along with new security initiatives, helped create a climate of distrust and irritation between Australia and China. Nonetheless, the government's approach to its major trading partner did not immediately provoke economic retaliation. It took Australia's COVID-19 decision to start that process. In the short term, however, China's response brought relatively minimal harm to Australian exporters. By the end of 2020, Australian exports to China reached $145.2 billion, just 2 per cent below its previous high in 2019 (Rajah, 2021).

Domestically, the BRI dispute created conflict between the federal government and Victoria, as well as between bureaucratic agencies. Debates about how Australia should respond to the BRI pitted ministers and policy-makers against each other. The federal government's determination to regain control of China policy resulted in an assertion of power to override international agreements negotiated by state governments and thereby centralised trade policy.

The BRI was a catalyst to review and strengthen external and internal controls. These actions reflected the perceived realities of the strategic context and the ascendancy of the Departments of Defence and Home Affairs, at the expense of DFAT, the traditional advocate of pragmatic liberalism and free trade. DFAT's influence was eroded by regular budget cuts along with its poor ministerial and bureaucratic leadership. In the new domestic and international contexts, advice from defence and intelligence agencies was given greater weight than the more measured advice of DFAT. Raby (2020) went so far as to claim that 'Australia's intelligence, security and military establishment has taken control of Australia's foreign policy towards China'.

No doubt prioritising security can have advantages in times of war, but during peace it can undermine *human* security more broadly. A former diplomat, senior public servant and security adviser, Dennis Richardson, set out the problem: 'If you're going to shut the gate in respect of China, well, that's fine, provided we are prepared to accept that puts at risk more than $100bn of exports that will impact on the living standards of Australians. This is the problem when you try to wrap the totality of government under an umbrella of national security.' (Cited in Kelly, 2020b, 18) Such a tendency presents obvious risks to Australia's economic and social welfare. Attempts to confine debate also limit policy flexibility, which is hardly in the national interest.

The larger significance of the BRI during this period lay in its contribution to an emerging paradox in Australian foreign economic policy. Reaffirming principles as a rationale for foreign policy, international trade and overseas development was commendable. By invoking them about the BRI, and restricting the flow of inbound foreign investment, however, the government took a step back from economic globalisation. Clearly, some types of investment were more welcome than others. With its more systematic approach to security, the government instigated a small retreat from the principles of globalisation and free trade that had been central to Australian foreign economic policy since the 1980s (see Stokes, 2009). The BRI controversy threatened to unravel a long-established consensus that economic openness was intrinsically in Australia's interests.

Possibly more important was the firming of Australia's choice between the United States and China. By presenting the BRI as part of China's larger geopolitical ambitions and as a security risk, Australia directly expressed hostility towards China's attempts at regional leadership and its model of economic development. In so doing, Australia signalled its commitment to the US alliance and its preference for the United States to remain the pre-eminent power in the Indo-Pacific (e.g. Payne & Reynolds, 2020). The consequences for Australian economic interests, however, remained to be seen.

Authors' note

Professor Geoffrey Stokes died in early November 2023, as this volume was being completed. He will be missed by his many colleagues, including his co-authors. They dedicate this chapter to the memory of Professor Stokes.

References

Abbott, T. (2014) Joint press statement with President Xi, Canberra. 17 November. https://pmtranscripts.pmc.gov.au/release/transcript-23977

ABC (2018) Prime Minister Scott Morrison, Victorian Premier Daniel Andrews clash over China deal. *ABC News*, 7 November. https://www.abc.net.au/news/2018-11-07/scott-morrison-daniel-andrews-clash-over-china-deal/10472026

ABC/Reuters (2017) One Belt One Road: Australia 'sees merit' in China's new Silk Road initiative. *ABC News*, 14 May. http://www.abc.net.au/news/2017-05-14/ciobo-sees-merit-in-chinas-new-silk-road-initiative/8525440

Adamson, F. (2017) Speech at Asialink Business and Macquarie University Thought Leadership Dinner. 1 November

Aedy, R. (2020) Made in Australia. *The Money*, ABC. 11 July. https://www.abc.net.au/radionational/programs/themoney/manufacturing/12344924

Australia–China OBOR Initiative (2016) Media release, 16 September

Australian Embassy, China (2012) Australia–China relationship overview. https://china.embassy.gov.au/bjng/relations1.html

Benson, S. & Packham, B. (2020) ASIO bans Chinese 'agents'. *Australian*, 10 September

Biggs, T. & Duke, J. (2018) China's Huawei, ZTE banned from 5G network. *Sydney Morning Herald*, 23 August. https://www.smh.com.au/technology/government-implies-5g-china-ban-in-new-security-advice-20180823-p4zz77.html

Birmingham, S. (2018) Interview on Sky News with David Speers. 6 November. https://www.trademinister.gov.au/minister/simon-birmingham/transcript/interview-sky-news-david-speers-2

Bishop, J. (2017) Change and uncertainty in the Indo-Pacific: Strategic challenges and opportunities. Singapore: International Institute for Strategic Studies, 13 March. https://www.foreignminister.gov.au/minister/julie-bishop/speech/change-and-uncertainty-indo-pacific-strategic-challenges-and-opportunities

——(2018) Australia, US and Japan announce trilateral partnership for infrastructure investment in the Indo-Pacific. Media release, 31 July. Canberra: Department of Foreign Affairs and Trade

Bishop, J. & Wang, Y. (2017) Australia–China foreign and strategic dialogue – joint press conference. 7 February. https://www.foreignminister.gov.au/minister/julie-bishop/transcript-eoe/australia-china-foreign-and-strategic-dialogue-joint-press-conference-chinese-foreign-minister-wang-yi

Brangwin, N. & Portillo-Castro, H. (2020) Cybersecurity. In Parliamentary Library (ed.), *Briefing Book: Key Issues for the 46th Parliament*, pp. 14–17. Canberra: Department of Parliamentary Services

Butterly, N. (2019) WA government won't sign up to China's Belt and Road initiative. *West Australian*, 11 June. https://thewest.com.au/politics/state-politics/wa-government-wont-sign-up-to-chinas-belt-and-road-initiative-ng-b881225762z

Cai, P. (2017) *Understanding China's Belt and Road Initiative*. Sydney: Lowy Institute for International Policy

Carr, A. (2020) Commonwealth? The state of Australian foreign policy. *Strategist*, 26 May. https://www.aspistrategist.org.au/common-wealth-the-state-of-australian-foreign-policy/

Collinson, E. (2017) *Australia and the Belt and Road Initiative: An Overview*. Sydney: Australia–China Relations Institute, University of Technology Sydney

——(2019) *Australian Perspectives on the Belt and Road Initiative*. Sydney: Australia–China Relations Institute, University of Technology Sydney

Commonwealth of Australia (2014) Address by the President of the People's Republic of China. *Hansard Parliamentary Debates*, 17 November, pp. 12717–20

Courtenay, A. (2018) The strategy of foreign investment. *In the Black*, 1 February. https://www.intheblack.com/articles/2018/02/01/foreign-investment-strategy

Department of Foreign Affairs and Trade (DFAT) (2017) *2017 Foreign Policy White Paper*. Canberra. www.fpwhitepaper.gov.au

——(2019) *Stepping up Australia's Engagement with our Pacific Family*. September. https://www.dfat.gov.au/sites/default/files/stepping-up-australias-engagement-with-our-pacific-family.pdf

——(2020a) China country brief. https://www.dfat.gov.au/geo/china/Pages/china-country-brief

——(2020b) Regional Comprehensive Economic Partnership. https://www.dfat.gov.au/trade/agreements/not-yet-in-force/rcep

Duffy, C. (2017) Donald Trump signs executive order withdrawing US from Trans-Pacific Partnership. *ABC News*, 24 January. https://www.abc.net.au/news/2017-01-24/trump-withdraws-from-tpp/8206356

Dutton, P. (2020) Doorstop interview. Transcript. Canberra: Parliament House. 4 December

Fenna, A. (2016) Shaping comparative advantage: The evolution of trade and industry policy in Australia. *Australian Journal of Political Science* 51(4): 618–35

Ferguson, R. (2020) US threatens to disconnect over Vic–China deal. *Australian*, 24 May. https://www.theaustralian.com.au/nation/coronavirus-australia-live-news-beer-wine-spirits-industry-loses-85bn-in-worst-month-on-record/news-story/d15a412bc88cab37f304728fdda747dd?keyevent=10.40am.

Frydenberg, J. (2020a) Changes to foreign investment framework. Media release. 29 March

——(2020b) Major reforms to Australia's foreign investment framework pass the parliament. Media release. 9 December

Fukuyama, F. (2016) One belt, one road: Exporting the Chinese model to Eurasia. *Australian*, 4 January

Galloway, A. (2020) 'Discourse control': Political leaders' language changes after signing up to Belt and Road, Clive Hamilton says. *Sydney Morning Herald*, 12 June. https://www.smh.com.au/politics/federal/discourse-control-political-leaders-language-changes-after-signing-up-to-belt-and-road-clive-hamilton-says-20200610-p551d0.html

Giles, A. (2016) Appropriation (2016–2017) Bill 2016. *Northern Territory Second Reading Speeches*

Government of Victoria (2019) *Framework Agreement between the Government of the State of Victoria of Australia and the National Development and Reform Commission of the People's Republic of China on Jointly Promoting the Silk Road Economic Belt and the 21st Century Maritime Silk Road*. https://www.vic.gov.au/bri-framework

Greene, A. & Probyn, A. (2017) One Belt, One Road: Australia's 'strategic' concerns over Beijing's bid for global trade dominance. *ABC News*, 23 October. http://www.abc.net.au/news/2017-10-22/australian-concerns-over-beijing-one-belt-one-road-trade-id/9074602

Gunner, M. (2018) Keynote speech, One Belt One Road in Australia Conference. Darwin Convention Centre, 10 July

Hanson, F., Currey, E. & Beattie, T. (2020) The Chinese Communist Party's Coercive Diplomacy. Policy Brief Report No. 36/2020, August. Canberra: International Cyber Policy Centre, Australian Strategic Policy Institute

Harrison, D. (2018) Victorian Government releases agreement with China on Belt and Road Initiative. *ABC News*, 12 November. https://www.abc.net.au/news/2018-11-12/victoria-china-belt-and-road-infrastructure-agreement-released/10487034

He, B. (2019) The domestic politics of the Belt and Road Initiative and its implications. *Journal of Contemporary China* 28(116): 180–95

Hundt, D. (2020) The changing role of the FIRB and the politics of foreign investment in Australia. *Australian Journal of Political Science* 55(3): 328–43

Joint Standing Committee on Foreign Affairs, Defence and Trade (2019) *Inquiry into Australia's Aid Program in the Indo-Pacific: First Report*. Canberra: Parliament of the Commonwealth of Australia

Karp, P. (2018) Scott Morrison rebukes Victoria for signing up to China's Belt and Road initiative. *Guardian*, 6 November. https://www.theguardian.com/world/2018/nov/06/scott-morrison-rebukes-victoria-for-signing-up-to-chinas-belt-and-road-initiative

Kearsley, J., Bagshaw, E. & Galloway, A. (2020) 'If you make China the enemy, China will be the enemy': Beijing's fresh threat to Australia. *Sydney Morning Herald*, 18 November

Keating, P. (2000) *Engagement: Australia Faces the Asia Pacific*. Sydney: Pan Macmillan

Kelly, P. (2017) Cabinet saw no gain in Xi [Jinping's] 'project of the century'. *Australian*, 29 May

——(2020a) Beijing shift was Malcolm Turnbull's gift to Scott Morrison. *Australian*, 29 April

——(2020b) China relations: 'National security cowboys' put nation's interests at unnecessary risk. *Australian*, 9 May

——(2020c) Sovereignty rules with the flex of constitutional muscle. *Weekend Australian*, 29–30 August

Lee, J. (2020) China: Petulant bully that can't quite work us out. *Australian*, 27 May

Maley, P. & Berkovic, N. (2017) When pushback comes to shove. *Weekend Australian*, 9–10 December

Morrison, S. (2019a) In our interest. Speech to the Lowy Institute. 3 October. Sydney Town Hall, NSW

——(2019b) Morrison gives his final 7:30 interview of the 2019 campaign. *ABC*, 17 May

——(2019c) Where we live. Asialink Bloomberg address, 26 June. University of Melbourne

Murray-Atfield, Y. (2020) Ambassador intervenes after Mike Pompeo warns US could 'disconnect' from Australia over Victoria's Belt and Road deal. *ABC News*, 24 May

Payne, M. (2018) Interview with Sabra Lane. *ABC AM*, 6 November

——(2020a) Coronavirus: Australia can lead the way for a global response. *Australian*, 22 April

——(2020b) Press conference, 18 May. https://www.foreignminister.gov.au/minister/marise-payne/transcript/press-conference-3

Payne, M. & Reynolds, L. (2020) Our special relationship with the US is a union of strength and shared values. *Weekend Australian*, 25–26 July

Raby, G. (2017) Xi Jinping's One Belt, One Road triumph and Australia's Sino confusion. *Australian Financial Review*, 17 May. https://www.afr.com/opinion/xis-one-belt-one-road-triumph-and-australias-sino-confusion-20170517-gw6qef

——(2020) Nation's approach to China being hijacked. *Weekend Australian*, 31 October–1 November

Rajah, R. (2021) The big bark but small bite of China's trade coercion. *Interpreter*, Lowy Institute, 8 April. https://www.lowyinstitute.org/the-interpreter/big-bark-small-bite-china-s-trade-coercion

SBS (2017) Turnbull downplays belt and road fears. *SBS News*, 23 October. https://www.sbs.com.au/news/article/turnbull-plays-down-belt-and-road-fears/zu3v5a7h6

Stokes, G. (1994) Towards a national trade strategy. *Australian Quarterly* 66(1): 74–95

——(2009) Neoliberal hyperglobalism in Australian political thought. In H. Löfgren & P. Sarangi (eds), *The Politics and Culture of Globalisation: India and Australia*, pp. 56–75. New Delhi: Social Science Press

Thurbon, E. (2016) The growing partisan divide in trade and industry policy. In M. Beeson & S. Hameiri (eds), *Navigating the New International Disorder: Australia in World Affairs 2011–2015*, pp. 137–57. Melbourne: Oxford University Press

Turnbull, M. (2016) Launch of the Defence White Paper. Transcript, 25 February

——(2017a) Visit to Australia by China's Premier Li Keqiang. Media statement, 24 March

——(2017b) Doorstop with the Minister for the Environment and Energy and Assistant Minister for Social Services and Multicultural Affairs, 23 October

——(2017c) Keynote address to the 2017 Asia Pacific Regional Conference. Perth, 4 November

——(2017d) Press conference at the launch of the government's Foreign Policy White Paper. Transcript, 23 November

——(2018) Speech at the University of New South Wales, Sydney, 7 August 2018. https://www.malcolmturnbull.com.au/media/speech-at-the-university-of-new-south-wales-sydney-7-august-2018

US Department of State (2019) Blue Dot Network: Frequently asked questions. Press release. https://www.state.gov/blue-dot-network-frequently-asked-questions/

Wade, G. (2016) China's 'One Belt, One Road' initiative. In Parliamentary Library (ed.), *Briefing Book: Key Issues for the 45th Parliament*, pp. 148–51. Canberra: Department of Parliamentary Services

White, H. (2016) The United States or China: 'We don't have to choose'. In M. Beeson & S. Hameiri (eds), *Navigating the New International Disorder: Australia in World Affairs 2011–2015*, pp. 93–108. Melbourne: Oxford University Press

Wroe, D. (2018a) Australia will compete with China to save Pacific sovereignty, says Bishop. *Sydney Morning Herald*, 18 June. https://www.smh.com.au/politics/federal/australia-will-compete-with-china-to-save-pacific-sovereignty-says-bishop-20180617-p4zm1h.html

——(2018b) How empires begin. *Sydney Morning Herald*, 22 June. https://www.smh.com.au/politics/federal/how-empires-begin-china-has-made-its-global-move-this-is-australia-s-response-20180620-p4zmpo.html

Yang, K. & Brennan, M. (2017) FIRB 2017 – changes under Australia's foreign investment regime. *Inhouse Counsel*, July, pp. 99–101

Index

5G telecommunications network
   Huawei and, 3, 19, 24, 38, 68, 100, 156, 165, 181, 196

Abbott government
   climate change and, 121
Abbott, Tony, 20, 63, 65, 122, 124, 131, 190
ANZUS alliance, 44, 81–2, 107, 190
   importance of to Asian Australians, 83
   public support for, 34
   See also US alliance
ASEAN, 10, 139, 162, 174–6, 182–3
   ASEAN Regional Forum, 175, 177
   Australia-ASEAN Summit 2018, 167
   Australian engagement with, 110–11
   Australian support for leadership of, 99
   Indo-Pacific concept and, 156–7
   'Outlook on the Indo-Pacific', 99, 157, 167, 181
ASEAN+3, 157
   Emerging Infectious Diseases Program, 134
Asia-Pacific community, 177–8
Asia-Pacific Economic Cooperation, 152, 175
Asian Australians
   attitudes to free trade, 83–4
   Australian-born and overseas-born views on foreign policy, 82–4
   importance of ANZUS alliance to, 83
   lack of inclusion in Australian public service, 76
   lack of involvement with foreign policy, 77–8
   lingering question of identity and place in Australia, 78–80
   perceptions of foreign policy threats, 82–3
   rhetoric versus reality of under-representation, 77–8
   See also Chinese Australians
Asian Infrastructure Investment Bank, 2–3, 20, 155, 191, 194
assessment of foreign interference laws
   alternatives and design weaknesses, 69–71
   correlation or causation, 67–9
asylum-seekers, 110, 131–4
Australia
   espionage and foreign interference threats to, 82–3
   as middle power, 4, 52–3, 55, 91, 149, 198
   rules-based order and, 9, 92–4
Australia-China policy
   changing of, 18–22
   reasons for new approach to, 20–1
   security dominance of, 22–5
Australia-China relations, 65, 80, 154–6
   assessment of foreign influence laws and, 67–9
   Australian balancing strategies, 97–100
   Chinese concept of regionalism and, 155
   concerns surrounding Chinese interference, 65–6
   enforcement of foreign interference laws and worsening relations, 65–7
   legislative defences to Chinese interference, 66
   trade sanctions, 197–8
Australia in the Asian Century White Paper, 25, 77
Australia-India relations, 153–4
   bilateral naval exercises, 154
   Comprehensive Strategic Partnership, 153
   Joint Declaration on a Shared Vision for Maritime Cooperation in the Indo-Pacific, 154
   Mutual Logistics Support Agreement, 153
Australia-Japan relations, 151–3
   bilateral military exercises, 152
   Joint Declaration on Security Cooperation, 24, 151
   mission statement for partnership, 152
   'Special Strategic Partnership', 151
Australia Pacific Security College, 194
Australia-Singapore relations, 174–8
   Comprehensive Strategic Partnership, 178–9
   joint military training and facilities, 179
   policy congruence, 179–80
   securing the Indo-Pacific and, 180–3
   security ties and enabling of US strategic presence, 178–80
   Singapore-Australia Free Trade Agreement, 178
   support for US and, 180
Australia-Solomon Islands Bilateral Security Treaty, 170
Australia-US alliance. *See* US alliance
Australian conventional security challenges
   reliability of US alliance, 107–8
   responses to, 109–11
   US alliance and great-power rivalry, 106–9
Australian Defence Force, 51, 169, 196
   Pacific Mobile Training Team, 168
Australian Election Study, 34, 40, 78
Australian Export Financing Agency, 157
Australian foreign policy
   Asian Australian perspective on, 81–4
   Australia-India relations. *See* Australia-India relations
   Australia-Japan relations, 151. *See also* Australia-Japan relations
   Australia-Singapore relations. *See* Australia-Singapore relations
   Australia-US relations. *See* US alliance
   Belt and Road Initiative and. *See* Belt and Road Initiative and Australian foreign policy
   bipartisan nature of, 48
   changing China policy. *See* Australia-China policy
   climate change and. *See* climate change and Australian foreign policy
   controls over foreign investment, 197
   COVID-19 vaccine assistance, 163, 167
   defence expenditure, 23, 97–8
   engagement of South-East Asia as enduring theme, 175–6
   engagement with ASEAN, 110–11
   expansion of political geography in, 94
   gender in. *See* gender in Australian foreign policy
   great-power rivalry and, 4
   health security and. *See* health security and Australian foreign policy
   independence of, 4–5
   Indo-Pacific construct, 25–6
   'Indo-Pacific Endeavour', 156
   Indo-Pacific engagement programs, 51–2
   infrastructural coalition in South Pacific, 99–100
   Joint Declaration on Security Cooperation, 24
   lack of Asian Australian involvement in, 77–8

Index

non-security expenditure, 23–4
options, reducing autonomy and breadth of, 4–5
regional security relations in the Indo-Pacific. *See* regional security relations in the Indo-Pacific
replacement of term Asia Pacific with Indo-Pacific, 25, 147–8
return to values in, 195–6
role of think tanks in, 27
'security/economic disconnect', 155–6
support of ASEAN leadership, 99
values in, 195–6
Australian foreign policy process
centralisation of, 6–7, 20–1
components of, 17–18
dominance by security concerns, 22–5
federalism and, 22
'reality check' on China, 20
role of Department of Foreign Affairs and Trade in, 6
Australian identity
corporate and social aspects of, 50–1
difference in the world and, 49–52
Australian Infrastructure Financing Facility for the Pacific, 157, 168, 170, 194
Australian Institute of Police Management, 168
Australian justification of Belt and Road Initiative decision, 194
foreign investment, 194
governance, 195
overseas development, 194
security concerns, 196–7
values, 195–6
Australian military spending, 23, 97–8
Defence White Paper 2016 and, 108
increase in during COVID-19 pandemic, 98
Australian Muslims
racial and ethnic prejudice towards, 79
Australian Pacific Security College, 157
Australian policy-makers
China's challenges to rules-based order and, 94–6
Chinese assertiveness in South China Sea and, 95–7
refrain from public criticism of US by, 96
US primacy in rules based order and, 92–3
Australian public opinion on foreign affairs, 31–2
public concerns about China. *See* public concerns about China
public opinion towards climate change, 40–2
role of social background, 42–4
trust in the United States, 32–4
Australian public service
gender imbalance in, 54–5, 77
lack of Asian Australian inclusion in, 76
non-white representation in, 78
racial or ethnic inequalities in, 77
Australian Strategic Policy Institute
'Uyghurs for Sale', 27
Australian unconventional security threats
climate change, 114–15
conventional responses to, 112–15
COVID-19 pandemic, 111–12
international telecommunications, 115
terrorism, 112–13
Australia's responses to great-power rivalry
adoption of Indo-Pacific strategy, 10
articulating values in foreign policy, 8–9
centralisation of foreign policy power, 6–7
criticism of China's human rights record, 7–8
promotion of gender equality in international policy, 9

revival of the Quad, 9–10
speaking out and to China, 7–8

Belt and Road Initiative, 2–4, 11, 109, 147, 155, 163, 167
Australian domestic discord and, 133–4
political and economic context of, 189–90
social discontent at presence of Chinese workers, 164–5
South-East Asia and, 164–5
South Pacific and, 99–100
Victorian memorandum of understanding, 7, 22, 67, 100, 155, 193–4
Belt and Road Initiative and Australian foreign policy, 188–9, 197–9
Australia's shifting position, 190–2
justification of decision. *See* Australian justification of Belt and Road Initiative decision
Northern Australia initiative and, 191
Biden administration, 127, 182–3
Biden, Joe, 125–7
Bishop, Julie, 6–7, 19, 25, 48, 51–5, 100, 136, 191, 194, 196
health security and, 134–5, 137
Boe Declaration on Regional Security, 169
Bretton Woods system, 92, 95, 101

challenges to rules-based order, 94–7
Australia's responses to, 97–100
China
Australian public opinion about. *See* public concerns about China
as challenger to rules-based order, 94–6
growth of influence in Pacific Islands, 166–7
hostility to Indo-Pacific concept, 155
influence in Indo-Pacific, 96
persistence of presence in South-East Asia, 164–6
presence in South-East Asia, 163
reaction to South China Sea ruling, 94, 107, 109, 155, 190
relations with Australia. *See* Australia-China relations
response to Australian foreign interference laws, 81, 84
role of in Australian climate change policy, 125
China-Australia Free Trade Agreement, 65, 84, 189–90
China-Australia relations. *See* Australia-China relations
China-Singapore relations, 181
China-US relations. *See* great-power rivalry
Chinese Australians.
COVID-19 pandemic and, 79
as 'fifth column' for Communist Party of China, 79
'guilt by association' and, 70
navigating China-US rivalry without, 80–1
securitisation of, 85
See also Asian Australians
Christchurch terrorist attack, 113
climate change
2019 federal election and, 122–3
Australian public opinion towards, 40–2, 123–5
Morrison government and, 42
security challenges of, 114–15
Turnbull government and, 41
climate change and Australian foreign policy, 119–20, 126–7
2019–20 bushfires and, 123–5
Australian emissions targets, 125–6
from 'Moderate Malcolm' to 'Scotty from Marketing', 121–3
from Rio to Paris, 120–1
international pressure and, 125–6
Pacific Islands Forum 2019, 123
Pacific Step-up commitment, 169–70

205

Index

climate change and Australian foreign policy (cont.)
  pressure from Pacific nations, 125
  role of China in, 125
Comprehensive and Progressive Agreement for Trans-Pacific Partnership, 93, 147, 152
Coral Sea Cable project, 115, 168
COVAX Advance Market Commitment, 10
COVAX vaccine facility, 138–9
COVID-19 pandemic, 3, 6, 22, 57, 95
  Australian emissions targets and, 126
  Australian response to, 138–9, 170
  Chinese Australians and, 79
  collective regional response to, 140
  increase in Australian military spending during, 98
  origins of, 20, 68, 165, 180, 189, 197–8
  'Quad plus' meeting, 10
  South-East Asia and, 165
  as unconventional security threat, 111–12
Critical Infrastructure Centre, 196
cyberattacks, 62, 100, 113–14

Dastyari, Sam, 65–6, 81
debt trap diplomacy, 152, 155
Defence Strategic Update 2020, 9, 23, 93, 96, 108, 138, 149, 179
Defence White Paper 2009, 18, 92
Defence White Paper 2013, 25, 92–3
Defence White Paper 2016, 9, 23, 25, 92–3, 97, 108, 149, 196
Department of Foreign Affairs and Trade, 21
  changes to organisational structure, 25–6
  erosion of influence of, 199
  Foreign Arrangements Taskforce, 64
  Indo-Pacific strategy, 181
  Office of the Pacific, 157
  role in foreign policy process, 6
  Women in Leadership strategy, 55
Department of Home Affairs, 28, 114, 199
  establishment of, 21, 25, 196
Dutton, Peter, 100, 122

East Asia Summit, 99, 167, 177
Ebola, 133–5
economic coercion, 4–5, 106, 109, 152
emerging infectious diseases, 133
Evans, Gareth, 50, 148, 150

Five Eyes alliance, 7, 51, 62, 177
Five Power Defence Arrangements, 178
foreign affairs
  Australian public opinion on. *See* Australian public opinion on foreign affairs
foreign interference laws, 19
  assessment of. *See* assessment of foreign interference laws
  Australia as 'first mover' legislator, 61
  Australia–China relations and, 65–7
  Australia's Foreign Relations (State and Territory Arrangements) Act 2020 (Cth), 61, 63–4, 80
  China's response to, 81, 84
  consequence of, 71
  effectiveness and potential dangers, 64–5
  Foreign Espionage and Interference Act 2018 (Cth), 80
  Foreign Influence Transparency Scheme Act 2018 (Cth), 61, 63
  as legislative defences to Chinese interference, 66
  National Security (Espionage and Foreign Interference) Act 2018 (Cth), 61–3
Foreign Interference Transparency Scheme, 63

foreign policy threats
  perceptions of by Asian Australians, 82–3
Foreign Policy White Paper 1997, 50
Foreign Policy White Paper 2016, 47
Foreign Policy White Paper 2017, 9, 25, 48, 51, 93–5, 114, 132–3, 136, 149, 174, 181, 191
foreign political donations, 38, 65–6
  ban on, 61, 66
Free and Open Indo-Pacific, 9–10, 150–5
free trade, 152–3, 156, 195, 198–9
  Asian Australian attitudes to, 83–4
  China-Australia Free Trade Agreement, 189–90
  Singapore-Australia Free Trade Agreement, 178

Gender Equality and Women's Empowerment Strategy, 53
gender in Australian foreign policy, 47–9
  critical assessment of 'soft power', 55–7
  good international citizenship and, 49–50
  human rights dialogue and, 50
  inclusive leadership and strategy and, 52–5
  strategy priorities, 53
  UN Human Rights Council membership and, 48, 53
  UN Security Council election campaign and, 48
Gender, Peace and Security Mandate 2020–30, 56
Gillard government
  aid-based foreign policy of, 51
  Indo-Pacific and, 25
  proclamation of Asian century by, 175
  rules-based order and, 9
Gillard, Julia, 6, 131
  climate change and, 121
Global Alliance for Vaccination and Immunisation, 135
Global Ambassador for Gender Equality, 48, 57
Global Financial Crisis, 40, 93
great-power rivalry, 2–3
  Australia and, 80
  Australia's responses to. *See* Australia's responses to great-power rivalry
  Australia's uneasy position amid, 5–6
  economic aspects of, 3–4
  global economic institutions and, 3–4
  navigation without Chinese Australians, 80–1
  prospects, 11
  public opinion of, 5–6
  US alliance and, 106–9

Hawke government
  emissions targets, 120
health diplomacy
  Australian investment in, 139–40
  Australian, technical-centred nature of, 140
  Australia's return to, 134–7
  ongoing role for Austalia in, 140–1
health security and Australian domestic policy, 133–4
health security and Australian foreign policy
  'A more effective global health response' program, 135
  'Access to clean water, sanitation, hygiene, and good nutrition as pre-conditions for health' program, 135–6
  Asia Pacific bilateral health security packages, 134, 136–7
  Australian engagement in, 133–4
  Australia's return to health diplomacy, 134–7
  'Combatting health threats that cross national borders' program, 135
  'Core public health systems and capacities in key partner countries' program, 135
  COVID-19, health diplomacy and Australia's regional role, 138–41

COVID-19 vaccine production submission and, 139
Foreign Policy White Paper 2017 and, 132–3, 136
'Health innovations and new approaches and solutions that benefit our region' program, 136
outward focus of, 134
priority of, 136
Health Security Initiative for the Indo-Pacific, 137
Hong Kong, 67–8, 80, 108, 153, 190
  Australian criticism of China's policy in, 7
  concerns about human rights in, 81
  erosions of democratic rights in, 109
  National Security Law and, 156
  pro-democracy protestors, support for, 2, 8, 165
  restrictions on personal freedom in, 36, 100
Howard government
  opposition to climate action, 120
Huawei, 3–4, 19, 24, 38, 68, 100, 115, 156, 165, 181, 196
human security, 132

Independent Panel for Pandemic Preparedness and Response, 138
India-Australia relations, 153–4
Indian Ocean Naval Symposium, 157
Indian Ocean Regional Association, 157
Indo-Pacific
  regional security relations in. *See* regional security relations in the Indo-Pacific
  as 'single strategic sysytem', 148–9
Indo-Pacific Centre for Health Security, 131, 137–8, 140–1
  2019–20 strategic framework challenges, 137
  priorities, 137
Indo-Pacific concept, 111, 147–51, 154, 156–8, 167
  ASEAN and, 156–7
  Chinese analysts and, 154
  Chinese hostility to, 155
  official US embrace of, 150–1, 153
  South-East Asia and, 156
  South Pacific and, 157
Indo-Pacific construct, 25–6
Indo-Pacific lens
  reconceptualising Australia's regions through, 148–9
Indo-Pacific strategy, 5, 26, 149–51, 154–5, 157, 181
  Australian adoption of, 10
  Foreign Policy White Paper 2017 and, 181
international telecommunications
  as security threat, 115

Japan-Australia relations, 151–3

Keating government
  climate activism during, 120
Keating, Paul, 148
Kyoto Protocol, 120

Liu, Gladys, 66, 81
Lombrum naval base, 168–9

Morrison government, 6, 9, 19, 140
  climate change and, 41–2
  COVID-19 origins and, 180
  engagement with Pacific, 24
  foreign interference laws, 80
  Indo-Pacific concept and, 167
  response to 2019–20 bushfires, 124
  'sovereignty first' approach to international relations, 110
  stance on multilateralism, 110

Morrison, Scott, 19, 21, 80–1, 95, 97–8, 125, 138, 192, 194
  climate change and, 122, 125
  Indo-Pacific and, 148
  negative globalism and, 198
  Pacific family and, 169
  Pacific Step-up and, 168
  Quad and, 99
  response to 2019–20 bushfires, 124
multiculturalism, 76, 81, 85

National Action Plan on Women, Peace and Security, 47
National Cabinet, 6, 112
National Defence Strategy, United States, 150
National Energy Guarantee, 41, 122
National Foundation for Australia–China Relations, 156
National Security Committee of Cabinet, 21, 191
National Security Strategy, United States, 111
  Trump administration, 2, 150
non-traditional security, 131–3
  Foreign Policy White Paper 2017 and, 132–3
North Atlantic Treaty Organization, 93, 178

Office for National Intelligence, Australia, 114
Operation COVID-19 Assist, 112

Pacific family, 169–70
Pacific Fusion Centre, 157
Pacific Islands
  growth of Chinese influence in, 166–7
Pacific Islands Forum, 163, 168
  Boe Declaration on Regional Security, 169
Pacific Labour Mobility Scheme, 125, 168
Pacific Maritime Security Program, 169
Pacific Step-up, 10, 24, 51, 109, 125, 157, 167, 171, 194
  Australian commitment to climate change and, 169–70
  COVID-19 recovery package, 140
  diplomatic and people-to-people links and, 168
  economic development aspect of, 168
  redevelopment of Lombrum naval base, 168–9
  reframing of security message of, 169
  security and, 168–9
Pandemic Influenza Preparedness Framework, 134
Paris Agreement, 41, 121, 123
Partnership for Recovery: Australia's COVID-19 Response, 138
Payne, Marise, 19–20, 49, 52–5, 57, 99–100, 123, 163, 166, 170, 193
Permanent Court of Arbitration
  South China Sea Arbitration, 94, 107, 109, 155, 190
Prime Minister's Office, 6, 20–1, 27
public concerns about China, 35–40, 154–5
  attitudes to Chinese investment, 38–9
  attitudes to military threat, 37–8
  economic partner or security threat, 39–40

Quad, 3, 154–5, 182
  revival of, 9–10, 24, 98–9, 110
Quadrilateral Dialogue. *See* Quad

refugee resettlement agreement, 107, 149
Regional Comprehensive Economic Partnership, 10, 93, 147, 152, 181, 189, 198
regional security relations in the Indo-Pacific, 149
  Australia–China, 154–6
  Australia–India, 153–4
  Australia–Japan, 151–3
  Australia–South-East Asia and South Pacific, 156–7
  US alliance, 149–51

Index

Reynolds, Linda, 49, 54, 98, 113, 151, 156
Rudd government
   aid-based foreign policy of, 51
   withdrawal from Quad, 98
Rudd, Kevin, 6, 18–19, 63, 66, 131, 157
   Asia-Pacific community and, 177–8
   climate activism by, 120–1
   National Security Speech 2008, 92
rules-based order, 4, 7–9, 51, 149, 152–3, 155
   Australia and, 92–4
   Australian advocation for, 9
   challenge to by China, 11
   challenges to. *See* challenges to rules-based order
   change in Australia's perception of, 93–4
   decrease in use of in official documents, 93
   definition, 92
   Singapore and, 182–3
   Trump administration and, 93, 96–7
   US primacy in, 92–3
rules-based order balancing strategies
   'ideological balancing', 100
   'institutional balancing', 99–100
   'military balancing', 97–9

securitisation, 7, 22, 81, 85
Severe Acute Respiratory Syndrome, 133–4, 140
Shanghai Cooperation Organisation, 3
Singapore
   2019 Shangri-La Dialogue and, 182
   prespective on Indo-Pacific, 181–2
   rules-based order and, 182–3
Singapore–Australia Free Trade Agreement, 178
Singapore-Australia relations. *See* Australia-Singapore relations
Singapore-China relations, 181
SingTel, 177
South China Sea, 3, 20, 36, 68, 80, 95, 152, 155, 165
   Freedom of Navigation Operations in, 109
   island-building in, 2, 109
   Permanent Court of Arbitration ruling, 94, 107, 109, 155, 181, 190
South-East Asia
   Australian bilateral partnerships in, 166
   Australian criticism of human rights abuses against Uyghurs and, 165
   Australian development aid to, 166
   China's presence in, 163
   COVID-19 pandemic and, 165
   persistence of Chinese presence in, 164–6
   recognition of Australian support to by regional partners, 167–8
South-East Asia and the Pacific
   Australian COVID-19 assistance to, 163, 167
   Australian development aid to, 167
   Australian elevated engagement in, 167–70
   Australia's security interests in, 161–2
   Australia's worldview and, 162–3
   traditions of regionalism, 162–3
strategic competition, 1
   hard and soft power and, 3
   technology and, 3
Strategic Defence Update 2020, 110, 147

terrorism, 112–13
   Australian 'foreign fighters', 113
   Christchurch terrorist attack, 113
   cyberattacks, 113–14

Trans-Pacific Partnership, 93, 152, 190, 198
   Trump administration withdrawal from, 108, 150
Trilateral Investment Fund, 151
Trump administration
   bilateral trade war with China, 96
   COVID-19 virus and, 165
   Freedom of Navigation Operations in South China Sea, 109
   global leadership and, 11
   National Security Strategy, 2, 111, 150
   rules-based order and, 93, 96–7
   security guarantees for treaty allies and, 150
   trade war with China, 2
   US alliance and, 180
   US-China relations and, 4
   withdrawal from Trans-Pacific Partnership, 108, 150
Trump, Donald, 2, 79, 91, 93, 107, 182–3, 189
   'alliance free-riding' and, 107
   antiglobalism and, 97
   climate change and, 121
   telephone exchange with Malcolm Turnbull, 33, 149
Turnbull government
   climate change and, 41
   South China Sea ruling and, 109
Turnbull, Malcolm, 81, 95, 107, 125, 148, 191, 194, 196
   assessment of China, 180
   China policy and, 19
   climate change and, 121–2
   foreign interference laws and, 66
   Pacific Step-up and, 168
   rules-based order and, 7, 9
   Shangri-La Dialogue, 7, 19, 96
   telephone exchange with Donald Trump, 33, 149

United Nations Convention on the Law of the Sea, 95, 190
United Nations Framework Convention on Climate Change, 120
US alliance, 6, 31, 33, 47, 111, 149–51, 180, 188, 200
   Australian public trust in, 32–4
   Coalition government reinforcement of, 108
   great-power rivalry and, 106–9
   reliability of, 107–8
   See also ANZUS alliance
US-China relations. *See* great-power rivalry
US–Japan–Australia Trilateral Strategic Dialogues, 153
Uyghurs, 27, 165

Vietnam War, 31, 37, 40

White Australia policy, 79, 191
White Paper on Northern Australia 2015, 191
Widodo, Joko, 34, 164
women
   violence against, 48
Women, Peace and Security, 50–1, 54, 58
   Australian embrace of, 55–7
   national action plans, 56–7
world affairs
   Australian public opinion on. *See* Australian public opinion on foreign affairs
World Health Assembly, 138, 165
World Health Organization, 79, 136, 138–9, 165
   Asia-Pacific Strategy for Emerging Diseases, 134

Xi, Jinping, 2, 20, 34, 65, 94, 107, 182–3, 190
Xinjiang, 8, 27, 68, 100, 108–9, 153, 156

ZTE, 19, 68

For EU product safety concerns, contact us at Calle de José Abascal, 56–1°,
28003 Madrid, Spain or eugpsr@cambridge.org.

www.ingramcontent.com/pod-product-compliance
Lightning Source LLC
LaVergne TN
LVHW080305260326
834688LV00039B/1150